CHILTON BOOK COMPANY

REPAIR MANUAL

CHRYSLER FRONT WHEEL DRIVE 1981-88

All U.S. and Canadian front wheel drive models of DODGE Aries, 400, 600, Daytona, Lancer, Shadow • PLYMOUTH Caravelle, Reliant, Sundance • CHRYSLER E-Class, Executive Sedan, 4-door sedan, Laser, LeBaron, Limousine, New Yorker, Towne & Country

Vice President and General Manager JOHN P. KUSHNERICK
Editor-in-Chief KERRY A. FREEMAN, S.A.E.
Managing Editor DEAN F. MORGANTINI, S.A.E.
Senior Editor RICHARD J. RIVELE, S.A.E.
Senior Editor W. CALVIN SETTLE, JR., S.A.E.
Editor JOHN M. BAXTER, S.A.E.

CHILTON BOOK COMPANY
Radnor, Pennsylvania
19089

CONTENTS

1 GENERAL INFORMATION and MAINTENANCE

2 ENGINE PERFORMANCE and TUNE-UP

3 ENGINE and ENGINE OVERHAUL

4 EMISSION CONTROLS

5 FUEL SYSTEM

6 CHASSIS ELECTRICAL

SAFETY NOTICE

Proper service and repair procedures are vital to the safe, reliable operation of all motor vehicles, as well as the personal safety of those performing repairs. This book outlines procedures for servicing and repairing vehicles using safe, effective methods. The procedures contain many NOTES, CAUTIONS and WARNINGS which should be followed along with standard safety procedures to eliminate the possibility of personal injury or improper service which could damage the vehicle or compromise its safety.

It is important to note that repair procedures and techniques, tools and parts for servicing motor vehicles, as well as the skill and experience of the individual performing the work vary widely. It is not possible to anticipate all of the conceivable ways or conditions under which vehicles may be serviced, or to provide cautions as to all of the possible hazards that may result. Standard and accepted safety precautions and equipment should be used during cutting, grinding, chiseling, prying, or any other process that can cause material removal or projectiles.

Some procedures require the use of tools specially designed for a specific purpose. Before substituting another tool or procedure, you must be completely satisfied that neither your personal safety, nor the performance of the vehicle will be endangered.

Although the information in this guide is based on industry sources and is as complete as possible at the time of publication, the possibility exists that the manufacturer made later changes which could not be included here. While striving for total accuracy, Chilton Book Company cannot assume responsibility for any errors, changes, or omissions that may occur in the compilation of this data.

PART NUMBERS

Part numbers listed in this reference are not recommendations by Chilton for any product by brand name. They are references that can be used with interchange manuals and aftermarket supplier catalogs to locate each brand supplier's discrete part number.

SPECIAL TOOLS

Special tools are recommended by the vehicle manufacturer to perform their specific job. Use has been kept to a minimum, but where absolutely necessary, they are referred to in the text by the part number of the tool manufacturer. These tools can be purchased, under the appropriate part number, from Miller Special Tools, A Division of Utica Tools Company, 32615 Park Lane, Garden City, Michigan 48135 or from your Dodge/Plymouth dealer or regional distributor or an equivalent tool can be purchased locally from a tool supplier or parts outlet. Before substituting any tool for the one recommended, read the SAFETY NOTICE at the top of this page.

ACKNOWLEDGMENTS

Chilton Book Company expresses appreciation to the Chrysler Plymouth Division, Chrysler Motor Corporation, Detroit, Michigan, and the Dodge Division, Chrysler Motors Corporation, Detroit, Michigan for their generous assistance.

Manufactured in the United States of America
 234567890   765432109

Chilton's Repair Manual: Chrysler Front Wheel Drive 1981–88
ISBN 0-8019-7827-0 pbk.
Library of Congress Catalog Card No. 87-47946

General Information and Maintenance

HOW TO USE THIS BOOK

Chilton's Repair Manual for Chrysler Front Wheel Drive cars is intended to help you learn more about the inner workings of your vehicle and save you money on its upkeep and operation.

The first two chapters will be the most used, since they contain maintenance and tune-up information and procedures. Studies have shown that a properly tuned and maintained car can get at least 10% better gas mileage than an out-of-tune car. The other chapters deal with the more complex systems of your car. Operating systems from engine through brakes are covered to the extent that the average do-it-yourselfer becomes mechanically involved. This book will not explain such things as rebuilding the differential for the simple reason that the expertise required and the investment in special tools make this task uneconomical. It will give you detailed instructions to help you change your own brake pads and shoes, replace spark plugs, and do many more jobs that will save you money, give you personal satisfaction, and help you avoid expensive problems.

A secondary purpose of this book is a reference for owners who want to understand their car and/or their mechanics better. In this case, no tools at all are required.

Before removing any bolts, read through the entire procedure. This will give you the overall view of what tools and supplies will be required. There is nothing more frustrating than having to walk to the bus stop on Monday morning because you were short one bolt on Sunday afternoon. So read ahead and plan ahead. Each operation should be approached logically and all procedures thoroughly understood before attempting any work.

All chapters contain adjustments, maintenance, removal and installation procedures, and repair or overhaul procedures. When repair is not considered practical, we tell you how to remove the part and then how to install the new or rebuilt replacement. In this way, you at least save the labor costs. Backyard repair of such components as the alternator is just not practical.

Two basic mechanic's rules should be mentioned here. One, whenever the left side of the car or engine is referred to, it is meant to specify the driver's side of the car. Conversely, the right side of the car means the passenger's side. Secondly, most screws and bolt are removed by turning counterclockwise, and tightened by turning clockwise.

Safety is always the most important rule. Constantly be aware of the dangers involved in working on an automobile and take the proper precautions. (See the section in this chapter Servicing Your Vehicle Safely and the SAFETY NOTICE on the acknowledgement page.)

Pay attention to the instructions provided. There are 3 common mistakes in mechanical work:

1. Incorrect order of assembly, disassembly or adjustment. When taking something apart or putting it together, doing things in the wrong order usually justs cost you extra time; however, it CAN break something. Read the entire procedure before beginning disassembly. Do everything in the order in which the instructions say you should do it, even if you can't immediately see a reason for it. When you're taking apart something that is very intricate (for example, a carburetor), you might want to draw a picture of how it looks when assembled at one point in order to make sure you get everything back in its proper position. (We will supply exploded view whenever possible). When making adjustments, especially tune-up adjustments, do them in order; often, one adjustment affects another, and you cannot expect even satisfac-

tory results unless each adjustment is made only when it cannot be changed by any order.

2. Overtorquing (or undertorquing). While it is more common for over-torquing to cause damage, undertorquing can cause a fastener to vibrate loose causing serious damage. Especially when dealing with aluminum parts, pay attention to torque specifications and utilize a torque wrench in assembly. If a torque figure is not available, remember that if you are using the right tool to do the job, you will probably not have to strain yourself to get a fastener tight enough. The pitch of most threads is so slight that the tension you put on the wrench will be multiplied many, many times in actual force on what you are tightening. A good example of how critical torque is can be seen in the case of spark plug installation, especially where you are putting the plug into an aluminum cylinder head. Too little torque can fail to crush the gasket, causing leakage of combustion gases and consequent overheating of the plug and engine parts. Too much torque can damage the threads, or distort the plug which changes the spark gap.

There are many commercial products available for ensuring that fasteners won't come loose, even if they are not torqued just right (a very common brand is Loctite®). If you're worried about getting something together tight enough to hold, but loose enough to avoid mechanical damage during assembly, one of these products might offer substantial insurance. Read the label on the package and make sure the products is compatible with the materials, fluids, etc. involved before choosing one.

3. Crossthreading. This occurs when a part such as a bolt is screwed into a nut or casting at the wrong angle and forced. Cross threading is more likely to occur if access is difficult. It helps to clean and lubricate fasteners, and to start threading with the part to be installed going straight in. Then, start the bolt, spark plug, etc. with your fingers. If you encounter resistance, unscrew the part and start over again at a different angle until it can be inserted and turned several turns without much effort. Keep in mind that many parts, especially spark plugs, used tapered threads so that gentle turning will automatically bring the part you're treading to the proper angle if you don't force it or resist a change in angle. Don't put a wrench on the part until its's been turned a couple of turns by hand. If you suddenly encounter resistance, and the part has not seated fully, don't force it. Pull it back out and make sure it's clean and threading properly.

Always take your time and be patient; once you have some experience, working on your car will become an enjoyable hobby.

TOOLS AND EQUIPMENT

It would be impossible to catalog each and every tool that you may need to perform all the operations included in this book. It would also not be wise for the amateur to rush out and buy an expensive set of tools on the theory that he may need one of them at some time. The best approach is to proceed slowly, gathering together a good quality set of those tools that are used most frequently. Don't be misled by the low cost of bargain tools. It is far better to spend a little more for quality, name brand tools. Forged wrenches, 10 or 12 point sockets and fine-tooth ratchets are by far preferable to their less expensive counterparts. As any good mechanic can tell you, there are few worse experiences than trying to work on a car or truck with bad tools. Your monetary savings will be far outweighed by frustration and mangled knuckles.

Begin accumulating those tools that are used most frequently; those associated with routine maintenance and tune-up. In addition to the normal assortment of screwdrivers and pairs of pliers, you should have the following tools for routine maintenance jobs:

1. SAE and Metric wrenches, sockets and combination open end/box end wrenches
2. Jackstands for support
3. Oil filter wrench
4. Oil filler spout or funnel
5. Grease gun for chassis lubrication
6. Hydrometer for checking the battery
7. A low flat pan for draining oil
8. Lots of rags for wiping up the inevitable mess.

In addition to the above items, there are several others that are not absolutely necessary, but are handy to have around. These include oil drying compound, a transmission funnel, and the usual supply of lubricants, antifreeze and fluids, although these can be purchased as needed. This is a basic list for routine maintenance, but only your personal needs can accurately determine your list of tools.

The next list of tools is for tune-ups. While the tools involved here are slightly more sophisticated, they need not be outrageously expensive. There are several inexpensive tach/dwell meters on the market that are every bit as good for the average mechanic as a $100.00 professional model. Just be sure that the one you buy shows at least 1,200-1,500 rpm on the tach scale, and that it works on 4, 6, and 8-cylinder engines. A basic list of tune-up equipment would include:

1. Tach/dwell meter.
2. Spark plug wrench.
3. Timing light (preferably a DC, power type light that works from the battery).

4. A set of flat feeler gauges.

5. A set of round wire spark plug gauges.

In addition to these basic tools, there are several other tools and gauges you may find useful. These include:

1. A compression gauge. The screw-in type takes more time to use, but eliminates the possibility of a faulty reading due to escaping pressure.

2. A manifold vacuum gauge.

3. A test light.

4. An induction meter. This is used for determining whether or not there is current in a wire. These are handy for use if a wire is broken somewhere in a wiring harness. As a final note, you will probably find a torque wrench necessary for all but the most basic work. The bar type models are perfectly adequate, although the newer click type are more precise.

Special Tools

Normally, the use of special factory tools is avoided for repair procedures, since these are not readily available for the do-it-yourself mechanic. When it is possible to perform the job with more commonly-available tools, this fact will be pointed out. Occasionally, a particular job just cannot be performed properly without a special tool designed specifically for that job. Before substituting another tool, you should be convinced that neither your safety nor the performance of the vehicle will be compromised.

Some special tools are available commercially from major tool manufacturers. Others for your Chyrsler car can be purchased from your dealer or from Utica Tool Co. (see the copyright page for the complete address).

SERVICING YOUR VEHICLE SAFELY

It is virtually impossible to anticipate all of the hazards involved with maintenance and service but care and common sense will prevent most accidents. The rules of safety for mechanics range from "don't smoke around gasoline" to "use the proper tool for the job". The trick to avoiding injuries is to develop safe work habits and take every possible precaution. Two critical items are working at a sensible pace and visualizing what you will be doing and what will happen before you perform each step of an operation.

Dos

● Do keep a fire extinguisher and first aid kit within easy reach.

● Do wear safety glasses or goggles when cutting, drilling, grinding or prying. If you wear glasses for the sake of vision, they should be made of hardened "safety" glass that can serve also as protection. If they are not of hardened glass, you should wear safety goggles over your regular glasses.

● Do shield your eyes whenever you work around the battery. Batteries contain sulphuric acid. In case of contact with the eyes or skin, flush the area with water or a mixture of water and baking soda and get medical attention immediately.

● Do use jackstands for any undercar service. The bumper jack which comes with the car is for raising the vehicle when the consequences of having it fall are minimal; jackstands are for making sure the vehicle stays raised until you want it to come down. Whenever your vehicle is raised, block the wheels remaining on the ground and set the parking brake.

● Do use adequate ventilation when working with any chemicals or hazardous materials.

● Do disconnect the negative battery cable when working on the electrical system. The secondary ignition system can contain up to 40,000 volts.

● Do follow manufacturer's directions whenever working with potentially hazardous materials. Both brake fluid and antifreeze are poisonous if taken internally.

● Do properly maintain your tools. Loose hammerheads, mushroomed punches and chisels, frayed or poorly grounded electrical cords, excessively worn screwdrivers, spread wrenches, cracked sockets, slipping ratchets, or faulty droplight sockets can cause accidents.

● Do use the proper size and type of tool for the job being done.

● Do, whenever possible, pull on a wrench handle rather than push on it, and adjust your stance to prevent a fall when a bolt suddenly breaks loose.

● Do be sure that adjustable wrenches are tightly closed on the nut or bolt and pulled so that the face is on the side of the fixed jaw.

● Do select a wrench or socket that fits the nut or bolt. The wrench or socket should sit straight, not cocked.

● Do strike squarely with a hammer; avoid glancing blows.

● Do set the parking brake and block the drive wheels if the work must be done with the engine running.

Don'ts

● Don't run an engine in a garage or anywhere else without proper ventilation—EVER! Carbon monoxide is poisonous; it takes a long time to leave the human body and you can build up a deadly supply of it in your system by simply breathing a little every day. You will not be bothered by a strong smell of exhaust and cannot smell carbon monoxide. You will not realize you are slowly poisoning yourself. Always use power vents, windows, fans or open the garage door.

• Don't work around moving parts while wearing a necktie or other loose clothing. Short sleeves are much safer than long, loose sleeves; hard-toed shoes with neoprene soles protect your toes and give a better grip on slippery surfaces. Jewelry such as watches, fancy belt buckles, beads or body adornment of any kind is not safe working around a truck. Long hair should be secured under a hat or cap.

• Don't use pockets for toolboxes. A fall or bump can drive a screwdriver deep into your body. Even a wiping cloth hanging from the back pocket can wrap around a spinning shaft or fan.

• Never attempt to pry out a part such as a freeze plug with a screwdriver. If the plug or other item suddenly comes loose, this, too, could drive the screwdriver into your body.

• Don't smoke when working around gasoline, cleaning solvent or other flammable material.

• Don't use gasoline to wash your hands; there are excellent soaps available. Gasoline may contain lead, and lead can enter the body through a cut, accumulating in the body until you are very ill. Gasoline also removes all the natural oils from the skin so that bone dry hands will absorb oil and grease.

• Don't use gasoline as a solvent, either. It is highly flammable. Use a non-volatile solvent intended for safe use in parts cleaning

• Don't service the air conditioning system unless you are equipped with the necessary tools and training. The refrigerant, R-12, when released into the air, will instantly freeze any surface it contacts, including your eyes. Although the refrigerant is normally non-toxic, R-12 becomes a deadly poisonous gas in the presence of an open flame. One good whiff of the vapors from burning refrigerant can be fatal. So, never smoke or have any other source of flame around when there may be leaking refrigerant gas.

MODEL IDENTIFICATION

Chrysler K cars include the Plymouth Reliant, Dodge Aries, Dodge 600 hardtop and convertible, and Chrysler LeBaron, Town & Country, and Limousine. The Reliant and Aries come in 2-door and 4-door sedan and station wagon styles. The Chrysler K cars may be either hardtops or convertibles.

The Chrysler E cars are the Plymouth Caravelle and Dodge 600 4-door sedans and the Chrysler New Yorker 4-door sedan and Turbo 4-door sedan. Model information is contained in digits 1-5 of the Vehicle Identification Number. See the chart below for a specific listing of the codes.

The P cars include the Plymouth Sundance and Dodge Shadow.

The Dodge Daytona and Chrysler Laser are G cars. The Chrysler Laser was produced only up until 1986.

The Dodge Lancer and LeBaron GTS are H cars.

SERIAL NUMBER IDENTIFICATION

Vehicle

The vehicle serial number is located on a plate on the top left side of the instrument panel and is visible through the windshield. The VIN consists of 17 elements embossed on a gray colored plate. The chart below interprets each letter or number according to its position in the sequence for each model year.

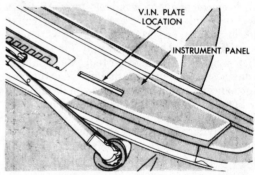

Location of V.I.N. plate

Body Code Plate

The 1988 body code plate lists information that may be helpful in identifying the paint colors and trim options on the car, if you should have to order paint or trim parts to do bodywork. On line 2, Digits 5, 6, 7, and 8 represent the code for the primary paint color. Digits 10, 11, 12, and 13 show the code for the secondary color, if the car is two-tone. Digits 15, 16, 17, and 18 represent the trim code, which may be helpful in ordering body trim items.

Engine Identification Number

All engine assemblies carry an engine identification number (EIN). The 135 cu. in. (2.2 Liter) engine identification number is located on the left rear face of the block directly under the head. The 156 cu. in. (2.6 Liter) identification number is located on the left side of the block between the core plug and the rear of the block on models through 1985. In 1986, the 2.6 liter Mitsubishi built engine was replaced by a 2.5 liter powerplant developed jointly by Mitsubishi and Chrysler and manufactured in the U.S. The 2.5 liter engine's identification tag is located on the left side of the block between the core plug and the rear face of the block (the "rear" face is the end of the block nearer the radiator).

Engine Serial Number

In addition to the EIN, each engine has a serial number, which must be referred to when ordering engine replacement parts. The serial number on the 135 cu. in. (2.2 Liter) engine is located on the rear face of the block directly below the head. On the 156 cu. in. (2.6 Liter) engine it is located on the right front side of the engine block, adjacent to the exhaust manifold. On the 2.5 liter engine, it is located on the right rear (dash panel) side of the block, adjacent to and near the exhaust manifold stud.

Transaxle Identification Number and Transaxle Serial Number

The Transaxle Identification Number is stamped on a boss located on the upper part of the transaxle housing. Every transaxle also carries an assembly part number, which is also required for parts ordering purposes. On the A-412 manual transaxle, it is located on the top of the housing, between the timing window and the differential.

On the A-460, A-465, and A-525 manual transaxles, this number is located on a metal tag attached to the front of the transaxle. On automatic models, it is stamped on a pad located just above the oil pan at the rear of the unit.

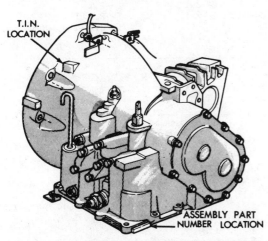

Location of the transaxle identification number (T.I.N.) on all transaxles, and the assembly part number for automatic transaxles

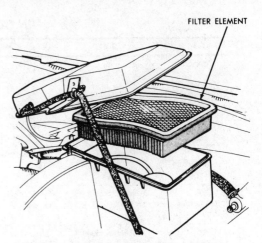

Air cleaner installation—2.2 carbureted engine

ROUTINE MAINTENANCE

Air Cleaner
REMOVAL AND INSTALLATION

On the 2.2 and 2.5 liter engines through 1986, replace the air cleaner element every 52,500 miles. Under dusty driving conditions, inspect the element frequently (about every 15,000 miles) and replace it as frequently as necessary. Generally, if you hold the element up to a strong light and you cannot see through it at all, it is clogged.

On the 2.6 liter engine and on all 1987-88 engines, replace the element every 30,000 miles under ordinary driving conditions. If you drive under extremely dusty conditions, inspect the filter every 15,000 miles and replace it as necessary.

When opening up the air cleaner housing to replace the air filter, wipe dust out of the air cleaner with a clean rag. Work carefully, to prevent the entry of dirt, dust, or foreign objects. Also, after you have reassembled the housing, inspect it to make sure the air cleaner is properly installed and sealed tightly. A vacuum leak here could allow dust to enter the engine and cause severely accelerated wear.

REMOVAL AND INSTALLATION
2.2 Liter Carbureted Engines

WARNING: *Make sure you perform the steps in exactly the sequence described below, or the air cleaner may leak, causing accelerated engine wear.*

On the 2.2 liter carbureted engine, replace the air cleaner element by removing the three wing nuts retaining the air cleaner-crossover cover to the carburetor and bracket. Lift the cover, pull the element out, and replace it, making sure you install it with the screen upward.

VIN Code Chart

Year	1981	1982	1983	1984
Position 1 Country of Origin	1—US	1—US	1—US	1—US 2—Canada 3—Mexico 4—Japan
2 Make	B—Dodge P—Plymouth	B—Dodge C—Chrysler P—Plymouth	B—Dodge C—Chrysler P—Plymouth	B—Dodge C—Chrysler P—Plymouth
3 Gen'l Vehicle Type	3—Pass. Car	3—Pass. Car	3—Pass. Car	3—Pass. Car
4 Passenger Safety System	B—Man. Seat Belts	B—Man. Seat Belts D—3000 lbs. GVW	B—Man. Seat Belts D—3000 lbs. GVW	B—Man. Seat Belts D—3000 lbs. GVW
5 Car Line	K—Aries & Reliant	C—Le Baron D—Aires P—Reliant V—400	C—Le Baron D—Aries E—600 D—Reliant T—New Yorker V—400	C—Le Baron D—Aries E—600 M—Horizon P—Reliant T—New Yorker/ E Class V—600
6 Series	1—Economy 2—Low 3—High 5—Premium	1—Economy 2—Low 4—High 5—Premium 6—Special	1—Economy 2—Low 4—High 5—Premium 6—Special	1—Economy 2—Low 4—High 5—Premium 6—Special
7 Body Style	1—2 Dr. Sedan 4—2 + 2 Hatchback 5—2 Dr. Convertible 6—4 Dr. Sedan 8—4 Dr. Hatchback 9—Dr. Wagon	1—2 Dr. Sedan 2—2 Dr. Specialty Hardtop 4—2 + 2 Hatchback 5—2 Dr. Convertible 6—4 Dr. Sedan 8—4 Dr. Hatchback 9—4 Dr. Wagon	1—2 Dr. Sedan 2—2 Dr. Specialty Hardtop 3—2 Dr. Hardtop 4—2 Dr. Hatchback 5—2 Dr. Convertible 6—4 Dr. Sedan 8—4 Dr. Hatchback 9—4 Dr. Wagon	1—2 Dr. Sedan 2—2 Dr. Specialty Hardtop 3—2 Dr. Hardtop 4—2 Dr. Hatchback 5—2 Dr. Convertible 6—4 Dr. Sedan 8—4 Dr. Hatchback 9—4 Dr. Wagon
8 Engine	B—2.2L D—2.6L	B—2.2L C—2.2L Turbocharged D—2.6L	C—2.2L G—2.6L	C—2.2L D—2.2L EFI E—2.2L Turbocharged G—2.6L
9 Check Digit	The digit in position 9 is used for VIN verification. "1–9", "0", or "X"			
10 Model Year	B—'81	C—'82	D—'83	E—'84
11 Assembly Plant	C—Jefferson D—Belvidere F—Newark	C—Jefferson D—Belvidere F—Newark G—St. Louis	C—Jefferson D—Belvidere F—Newark G—St. Louis	C—Jefferson D—Belvidere F—Newark G—St. Louis X—Missouri
12–17 Sequence Number	These digits identify your particular car			

VIN Code Chart (cont.)

1985	1986	1987	1988
1—US	1—US	1—US	1—US
2—Canada	2—Canada	2—Canada	2—Canada
3—Mexico	3—Mexico	3—Mexico	3—Mexico
4—Japan	J—Japan	J—Japan	J—Japan
B—Dodge	B—Dodge	B—Dodge	B—Dodge
C—Chrysler	C—Chrysler	C—Chrysler	C—Chrysler
P—Plymouth	P—Plymouth	P—Plymouth	P—Plymouth
3—Pass. Car	3—Pass. Car	3—Pass. Car	3—Pass. Car
			7—Truck
B—Man. Seat Belts	B—Man. Seat Belts	B—Man. Seat Belts	B—Man. Seat Belts
D—3000 lbs. GVW	D—1–3000 lbs. GVW	D—1–3000 lbs. GVW	D—1–3000 lbs. GVW
C—Le Baron/ET5	C—Le Baron	C—Le Baron	D—Dynasty
D—Aries	D—Aries	D—Aries	C—New Yorker Landau
E—600	E—600	E—600	J—Caravelle
T—New Yorker	T—New Yorker	T—New Yorker	E—600
P—Reliant	P—Reliant	X—Lancer	T—New Yorker Turbo
V—600	V—600	L—Caravelle (Canada)	V—Daytona
	A—V Daytona	M—Horizon	X—Lancer
	A—C Laser	P—Reliant	H—Le Baron GTS
	H—Le Baron GTS	J—Caravelle (U.S.)	J—Le Baron
		Z—Omni	P—Reliant
		A—V Daytona	D—Aries
		H—Le Baron GTS	C—Le Baron
		S—Sundance	S—Sundance
		S—Shadow	S—Shadow
		J—Le Baron	
1—Economy	1—Economy	1—Economy	1—Economy
2—Low	2—Low	2—Low	2—Low
4—High	4—High	3—Medium	3—Medium
5—Premium	5—Premium	4—High	4—High
6—Special	6—Special	5—Premium	5—Premium
		6—Special	6—Special
1—2 Dr. Sedan	1—2 Dr. Sedan	1—2 Dr. Sedan	1—2 Dr. Sedan
2—2 Dr. Specialty Hardtop	2—2 Dr. Specialty Hardtop	3—2 Dr. Hardtop	3—2 Dr. Hardtop
3—2 Dr. Hardtop	3—2 Dr. Hardtop	4—2 Dr. Hatchback	4—2 Dr. Hatchback
4—2 Dr. Hatchback	4—2 Dr. Hatchback	5—2 Dr. Convertible	5—2 Dr. Convertible
5—2 Dr. Convertible	5—2 Dr. Convertible	6—4 Dr. Sedan	6—4 Dr. Sedan
6—4 Dr. Sedan	6—4 Dr. Sedan	8—4 Dr. Hatchback	8—4 Dr. Hatchback
8—4 Dr. Hatchback	8—4 Dr. Hatchback	9—4 Dr. Wagon	9—4 Dr. Wagon
9—4 Dr. Wagon	9—4 Dr. Wagon		
C—2.2L	C—2.2L	C—2.2L	C—2.2L
D—2.2L EFI	D—2.2L EFI	D—2.2 EFI	D—2.2L E.F.I.
E—2.2L Turbocharged	E—2.2L Turbo	E—2.2L Turbo	E—2.2L Turbo
G—2.6L	K—2.5L	K—2.5L	K—2.5L
			3—3.0L
F—'85	G—'86	H—1987	J—1988
C—Jefferson	A—Outer Drive	A—Outer Drive	A—Outer Drive
D—Belvidere	C—Jefferson	C—Jefferson	C—Jefferson
F—Newark	D—Belvidere	D—Belvidere	D—Belvidere
G—St. Louis 1	F—Newark	F—Newark	E—Modena
K—Pillette Road	G—St. Louis	G—St. Louis	F—Newark
N—Sterling	K—Pillette Road	K—Pillette Road	G—St. Louis 1
R—Windsor	N—Sterling	N—Sterling Heights	N—Sterling
T—Toluca	R—Windsor	R—Windsor	R—Windsor
W—Clairpointe	T—Toluca	T—Toluca	T—Toluca
X—St. Louis 2	X—St. Louis 2	X—St. Louis 2	W—Kenosha
			X—St. Louis 2

FILTER ELEMENT

2.6L engine air cleaner filter

Position the cover on top, aligning the three clips and making sure the element seals all around. Let the three studs stick upward through the whole for each in the cover. Then, install both of the plastic wing nuts onto the two studs on the carburetor and tighten each just finger tight (14 in.lb.). After those nuts have been properly torqued, install the other wingnut—the one that fastens the air cleaner to the support bracket—and tighten it in a simi-

lar manner. Finally, close the three hold-down clips.

1981-86 2.2 Liter Electronic Fuel Injection Engine

To remove the air cleaner, remove the clamp fastening the air hose at the throttle body and unclip the five clips that fasten the top of the air cleaner to the lower housing. Pull the air hose off the throttle body and then lift the cover and hose off the bottom of the air cleaner. Now remove the filter.

To install the filter, drop it screen side up into the plastic bottom section of the lower housing. Install the clamp loosely onto the throttle body hose and connect the hose onto the throttle body. Slide the top of the air cleaner squarely down over the seal of the filter element, making sure it is not pinching the seal anywhere but lies flat all around. Clip the five hold-down clips and then tighten the clamp around the hose at the throttle body until it is just snug – 25 in.lb.

2.6 Liter Engine

To replace the air cleaner cartridge, simply unclip the four clips fastening the top in place, lift the top off the lower housing (the intake hose is flexible enough to permit this) and remove the filter. Install in reverse order, making sure all parts are positioned correctly to prevent leaks. Clean the inside of the air cleaner housing before installing the air filter.

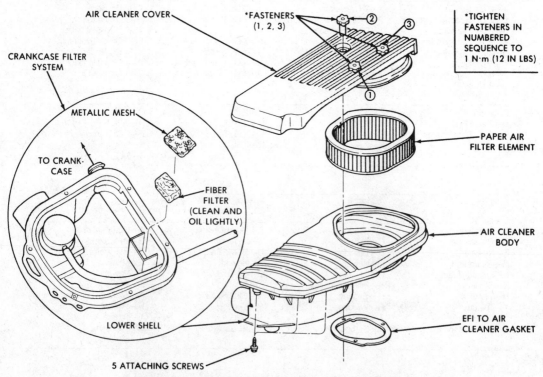

AIR CLEANER COVER

*FASTENERS
(1, 2, 3)

*TIGHTEN
FASTENERS IN
NUMBERED
SEQUENCE TO
1 N·m (12 IN LBS)

CRANKCASE FILTER
SYSTEM

METALLIC MESH

TO CRANK-
CASE

FIBER
FILTER
(CLEAN AND
OIL LIGHTLY)

PAPER AIR
FILTER ELEMENT

AIR CLEANER
BODY

LOWER SHELL

EFI TO AIR
CLEANER GASKET

5 ATTACHING SCREWS

The air cleaner used on 1987–88 2.2 and 2.5 Liter Engines

1987-88 2.2 and 2.5 Liter Engines

When changing the filter element in this air cleaner, the body of the unit remains mounted on the intake manifold. Only the top cover need be removed unless the crankcase ventilation filter must be serviced. To replace the air cleaner, remove the three attaching thumbscrews and remove the air cleaner top cover. Then, grab the paper element at two locations on the inside diameter to lift it out of the housing.

Install in reverse order, turning the element so its flat sides line up with those in the housing. Be careful to tighten the three fasteners for the top cover in the numbered order shown in the illustration. They need not be extremely tight (recommended torque is only 12 in.lb.).

2.2 Liter Turbocharged Engines

To remove the air cleaner element, first unclip the hold-down bails attaching the top cover of the air cleaner to the main housing. Then, gently pull the cover off the housing. If the intake hose restricts the movement of the air cleaner cover so that you cannot gain access to the element without putting a lot of stress on the hose, loosen the hose clamp and pull the air intake hose off the housing cover. Remove the element, noting that the rubber seal goes in last and fits into the groove around the top or intake side of the lower housing.

Install the new element in reverse order. Check that the rubber seal fits properly in the groove all around. Install the top cover over the element so it fits down squarely over the rubber seal and attach all the bails securely. If necessary, reconnect the intake hose and tighten the clamp securely.

Fuel Filter

CAUTION: *Never smoke when working around gasoline! Avoid all sources of sparks or ignition. Gasoline vapors are EXTREMELY volatile!*

REMOVAL AND INSTALLATION

Carbureted Engines

There are two fuel filters in the present system. One is part of the gauge unit assembly located inside the fuel tank on the suction end of the tube. This filter normally does not need servicing, but may be replaced or cleaned if a very large amount of extremely coarse material gets into the tank and clogs it.

The 2.2 liter engine usually uses a disposable filter-vapor separator that is located on the front side of the engine block between the fuel pump and carburetor. On some applications, this filter has not only inlet and outlet connections, but a third connection designed to permit

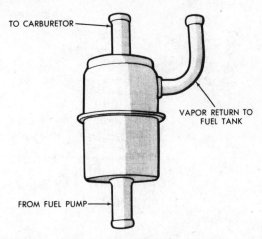

TO CARBURETOR

VAPOR RETURN TO FUEL TANK

FROM FUEL PUMP

Fuel filter vapor separator 2.2L engine

fuel to return to the tank so that vapor that accumulates in hot weather will not interfere with carburetion.

The 2.6 liter engine uses a disposable, canister type filter in most applications. This type filter has only two connections.

A few models use a filter-reservoir assembly that attaches to the air cleaner and also has three connections, one for the elimination of vapor.

A plugged fuel filter can limit the speed at which a vehicle can be driven and may cause hard starting. The most critical symptom will usually be suddenly reduced engine performance at maximum engine power levels, as when passing.

Remove the filter as follows:

1. Have a metal container ready to catch spilled fuel. Make sure the engine is cool.

2. Remove the hose clamps from each end of the filter. Then, disconnect the hoses, collecting the fuel in the metal container.

3. Remove the old filter and hoses. On the non-return (two connection) type filter used on 2.6 liter engines, this requires unfastening the mounting bracket. On the reservoir type filter,

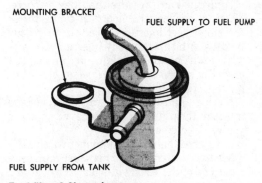

MOUNTING BRACKET

FUEL SUPPLY TO FUEL PUMP

FUEL SUPPLY FROM TANK

Fuel filter 2.6L engine

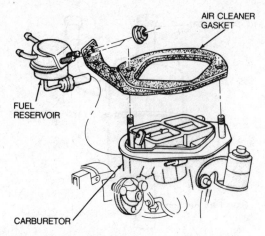

The fuel reservoir type filter used on some models

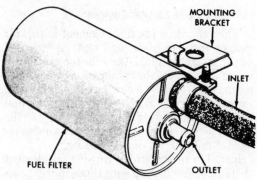

The fuel filter used on fuel injected models through the 1987 model year

remove the two mounting nuts inside the air cleaner.

4. Put the new filter into position. If it has mounting studs, pass them through the mounting bracket and then install the attaching nuts snugly. Connect the hoses, and install and tighten the hose clamps (if the hoses are hard to force onto the nipples, you can wet them inside just very slightly). Make sure the clamps are located a short distance away from the ends of the hoses and on the inside of the nipples located on the ends of the filter connections.

5. Start the engine and check for leaks.

Fuel Injected Engines

CAUTION: *Fuel injected engines use high pressure in their operation. This pressure is maintained through the action of check valves even when the engine is off. Therefore, you must be sure to work on the fuel carrying parts of injected cars only when the engine has cooled off and only after you have properly bled the pressurized fuel from the system. Failure to do this could readily cause a fire!*

1. Relieve fuel system pressure as follows:

a. Loosen the fuel tank cap to release any accumulated air pressure that may be there. Then, disconnect the electrical connector at the single fuel injector on the throttle body on cars with throttle body injection. On cars with multi-point injection, disconnect the electrical connector on the injector closest to the battery.

b. Use a jumper wire to ground one of the injector terminals for whichever injector you've disconnected.

c. Connect one end of a jumper wire to the other injector terminal. Then, just touch the other end of the second jumper to the battery positive post for nearly 10 seconds. *Make sure*

you do not maintain this connection for more than the maximum of 10 seconds or the injector could be damaged.

2. Remove the retaining screw that mounts the filter to its retaining bracket so you can reach the hose clamps.

3. Then, loosen the clamps for both the inlet and outlet lines. Quickly wrap a shop towel around these connections to collect escaping fuel safely. Then, dispose of this towel in such a way as to protect it from heat the the chance of fire.

4. Note the routing of the hoses. The high pressure hose from the tank and pump goes to the inlet connection, which is always located toward the outer edge of the filter. The outlet hose to the engine is labeled on some filters and is always at the center. Pull the hoses off the connections on the filter. Replace the filter, draining fuel into a metal container and disposing of it safely. Inspect the hoses and clamps and replace defective parts as necessary.

WARNING: *Chrysler uses and recommends hoses that meet their specifications and are labeled "EFM/EFI18519". Make sure you use either this type of hose or an equivalent, high pressure (up to 55 psi) type of fuel hose available in the automotive aftermarket. Be sure not to use ordinary rubber fuel hose, as this is not tough enough for high pressure use and may not be able to resist the destruction caused by certain types of contamination. Also, if hose clamps require replacement, note that the original equipment clamps have rolled edges to keep the edge of the band from cutting into this hose, due to the necessary use of high clamping forces with a high pressure fuel system. Make sure that you use either an original equipment clamp or a similar type of clamp available in the aftermarket.*

5. Reconnect the hoses, using the proper routing noted as you disconnected them. You may want to very slightly wet the inside diameter of the hoses to make it easier to install them

onto the filter connections. Install them as far as possible, until they are well over the bulges at the ends of the connectors. Install the clamps so they are a short distance away from the ends of the hoses but well over the bulged areas at the ends of the filter connections. Tighten both clamps securely. If you have an inch lb. torque wrench torque them to 10 in.lb.

6. Remount the filter on the bracket snugly with the screw. Start the engine and check for leaks, tightening the hose clamps, replacing parts, or forcing the hoses farther onto the connectors, if necessary.

PCV Valve and System Components

The PCV system draws a small amount of air through the engine crankcase in order to remove and reburn a small amount of incompletely burned fuel that accumulates there. A vehicle run on unleaded fuel and receiving frequent oil changes and tune-ups will rarely exhibit trouble with this system. Because a clogged PCV system not only increases emissions but can contribute to engine wear, or may cause rough idle or stalling, it should be inspected regularly. In addition, all cars equipped with a crankcase vent module require that it be cleaned at 50,000 miles.

To inspect the system pull the PCV valve out of the crankcase vent module, valve cover, or crankcase vent valve hose and shake it. If the valve rattles, this is a partial indication that it is okay; if there is no sound, it must be replaced and the PCV hose cleaned by spraying solvent through it.

If the valve rattles, you should still check the PCV valve with the engine idling. Pull it out of the vent module and place your finger or thumb over the end to stop air flow. You should feel some suction, and the engine speed should drop slightly. If there is no suction, or if the engine idle speeds up and smooths out considerably, replace the valve. Inspect the PCV hose and clean it by spraying solvent through it, if the inside is coated with gum and varnish.

Check the vacuum at the PCV inlet tube, as well. Disconnect this tube from the air cleaner and loosely hold a piece of paper over the tube. After about a minute, enough vacuum should build up to cause the paper to be sucked against the opening with a noticeable amount of force. This test proves whether or not the suction side of the system is clear.

Regardless of PCV valve or system performance, the valve itself should be replaced at specified intervals. At this time, you should inspect the hoses for clogging and spray a small amount of a safe cleaning solvent designed for this purpose through the hoses to remove any accumulated sludge or varnish.

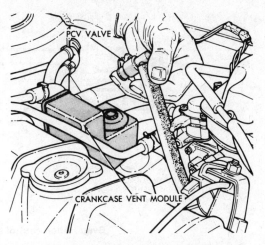

Servicing the PCV valve—2.2 liter engine shown

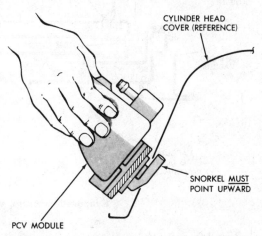

Removing or installing the PCV module on the 2.2 liter engine

If the car has the PCV module used on carbureted 2.2L engines and has 50,000 miles on it or a multiple of that figure, the module must be cleaned. First, remove the PCV valve and vent hose from the module. Then, depress the retaining clip and turn the module counterclockwise to remove it. Use kerosene or a similar cleaning solvent (not gasoline!) to flush the filter inside the module. Allow to dry. Then, invert the module and fill it with SAE 30 engine oil. Turn it right side up and permit the oil to drain through the vent located on top of the air cleaner. Then, carefully depress the retaining clip, insert the module and turn it clockwise until it reaches its normal position to install it. Do not force the module in or to turn. Note that the snorkel must end up pointing upward and must not be free to rotate. Reconnect the vent hose and PCV valve.

On 1987-88 models, the air drawn into the PCV system passes through a foam or metal

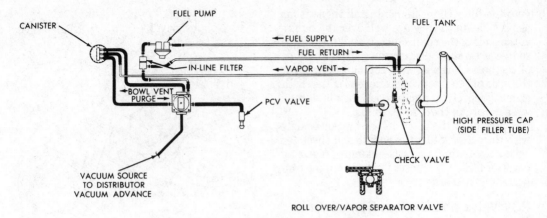

Evaporation control system—2.2L engine

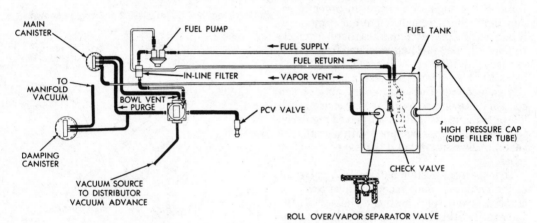

Evaporation control system—2.6L engine

mesh and foam filtration system. At the maintenance interval when PCV valve replacement is required, you should remove this element (or these elements) and replace it (or them). These elements are typically located in a corner of the air cleaner housing where you can see them as soon as the air filter element has been removed. If they become clogged before the normal service interval, they may be cleaned in a solvent such as kerosene and then coated with engine oil. When the car has reached the normal maintenance interval for the PCV system, these filters should be replaced.

Evaporative Control System

The function of the Evaporative Control System is to prevent gasoline vapors from the fuel tank from escaping into the atmosphere. Periodic maintenance is required only on 1981-82 models. The fiberglass filter on the bottom of the canister must be replaced on these models, but only if the vehicle is driven under dusty conditions.

To replace the filter, note locations of the hoses going to the canister, and then disconnect

them. Unclamp the canister, pull the filter out as shown, and replace it in reverse order.

In spite of the fact that this system requires no periodic maintenance, it is a good idea to quickly look over the hoses when servicing the PCV system. If any of these hoses is cracked, torn, or rotted, the result could be vacuum

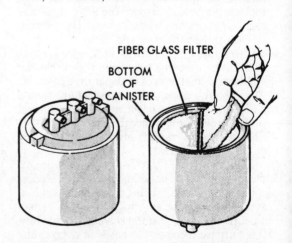

Replacing evaporative canister filter (1981–82 models)

leaks and consequent poor engine operation or an annoying smell of fuel vapor. If any of these hoses should require replacement, make sure to use a high quality replacement hose of a material approved for use in fuel bearing applications. Ordinary vacuum type rubber hose will not give satisfactory life or reliable performance.

Battery

Two types of batteries are used, Standard and Maintenance Free. Both batteries are equipped with a Test Charge Indicator. This indicator is a built-in hydrometer, which replaces one of the battery filler caps in the Standard battery and is permanently installed in the cover on the Maintenance Free battery.

Visual inspection of the indicator sight glass will aid in determining battery condition. The indicator shows green if the battery is above 76-80 percent of being fully charged, and dark if it needs charging. A light yellow means the battery requires water or may need replacing.

For Standard batteries, check the fluid level in each cell every 2 months (more often in hot weather or on long trips). If the water is low, fill it to the bottom of the filler well with distilled water.

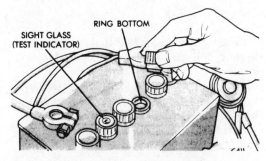

Check the fluid level—standard battery

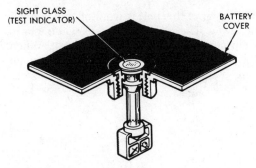

Test indicator—maintenance free battery

Drive Belts
INSPECTION

Check the drive belts every 15,000 miles for evidence of wear such as cracking, fraying, and incorrect tension. Determine the belt tension at a point half-way between the pulleys by pressing on the belt with moderate thumb pressure. The belt should deflect about ¼-½" at this point. Note that "deflection"is not play, but the ability of the belt, under actual tension, to stretch slightly and give.

Although it is generally easier on the component to have the belt too loose than too tight, a very loose belt may place a high impact load on a bearing due to the whipping or snapping action of the belt. A belt that is slightly loose may slip, especially when component loads are high. This slippage may be hard to identify. For example, the generator belt may run okay during the day, and then slip at night when headlights are turned on. Slipping belts wear quickly not only due to the direct effect of slippage but also because of the heat the slippage generates. Extreme slippage may even cause a belt to burn. A very smooth, glazed appearance on the belt's sides, as opposed to the obvious pattern of a fabric cover, indicates that the belt has been slipping.

ADJUSTMENT

WARNING: *Be careful not to overtighten the drive belts, as this will damage the driven component's bearings.*

Except Alternator/Water Pump Drive Belt

If the deflection is found to be too much or too little, loosen the accessory's slotted adjusting bracket bolt. If the hinge bolt is very tight, it too may have to be loosened. Use a wooden hammer handle or a broomstick to lever the accessory closer to or farther away from the engine to provide the correct tension. Do not use a metal prybar, which may damage the component by springing the housing. When the belt tension seems correct, tighten the bolts and then recheck the adjustment, in case the component has moved slightly.

Alternator/Water Pump Drive Belt

On most of the engines covered in this guide, the alternator/water pump drive belt is tensioned by a more sophisticated screw type tensioner which makes precise tension adjustment much easier. If the belt deflection is found to be incorrect, first loosen the locknut located on the locking screw or the lockbolt. On all but 1988 models, this is located in a slotted portion of the outboard alternator mounting bracket. On '88 models, loosen the T-bolt located in the center of the disc shaped portion of the outboard alternator bracket. Then, on all models, tighten or loosen the tensioning bolt located outboard of the alternator. This bolt is tightened (turned clockwise) to increase belt tension and loosened

HOW TO SPOT WORN V-BELTS

V-Belts are vital to efficient engine operation—they drive the fan, water pump and other accessories. They require little maintenance (occasional tightening) but they will not last forever. Slipping or failure of the V-belt will lead to overheating. If your V-belt looks like any of these, it should be replaced.

Cracking or weathering

This belt has deep cracks, which cause it to flex. Too much flexing leads to heat build-up and premature failure. These cracks can be caused by using the belt on a pulley that is too small. Notched belts are available for small diameter pulleys.

Softening (grease and oil)

Oil and grease on a belt can cause the belt's rubber compounds to soften and separate from the reinforcing cords that hold the belt together. The belt will first slip, then finally fail altogether.

Glazing

Glazing is caused by a belt that is slipping. A slipping belt can cause a run-down battery, erratic power steering, overheating or poor accessory performance. The more the belt slips, the more glazing will be built up on the surface of the belt. The more the belt is glazed, the more it will slip. If the glazing is light, tighten the belt.

Worn cover

The cover of this belt is worn off and is peeling away. The reinforcing cords will begin to wear and the belt will shortly break. When the belt cover wears in spots or has a rough jagged appearance, check the pulley grooves for roughness.

Separation

This belt is on the verge of breaking and leaving you stranded. The layers of the belt are separating and the reinforcing cords are exposed. It's just a matter of time before it breaks completely.

to decrease it. When the belt tension is correct, tighten the lockbolt.

Hoses

REMOVAL AND INSTALLATION

All Models

CAUTION: *Do not perform this procedure on a hot or warm engine. Otherwise, serious injury could result.*

1. Drain the cooling system through the bottom of the radiator (the block need not be drained to replace the hoses.

2. Remove the top hose from the radiator neck and the thermostat housing.

3. Remove the bottom hose from the water pump and the bottom of the radiator.

4. Remove the heater hoses from the core connections near the firewall and the nipples on the cylinder head and thermostat housing. Remove any bypass hoses from the thermostat housing and intake manifold.

5. Check the hoses for damage. Hoses that are brittle, cracked, or extremely soft and pliable require replacement. Replace them as necessary.

6. Inspect the clamps for corrosion, fatigue (causing them to lose their springiness), or, in the case of aircraft type clamps, stripped threads. Replace any clamps that are questionable.

7. Installation is the reverse of removal. Refill and bleed the cooling system.

Air Conditioning

SAFETY WARNINGS

The compressed refrigerant used in the air conditioning system expands into the atmosphere at a temperature of –21.7°F or lower. This will freeze any surface, including your eyes, that it contacts. In addition, the refrigerant decomposes into a poisonous gas in the presence of flame. Further, the refrigerant normally produces high pressure in the system, especially when it is running.

For these reasons, any repair work to an air conditioning system should be left to a professional. Do not, under any circumstances, attempt to loosen or tighten any fittings or perform any work other than that outlined here.

SYSTEM INSPECTION

Checking for Oil Leaks

Refrigerant leaks show up as oily areas on the various components because the compressor oil is transported around the entire system along with the refrigerant. Look for oil spots on all the hoses and lines, and especially on the hose

and tubing connections. If there are oily deposits, the system may have a leak, and you should have it checked by a qualified repairman.

NOTE: *A small area of oil on the front of the compressor is normal and no cause for alarm.*

Checking the Compressor Belt

Inspect the belt carefully for glazing on the V surfaces, which indicates slippage (there should be a slight crosshatch or fabric appearance), cracks (which usually start at the center) or any other damage, including being too stretched to permit a tight adjustment. Replace the A/C belt if there is any sign at all of damage, as this belt carries a great deal of load.

On most air conditioning installations (2.2 and 2.5L engines), the compressor is mounted directly to the block or cylinder head and remains in the same position regardless of the belt adjustment. An idler bracket is locked in place by two locknuts and a pivot bolt. It is rotated via a nut that is welded onto its front surface to adjust the compressor drive belt.

Check the belt tension by depressing the belt in the center of its longest span with your thumb. It should depress approximately $\frac{7}{16}''$. If the tension is incorrect, loosen the two lockbolts and the pivot bolt. Then, turn the bracket via the weld nut until tension is correct. Hold the bracket in position as you first tighten the locking bolts and then tighten the pivot bolt. Recheck the tension to make sure it has not changed. Readjust if necessary.

On the 2.6L engine, the air conditioning compressor drive belt is adjusted by adjusting the position of the alternator. Check the tension as described in the paragraph above. Then, if the belt needs adjustment, loosen the locking screw on the front of the slotted alternator bracket, the jamnut on the adjusting bolt, and the pivot nut on the pivot through bolt. Turn the adjusting bolt clockwise to increase belt tension or counterclockwise to reduce it. When tension is correct, tighten the three nuts. Recheck the tension and readjust it if necessary.

Checking Refrigerant Level

The first order of business when checking the sight glass is to find it. It will be in the head of the receiver/drier. In some cases, it may be covered by a small rubber plug designed to keep it clean. Once you've found it, remove the cover, if necessary, wipe it clean and proceed as follows:

1. With the engine and the air conditioning system running, look for the flow of refrigerant through the sight glass. If the air conditioner is working properly, you'll be able to see a continuous flow of clear refrigerant through the sight

HOW TO SPOT BAD HOSES

Both the upper and lower radiator hoses are called upon to perform difficult jobs in an inhospitable environment. They are subject to nearly 18 psi at under hood temperatures often over 280°F., and must circulate nearly 7500 gallons of coolant an hour—3 good reasons to have good hoses.

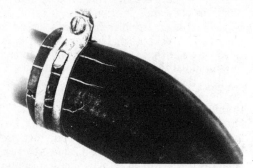

A good test for any hose is to feel it for soft or spongy spots. Frequently these will appear as swollen areas of the hose. The most likely cause is oil soaking. This hose could burst at any time, when hot or under pressure.

Swollen hose

Cracked hoses can usually be seen but feel the hoses to be sure they have not hardened; a prime cause of cracking. This hose has cracked down to the reinforcing cords and could split at any of the cracks.

Cracked hose

Weakened clamps frequently are the cause of hose and cooling system failure. The connection between the pipe and hose has deteriorated enough to allow coolant to escape when the engine is hot.

Frayed hose end (due to weak clamp)

Debris, rust and scale in the cooling system can cause the inside of a hose to weaken. This can usually be felt on the outside of the hose as soft or thinner areas.

Debris in cooling system

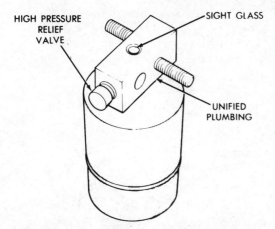

HIGH PRESSURE RELIEF VALVE

SIGHT GLASS

UNIFIED PLUMBING

The refrigerant sightglass on air conditioned vehicles is located in the top of the receiver-drier

glass, with perhaps an occasional bubble at very high outside temperatures.

2. Cycle the air conditioner on and off to make sure what you are seeing is a pure stream of liquid refrigerant. Since the refrigerant is clear, it is possible to mistake a completely discharged system for one that is fully charged. Turn the system off and watch the sight glass. If there is refrigerant in the system, you'll see bubbles during the off cycle. Also, the lines going into and out of the compressor will be at radically different temperatures (be careful about touching the line going forward to the condenser, which is in front of the radiator, as it will be very hot). If the bubbles disappear just after you start the compressor, there are no bubbles when the system is running, and the air flow from the unit in the car is cold, everything is O.K.

3. If you observe bubbles in the sight glass while the system is operating, the system is low on refrigerant. You may want to charge it yourself, as described later. Otherwise, have it checked by a professional.

4. If all you can see in the sight glass is oil streaks, this is an indication of trouble. This is true because there is no liquid refrigerant in the system (otherwise, the oil would mix with the refrigerant and would be invisible). Most of the time, if you see oil in the sight glass, it will appear as a series of streaks, although occasionally it may be a solid stream of oil. In either case, it means that part of the charge of refrigerant has been lost.

USING THE BAR GAUGE MANIFOLD

WARNING: *Refrigerant work is usually performed by highly trained technicians. Improper use of the gauges can result in a leakage of refrigerant liquid, damage to the compressor, or even explosion of a system part.*

The do-it-yourselfer must be very careful to insure that he proceeds with extreme care and understands what he is doing before proceeding. The best insurance for safety is a complete understanding of the system and proper techniques for servicing it. A careful study of a complete text such as CHILTON'S GUIDE TO AIR CONDITIONING SERVICE AND REPAIR, book part No. 7580, is the best insurance against either dangerous or system-damaging problems.

To use the bar gauge manifold, follow the procedures outlined below.

1. It is first necessary to clear the manifold itself of air and moisture, especially if the fittings have been left open. You should follow this procedure, unless you know that the hoses and gauge manifold have recently been bled with refrigerant and capped off tightly. Otherwise, you may actually force air and moisture into the system when you are testing or charging it. Begin with both the service valves on the refrigerant gauge set *closed.*

a. First, tap a can of refrigerant. To do this, first unscrew the tap's cutting tool all the way. Turn the rotatable locking lever so it leaves one side of the collar assembly open. Then, slide the tap onto the top of the can so the collar tabs fit over the rim that runs around the top of the can. Turn the locking lever so that it secures the collar. Then, turn the cutting tool all the way down to tap the can.

b. Remove any plugs that may be present and then screw the *center* hose to the screw fitting on top of the tap. Now, slightly loosen the plugs in the ends of the other two lines.

c. Sit the can of refrigerant down right side up on a flat surface. *Make sure the can does not get pulled up off the surface as you work, or you could be splattered by liquid refrigerant.* Then, open the tap by unscrewing the tapping tool handle all the way. Crack both of the bar gauge manifold valves just a little-- just until you hear a slight hiss at the plug at the end of the hose on either side. Allow the refrigerant to enter the system until you are sure it has reached the ends of the hoses (30 seconds). Tighten the plugs at the bottom of the hoses and then *immediately* turn off both manifold valves.

2. Using a wrench if the cap has flats, uncap the low and high pressure, Schrader valve type fittings for the system. The low pressure fitting is located on the suction port of the compressor. In a typical mounting of the unit with the ports facing the front of the car, this is the lower port. You'll find that there is a line connecting with this port that comes from the evaporator (located behind the cowl). The high pressure fitting is

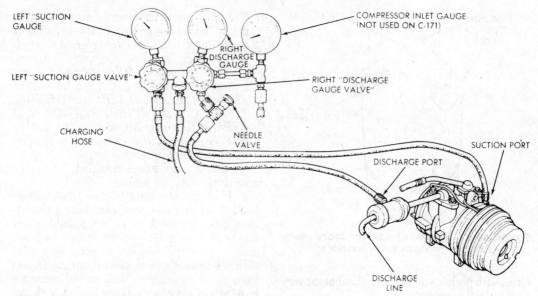

Hook the gauges up as shown. Note that you can use a bar gauge manifold set that has only two gauges— you do not need the "compressor inlet" gauge shown on the right.

located on the muffler, which, in turn is located on the line coming out of the commpressor and heading toward the condenser. There is a low pressure gauge on the left side of the manifold, which shows pressures up to about 100 psi *and* vacuum. Connect the line on this side to the low pressure side of the system. The gauge on the right or high pressure side of the manifold reads only pressure and, typically, the scale goes up to 500 psi. or higher. On some gauge sets sold for use with Chrysler systems, there is a third gauge, known as the "compressor inlet gauge" to the right of the discharge or high pressure gauge. This gauge is for testing systems that use a special pressure regulating valve in the compressor. Since none of the front wheel drive cars covered by this guide use this type of compressor, you will not use this gauge. If you are shopping for gauges, you can use a conventional set which has only two gauges.

On many newer systems, the threads on high and low pressure Schrader valves are of different sizes to prevent improper hookup.

If you have an older set of gauges, you can get an adapter or a different hose that will convert your gauges to the new thread sizes. Consult a heating, air conditioning and refrigeration supply source.

WARNING: *When making connections, start the threads carefully and, once you are sure they are not crossthreaded, turn the fitting as fast as you can in order to avoid getting sprayed by refrigerant. Sometimes the Schrader valve will open early--before the fitting is tight, and this will cause a little refrigerant to be sprayed out.*

3. Use of the gauges once they are bled and installed typically includes reading high and low side pressures with both valves closed, charging the system with the low side valve cracked partly open, and discharging it with both valves partly open. Refer to the section just below on "Charging the System" for specifics.

4. To disconnect the gauges, turn the fittings as quickly as possible so as to close the Schrader valves as quickly as possible. Note that liquid refrigerant and oil may be sprayed out for a short time as this is done, especially on the low pressure side. Turn the fittings by reaching down from above, as liquid will be sprayed out underneath the gauge connection. Less refrigerant will be sprayed out on the high side if the connection is broken a few minutes after the system is turned off. Cap the open ends of the gauges immediately. If, for any reason, the ends are left open for a minute or two, repeat the bleeding procedure above. Tightly cap the system openings right away.

DISCHARGING THE SYSTEM

NOTE: *Fluorocarbon refrigerants like that used in car air conditioners damage the upper atmosphere, destroying its ability to screen off dangerous solar radiation. For this reason, air conditioning service shops will soon be required to use special charging/evacuating stations to condense and recover refrigerants rather than releasing them to the atmosphere. While these environmental regulations may not apply to the do-it-yourselfer, you may wish to have your system discharged by a professional equipped to recover the refrigerant if you are concerned about the environment.*

1. Connect the gauges to the high and low sides of the system, as described above. Do not connect a refrigerant can to the center hose.

2. Insert the center hose into a glass bottle with an opening that is slightly larger in diameter than the hose. *Do not attempt to cap or seal the opening in the top of the bottle in any way.* This bottle will collect oil discharged from the system so that it can be measured and replaced when the system is recharged. Make sure you keep the bottle upright to avoid spilling any of this oil out.

3. Make sure the compressor is turned off and remains off throughout the procedure. Crack the low side manifold valve until refrigerant gas is expelled at a steady, moderate rate. Don't open the valve all the way, or too much refrigerant oil will be expelled from the system.

4. As refrigerant pressure drops and the gas begins to be expelled only very slowly, open the low side manifold valve more and more to compensate and keep the refrigerant moving out of the system.

5. Once *all* the pressure is discharged, slowly open the high side service valve, repeating Steps 3 and 4 until the system is clear. Close it after any pressure has escaped.

6. Disconnect the gauges and recap the openings. Retain the bottle of oil. If you have the system evacuated and recharged by a professional, give him the bottle of oil. He will measure the amount it contains and replace it with a like amount.

CHARGING THE SYSTEM

WARNING: *Charging the system can prove to be very dangerous. You must satisfy yourself that you are fully aware of all risks before starting. Although most systems use a high pressure cutoff switch for the compressor, overcharging the system, attempting to charge it when it contains air, or charging it when there is inadequate cooling of the condenser could cause dangerous pressures to develop if this switch should fail. Overcharging could also damage the compressor.*

The safest way to charge the system is with a set of gauges installed and reading both low and high side pressures so that you can monitor pressures throughout the procedure. It is best to refer to a text on refrigeration and air conditioning first, so that you understand what will happen. Using the simple hose sold for do-it-yourself charging of the system can be safe, provided three precautions are taken:

a. Make sure the system has been completely evacuated by a professional with a good vacuum pump. Eliminating air in the system is a vital step toward maintaining safe pressures during the charging process and ensuring reliable and effective operation later.

b. Charge the system with precisely the amount of refrigerant it is specified to use *and no more.* Consult the label on the compressor. Purchase the right number of cans. You can precisely estimate what percentage of a can has been charged into the system by noting the frost line on the can.

c. Run the engine at a moderate speed during charging (not too fast), valve the refrigerant into the system at a controlled rate, and keep a fan blowing across the condenser at all times.

Charge the system by following these steps:

1. Make sure the system has been completely evacuated with a good vacuum pump. This should be done with gauges connected and the pump must be able to create a vacuum of 28-29 in.Hg near sea level. Lower this specification one in.Hg for each 1,000 feet above sea level at your location.

2. Connect the gauges as described above, including tapping in a new can of refrigerant. If you are using a gaugeless hose that is part of a charging kit, follow the directions on the package; in any case, make sure to hook up the hose to the low pressure side of the system--to the accumulator or POA valve.

3. Situate a fan in front of the condenser and use it to blow air through the condenser and radiator throughout the charging process.

4. Unless the system has a sight glass, get the exact refrigerant capacity off the compressor label. Make sure you have only the proper number of cans available to help avoid unnecessary overcharge.

5. It will speed the process to place the cans, top up, in warm water. Use a thermometer and make sure the water is *not over 120°F.* You will need to warm the water as the process goes on. Monitor the temperature to make sure it does not go too high, as warm water will almost immediately create excessive pressure inside the can—pressure that will not be reflected in gauge readings. Make sure the cans *always* stay top up. This requires a lot of attention because as the cans run low on refrigerant, they begin to float and may turn upside down. Charging the system with the can upside down may cause liquid refrigerant to enter the system, damaging the compressor. If the bar gauge manifold or charging line suddenly frosts up, check the position of the can immediately and rectify it, if necessary!

6. Start the process with the engine off. Open the charging valve (if you are using a kit)

or the low side bar gauge manifold valve slightly until the pressures equalize. Then, close the charging valve or bar gauge manifold back off. Place an electric fan in front of the condenser. Then, start the engine and run it at idle speed or just very slightly above. Turn the blower to the lowest speed. Then, turn the air conditioner on in the normal operating mode. If the system has no refrigerant in it, the low pressure cutout switch on the compressor will keep it from starting until some pressure is created in the system.

7. If you're working with a charging kit, follow the manufacturer's instructions as to how far to open the charging valve. If you're working with a bar gauge manifold, and the system has a lot of refrigerant in it (you're just topping it off) follow the rest of this step. Otherwise, skip to 8. Note the operating pressure (the average if the compressor is cycling). Then, open the manifold valve until system low side pressure rises 10 psi. Throughout the charging procedure, maintain this pressure by opening or closing the valve to compensate for changes in the temperature of the refrigerant can. Also, keep your eye on the high side pressure and make sure it remains at a moderate level (usually less than 200 psi).

8. Gradually open the valve on the suction (left) side of the bar gauge manifold, as you watch the low side gauge. Allow the pressure to build until the compressor comes on and runs continuously. Keep permitting it to rise until it reaches 50 psi. Then, carefully control the position of the valve to maintain this pressure. You will have to change the position of the valve to compensate for cooling of the refrigerant can and surrounding water and to help empty the can.

9. When the first can runs out of refrigerant, close off the manifold valve or charging line valve. Tap in a new can, immerse it in liquid, keeping it right side up, and then open the charging line valve if you're working without gauges. If you are working with gauges, open the valve on the tap and then open the low side manifold valve as described in Step 8 to maintain the pressure as before.

10. Continue with the process until the last can is hooked up. Measure in a fraction of a can, if necessary, by watching the frost line on the can and stopping appropriately. Watch for the time when bubbles just disappear from the sight glass. If you're just topping off the system, stop charging just after this occurs. Otherwise, this is a sign that you should expect the system to be completely charged and find that you have just about measured the right amount of refrigerant in. Be ready to stop charging! If you're just topping off the system, turn off the charging valve or low side manifold valve and then run the system with the fan on high and the engine accelerated to about 1,500 rpm to check the charge. If bubbles appear, charge the system slightly more until just after all the bubbles disappear.

11. When charging is complete, turn off the manifold or charging line valves and any valve on the can. Disconnect the low side line *at the suction line and not at the gauges*, grabbing the connection from above, watching for liquid refrigerant to spray out, and unscrewing the con-

Troubleshooting Basic Air Conditioning Problems

Problem	Cause	Solution
There's little or no air coming from the vents (and you're sure it's on)	• The A/C fuse is blown • Broken or loose wires or connections • The on/off switch is defective	• Check and/or replace fuse • Check and/or repair connections • Replace switch
The air coming from the vents is not cool enough	• Windows and air vent wings open • The compressor belt is slipping • Heater is on • Condenser is clogged with debris • Refrigerant has escaped through a leak in the system • Receiver/drier is plugged	• Close windows and vent wings • Tighten or replace compressor belt • Shut heater off • Clean the condenser • Check system • Service system
The air has an odor	• Vacuum system is disrupted • Odor producing substances on the evaporator case • Condensation has collected in the bottom of the evaporator housing	• Have the system checked/repaired • Clean the evaporator case • Clean the evaporator housing drains
System is noisy or vibrating	• Compressor belt or mountings loose • Air in the system	• Tighten or replace belt; tighten mounting bolts • Have the system serviced

Troubleshooting Basic Air Conditioning Problems (cont.)

Problem	Cause	Solution
Sight glass condition		
Constant bubbles, foam or oil streaks	• Undercharged system	• Charge the system
Clear sight glass, but no cold air	• No refrigerant at all	• Check and charge the system
Clear sight glass, but air is cold	• System is OK	
Clouded with milky fluid	• Receiver drier is leaking dessicant	• Have system checked
Large difference in temperature of lines	• System undercharged	• Charge and leak test the system
Compressor noise	• Broken valves	• Replace the valve plate
	• Overcharged	• Discharge, evacuate and install the correct charge
	• Incorrect oil level	• Isolate the compressor and check the oil level. Correct as necessary.
	• Piston slap	• Replace the compressor
	• Broken rings	• Replace the compressor
	• Drive belt pulley bolts are loose	• Tighten with the correct torque specification
Excessive vibration	• Incorrect belt tension	• Adjust the belt tension
	• Clutch loose	• Tighten the clutch
	• Overcharged	• Discharge, evacuate and install the correct charge
	• Pulley is misaligned	• Align the pulley
Condensation dripping in the passenger compartment	• Drain hose plugged or improperly positioned	• Clean the drain hose and check for proper installation
	• Insulation removed or improperly installed	• Replace the insulation on the expansion valve and hoses
Frozen evaporator coil	• Faulty thermostat	• Replace the thermostat
	• Thermostat capillary tube improperly installed	• Install the capillary tube correctly
	• Thermostat not adjusted properly	• Adjust the thermostat
Low side low—high side low	• System refrigerant is low	• Evacuate, leak test and charge the system
	• Expansion valve is restricted	• Replace the expansion valve
Low side high—high side low	• Internal leak in the compressor—worn	• Remove the compressor cylinder head and inspect the compressor. Replace the valve plate assembly if necessary. If the compressor pistons, rings or cylinders are excessively worn or scored replace the compressor
	• Cylinder head gasket is leaking	• Install a replacement cylinder head gasket
	• Expansion valve is defective	• Replace the expansion valve
	• Drive belt slipping	• Adjust the belt tension
Low side high—high side high	• Condenser fins obstructed	• Clean the condenser fins
	• Air in the system	• Evacuate, leak test and charge the system
	• Expansion valve is defective	• Replace the expansion valve
	• Loose or worn fan belts	• Adjust or replace the belts as necessary
Low side low—high side high	• Expansion valve is defective	• Replace the expansion valve
	• Restriction in the refrigerant hose	• Check the hose for kinks—replace if necessary
	• Restriction in the receiver/drier	• Replace the receiver/drier
	• Restriction in the condenser	• Replace the condenser
Low side and high side normal (inadequate cooling)	• Air in the system	• Evacuate, leak test and charge the system
	• Moisture in the system	• Evacuate, leak test and charge the system

nection as fast as you can. Turn off the engine and allow the pressure on the high side to drop until it stabilizes. Then, disconnect the high side gauge connection (if necessary) as quickly as possible. Cap both system openings and all gauge openings as soon as possible.

Windshield Wipers

For maximum effectiveness and longest element life, the windshield and wiper blades should be kept clean. Dirt, tree sap, road tar and so on will cause streaking, smearing and blade deterioration if left on the glass. It is advisable to wash the windshield carefully with a commercial glass cleaner at least once a month. Wipe off the rubber blades with the wet rag afterwards. Do not attempt to move the wipers by hand; damage to the motor and drive mechanism will result.

If the blades are found to be cracked, broken or torn, they should be replaced immediately. Replacement intervals will vary with usage, although ozone deterioration usually limits blade life to about one year. If the wiper pattern is smeared or streaked, or if the blade chatters across the glass, the elements should be replaced. It is easiest and most sensible to replace the elements in pairs.

There are basically three different types of refills, which differ in their method of replacement. One type has two release buttons, approximately 1/3 of the way up from the ends of the blade frame. Pushing the buttons down releases a lock and allows the rubber filler to be removed from the frame. The new filler slides back into the frame and locks in place.

The second type of refill has two metal tabs which are unlocked by squeezing them together. The rubber filler can then be withdrawn from the frame jaws. A new refill is installed by inserting the refill into the front frame jaws and sliding it rearward to engage the remaining frame jaws. There are usually four jaws. Be certain when installing that the refill is engaged in all of them. At the end of its travel, the tabs will lock into place on the front jaws of the wiper blade frame.

The third type is a refill made from polycarbonate. The refill has a simple locking device at one end which flexes downward out of the groove into which the jaws of the holder fit, allowing easy release. By sliding the new refill through all the jaws and pushing through the slight resistance when it reaches the end of its travel, the refill will lock into position.

Regardless of the type of refill used, make sure that all of the frame jaws are engaged as the refill is pushed into place and locked. The metal blade holder and frame will scratch the glass if allowed to touch it.

ARM AND BLADE REPLACEMENT

A detailed description and procedures for replacing the wiper arm and blade is found in Chapter 6.

TIRES AND WHEELS

Inspect the tires regularly for wear and damage. Remove stones or other foreign particles which may be lodged in the tread. If tread wear is excessive or irregular it could be a sign of front end problems, or simply improper inflation.

The inflation should be checked at least once per month and adjusted if necessary. The tires must be cold (driven less than one mile) or an inaccurate reading will result. Do not forget to check the spare.

The correct inflation pressure for your vehicle can be found on a decal mounted to the car. Depending upon model and year, the decal can be located at the driver's door, the passenger's door or the glove box. If you cannot find the decal a local automobile tire dealer can furnish you with information.

Inspect tires for uneven wear that might indicate the need for front end alignment or tire rotation. Tires should be replaced when a tread wear indicator appears as a solid band across the tread.

When you buy new tires, give some thought to these points, especially if you are switching to larger tires or to another profile series (50, 60, 70, 78):

1. The wheels must be the correct width for the tire. Tire dealers have charts of tire and rim compatibility. A mismatch can cause sloppy handling and rapid tread wear. The old rule of thumb is that the tread width should match the rim width (inside bead to inside bead) within an inch. For radial tires, the rim width should be 80% or less of the tire (not tread) width.

2. The height (mounted diameter) of the new tires can greatly change speedometer accuracy, engine speed at a given road speed, fuel mileage, acceleration, and ground clearance. Tire makers furnish full measurement specifications. Speedometer drive gears are available from Ford dealers for correction.

NOTE: *Dimensions of tires marked the same size may vary significantly, even among tires from the same maker.*

3. The spare tire should be usable, at least for low speed operation, with the new tires.

4. There shouldn't be any body interference when loaded, on bumps, or in turning.

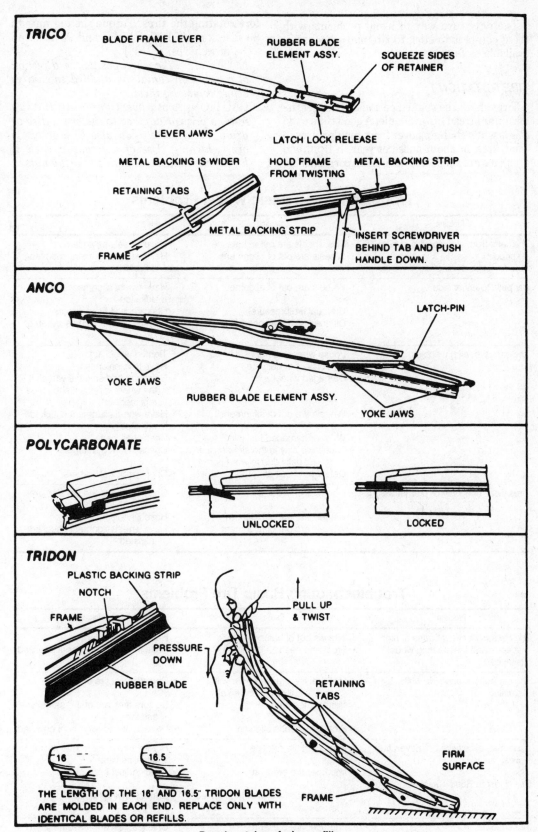

Popular styles of wiper refills

The only sure way to avoid problems with these points is to stick to tire and wheel sizes available as factory options.

TIRE ROTATION

Tires should be rotated periodically to get the maximum tread life available. A good time to do this is when changing over from regular tires to snow tires, or about once per year. If front end problems are suspected have them corrected be-fore rotating the tires. Torque the lug nuts to 80 ft.lb. on 1981-82 vehicles and 95 ft.lb. on 1983-88 vehicles.

NOTE: *Mark the wheel position or direction of rotation on radial, or studded snow tires before removing them.*

CAUTION: *Avoid overtightening the lug nuts to prevent damage to the brake disc or drum. Alloy wheels can also be cracked by overtightening. Use of a torque wrench is highly recommended. Tighten the lug nuts in*

Troubleshooting Basic Wheel Problems

Problem	Cause	Solution
The car's front end vibrates at high speed	• The wheels are out of balance • Wheels are out of alignment	• Have wheels balanced • Have wheel alignment checked/adjusted
Car pulls to either side	• Wheels are out of alignment • Unequal tire pressure • Different size tires or wheels	• Have wheel alignment checked/adjusted • Check/adjust tire pressure • Change tires or wheels to same size
The car's wheel(s) wobbles	• Loose wheel lug nuts • Wheels out of balance • Damaged wheel • Wheels are out of alignment • Worn or damaged ball joint • Excessive play in the steering linkage (usually due to worn parts) • Defective shock absorber	• Tighten wheel lug nuts • Have tires balanced • Raise car and spin the wheel. If the wheel is bent, it should be replaced • Have wheel alignment checked/adjusted • Check ball joints • Check steering linkage • Check shock absorbers
Tires wear unevenly or prematurely	• Incorrect wheel size • Wheels are out of balance • Wheels are out of alignment	• Check if wheel and tire size are compatible • Have wheels balanced • Have wheel alignment checked/adjusted

Troubleshooting Basic Tire Problems

Problem	Cause	Solution
The car's front end vibrates at high speeds and the steering wheel shakes	• Wheels out of balance • Front end needs aligning	• Have wheels balanced • Have front end alignment checked
The car pulls to one side while cruising	• Unequal tire pressure (car will usually pull to the low side) • Mismatched tires • Front end needs aligning	• Check/adjust tire pressure • Be sure tires are of the same type and size • Have front end alignment checked
Abnormal, excessive or uneven tire wear See "How to Read Tire Wear"	• Infrequent tire rotation • Improper tire pressure • Sudden stops/starts or high speed on curves	• Rotate tires more frequently to equalize wear • Check/adjust pressure • Correct driving habits
Tire squeals	• Improper tire pressure • Front end needs aligning	• Check/adjust tire pressure • Have front end alignment checked

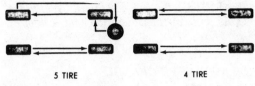

5 TIRE   **4 TIRE**

Radial ply tire rotation

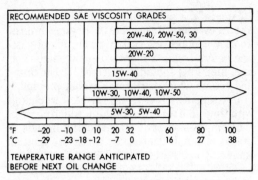

Oil viscosity recommendations for 1981–87 models

a criss-cross sequence shown to the figures quoted in the paragraph above.

TIRE DESIGN

Most automotive experts are in agreement that radial tires are better all-around performers, giving prolonged wear and better handling. An added benefit which you should consider when purchasing tires is that radials have less rolling resistance and can give up to a 10% increase in fuel economy over a bias-ply tire.

Tires of different construction should never be mixed. Always replace tires in sets of four or five when switching tire types and never substitute a belted tire for a bias-ply, a radial for a belted tire, etc. An occasional pressure check and periodic rotation could make your tires last much longer than a neglected set and maintain the safety margin which was designed into them.

CARE OF ALUMINUM WHEELS

Normal appearance maintenance of aluminum wheels includes frequent washing and waxing. However, you *must be careful to avoid the use of abrasive cleaners*. Failure to heed this warning will cause the protective coating to be damaged.

The special coating may also be abraded by repeated washing of the car in an automatic car wash using certain types of brushes. Once the finish abrades, it will provide less protection; then, even normal exposure to either caustic cleaners or road salt will cause the process to continue. If the wheel reaches this point it will require refinishing.

FLUIDS AND LUBRICANTS

Fuel and Engine Oil Recommendations

Chrysler Corporation recommends the use of a high quality, heavy duty detergent oil with the proper viscosity for prevailing conditions. Oils labeled "For Service SF/CC" on the top of the can are satisfactory for use in all engines; however, a higher quality oil, labeled "For Service SF/CD" is preferred for use in turbocharged engines.

It's important to recognize the distinctions between these oil types and the additional stresses put on oil used in turbocharged engines. Since the turbocharger bearings receive heat conducted directly from the unit's turbine, which may reach a cherry-red heat, oil passing through these bearings may reach temperatures high enough to cause chemical breakdown. This problem is especially severe right when the engine is shut down. Also, the additional power a turbocharged engine produces translates to higher mechanical loads and oil temperatures within the rest of the engine.

The CD designated oil has chemical additives capable of resisting this breakdown and countering its effects. If your car is turbocharged, it will almost surely pay you to use the better designation.

Oil must also meet viscosity standards. Follow the chart below precisely. Make sure the oil you buy is clearly labeled so as to confirm to both these basic standards.

A prime requirement is the use of unleaded fuel only. All the vehicles covered in this manual require the use of unleaded fuel exclusively, to protect the catalytic converter. Failure to follow this recommendation will result in failure of the catalyst and consequent failure to pass the emission test many states are now requiring. The use of unleaded fuel also prolongs the life of spark plugs, the engine as a whole, and the exhaust system.

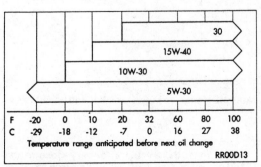

Oil viscosity recommendations for 1988 models

Fuels of the same octane rating have varying anti-knock qualities. Thus, if your engine knocks or pings, try switching brands of gasoline before trying a more expensive higher octane fuel. Fuel should be selected for the brand and octane which performs without pinging.

Your engine's fuel requirements can change with time, due to carbon buildup which changes the compression ratio. If switching brands or grades of gas doesn't work, check the ignition timing. If it is necessary to retard timing from specifications, don't change it more than about 2°. Retarded timing will reduce power output and fuel mileage and increase engine temperature.

Basic engine octane requirements, to be used in your initial choice of fuel, are 87 octane, unleaded. This rating is an average of Research and Motor methods of determination (R plus M/2). For increased vehicle performance and gas mileage, turbocharged engines, use a premium unleaded fuel – that is, one with a rating of 91 octane. More octane results in better performance and economy in these engines because the ignition system will compensate for their characteristics by advancing the timing.

Gasohol consisting of 10% ethanol and gasoline may be used in your car, but gasolines containing methanol (wood alcohol) are not approved. They can damage fuel system parts and cause operating problems.

Engine
OIL LEVEL CHECK

The engine oil level is checked with the dipstick, which is located on the radiator side of the engine. The oil should be checked either before the engine is started or five minutes after it has been shut off. This gives the oil time to drain back to the oil pan and prevents an inaccurate oil level reading. Remove the dipstick from the tube, wipe it clean, and insert it back into the tube. Remove it again and observe the oil level. It should be maintained within the indicated range on the dipstick, that is from the maximum level to one quart low.

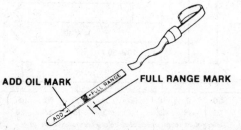

ADD OIL MARK   **FULL RANGE MARK**

Add oil when the level is at or very close to the "Add oil" mark. One quart will bring it into the "Full Range" as marked.

WARNING: *Do not overfill the crankcase. This will cause oil aeration and loss of oil pressure.*
Be sure to use only oil with an SE rating.

OIL AND FILTER CHANGE

CAUTION: *The EPA warns that prolonged contact with used engine oil may cause a number of skin disorders, including cancer! You should make every effort to minimize your exposure to used engine oil. Protective gloves should be worn when changing the oil. Wash your hands and any other exposed skin areas as soon as possible after exposure to used engine oil. Soap and water, or waterless hand cleaner should be used.*

NOTE: *The manufacturer recommends that the oil filter be changed at every other oil change, after the initial change. This can prove to be effective maintenance, especially if the change interval is carefully adapted to the driving conditions. However, Chilton's philosophy is that changing the filter at every oil change is excellent insurance against filter clogging and the consequent drastically increased wear this will cause. Further, replacing the filter removes a substantial amount of dirty oil whose additives are depleted – an amount that otherwise remains in the system. We recommend, therefore, that the engine oil and oil filter should be changed at the same time, at the intervals recommended on the Maintenance Intervals Chart.*

1. Run the engine until it reaches normal operating temperature.
2. Shut it off, firmly apply the parking brake, and block the wheels.
3. Raise and support the front end on jackstands.
4. Place a drip pan beneath the oil pan and remove the drain plug.
CAUTION: *The oil could be very hot! Protect yourself by using rubber gloves if necessary.*
5. Allow the engine to drain thoroughly.
6. While the oil is draining, replace the filter as described below.
7. When the oil has completely drained, wipe the threads of the plug clean and install it. Tighten it snugly.
WARNING: *The threads in the oil pan are easily stripped! Do not overtighten the plug!*
8. Fill the crankcase with the proper amount of oil shown in the Capacities Chart in this chapter.
9. Start the engine and check for leaks.

Replacing The Oil Filter

1. Place the drip pan beneath the oil filter.
2. Using an oil filter wrench, turn the filter counterclockwise to remove it.

CAUTION: *The oil could be very hot! Protect yourself by using rubber gloves if necessary.*

3. Wipe the contact surface of the new filter clean and coat the entire inner surface of the rubber gasket with clean engine oil.

4. Wipe the mating surface of the adapter on the block with a clean rag or paper towel.

5. Refer to the instructions on the filter or filter box to determine how tight to make the filter. It will say to turn the filter a certain distance past the point where its gasket touches the block — say ½-¾ turn.

WARNING: *Do not use a strap wrench to install the filter!*

6. Screw the new filter into position on the block until the gasket just touches the block sealing surface. Then hand-turn the filter the additional distance specified on the installation instructions *and no farther.*

Manual Transaxle

FLUID RECOMMENDATIONS

Some early vehicles may be equipped with the A-412 manual transaxle. This unit can be identified by locating the position of the starter which is found on the radiator side of the engine compartment. If it becomes necessary to add fluid to this unit, SAE 80W-90 gear lube is recommended.

If your vehicle has the A-460 or A-465 manual transaxle (4- and 5-speed transaxles respectively), the starter will be next to the firewall. When it becomes necessary to add fluid to this unit, Dexron®II is recommended. On the A-520 and A-555 manual transaxles used in 1987-88 models, add SAE 5W-30 SF or SF/CC or the equivalent.

LEVEL CHECK

The manual transmission fluid level is checked by removing the filler plug. This plug is located on the left side of the unit—at what would normally be the rear of the unit on a front engine, rear drive car, or the side opposite the clutch housing.

1. If you have the right size solid wrench, use that rather than an adjustable one. If you use an adjustable wrench, fit it very snugly and make sure the movable jaw is on the side toward which you are turning (that is, on the right side, if the wrench handle is below the plug). The 1986-88 cars use a filler plug with a finger grip. Just grab the plug with your fingers rather than using a wrench. Loosen the plug and remove it.

2. If a little fluid runs out, the level is, of course, okay. If not, feel for the presence of fluid by sticking your finger or a clean object into the hole. The level must be within ³⁄₁₆″ of the

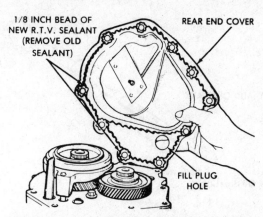

Forming a bead of sealer on the manual transaxle rear cover

bottom of the hole. If necessary, add fluid with a clean syringe. Wipe off the threads, replace the filler plug, and tighten it just snug.

DRAIN AND REFILL

1. The unit has no drain plug. To drain the fluid, you will need a tube of RTV sealant and a supply of clean rags. Place a drain pan under the cover at the rear of the unit (the side away from the engine and clutch).

2. Remove the bolts or studs. Gently pull the cover away from the transaxle and remove it to allow the fluid to drain.

3. Clean the magnet and the inside surface of the cover. Make sure to remove all old sealant. Then, use the tube of sealant to form a new gasket on the inside of the cover, as shown in the illustration.

4. Install the cover mounting bolts and torque them to 21 ft.lb. on the A-460/465/525 models and to 40 ft.lb. on the A-520 and A-555 manual transaxles used in 1987-88 models. Refill the unit with the approved fluid until it appears at the filler plug and install and tighten the plug.

Automatic Transaxle

FLUID RECOMMENDATIONS

ATF bearing the designation "Dexron®II" should be used for all automatic transaxles up through 1986. For 1987-88 models, Chrysler recommends the use of Mopar ATF fluid type 7176 "...for optimum transmission performance." Dexron®II may be used if the Chrysler fluid is not available.

On 1983 and earlier models, the automatic transaxle fluid level must be checked when the transmission is at normal operating temperature. Otherwise, the fluid will not have expanded enough to give an accurate reading. Drive the car at least 10 miles to ensure the transmission has warmed up.

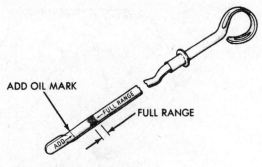

Oil dipstick

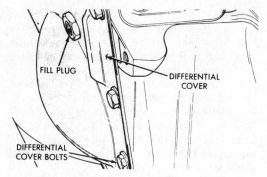

Differential (cover) fill plug location

On 1984-88 models, the fluid can be checked after a short drive (3-4 miles), at which time it is considered to be "Warm" or after 15 miles or more of operation, at which time it will have reached about 180°F and is considered to the "Hot". If the fluid is warm, it will be comfortable to grab the wet end of the dipstick just after pulling it out (just be sure not to check the level if the dipstick feels cold). If the fluid is hot, you will not be able to hold the wet end of the dipstick comfortably. *Be careful in checking it to pinch it very briefly so you will not be burned.* Once temperature is determined, fluid level is checked in the following manner:

1. With the parking brake engaged and the engine idling shift the transmission through the shift pattern and return it to the Park position. Make sure the transmission runs for at least 60 seconds before attempting to check fluid level.

2. Remove the dipstick. The fluid level should be between the ADD and FULL marks. On the models with two fluid level ranges, just read the "Warm" or "Hot" section of the stick, as appropriate. Add fluid (with a funnel, if necessary), right through the dipstick tube, until the level reaches the "FULL" mark, but never until it goes above it. Note that it is *vitally* important not to overfill the transmission. This is because overfilling will cause the moving parts to aerate or foam the oil so that shifting charac-

teristics will change and the transmission may be damaged due to poor lubrication.

DIFFERENTIAL FLUID CHECK AUTOMATIC TRANSAXLE

1981-82 Models

Under normal operating conditions, lubricant changes are not required for this unit. However, fluid level checks are required every 7500 miles or 12 months whichever comes first. The fluid level should be within ⅜" of the bottom of the fill plug.

NOTE: *A rod with a U-bend at the end can be made to check the fluid level. If it becomes necessary to add or replace the fluid use only Dexron®II automatic transmission fluid.*

Cooling System
FLUID RECOMMENDATIONS

The cooling system was filled at the factory with a high quality coolant solution that is good for year around operation and protects the system from freezing. If coolant is needed, a 50/50 mix of ethylene glycol antifreeze and water should be used. Alcohol or methanol base coolants are specifically not recommended. Antifreeze solution should be used all year, even in summer, to prevent rust and to take advantage of the solution's higher boiling point compared to plain water. This is imperative on air conditioned models; the heater core can freeze if·it isn't protected.

Level Check

The coolant should be checked at each fuel stop, to prevent the possibility of overheating and serious engine damage. To check the coolant level simply look into the expansion tank.

CAUTION: *The radiator coolant is under pressure when hot. To avoid the danger of physical injury, coolant should be checked or replenished only when cool. To remove the cap, slowly rotate it counterclockwise to the stop, but do not press down. Wait until all*

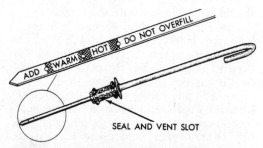

On 1984–88 models, the dipstick has a "Warm" and a "Hot" fluid level range. Read the stick according to the temperature of the transmission fluid.

pressure is released (indicated when the hissing sound stops) then press down on the cap while continuing to rotate it counterclockwise. Wear a glove or use a thick rag for protection.

WARNING: *Never add large quantities of cold coolant to a hot engine. A cracked engine block may result. If it is absolutely necessary to add coolant to a hot engine, do so only with the engine idling and add only small quantities at a time.*

Simply add coolant mixture to the tank until the upper level line is reached. If the system shows signs of overheating and, possibly, a small leak, you may want to check the level in the radiator *when the engine is cold.* If the radiator is not full, replace the cap, as it has lost the ability to retain vacuum or is of improper design for a coolant overflow tank type of system, such as that used on your car.

Each year, the cooling system should be serviced as follows:

1. Wash the radiator cap and filler neck with clean water.

2. Check the coolant for proper level and freeze protection.

3. Have the system pressure tested. If a replacement cap is installed, be sure that it conforms to the original specifications.

4. Tighten the hose clamps and inspect all hoses. Replace hoses that are swollen, cracked or otherwise deteriorated.

5. Clean the frontal area of the radiator core and the air conditioning condenser, if so equipped.

DRAIN AND REFILL

Every 2 years, the system should be serviced as follows:

1. Run the engine with the cap removed and the heater on until operating temperature is reached (indicated by heat in the upper radiator hose).

2. With the engine stopped, open the radiator drain cock located at the bottom of the radiator, and (to speed the draining) the engine block drains, if any (most of the cars covered in this manual do not have block drains).

3. Completely drain the coolant, and close the drain cocks.

4. Add sufficient clean water to fill the system. Run the engine and drain and refill the system as often as necessary until the drain water is nearly colorless.

5. Add sufficient ethylene glycol coolant to provide the required freezing and corrosion protection (at least a 44% solution protecting to -20°F). Fill the radiator to the cold level. Run the engine with the cap removed until normal operating temperature is reached.

6. Check the hot level.

7. Install the cap.

FLUSHING AND CLEANING THE SYSTEM

A well maintained system should never require aggressive flushing or cleaning. However, you may find that you (or a previous owner) has neglected to change the antifreeze often enough to fully protect the system. It may have obviously accumulated rust inside, or you there may be visible clogging of the radiator tubes.

There are two basic means of rectifying this situation for the do-it-yourselfer. One is to purchase a kit designed to allow you to reverse-flush the system with the pressure available from a garden hose. This kit comes with special fittings which allow you to force water downward inside the engine block and upward (or in reverse of normal flow) in the radiator. It will have complete instructions.

The other means is to purchase a chemical cleaner. The cleaner is installed after the system is flushed and filled with fresh water and cleans the system as you drive a short distance or idle the engine hot. In all cases, the cleaner must be flushed completely from the system after use. In some cases, it may be necessary to follow up with use of a neutralizer. Make sure to follow the instructions very carefully. These cleaners are quite potent, chemically, and work very well; because of that fact, you must be careful to flush and, if necessary, neutralize the effect of the cleaner to keep it from damaging your cooling system.

If the radiator is severely clogged, it may be necessary to have the tubes rodded out by a professional radiator repair shop. In this case, the radiator must be removed and taken to the shop for this highly specialized work. You can save money on the job by removing and replacing the radiator yourself, as described in Chapter 3.

Brake Master Cylinder

FLUID RECOMMENDATIONS

Use *only* brake fluid conforming to Federal DOT 3 specifications.

LEVEL CHECK

Once every 7500 miles or 12 months check the brake fluid level in the master cylinder. The master cylinder is mounted either on the firewall or the brake booster, and is divided into two reservoirs. The fluid must be maintained at the bottom of the split ring.

Remove the two master cylinder caps and fill to the bottom of the split rings using DOT 3 brake fluid. If the brake fluid level is chronically low there may be a leak in the system which should be investigated immediately.

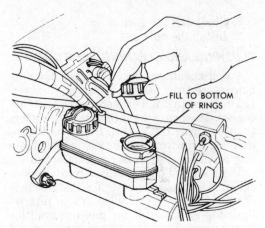

Checking the master cylinder fluid level

NOTE: *Brake fluid absorbs moisture from the air, which reduces its effectiveness and causes corrosion. Never leave the brake fluid can or master cylinder uncovered any longer than necessary. Brake fluid also damages paint. If any is spilled, it should be washed off immediately with clear, cold water.*

Power Steering Pump

FLUID RECOMMENDATIONS

Use power steering fluid, Part No. 2084329 on 1981-83 models, and 4318055 on later models, or its equivalent.

LEVEL CHECK

Maintain the proper fluid level as indicated on the cap of the reservoir. Check the level with the engine off and at normal ambient temperature (overnight cold). The dipstick should indicate FULL COLD. If the reservoir needs fluid refill with the approved fluid.

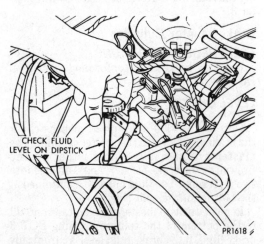

Checking the power steering fluid level

Manual Steering Gear

FLUID RECOMMENDATIONS

The approved lubricant for the steering gear is API GL-5. However, the rack and pinion manual steering units used on this car are permanently sealed. The lubricant is replenished only in connection with a major rebuild of the unit not covered by this manual.

LEAK CHECK

The manual steering gear is permanently lubricated at the factory and periodic replenishment of lubricant is not needed. However, you should inspect the two rubber boots that seal between the housing and the tie rod ends when checking the engine oil and other fluid levels. Make sure there is no leakage and that the boots are intact. Have the boots replaced if necessary. Check also for leakage where the steering shaft passes into the gearbox.

Chassis Greasing

Chassis greasing can be performed with a pressurized grease gun or it can be performed at home using a hand-operated grease gun. Wipe the fittings clean before greasing, in order to prevent the possibility of forcing any dirt into the component.

Ball joint and steering linkages are semi-permanently lubricated at the factory with a special grease. They should be regreased every 30,000 miles or 3 years whichever comes first. When regreasing is necessary, use only special long life chassis grease such as Multi-Mileage lubricant Part No. 2525035 or its equivalent.

Body Lubrication

Body hinges and latches should be lubricated, as necessary, to maintain smooth operation of

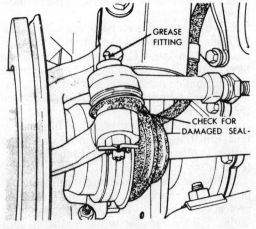

Tie rod seal and grease fitting

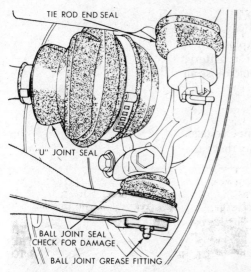

TIE ROD END SEAL

"U" JOINT SEAL

BALL JOINT SEAL
CHECK FOR DAMAGE

BALL JOINT GREASE FITTING

Front suspension ball joint seal and grease fitting

doors and the front and rear hoods. Wipe all parts with a clean rag prior to lubrication. *Pay particular attention to the smooth operation of hood latch components as failure to operate can produce an extreme safety hazard − inspect and lubricate these with great care. If any problems appear, have them corrected immediately.* Lubricate each part with the grease specified below:

- Door hinges − Engine oil.
- Door latches, rotors, and strikers − Wheel bearing grease.
- Hood latch, release mechanism, and safety catch − apply sparingly to all contact areas − Multipurpose lubricant NLGI Grade 2.
- Hood hinges and counterbalance springs − Mopar Multi-mileage Lubricant 4318062 or equivalent.
- Seat regulator and track adjusters − Mopar Spray White Lube 4318066 or equivalent.
- Tailgate − all pivot and slide contact surfaces on hinges, quick release pins, and release handles − Spray White Lube.
- Tailgate check arms − Engine oil.

Wheel Bearings

Your Chrysler K- or E-car is equipped with permanently sealed front wheel bearings. There is no periodic adjustment for these units.

The rear wheel bearings should be inspected whenever the drums are removed to inspect or service the brakes, or at least every 22,500 miles. For lubrication procedures of these bearings refer to Chapter 8.

TRAILER TOWING

Trailer towing is best performed by vehicles equipped with special towing packages to improve engine and transmission cooling and to help the suspension system carry the extra weight. However, towing is permitted without these special systems, provided the road conditions are normal (both ascending and descending steep hills must be avoided) and the temperatures are moderate (extreme heat must also be avoided). The sole exception is that towing is *strictly prohibited with a turbocharged engine.* This is because of the tremendous ability of the turbocharged engine to produce high power output, which, in the absence of towing a trailer, can usually be sustained for only very short periods.

The Maximum loads depend on the engine and transmission in use. They are:
- 2.2L manual transmission − 1,000 lbs.
- 2.2L automatic transmission − 1,500 lbs.
- 2.5L manual transmission − 1,000 lbs.
- 2.5L automatic transmission − 2,000 lbs.
- 2.6L Mitsubishi engine − 2,000 lbs.

The trailer tongue load must not cause the total weight permitted for your car to be exceeded. Note also that, if the trailer weighs more than 1,000 lbs., it must not be towed without its own brakes, as the capacity of the vehicle's brakes will be substantially exceeded.

Check the automatic transmission fluid level and color. Make sure the fluid level is correct. If the fluid is burnt, replace the fluid and filter. Should the temperature gauge rise above the normal indication while driving on the highway, reduce your speed. If the engine begins to get hot in traffic, put the (automatic) transmission in neutral and allow the engine to idle and normal idle speed.

PUSHING AND TOWING

The vehicle can be towed from either the front or rear. If the vehicle is towed from the front for an extended distance make sure the parking brake is completely released.

Manual transmission vehicles may be towed on the front wheels at speeds up to 35 mph, for a distance not to exceed 15 miles, provided the transmission is in neutral and the driveline has not been damaged. The steering wheel must be clamped in a straight ahead position.

WARNING: *Do not use the steering column lock to secure front wheel position for towing.*

Automatic transmission vehicles may be towed on the front wheels at speeds not to exceed 25 mph for a period of 15 miles.

JUMP STARTING A DEAD BATTERY

The chemical reaction in a battery produces explosive hydrogen gas. This is the safe way to jump start a dead battery, reducing the chances of an accidental spark that could cause an explosion.

Jump Starting Precautions

1. Be sure both batteries are of the same voltage.
2. Be sure both batteries are of the same polarity (have the same grounded terminal).
3. Be sure the vehicles are not touching.
4. Be sure the vent cap holes are not obstructed.
5. Do not smoke or allow sparks around the battery.
6. In cold weather, check for frozen electrolyte in the battery. Do not jump start a frozen battery.
7. Do not allow electrolyte on your skin or clothing.
8. Be sure the electrolyte is not frozen.

CAUTION: *Make certain that the ignition key, in the vehicle with the dead battery, is in the OFF position. Connecting cables to vehicles with on-board computers will result in computer destruction if the key is not in the OFF position.*

Jump Starting Procedure

1. Determine voltages of the two batteries; they must be the same.
2. Bring the starting vehicle close (they must not touch) so that the batteries can be reached easily.
3. Turn off all accessories and both engines. Put both cars in Neutral or Park and set the handbrake.
4. Cover the cell caps with a rag—do not cover terminals.
5. If the terminals on the run-down battery are heavily corroded, clean them.
6. Identify the positive and negative posts on both batteries and connect the cables in the order shown.
7. Start the engine of the starting vehicle and run it at fast idle. Try to start the car with the dead battery. Crank it for no more than 10 seconds at a time and let it cool off for 20 seconds in between tries.
8. If it doesn't start in 3 tries, there is something else wrong.
9. Disconnect the cables in the reverse order.
10. Replace the cell covers and dispose of the rags.

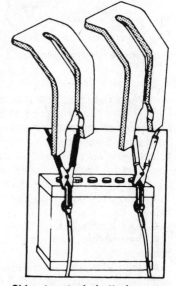

Side terminal batteries occasionally pose a problem when connecting jumper cables. There frequently isn't enough room to clamp the cables without touching sheet metal. Side terminal adaptors are available to alleviate this problem and should be removed after use.

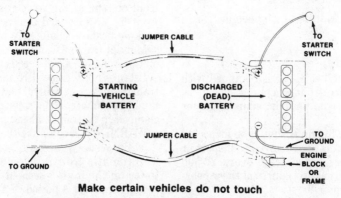

TO STARTER SWITCH

JUMPER CABLE

TO STARTER SWITCH

STARTING VEHICLE BATTERY

DISCHARGED (DEAD) BATTERY

TO GROUND

JUMPER CABLE

TO GROUND

ENGINE BLOCK OR FRAME

Make certain vehicles do not touch

This hook-up for negative ground cars only

WARNING: *If this requirement cannot be met, the front wheels must be placed on a dolly.*

JACKING

The standard jack utilizes special receptacles located at the body sills to accept the scissors jack supplied with the vehicle for emergency road service. The jack supplied with the car should never be used for any service operation other than tire changing. Never get under the car while it is supported by only a jack. Always block the wheels when changing tires.

The service operations in this book often require that one end or the other, or both, of the car be raised and safely supported. The ideal method, of course, would be a hydraulic hoist. Since this is beyond both the resource and requirement of the do-it-yourselfer, a small hydraulic, screw or scissors jack will suffice for the procedures in this guide. Two sturdy jackstands should be acquired if you intend to work under the car at any time. An alternate method of raising the car would be drive-on ramps. These are available commercially or can be fabricated from heavy boards or steel. Be sure to block the wheels when using ramps.

CAUTION: *Concrete blocks are not recommended for supporting the car. They are likely to crumble if the load is not evenly distributed. Boxes and milk crates of any description must not be used to support the car!*

Capacities

Year	Engine Displacement Cu In.	Engine Crankcase (qts) With Filter	Engine Crankcase (qts) Without Filter	Transaxle (pts) Manual	Transaxle (pts) Automatic	Differential (pts)	Gasoline Tank (gals)	Cooling System (qts) W/AC	Cooling System (qts) W/O AC
1981	135	4	4	4	15	2	13	7	7
	156	5	4½	4	17	2	13	8½	8½
1982	135	4	4	4	15	2	13	7	7
	156	5	4½	4	15	2	13	8½	8½
1983	135	4	4	4①	17.8	②	13③	9	9
	156	5	4½	4①	17.8	②	13③	9	9
1984	135	4	4	4①	17.8	②	14	9	9
	156	5	4½	4①	17.8	②	14	9	9
1985	135	4④	4④	⑤	17.8⑥	②	14	9	9
	156	5	5	⑤	18.4⑥	②	14	9	9
1986	135	4④	4④	4.6	17.8⑦	②	14	9	9
	150	4	4	4.6	17.8⑦	②	14	9	9
1987	135	4④	4④	5⑦	17.8⑦	②	14	9	9
	150	4	4	5	17.8⑦	②	14	9	9
1988	135	4	4	5⑦	17.8	②	14⑧	9	9
	150	4	4	5	17.8	②	14⑧	9	9

① With the 412 transaxle—1.5 qts.
   With the 465 5-speed—2.3 qts.
② The differential is combined with the transmission sump on 1983 and later models
③ Models with Electronic Fuel Injection—14
④ The 135 cu. in. engine with Turbocharging holds 5 qts with or without filter change
⑤ With the 460 transaxle—4.0
   With the 525 5-speed transaxle—4.6
⑥ To refill after changing fluid, add 8.0 pts.
⑦ Both the A520 and A555 5-speed transaxles hold this amount of fluid (the A555 is used only with Turbo II engines)
⑧ The Le Baron and Le Baron GTS hold 16 gallons

Maintenance Intervals Chart 1981–87

Operation	Mileage Interval (in thousands)
Engine Oil/Filter Change (without Turbocharger)	7.5 (12 months) ①
Engine Oil/Filter Change (with Turbocharger)	7.5 (6 months)
Carburetor Air Filter (2.6L engine)	30
Apply Solvent to Choke/Fast Idle Cam (Carb. only)	30
Replace Spark Plugs (with Cat. Conv.)	30
Replace Spark Plugs (without Cat. Conv.)	15
Adjust Valve Lash (2.6L Engine)	15
Adjust/Inspect Drive Belts	15
Drain and Flush Cooling System	30 (24 months) ②
Inspect Brake Hoses	7.5 (12 months, 6 months on Turbos)
Inspect Front and Rear Brake Linings	22.5
Inspect Rear Wheel Bearings	22.5
Lubricate Tie Rod Ends and Steering Linkage	48 (3 years)
Lubricate Ball Joints (1981–83 only)	48 (3 years)
Check Auto Transaxle Differential Fluid Level (1981–83 only)	7.5 (12 months)

① In severe service, change at 3000 miles, 3 months. This includes stop and go driving in extreme cold, driving in dusty conditions, extensive idling, operating at sustained high speeds with temperatures above 90°F.
② Original factory fill may be used for 52,500 miles and 36 months.

Maintenance Intervals Chart 1988

Operation	Mileage Intervals (in thousands)
Change Engine Oil and Filter ①	7.5 (12 months)
Inspect/Adjust Drive Belts	15
Replace Spark Plugs	30
Replace Engine Air Filter	30
Replace Oxygen Sensor	52.5
Replace EGR Valve and Tube and Clean Passages	52.5 (60 months)
Replace PCV Filter	30
Replace PCV Valve	60 (60 months)
Replace Vacuum Operated Emission Controls	52.5 (60 months)
Adjust Idle Mixture (with Propane)	52.5
Check/Adjust Ignition Timing	60
Replace Ign. Wires, Cap, and Rotor	60
Flush/Replace Coolant	52.5 (36 months) ②
Replace Alternator Brushes	75
Inspect Brake Hoses	7.5 (12 months non-turbo, 6 months turbo)
Inspect Brake Linings Front and Rear	22.5
Inspect Rear Wheel Bearings	82.5 (then every 30,000 miles)
Lubricate Tie Rod Ends and Steering Linkage	90 (36 months)

① At this time, inspect driveshaft boots for leaks and replace as necessary.
② After first change, replace at 24 months/30,000 miles. Check hoses, cap, clamps, and coolant for cleanliness every 12 months.

Engine Performance and Tune-Up

2

TUNE-UP PROCEDURES

Neither tune-up nor troubleshooting can be considered independently since each has a direct relationship with the other.

It is advisable to follow a definite and thorough tune-up procedure.

Tune-up consists of three separate steps: Analysis, the process of determining whether normal wear is responsible for performance loss, and whether parts require replacement or service and adjustment.

The manufacturer's recommended interval for tune-ups is every 30,000 miles. This interval should be shortened if the car is subjected to severe operating conditions such as trailer pulling or stop and start driving, or if starting and running problems are noticed. It is assumed that the routine maintenance described in Chapter 1 has been kept up, as this will have an effect on the results of the tune-up. All the applicable tune-up steps should be followed, as each adjustment complements the effects of the others. If the tune-up (emission control) sticker in the engine compartment disagrees with the information presented in the "Tune-up Specifications" chart in this chapter, the sticker figures must be followed. The sticker information reflects running changes made by the manufacturer during production.

Troubleshooting is a logical sequence of procedures designed to locate a particular case of trouble.

It is advisable to read the entire chapter before beginning a tune-up, although those who are more familiar with tune-up procedures may wish to go directly to the instructions.

Spark Plugs

A typical spark plug consists of a metal shell surrounding a ceramic insulator. A metal electrode extends downward through the center of the insulator and protrudes a small distance. Located at the end of the plug and attached to the side of the outer metal shell is the side electrode. The side electrode bends in at a 90° angle so that its tip is even with, and parallel to, the tip of the center electrode. The distance between these two electrodes (measured in thousandths of an inch) is called the spark plug gap. The spark plug in no way produces a spark but merely provides a gap across which the current can arc. The coil produces anywhere from 20,000 to 40,000 volts which travels to the distributor where it is distributed through the spark plug wires to the spark plugs. The current passes along the center electrode and jumps the gap to the side electrode, and, in do doing, ignites the air/fuel mixture in the combustion chamber.

SPARK PLUG HEAT RANGE

Spark plug heat range is the ability of the plug to dissipate heat. The longer the insulator (or the farther it extends into the engine), the hotter the plug will operate; the shorter the insulator the cooler it will operate. A plug that absorbs little heat and remains too cool will quickly accumulate deposits of oil and carbon since it is not hot enough to burn them off. This leads to plug fouling and consequently to misfiring. A plug that absorbs too much heat will have no deposits, but, due to the excessive heat, the electrodes will burn away quickly and in some instances, preignition may result. Preignition takes place when plug tips get so hot that they glow sufficiently to ignite the fuel/air mixture before the actual spark occurs. This early ignition will usually cause a pinging during low speeds and heavy loads.

The general rule of thumb for choosing the correct heat range when picking a spark plug is: if most of your driving is long distance, high speed travel, use a colder plug; if most of your driving is stop and go, use a hotter plug. Origi-

Tune-Up Specifications

When analyzing compression test results, look for uniformity among cylinders rather than specific pressures

Year	No. Cyl Displacement (cu. in.)	Emission◆ Control Classification	Spark Plugs Type	Gap (in.)	Ignition Timing (deg.)▲ Man. Trans.	Auto Trans●	Valves Intake Opens (deg.)■	Fuel Pump Pressure (psi)	Idle Speed (rpm)▲ Man Trans.	Auto Trans●
1981	4-135	All	P-65-PR4	.035	10B	10B	12	4½–6	900	900
	4-156	All	P-65-PR4	.035	—	7B	25	4½–6	—	800
1982	4-135	All	P-65-PR4	.035	12B	12B	14	4½–6	900	900
	4-156	All	RN-12Y	.035	—	7B	25	4½–6	—	800
1983	4-135	Fed-Aut	RN-12Y	.035	—	10B	16	4½–6	—	900 ①
	4-135	Fed-Man	RN-12Y	.035	10B	—	16	4½–6	775 ①	—
	4-135	Cal-Aut	RN-12Y	.035	—	10B	16	4½–6	—	900 ①
	4-135	Cal-Man	RN-12Y	.035	10B	—	16	4½–6	775	—
	4-135	Hi Alt.	RN-12Y	.035	6B	6B	16	4½–6	850	850
	4-156	Fed	RN-12Y	.040	7B	7B	25	4½–6	—	800
	4-156	Cal	RN-12Y	.040	7B	7B	25	4½–6	—	800
1984	4-135	Fed-Man	RN-12Y	.035	10B	—	16	4½–6	800	—
	4-135	Cal-Man	RN-12Y	.035	10B	—	16	4½–6	800	—
	4-135	Fed 8 Hi Alt-Aut	RN-12Y	.035	—	10B	16	4½–6	—	900
	4-135	Cal-Aut	RN-12Y	.035	—	10B	16	4½–6	—	900
	4-135	Man-EFI	RN-12Y	.035	6B	—	16	4½–6	850	—
	4-135	Auto-EFI	RN-12Y	.035	—	6B	16	4½–6	—	750
	4-135	TC	RN-12Y	.035	12B	12B	10	4½–6	990	950
	4-156	All	RN-12Y	.035–.040	—	7B	25	4½–6	—	800
1985	4-135	Man	RN-12Y	.035	10B	—	16	4½–6	800	—
	4-135	Aut	RN-12Y	.035	—	10B	16	4½–6	—	900
	4-135	Man-EFI	RN-12Y	.035	12B	—	16	4½–6	850	—
	4-135	Aut-EFI	RN-12Y	.035	—	12B	16	4½–6	—	750
	4-135	TC	RN-12Y	.035	12B	12B	10	4½–6	950	950
	4-156	All	RN-12Y	.035–.040	7B	7B	25	4½–6	800	800
1986	4-135	Non-Turbo	RN-12YC	.035	②	②	16	4½–6	②	②
	4-135	Turbo	RN-12YC	.035	②	②	10	55	②	②
	4-153	All	RN-12YC	.035	②	②	12	14.5	②	②
1987	4-135	Non-Turbo	RN-12YC	.035	10B	10B	16	4½–6	900	900
	4-135	Turbo	R-12YC	.035	10B	10B	10	55	900	900
	4-153	All	RN12-YC	.035	10B	10B	12	14.5	900	900
1988	4-135	Non-Turbo	RN-12Y	.035	12B	12B	16	14.5	850	850
	4-135	Turbo	RN-12Y	.035	12B	12B	10	55	900	900
	4-135	Turbo II	RN-12Y	.035	12B	12B	10	55	900	900
	4-153	All	RN-12Y	.035	12B	12B	12	14.5	850	850

▲ See text for procedure
● Figure in parentheses indicates California engine
■ All figures Before Top Dead Center
◆ Emission control classification abbreviations:
  Fed—Federal, 49 states (except California)
  CA—California cars only
  Aut—Automatic transmission

Man—Manual transmission
Hi. Alt—High altitude emissions package only
EFI—Electronic Fuel Injection
TC—Turbocharged
Sh—Shelby
① Set idle speed with vacuum advance line connected
② Refer to engine compartment sticker

nal equipment plugs are compromise plugs, but most people never have occasion to change their plugs from the factory-recommended heat range.

REMOVAL AND INSTALLATION

Rough idle, hard starting, frequent engine miss at high speeds and physical deterioration are all indications that the plugs should be replaced.

The electrode end of a spark plug is a good indicator of the internal condition of your car's engine. If a spark plug is fouled, causing the engine to misfire, the problem will have to be found and corrected. Often, "reading" the plugs will lead you to the cause of the problem. Spark plug conditions and probable causes are listed in the color section.

NOTE: *A small amount of light tan or rust red colored deposits at the electrode end of the plug is normal. These plugs need not be renewed unless they are severely worn.*

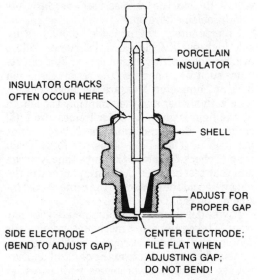

PORCELAIN INSULATOR

INSULATOR CRACKS OFTEN OCCUR HERE

SHELL

ADJUST FOR PROPER GAP

SIDE ELECTRODE (BEND TO ADJUST GAP)

CENTER ELECTRODE; FILE FLAT WHEN ADJUSTING GAP; DO NOT BEND!

Cross section of a spark plug

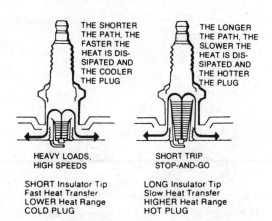

THE SHORTER THE PATH, THE FASTER THE HEAT IS DISSIPATED AND THE COOLER THE PLUG

THE LONGER THE PATH, THE SLOWER THE HEAT IS DISSIPATED AND THE HOTTER THE PLUG

HEAVY LOADS, HIGH SPEEDS

SHORT Insulator Tip
Fast Heat Transfer
LOWER Heat Range
COLD PLUG

SHORT TRIP STOP-AND-GO

LONG Insulator Tip
Slow Heat Transfer
HIGHER Heat Range
HOT PLUG

Spark plug heat range

Pull on the rubber boot to remove the spark plug wire, not the wire itself

Keep the socket straight on the plug

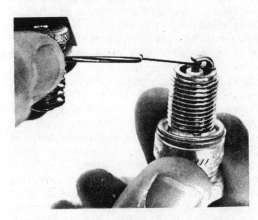

Use a wire gauge to check the electrode gap

1. Before removing the spark plugs, number the plug wires so that the correct wire goes on the plug when replaced. This can be done with pieces of adhesive tape.

2. Next, clean the area around the plugs by brushing or blowing with compressed air. You can also loosen the plugs a few turns and crank the engine to blow the dirt away.

3. Disconnect the plug wires by twisting and pulling on the rubber cap, not on the wire.

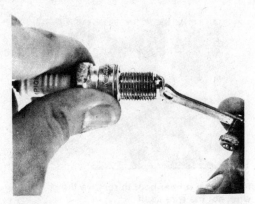
Adjust the electrode gap by bending the side electrode.

4. Remove each plug with a rubber-insert spark plug socket. Make sure that the socket is all the way down on the plug to prevent it from slipping and cracking the porcelain insulator.

5. After removing each plug, evaluate its condition. A spark plug's useful life is approximately 30,000 miles with electronic ignition. Thus, it would make sense to replace a plug if it has been in service that long. If the plug is to be replaced, refer to the Tune-up Specifications chart for the proper spark plug type. The numbers indicate heat range; hotter running plugs have higher numbers.

6. If the plugs are to be reused, file the center and side electrodes flat with a fine, flat point file. Heavy or baked on deposits can be carefully scraped off with a small knife blade or the scraper tool on a combination spark plug tool. It is often suggested that plugs be tested and cleaned on a service station sandblasting machine; however, this piece of equipment is becoming rare. Check the gap between the electrodes with a round wire spark plug gapping gauge. Do not use a flat feeler gauge; it will give an inaccurate reading. if the gap is not as specified, use the bending tool on the spark plug gap gauge to bend the outside electrode. Be careful not to bend the electrode too far or too often, because excessive bending may cause the electrode to break off and fall into the combustion chamber. This would require removing the cylinder head to reach the broken piece and could also result in cylinder wall, piston ring, or valve damage.

CAUTION: *Never bend the center electrode of the spark plug. This will break the insulator and render the plug useless.*

7. Clean the threads of old plugs with a wire brush. Lubricate the threads with a drop of oil.

8. Screw the plugs in finger tight, and then tighten them with the spark plug socket. Be very careful not to overtighten them. Just snug them in.

9. Reinstall the wires. If, by chance, you have forgotten to number the plug wires, refer to the Firing Order illustrations.

Spark Plug Wires

The plug wires carry a very tiny amount of current under extremely high voltage. The conductors inside must offer some resistance to flow of current, or operation of a radio in the car or even nearby would be impossible. For these reasons, these wires deteriorate steadily and often produce puzzling and unexpected lapses in performance. The most typical evidence of wire problems is the sudden failure of the car to start on a damp morning.

The wires should be inspected frequently for full seating at the plugs and distributor cap towers. Before inspection, wipe the wires carefully with a cloth slightly moistened with a non-flammable solvent so it will be easier to see cracks or other damage. The insulation and all rubber boots should be flexible and free of cracks. Replace the wires as a set as soon as any such problems develop.

Unfortunately, the invisible conductors inside high quality wires can deteriorate before evidence of poor insulation exists. You can remove such wires and test the resistance if you have an ohmmeter. Measure the length of each wire with a ruler and then multiply the length by the figures given, in order to measure total resistance. Resistance must be 250-600 ohms per inch or 3,000-7200 ohms per foot. If you wish to check the cap at the same time, you can run your test between the spark plug end of the plug wire and the contact at the center of the inside of the cap.

If you do not have an ohmmeter, you may want to take you car to a mechanic or diagnostic center with an oscilloscope type of diagnosis system. This unit will read the curve of ignition voltage and uncover problems with wires, or any other component, easily. You may also

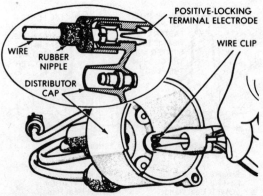
Removing the plug wires from the cap on late model cars

want to refer to the color section on spark plug analysis, as looking at the plugs may help you to identify wire problems.

To replace the wires, note first that on most of the models covered by this book, original equipment Chrysler wires cannot be pulled out of the distributor cap. Remove the cap and release each wire from inside by pinching the locking jaws together with a pair of needle-nose pliers. Replace the wires one at a time in order to avoid having to study and follow the firing order diagrams.

Firing Orders

NOTE: *To avoid confusion, remove and tag and wires one at a time, for replacement.*

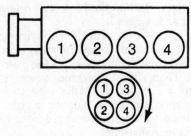

2.2L and 2.5L firing order: 1-3-4-2 distributor rotation clockwise

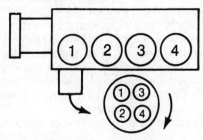

2.6L engine firing order: 1-3-4-2 distribution rotation: clockwise

Electronic Ignition

Models using the 2.2 Liter and 2.5 Liter engines are equipped with the "Electronic Fuel Control System". This consists of a Spark Control Computer, various engine sensors, and a specially calibrated carburetor with an electronically controlled fuel metering system. On fuel injected engines, the computer controls the total amount of fuel injected by slightly modifying the pulses that operate the injectors. The function of this system is to provide a way for the engine to burn a correct air-fuel mixture.

The Spark Control Computer is the heart of the entire system. It has the capability of igniting the fuel mixture according to different models of engine operation by delivering an infinite

number of different variable advance curves. The computer consists of one electronic printed circuit board, which simultaneously received signals from all the sensors and within milliseconds, analyzes them to determine how the engine is operating and then advances or retards the timing.

For 1988, this system has been renamed the SMEC ("Single Module Engine Controller") system. It functions similarly to the Electronic Fuel Control System, using coolant temperature, engine rpm, and available manifold vacuum for inputs. On turbo engines, it synchronizes the injection pulses with the ignition pulses by reading signals from the Hall Effect pickup in the distributor. Both systems use the oxygen sensor to fine-tune the mixture to actual operating conditions.

The 2.6 Liter engine uses a system that consists of the battery, ignition switch, coil, and IC igniter (electronic control unit), built into the distributor, spark plugs and inter-component wiring. Primary current is switched by the IC igniter in response to timing signals produced by a magnetic pickup.

The distributor is equipped with both centrifugal and vacuum advance mechanisms on 1981-83 models. The centrifugal advance is located below the rotor assembly, and has gover-

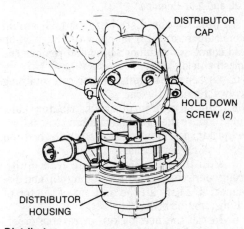

Distributor

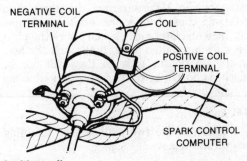

Ignition coil

nor weights that move in and out with changes in engine speed. As speed increases the weights move outward and cause the reluctor to rotate ahead of the distributor shaft, this advances ignition timing. The vacuum advance has a spring loaded diaphragm connected to the breaker assembly. The diaphragm is actuated by intake manifold vacuum. As the vacuum increases, the diaphragm causes the movable breaker assembly to pivot in a direction opposite to distributor rotation, advancing the ignition timing.

On 1984-89 models, the vacuum advance mechanism has been replaced by a vacuum transducer, located on top of the computer. This unit responds to engine vacuum the way the vacuum advance unit does, but produces an electronic signal that is fed to the computer, instead of acting to advance the ignition timing directly. This allows the computer to tailor the advance curve—the amount of advance the distributor gives—to the operating conditions.

On 1988 vehicles, the new SMEC system measures vacuum via a Manifold Absolute Pressure sensor and controls spark advance via the computer without the use of a separate vacuum transducer.

HALL-EFFECT PICKUP ASSEMBLY REPLACEMENT

2.2L and 2.5L Engines

1. Remove the distributor splash shield mounting screws (2) along with the pick-up lead connector retainer screw and remove the splash shield.

2. Loosen the two distributor cap retaining screws. Remove the cap.

3. Pull the rotor up off the distributor shaft.

4. Remove the two clips retaining the hall-effect pickup assembly to the distributor body on 1985 and earlier models.

5. Pull the hall-effect pickup lead multi-prong connector out of its retaining clip and disconnect it. Then, lift the unit out of the top of the distributor body.

6. Install the new pickup in reverse order. Make sure the multi-prong connector is securely plugged in and then securely mounted in its retaining clip. Make sure, too, that the pickup retaining clips, if used, are installed securely. On 1986 and later models, make sure the pickup wires are routed properly through the hole in the distributor body so they will not be pinched and damaged when the distributor cap is reinstalled.

2.6L Engine

1. Unscrew the two phillips type retaining screws and remove the cap.

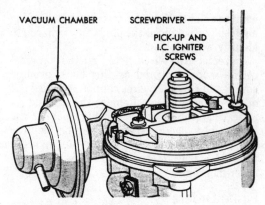

VACUUM CHAMBER   SCREWDRIVER

PICK-UP AND I.C. IGNITER SCREWS

Removing the pick-up and igniter—2.6 L engine distributor

2. Unscrew the two similar screws retaining the rotor and remove it.

3. *Using a box or socket wrench for maximum torque,* remove the governor assembly retaining bolt from the upper end of the distributor shaft. Then, slide the governor assembly upward and off the shaft. Make sure to keep governor springs either in place or in order for proper installation in the same positions (they are not interchangeable).

4. Remove the wire retaining screw from the retaining clamp on the side of the distributor.

5. Remove the pickup/igniter mounting screws from the clip on the side of the distributor. Unplug the pickup/wiring connector from the harness. Then, remove both the pick-up coil and igniter, keeping them together. Pull the wiring conduit out of the side of the distributor.

6. If you are replacing the breaker assembly or pole piece underneath, remove the two retaining screws and remove it.

7. Installation is the reverse of removal.

Ignition Timing

Timing should be checked at each tune-up. Timing isn't likely to change very much with electronic ignition.

On 1981-83 models with the 2.2L engine, and on 1986-88 models with the 2.2 and 2.5L engines, the timing marks are located on the flywheel with the pointer on an access hole in the transaxle, or on the edge of the access hole with a line on the flywheel. On 1984-85 2.2L engines, the timing marks are on the timing belt cover with a notch on the front pulley. On 2.6L engines, the timing marks are on a special bracket mounted on the front of the block and there is a notch in the front pulley.

A stroboscopic (dynamic) timing light must be used, because static lights are too inaccurate for emission controlled engines.

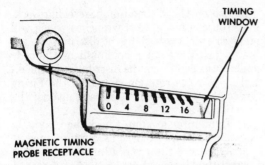

Timing window for the 1988 2.2 and 2.5 L engines.

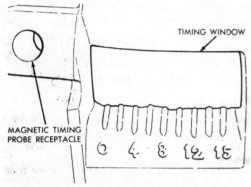

Timing mark location all manual and automatic transaxles except A-412

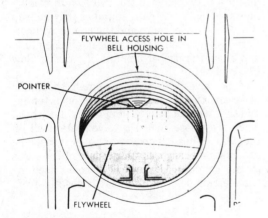

Timing mark location A-412 transaxle

There are three basic types of timing light available. The first is a simple neon bulb with two wire connections. One wire connects to the spark plug terminal and the other plugs into the end of the spark plug wire for the No. 1 cylinder, thus connecting the light in series with the spark plug. This type of light is pretty dim and must be held close to the timing marks to be seen. It has the advantage of low price. The second type operates from the car's battery; two alligator clips connect to the battery termi-

nals, while an adapter enables a third clip to be connected to the No. 1 spark plug and wire. This type provides a bright flash which can be seen even in bright sunshine. The third type replaced the battery current with 110 volt house current.

Some timing lights have other features built into them, such as dwell meters or tachometers. These are nice, in that they reduce the tangle of wires under the hood when you're working, but may duplicate the functions of tools you already have. One worthwhile feature, which is becoming more of a necessity with higher voltage ignition systems, is an inductive pickup. The inductive pickup clamps around the No. 1 spar plug wire, sensing the surges of high voltage electricity as they are sent to the plug. The advantage is that no mechanical connection is inserted between the wire and the plug, which eliminates false signals to the timing light. A timing light with an inductive pickup should be used on electronic ignition systems.

NOTE: *For 1985 models with both Throttle Body and Multi-Point injection, refer to the special timing procedure at the end of Chapter 5.*

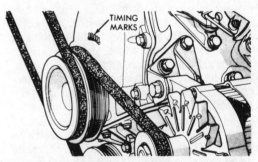

Location of timing marks on 1984 and later 2.2 liter engines. On these engines, the marks are located on the front engine timing cover, rather than on the flywheel.

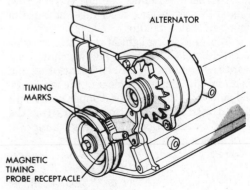

Timing marks 2.6L engine

To check and adjust the timing:

1. Warm the engine to normal operating temperature. Shut off the engine and connect the timing light to the No. 1 spark plug. Do not under any circumstances pierce a wire to hook up a light.

2. Clean off the timing marks and mark the pulley or damper notch and the timing scale with white chalk or paint. The timing notch on the damper or pulley can be elusive. Bump the engine around with the starter or turn the crankshaft with a wrench on the front pulley bolt to get it to an accessible position.

NOTE: *The 2.2 and 2.5 Liter engines have their timing marks on the flywheel and bell housing.*

3. Disconnect and plug the vacuum advance hose at the distributor or, at the spark advance computer vacuum transducer on (carbureted) models that have one in all years through 1987, to prevent any distributor advance. The computer is located in the air intake on the driver's side fender well, with the vacuum transducer's diaphragm clearly in view on top. The vacuum line is the rubber hose connected to the metal cone-shaped canister on the side of the distributor or the top/center of the transducer diaphragm. A short screw, pencil, or a golf tee can be used to plug the hose. On 1986 models equipped with a carburetor switch, connect a jumper wire between the carburetor switch and ground. On 1987 2.2 and 2.5L engines with Electronic Fuel Injection, and all 1988 models, disconnect the coolant temperature sensor electrical lead at the sensor, which is located on the thermostat housing.

4. Make sure the idle screw rests against its stop. If necessary, open and close the throttle to make sure the linkage is not binding. Start the engine and adjust the idle speed to that specified in the "Tune-up Specifications" chart. Some cars require that the timing be set with the transmission in Neutral. You can disconnect the idle solenoid, if any, to get the speed down. Otherwise, adjust the idle speed screw. This is to prevent any centrifugal advance of timing in the distributor.

5. Aim the timing light at the timing marks. Be careful not to touch the fan, which may appear to be standing still. Keep your clothes and hair, and the light's wire clear of the fan, belts, and pulleys. If the pulley or damper notch isn't aligned with the proper timing mark (see the Tune-up Specifications chart), the timing will have to be adjusted.

NOTE: *TDC or Top Dead Center corresponds to 0°, B, or BTDC, or Before Top Dead Center, may be shown as BEFORE; A, or ATDC, or After Top Dead Center, may be shown as AFTER.*

6. Loosen the distributor base clamp locknut. You can buy special wrenches which will make this task easy. Turn the distributor slowly to adjust the timing, holding it by the body and not the cap. Turn the distributor in the direction of rotor rotation (found in the Firing Order illustrations) to retard, and against the direction to advance.

7. Tighten the locknut. Check the timing, in case the distributor moved as you tightened it.

8. Reconnect the distributor vacuum hose. Correct the idle speed.

9. Shut off the engine and disconnect the light. Reconnect the coolant temperature sensor connector, if necessary. On 1988 models only, some fault codes may be set. They can be cleared immediately only with a special test instrument. However, as the ignition is turned off 25-50 times in normal use, they will automatically be cleared by the system.

Valve Lash

Valve adjustment determines how far the valves enter the cylinder and how long they stay open and closed.

If the valve clearance is too large, part of the lift of the camshaft will be used in removing the excessive clearance. Consequently, the valve will not be opening as far as it should. This condition has two effects: the valve train components will emit a tapping sound as they take up the excessive clearance and the engine will perform poorly because the valves don't open fully and allow the proper amount of gases to flow into and out of the engine.

If the valve clearance is too small, the intake valve and the exhaust valves will open too far and they will not fully seat on the cylinder head when they close. When a valve seats itself on the cylinder head, it does two things: it seals the combustion chamber so that none of the gases in the cylinder escape and it cools itself by transferring some of the heat it absorbs from

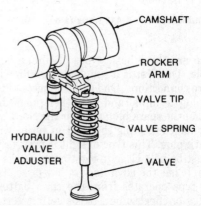

Hydraulic valve adjuster used on 2.2L engine

the combustion in the cylinder to the cylinder head and to the engine's cooling system. If the valve clearance is too small, the engine will run poorly because of the gases escaping from the combustion chamber. The valves will also become overheated and will warp, since they cannot transfer heat unless they are touching the valve seat in the cylinder head.

NOTE: *While all valve adjustments must be made as accurately as possible, it is better to have the valve adjustment slightly loose than slightly tight as a burned valve may result from overly tight adjustments.*

2.2L and 2.5L Engines

The 2.2L and 2.5L engines use hydraulic lash adjusters. No periodic adjustment or checking is necessary.

2.6L Engine

The 2.6L engine has a jet valve located beside the intake of each cylinder.

NOTE: *When adjusting valve clearances, the jet valve must be adjusted before the intake valve.*

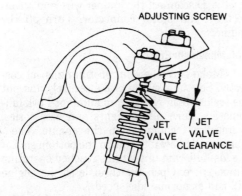

Adjusting the jet valve on 2.6L engines

Adjusting the valve lash on 2.6L engines

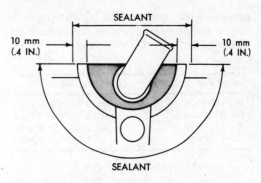

Applying sealant on the 2.6 liter valve cover

1. Start the engine and allow it to reach normal operating temperature.

2. Stop the engine and remove the air cleaner and its hoses. Remove any other cables, hoses, wires, etc., which are attached to the valve cover, and remove the valve cover.

3. Disconnect the high tension coil-to-distributor wire at the coil.

4. Watch the rocker arms for No. 1 cylinder and rotate the crankshaft until the exhaust valve is closing and the intake valve has just started to open. At this point, no. 4 cylinder will be at Top Dead Center (TDC) commencing its firing stroke.

5. Loosen the locknut on cylinder no. 4 intake valve adjusting screw 2 or more turns.

6. Loosen the locknut on the jet valve adjusting screw.

7. Turn the jet valve adjusting screw counter-clockwise and insert a 0.006" feeler gauge between the jet valve stem and the adjusting screw.

8. Tighten the adjusting screw until it touches the feeler gauge.

WARNING: *Take care not to press on the valve while adjusting because the jet valve spring is very weak.*

If the adjusting screw is tight, special care must be taken to avoid pressing down on the jet valve when adjusting the clearance or a false reading will result.

9. Tighten the locknut securely while holding the rocker arm adjusting screw with a screwdriver to prevent it from turning.

10. Make sure that a 0.006" feeler gauge can be easily inserted between the jet valve and the rocker arm.

11. Adjust no. 4 cylinder's intake valve to 0.006" and its exhaust valve to 0.010". Tighten the adjusting screw locknuts and recheck each clearance.

12. Perform step 4 in conjunction with the chart below to set up the remaining three cylinders for valve adjustments.

13. Replace the valve cover and all other com-

ponents. Apply sealer to the top surface of the semi-circular packing. Run the engine and check for oil leaks at the valve cover.

Exhaust Valve Closing	Adjust
No. 1 Cylinder	No. 4 Cylinder Valves
No. 2 Cylinder	No. 3 Cylinder Valves
No. 3 Cylinder	No. 2 Cylinder Valves
No. 4 Cylinder	No. 1 Cylinder Valves

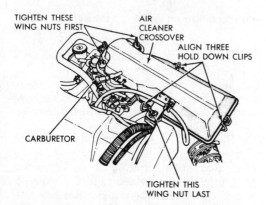

TIGHTEN THESE WING NUTS FIRST

AIR CLEANER CROSSOVER

ALIGN THREE HOLD DOWN CLIPS

CARBURETOR

TIGHTEN THIS WING NUT LAST

Idle Speed and Mixture Adjustment

Carbureted vehicles use the Holley 5220/6250/6520 Series carburetors. Idle speed is adjusted on the top of the idle stop solenoid. Fuel injected cars, whether equipped with Throttle Body or Multi-Point injection use an Automatic Idle Speed motor. This is a throttle bypass system that is computer controlled, and does not require periodic adjustment. To adjust the idle speed on carbureted vehicles, follow the appropriate procedure below.

2.2L and 2.5L Carbureted Engines

1. Make sure the ignition timing is sect correctly. Set the parking brake securely and put the transaxle in Neutral (manual) or Park (automatic). Turn off all lights and accessories. Connect a tachometer to the engine. Then, start it and allow it to run on the bottom step of the fast idle cam until it has reached operating temperature. Open the throttle so the engine will run at normal idle speed.

2. Unplug the radiator fan electrical connector and jumper the connector to ground to make the fan run continuously.

3. Pull the PCV valve out of the crankcase vent module.

4. Disconnect the oxygen feedback system test connector located on the left fender shield. Also disconnect the wiring from the kicker vacuum solenoid—the connector is also located on the left fender shield.

5. Turn the idle speed screw on top of the so-

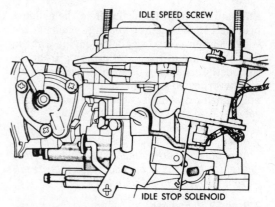

IDLE SPEED SCREW

IDLE STOP SOLENOID

Adjust the idle speed on carbureted cars with the idle speed screw, located on top of the idle stop solenoid

lenoid kicker to obtain the correct idle speed, as shown in the Tune-Up Specifications chart.

6. Reconnect the two disconnect connectors and install the PCV valve back into the vent module.

7. Increase rpm to about 2500 for 15 seconds and then return it to idle speed. Even though idle speed might be different now, you need not reset it. Disconnect the jumper wire and reconnect the fan motor connector. Turn off the engine.

2.6L Mitsubishi Engines

1. Make sure the ignition timing is set correctly. Set the parking brake securely and put the transaxle in Neutral (manual) or Park (automatic). Turn off all lights and accessories. Connect a tachometer to the engine. Then, start it and allow it to run on the bottom step of the fast idle cam until it has reached operating temperature. Open the throttle so the engine will run at normal idle speed.

2. Unplug the radiator fan electrical connector. On 1983 and earlier models, allow the engine to idle for 1 minute to stabilize rpm.

3. On 1984 models, turn the engine off and then disconnect the negative battery cable for 3 seconds and reconnect it. Disconnect the engine harness lead from the O$_2$ sensor connector at the bullet connector. Avoid pulling on the sensor wire when doing this.

4. On 1983-85 models, open the throttle and allow the engine to run at 2500 rpm for 10 seconds. Then, return the engine to normal idle speed.

5. Wait two minutes.

6. Read the idle speed on the tach. If the rpm is not correct, and if the car has electronic feedback control, disconnect the idle switch connector. Now, if the rpm is not correct, turn the idle speed screw, accessible through the bracket on the carburetor body, to get the correct idle rpm.

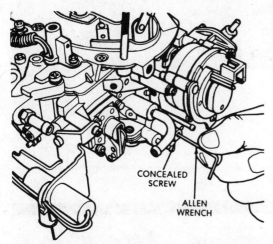

Adjusting propane enrichment rpm—carbureted engine idle mixture adjustment

7. If the car has air conditioning, set the temperature control level to the coldest position and turn the air conditioner on. Then, set the idle-up speed screw to obtain 900 rpm with the compressor running.

8. Turn off the engine, reconnect the fan, disconnect the tachometer, and reconnect the idle switch connector.

IDLE MIXTURE ADJUSTMENT

Chrysler recommends the use of propane enrichment procedure to adjust the mixture. The equipment needed for this procedure is not readily available to the general public. The procedure is included here for reference purposes:

1. Remove the concealment plug located under the choke housing.

2. Set the parking brake and make sure a manual transaxle is in Neutral and an automatic one is in Park.

3. Connect a tachometer to the engine. Then, start it and allow it to run on the bottom

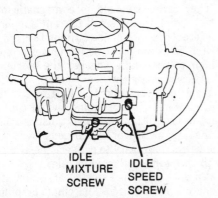

IDLE MIXTURE SCREW   **IDLE SPEED SCREW**

Location of idle speed and mixture adjusting screws on 2.6L engines

step of the fast idle cam until it has reached operating temperature. Open the throttle so the engine will run at normal idle speed.

2. Unplug the radiator fan electrical connector and install a jumper wire so the fan runs continuously.

3. Pull the PCV valve out of the crankcase vent module so it will draw underhood air.

4. Disconnect the oxygen feedback system test connector located on the left fender shield.

5. Disconnect the vacuum harness from the CVSCC valve and plug both hoses. On the 2.2L engine only, disconnect the wiring from the single solenoid kicker vacuum control solenoid, which is located on the left fender shield.

6. Disconnect the vacuum hose which leads to the heated air sensor at the three-way connector and install the supply hose from the propane bottle where it was connected. Make sure the propane valves are fully closed and that the bottle is in a safe and secure position that will maintain it upright.

7. Open the propane main valve. Leaving the air cleaner in place, slowly and very steadily open the propane metering valve while you watch the tach, until maximum rpm is reached. You will note that there will be an optimum mixture, after which further addition of propane will cause the engine rpm to begin falling. Note what this rpm is and carefully adjust the propane valve to produce this exact rpm.

8. Adjust the idle speed screw on top of the solenoid kicker (without changing the propane setting) so that the tach reads the propane enrichment rpm shown on the engine compartment sticker.

9. Increase the engine speed to 2500 rpm for 15 seconds and then return it to idle. Read the rpm and, if it has changed, readjust the idle speed to give the specified rpm.

10. Turn off the propane system main valve and allow the engine speed to stabilize. With the air cleaner in place, slowly adjust the mixture screw to achieve the specified idle set rpm with an Allen wrench. Work very slowly and pause after slight adjustment increments to allow the engine rpm to stabilize. Again, increase the engine speed to 2500 rpm for 15 seconds and then return it to idle. Recheck the rpm.

11. Repeat the procedure of Step 7 to get optimum propane enrichment rpm at these new basic settings. Reread the tach. If this rpm is more than 25 rpm either side of the specified propane enrichment rpm, repeat the procedure starting with Step 7. The adjustment is correct when the test in this step is passed.

12. Turn off both propane valves, remove the propane supply hose, and reinstall the vacuum hose. Reinstall the concealment plug into the carburetor.

Engine and Engine Overhaul

3

ENGINE ELECTRICAL

Understanding the Engine Electrical System

The engine electrical system can be broken down into three separate and distinct systems:

1. The starting system.
2. The charging system.
3. The ignition system.

BATTERY AND STARTING SYSTEM

Basic Operating Principles

The battery is the first link in the chain of mechanisms which work together to provide cranking of the automobile engine. In most modern cars, the battery is a lead/acid electrochemical device consisting of six 2v subsections connected in series so the unit is capable of producing approximately 12v of electrical pressure. Each subsection, or cell, consists of a series of positive and negative plates held a short distance apart in a solution of sulfuric acid and water. The two types of plates are of dissimilar metals. This causes a chemical reaction to be set up, and it is this reaction which produces current flow from the battery when its positive and negative terminals are connected to an electrical appliance such as a lamp or motor. The continued transfer of electrons would eventually convert the sulfuric acid in the electrolyte to water, and make the two plates identical in chemical composition. As electrical energy is removed from the battery, its voltage output tends to drop. Thus, measuring battery voltage and battery electrolyte composition are two ways of checking the ability of the unit to supply power. During the starting of the engine, electrical energy is removed from the battery. However, if the charging circuit is in good condition and the operating conditions are normal, the power removed from the battery will be replaced by the generator (or alternator) which will force electrons back through the battery, reversing the normal flow, and restoring the battery to its original chemical state.

The battery and starting motor are linked by very heavy electrical cables designed to minimize resistance to the flow of current. Generally, the major power supply cable that leaves the battery goes directly to the starter, while other electrical system needs are supplied by a smaller cable. During starter operation, power flows from the battery to the starter and is grounded through the car's frame and the battery's negative ground strap.

The starting motor is a specially designed, direct current electric motor capable of producing a very great amount of power for its size. One thing that allows the motor to produce a great deal of power is its tremendous rotating speed. It drives the engine through a tiny pinion gear (attached to the starter's armature), which drives the very large flywheel ring gear at a greatly reduced speed. Another factor allowing it to produce so much power is that only intermittent operation is required of it. This, little allowance for air circulation is required, and the windings can be built into a very small space.

The starter solenoid is a magnetic device which employs the small current supplied by the starting switch circuit of the ignition switch. This magnetic action moves a plunger which mechanically engages the starter and electrically closes the heavy switch which connects it to the battery. The starting switch circuit consists of the starting switch contained within the ignition switch, a transmission neutral safety switch or clutch pedal switch, and the wiring necessary to connect these in series with the starter solenoid or relay.

A pinion, which is a small gear, is mounted to a one-way drive clutch. This clutch is splined to the starter armature shaft. When the ignition switch is moved to the **start** position, the solenoid plunger slides the pinion toward the fly-wheel ring gear via a collar and spring. If the teeth on the pinion and flywheel match proper-ly, the pinion will engage the flywheel immedi-ately. If the gear teeth butt one another, the spring will be compressed and will force the gears to mesh as soon as the starter turns far enough to allow them to do so. As the solenoid plunger reaches the end of its travel, it closes the contacts that connect the battery and start-er and then the engine is cranked.

As soon as the engine starts, the flywheel ring gear begins turning fast enough to drive the pinion at an extremely high rate of speed. At this point, the one-way clutch begins allow-ing the pinion to spin faster than the starter shaft so that the starter will not operate at ex-cessive speed. When the ignition switch is re-leased from the starter position, the solenoid is de-energized, and a spring contained within the solenoid assembly pulls the gear out of mesh and interrupts the current flow to the starter.

Some starter employ a separate relay, mount-ed away from the starter, to switch the motor and solenoid current on and off. The relay thus replaces the solenoid electrical switch, buy does not eliminate the need for a solenoid mounted on the starter used to mechanically engage the starter drive gears. The relay is used to reduce the amount of current the starting switch must carry.

THE CHARGING SYSTEM

Basic Operating Principles

The automobile charging system provides electrical power for operation of the vehicle's ig-nition and starting systems and all the electri-cal accessories. The battery services as an elec-trical surge or storage tank, storing (in chemi-cal form) the energy originally produced by the engine driven generator. The system also pro-vides a means of regulating generator output to protect the battery from being overcharged and to avoid excessive voltage to the accessories.

The storage battery is a chemical device in-corporating parallel lead plates in a tank con-taining a sulfuric acid/water solution. Adjacent plates are slightly dissimilar, and the chemical reaction of the two dissimilar plates produces electrical energy when the battery is connected to a load such as the starter motor. The chemi-cal reaction is reversible, so that when the gen-erator is producing a voltage (electrical pres-sure) greater than that produced by the bat-tery, electricity is forced into the battery, and the battery is returned to its fully charged state.

The vehicle's generator is driven mechanical-ly, through V-belts, by the engine crankshaft. It consists of two coils of fine wire, one stationary (the stator), and one movable (the rotor). The rotor may also be known as the armature, and consists of fine wire wrapped around an iron core which is mounted on a shaft. The electric-ity which flows through the two coils of wire (provided initially by the battery in some cases) creates an intense magnetic field around both rotor and stator, and the interaction between the two fields creates voltage, allowing the gen-erator to power the accessories and charge the battery.

There are two types of generators: the earlier is the direct current (DC) type. The current produced by the DC generator is generated in the armature and carried off the spinning ar-mature by stationary brushes contacting the commutator. The commutator is a series of smooth metal contact plates on the end of the armature. The commutator is a series of smooth metal contact plates on the end of the armature. The commutator plates, which are separated from one another by a very short gap, are connected to the armature circuits so that current will flow in one directions only in the wires carrying the generator output. The gen-erator stator consists of two stationary coils of wire which draw some of the output current of the generator to form a powerful magnetic field and create the interaction of fields which gener-ates the voltage. The generator field is wired in series with the regulator.

Newer automobiles use alternating current generators or alternators, because they are more efficient, can be rotated at higher speeds, and have fewer brush problems. In an alterna-tor, the field rotates while all the current pro-duced passes only through the stator winding. The brushes bear against continuous slip rings rather than a commutator. This causes the cur-rent produced to periodically reverse the direc-tion of its flow. Diodes (electrical one-way switches) block the flow of current from travel-ing in the wrong direction. A series of diodes is wired together to permit the alternating flow of the stator to be converted to a pulsating, but unidirectional flow at the alternator output. The alternator's field is wired in series with the voltage regulator.

The regulator consists of several circuits. Each circuit has a core, or magnetic coil of wire, which operates a switch. Each switch is con-nected to ground through one or more resis-tors. The coil of wire responds directly to sys-tem voltage. When the voltage reaches the re-quired level, the magnetic field created by the winding of wire closes the switch and inserts a resistance into the generator field circuit, thus reducing the output. The contacts of the switch cycle open and close many times each second to precisely control voltage.

While alternators are self-limiting as far as maximum current is concerned, DC generators employ a current regulating circuit which responds directly to the total amount of current flowing through the generator circuit rather than to the output voltage. The current regulator is similar to the voltage regulator except that all system current must flow through the energizing coil on its way to the various accessories.

Ignition Coil
TESTING

NOTE: *To perform a reliable test of the coil, you must make up several jumper wires. You'll need two simple wires several feet long with alligator clips on the ends. A third wire must incorporate a capacitor of 0.33 MicroFarad capacitance. The materials and components needed to make up such jumpers should be available at a reasonable price in a local electronics store.*

1. Turn the ignition key off. Disconnect the negative battery cable. Then, carefully remove the retaining nuts and disconnect the two coil primary leads. Wrap the positive (+) lead in electrician's tape or otherwise ensure that it cannot accidentally ground during the test.

2. Run a jumper wire from the battery positive (+) terminal directly to the coil positive (+) terminal. Run the jumper wire incorporating the capacitor from the coil negative terminal to a good ground. Reconnect the battery negative cable and turn on the ignition switch. Fasten one end of the remaining standard jumper wire in a position where the clip cannot ground. Then connect the other end of it to the coil negative terminal. Turn on the ignition key.

3. Unclip the coil high tension lead from inside the distributor cap and pull it out. Hold the distributor end of the lead ¼" from a good ground. Ground the standard jumper wire coming from the coil negative terminal.

4. Break the ground in the standard lead coming from the coil negative as you watch for spark. The coil should produce a hot, blue-white spark. Repeat the test looking at the coil tower. If sparks are visible there, replace the ignition wires if the rubber boots are deteriorated, or the coil, if the tower is burned and tracked.

5. If the coil tower and wire boots are okay, and this test fails to produce a spark, replace the coil.

On 1987-88 cars, you can confirm the problem with an ohmmeter. Turn off the ignition switch, and disconnect the negative battery cable. With the coil primary wires still disconnected, test the resistance between positive and negative primary terminals. It must be 1.35-1.55Ω. For secondary resistance, first determine whether the coil is a Chrysler Prestolite, Chrysler Essex, or Diamond brand coil by wiping off the coil and looking for appropriate lettering. Then, pull the high tension lead out of the coil tower and run the ohmmeter lead between the coil negative primary terminal and the brass connector down inside the tower. Resistance ranges must be as follows:
- Chrysler Prestolite – 9,400-11,700
- Chrysler Essex – 9,000-12,200
- Diamond – 15,000-19,000

CAUTION: *If the coil tests okay, you must be sure to turn off the ignition switch and have the battery negative cable disconnected before reconnecting the primary leads.*

Distributor
REMOVAL AND INSTALLATION

1. Disconnect the distributor pickup lead wire at the harness connector. Remove the two retaining screws and remove the distributor splash shield.

2. Remove the two distributor cap retaining screws and then remove the distributor cap.

3. Rotate the engine crankshaft (in the direction of normal rotation) until No. 1 cylinder is at TDC on compression stroke. At this point, the timing marks will line up at TDC and, *at the same time* the rotor will point to the high tension wire terminal for No. 1. cylinder in the cap. If the rotor does not line up properly, turn the engine crankshaft another 360°. Make a mark on the block where the rotor points for installation reference. Also mark the relationship between the body of the distributor and the block so you can install the distributor with the ignition timing nearly correct.

4. Remove the distributor holddown bolt.

5. Carefully lift the distributor from the engine. The shaft will rotate slightly as the distributor is removed because of the curvature in the teeth of the drive gear. Note the angle at which the rotor sits as the shaft stops rotating and mark it.

6. Installation is the reverse of removal. When installing the distributor, start inserting it with the rotor lined up with the second mark you made. If the distributor drive gear does not immediately engage with the accessory shaft, turn the rotor back and forth very slighty, keeping it as nearly aligned with the second mark as possible, until it engages easily, making it easy

to slide the distributor into the block. Then, when the distributor seats on the block, verify that the first mark and the rotor tip are lined up. Make sure the distributor seats so the gasket at its base will seal.

7. Adjust the ignition timing, as described in Chapter 2.

NOTE: *The following procedure is to be used if the engine was cranked with the distributor removed.*

1. If the engine has been cranked over while the distributor was out of the engine, rotate the crankshaft until the number one piston is at TDC on the compression stroke. This will be indicated by the 0 mark on the flywheel or crank pulley aligning with the pointer on the clutch housing or engine front cover. Now, you must verify that No. 1 cylinder is at Top Dead Center firing position, and not at the top of the exhaust stroke. Do this in one of two ways:

a. Remove the valve cover and check the positions of No. 1 valve springs and rockers. The valves should be closed (with springs up all the way) and the rockers should be in contact with the base circles of the cams, rather than the cam lobes. If the cam is actuating the valves, rotate the engine another 360° until the timing marks are again at Top Dead Center.

b. Remove the No. 1 Cylinder spark plug and put your finger over the spark plug hole as you crank the engine toward Top Dead Center. If the engine is approaching the firing position, you will feel air being forcibly expelled from the cylinder because the valves will be closed, sealing off the cylinder. If the engine is approaching Top Dead Center of the exhaust stroke, air will not be forcibly expelled. If this latter situation is the case, turn the engine another 360°, and feel for air pressure.

Once the engine is at TDC No. 1 firing position:

2. Position the rotor just ahead of the #1 terminal of the cap, at the second mark made earlier, and lower the distributor into the engine. With the distributor fully seated, the rotor should be directly under the #1 terminal in the cap.

3. If the engine was not disturbed while the distributor was out, lower the distributor into the engine, engaging the gears by rocking the shaft back and forth, if necessary, and making sure that the gasket is properly seated in the block. The rotor should line up with the mark made before removal.

4. Tighten the holddown bolt and connect the wires.

5. Check and, if necessary, adjust the ignition timing.

Ignition Computer/Power Module (1981-87)

REMOVAL AND INSTALLATION

WARNING: *The grease located in the 10 or 14 way connector cavity in the computer is necessary to prevent moisture from corroding the terminals. Not only should this grease be left in place, but if the layer is less than ⅛″ thick, spread Mopar Multi-purpose grease Part No. 2932524 or an equivalent available in the aftermarket in an even layer over the end of each connector plug before reconnecting them.*

1. Disconnect the negative battery cable. Then, disconnect the 10 and 14-way dual connectors.

2. Disconnect the outside air duct at the computer housing. Disconnect the vacuum line at the vacuum transducer on top of the housing.

3. Remove the 3 mounting screws that fasten the computer to the inside of the left front fender and remove it.

4. Installation is the reverse of removal.

SMEC Controller (1988)

1. Disconnect both battery cables (negative first).

2. Disconnect the air cleaner duct at the SMEC.

3. Remove the two mounting screws by which the module hangs onto the fender well.

4. Move the unit out slightly for access and then disconnect both the 14 and 60-way wiring connectors. Remove the SMEC from the engine compartment.

5. Install the module in reverse order, making sure to connect the electrical connectors before attempting to mount it.

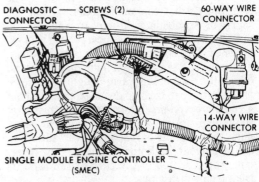

Removing the SMEC controller used on 1988 models

Alternator

ALTERNATOR PRECAUTIONS

Several precautions must be observed with alternator equipped vehicles to avoid damaging the unit. They are as follows:

1. If the battery is removed for any reason, make sure that it is reconnected with the correct polarity. Reversing the battery connections may result in damage to the one-way rectifiers.

2. When utilizing a booster battery as a starting aid, always connect it as follows: positive to positive, and negative (booster battery) to a good ground on the engine of the car being started.

3. Never use a fast charger as a booster to start cars with alternating current (AC) circuits.

4. When servicing the battery with a fast charger, always disconnect the car battery cables.

5. Never attempt to polarize an alternator.

6. Avoid long soldering times when replacing diodes or transistors. Prolonged heat is damaging to alternators.

7. Do not use test lamps of more than 12 volts (V) for checking diode continuity.

8. Do not short across or ground any of the terminals on the alternator.

9. The polarity of the battery, alternator, and regulator must be matched and considered before making any electrical connections within the system.

10. Never separate the alternator on an open circuit. Make sure that all connections within the circuit are clean and tight.

11. Disconnect the battery terminals when performing any service on the electrical system. This will eliminate the possibility of accidental reversal of polarity.

12. Disconnect the battery ground cable if arc welding is to be done on any part of the car.

CHARGING SYSTEM TROUBLESHOOTING

There are many possible ways in which the charging system can malfunction. Often the source of a problem is difficult to diagnose, requiring special equipment and a good deal of experience. This is usually not the case, however, where the charging system fails completely and causes the dash board warning light to come on or the battery to become dead. To troubleshoot a complete system failure only two pieces of equipment are needed: a test light, to determine that current is reaching a certain point; and a current indicator (ammeter), to determine the direction of the current flow and its measurement in amps.

This test works under three assumptions:

1. The battery is known to be good and fully charged.

2. The alternator belt is in good condition and adjusted to the proper tension.

3. All connections in the system are clean and tight.

NOTE: *In order for the current indicator to give a valid reading, the car must be equipped with battery cables which are of the same gauge size and quality as original equipment battery cables.*

1. Turn off all electrical components on the car. Make sure the doors of the car are closed. If the car is equipped with a clock, disconnect the clock by removing the lead wire from the rear of the clock. Disconnect the positive battery cable from the battery and connect the ground wire on a test light to the disconnected positive battery cable. Touch the probe end of the test light to the positive battery post. The test light should not light. If the test light does light, there is a short or open circuit on the car.

2. Disconnect the voltage regulator wiring harness connector at the voltage regulator. Turn on the ignition key. Connect the wire on a test light to a good ground (engine bolt). Touch the probe end of a test light to the ignition wire connector into the voltage regulator wiring connector. This wire corresponds to the **I** terminal on the regulator. If the test light goes on, the charging system warning light circuit is complete. If the test light does not come on and the warning light on the instrument panel is on, either the resistor wire, which is parallel with the warning light, or the wiring to the voltage regulator, is defective. If the test light does not come on and the warning light is not on, either the bulb is defective or the power supply wire form the battery through the ignition switch to the bulb has an open circuit. Connect the wiring harness to the regulator.

3. Examine the fuse link wire in the wiring harness from the starter relay to the alternator. If the insulation on the wire is cracked or split, the fuse link may be melted. Connect a test light to the fuse link by attaching the ground wire on the test light to an engine bolt and touching the probe end of the light to the bottom of the fuse link wire where it splices into the alternator output wire. If the bulb in the test light does not light, the fuse link is melted.

4. Start the engine and place a current indicator on the positive battery cable. Turn off all electrical accessories and make sure the doors are closed. If the charging system is working properly, the gauge will show a draw of less than 5 amps. If the system is not working properly, the gauge will show a draw of more than 5 amps. A charge moves the needle toward the

battery, a draw moves the needle away from the battery. Turn the engine off.

5. Disconnect the wiring harness from the voltage regulator at the regulator at the regulator connector. Connect a male spade terminal (solderless connector) to each end of a jumper wire. Insert one end of the wire into the wiring harness connector which corresponds to the **A** terminal on the regulator. Insert the other end of the wire into the wiring harness connector which corresponds to the **F** terminal on the regulator. Position the connector with the jumper wire installed so that it cannot contact any metal surface under the hood. Position a current indicator gauge on the positive battery cable. Have an assistant start the engine. Observe the reading on the current indicator. Have your assistant slowly raise the speed of the engine to about 2,000 rpm or until the current indicator needle stops moving, whichever comes first. Do not run the engine for more than a short period of time in this condition. If the wiring harness connector or jumper wire becomes excessively hot during this test, turn off the engine and check for a grounded wire in the regulator wiring harness. If the current indicator shows a charge of about three amps less than the output of the alternator, the alternator is working properly. If the previous tests showed a draw, the voltage regulator is defective. If the gauge does not show the proper charging rate, the alternator is defective.

REMOVAL AND INSTALLATION

1. Disconnect the negative battery terminal.
2. Disconnect the wiring and label it for easy reinstallation.
3. Loosen the alternator adjusting bracket bolt, or adjusting nut and bolt.
4. Remove all necessary drive belts.
5. Remove the adjusting bolt or bolt and nut and the pivot bolt.
6. Remove the alternator.
7. Installation is the reverse of removal. Adjust the belt tension to allow ½" of play on the longest run.

Regulator

REMOVAL AND INSTALLATION

NOTE: *The alternator on the 2.6 liter engine has an integral regulator. No adjustments are possible. The voltage of many late model and all 1988 alternators is regulator via the Power Module or SMEC controller. Other alternators used with the 2.2L and 2.5L engines may incorporate a separate regulator.*
1. Disconnect the negative battery terminal.
2. Remove the electrical connection.

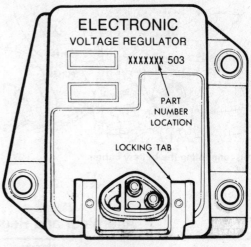

Electronic voltage regulator

3. Remove the mounting bolts and remove the regulator.
4. This regulator is not adjustable and must be replaced as a unit if found to be defective.
5. Installation is the reverse of removal.

Battery

REMOVAL AND INSTALLATION

CAUTION: *Batteries often develop acid leaks! In all battery handling, you should wear thick (not medical or household) rubber gloves. Failure to do this could result in acid burns!*
1. Make *sure* that the ignition switch is off.
2. Disconnect both of the battery cables, negative (-) first, as follows:

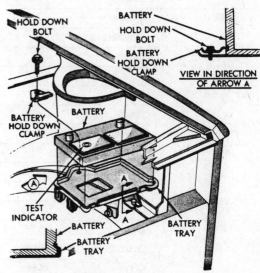

The battery mounting system

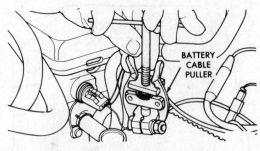

Disconnecting the battery cables

a. Loosen the nuts which secure the cable ends to the battery terminals.

b. Lift the battery cables from the terminals with a twisting motion. If there is a battery cable puller available, make use of it.

3. Remove its bolt and remove the battery holddown clamp.

4. Carefully lift the battery out of the vehicle.

5. Clean the battery tray with a mild solution of baking soda and water, using a stiff, bristle

Alternator and Regulator Specifications

Year	Alternator Manufacturer	Rating	Minimum Output (amps)	Regulator Type	Volts @ 80°F
1981–83	Chrysler	65	62	Chrysler	13.9–14.6
	Chrysler	60	57	Chrysler	13.9–14.6
	Mitsubishi	—	74	Integral	
1984	Chrysler	78	56	Chrysler	13.9–14.6
	Bosch	60	45	Chrysler	13.9–14.6
	Bosch	90	89	Integral	
	Mitsubishi	75	74	Integral	
1985	Chrysler	60	45	Chrysler	13.9–14.6
	Bosch	65	50	Chrysler	13.9–14.6
	Bosch	90	89	Integral	
	Mitsubishi	75	74	Integral	
	Chrysler	40/90	96	In Engine Electronics	
	Bosch	40/90	87	In Engine Electronics	
1986	Chrysler	78	56	Chrysler	13.9–14.6
	Chrysler	60	45	Chrysler	13.9–14.6
	Bosch	65	50	Chrysler	13.9–14.6
	Chrysler	40/90	87	In Engine Electronics	
	Bosch	40/90	80	In Engine Electronics	
	Bosch	40/100	87	In Engine Electronics	
1987	Chrysler	78	56	Chrysler	13.9–14.6
	Chrysler	78	56	In Engine Electronics	
	Chrysler	40/90	87	In Engine Electronics	
	Bosch	40/90	80	In Engine Electronics	
	Chrysler	50/120	98	In Engine Electronics	
1988	Bosch	35/75	30	In Engine Electronics	
	Bosch	40/90	40	In Engine Electronics	
	Chrysler	40/90	87	In Engine Electronics	
	Chrysler	50/120	98	In Engine Electronics	

brush. If the battery is to be reinstalled, clean it as well, and then wipe it with a rag dampened in ammonia.

6. Install the battery in reverse order, tightening the clamp bolt to 12 ft.lb.

7. Install the battery cables so that the tops of the clamps are flush with the terminals and torque the nuts to 12 ft.lb. Coat the terminals with a petroleum grease.

Starter

REMOVAL AND INSTALLATION

1. Disconnect the negative battery terminal.
2. Remove the bolts attaching the starter to the flywheel housing and the rear bracket to the engine or transaxle.
3. On the 2.2 liter engine loosen the air pump tube at the exhaust manifold and move the tube bracket away from the starter.
4. Remove the heat shield and its clamp if so equipped.
5. Remove the electrical connections from the starter.
6. Remove the starter.
7. Installation is the reverse of removal.

SOLENOID REPLACEMENT

1. Remove the starter as previously outlined.
2. Disconnect the field coil wire from the solenoid by removing the nut and pulling the connector off.
3. Remove the solenoid mounting screws.
4. Remove the solenoid by working the plunger stem off the shift fork.
5. Installation is the reverse of removal.

OVERHAUL

Nippondenso/Mitsubishi Reduction Starter (2.6L engine)

1. Position the assembly in a suitable holding fixture. Disconnect the wire terminal from

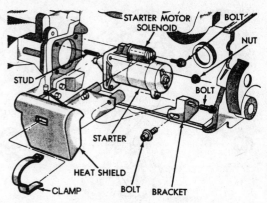

Starter mounting for the 2.2 and 2.5 L engines

the field coil stud and move the rubber shield away from the wire end.

2. Remove the two through bolts from the end frame. Remove the two screws from the end of the frame cap. Remove the upper left solenoid screw and remove the wire retainer.
3. Remove the end shield. Remove the two field frame brushes from the brush plate.
4. Remove the brush plate and slide the armature out of the field frame and remove the field frame.
5. Remove the two screws from the gear housing and remove the gear housing from the solenoid.
6. Remove the clutch rollers and retainer. Remove the pinion and clutch. Remove the solenoid steel ball and spring.
7. Remove the solenoid cover screws, remove the solenoid cover and remove the solenoid plunger.
8. Do not immerse parts in cleaning solvent. Immersing the field frame and coil assembly and armature will damage insulation. Wipe these parts with a cloth only.
9. Do not immerse drive unit in cleaning solvent. Drive clutch is prelubricated at the fac-

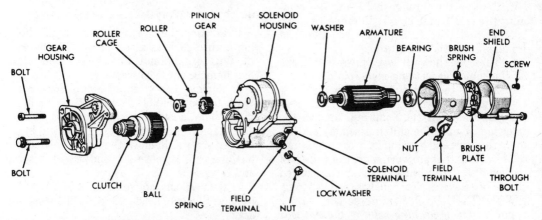

Exploded view of the gear reduction type starter used with the 2.6 L engine

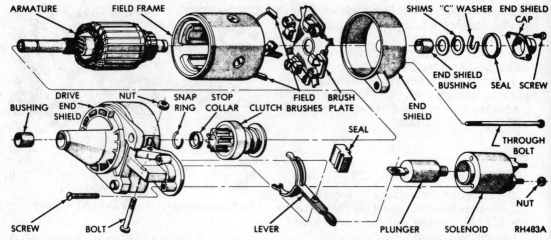

ARMATURE FIELD FRAME SHIMS "C" WASHER END SHIELD CAP

END SHIELD BUSHING SEAL SCREW

DRIVE END SHIELD NUT SNAP RING STOP COLLAR CLUTCH FIELD BRUSHES BRUSH PLATE END SHIELD

BUSHING

SEAL

THROUGH BOLT

NUT

SCREW BOLT LEVER PLUNGER SOLENOID RH483A

Exploded view of the reduction gear Bosch reduction starter used with the 2.2 L engine through 1986

tory and solvent will wash lubrication from clutch.

10. The drive unit may be cleaned with a brush moistened with cleaning solvent and wiped dry with a cloth. Brushes that are worn more than ½ the length of new brush, or are oil soaked, should be replaced.

11. Field brushes are serviced as part of the field and frame assembly. Ground brushes and all springs come as part of the brush plate assembly.

12. The assembly is the reverse of the disassembly procedure.

Bosch Reduction Gear Starter (2.2L Engine — 1981-86)

1. Position the assembly in a soft-jawed holding fixture. Disconnect the field coil wire from the solenoid terminal.

2. Remove the solenoid mounting screws and work the solehoid plunger off the shift fork.

3. Remove the two screws holding down the end shield bearing cap, and remove the cap and washers.

4. Remove the through bolts and the commutator end frame cover. Remove the two brushes and the brush plate. Slide the field frame off over the armature.

5. Take out the shift lever pivot bolt. Take off the rubber gasket and metal plate.

6. Remove the armature assembly and shift lever from the drive end housing. Then, press the stop collar off the snapring, remove the snapring, remove the clutch assembly and remove the drive end housing from the armature.

7. Brushes that are worn more than one half the length of new brushes, or are oil soaked should be replaced. New brushes are $^{11}/_{16}$" long.

WARNING: *Do not immerse the starter clutch unit in cleaning solvent. Solvent will wash the lubricant from the clutch.*

8. Place the drive unit on the armature shaft and while holding the armature rotate the pinion. The drive pinion should rotate smoothly in one direction only. The pinion may not rotate easily but as long as it rotates smoothly it is in good condition. If the clutch unit does not function properly or if the pinion is worn, chipped or burred replace the unit.

9. Assembly is the reverse of the disassembly procedure. Lubricate the armature shaft and splines with SAE 10W or 30W oil.

10. On all except the Bosch (manual transmission) install the clutch, stop collar, lock ring and shaft fork on the armature. On the Bosch (manual transmission) install the drive end housing on the armature then install the clutch, stop collar and snapring on the armature.

11. On all except the Bosch (manual transmission) install the armature assembly and shift fork in the drive end housing. On Bosch units install the shim and armature shaft lock. Check the end play. It should be 0.002-0.021".

Bosch Starter (Chrysler 2.5 Liter Engine)

1. Position the assembly in a suitable holding fixture such as a soft-jawed vice. Remove the field terminal nut. Remove the field terminal. Remove the field washer.

2. Remove the solenoid mounting screws. Work the solenoid off of the shift fork and remove the solenoid from the starter.

3. Remove the two starter end shield bushing cap screws. Remove the starter end shield bushing cap. Remove the end shield bushing and C-washer.

4. Remove the starter end shield bushing washer. Remove the starter end shield bushing seal.

5. Remove the two starter through bolts. Re-

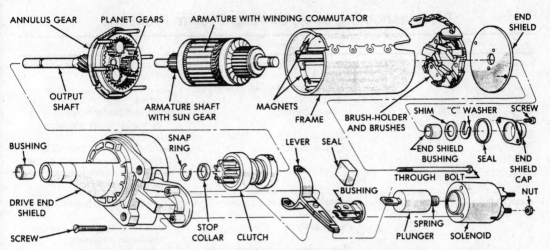

Exploded view of the Bosch Reduction Gear Starter used with the Chrysler 2.5 L engine

move the starter end shield. Remove the brush plate.

6. Slide the field frame off of the starter and over the armature. Remove the armature assembly from the drive end housing.

7. Remove the rubber seal from the drive end housing. Remove the starter drive gear train.

8. Remove the dust plate. Press the stop collar downward until it sits below the snapring using a socket wrench which just fits over the output shaft. Work the snapring out of its groove in the output shaft using a pair of snapring pliers.

9. Remove the output shaft snapring. Re-

Starter Specifications

Year	Part No.	Application	Cranking Amps	No-Load Test		
				Volts	Amps	RPM
1981–83	5213045	2.2—All	120–160	11	47	6600
1984–85	5213045	2.2 Non-Turbo (Bosch)	120–160	11	47	6600
	5213645	2.2 Non-Turbo (Nippondenso)	120–160	11	47	6600
	5213450	2.2 Turbo	120–160	11	47	6600
	5213235	2.6—All	150–210	11	85	3700
1986	5226442	2.2 Non-Turbo (Bosch)	120–160	11	47	6600
	5226742	2.2 Non-Turbo (Nippondenso)	120–160	11	47	6600
	5226441	2.2 Turbo	120–160	11	47	6600
	5226444	2.6—All	150–210	11	85	3700
1987	5226442	2.2 Non-Turbo (Bosch)	150–210	11	47	6600
	5226441	2.2 Turbo (Bosch)	150–210	11	47	6600
	5226844	2.2 EFI (Bosch)	160–220	11	85	3700
	5226842	2.2 Turbo (Bosch)	150–210	11	75	4020
	5227282	2.2 Non-Turbo (Nippondenso)	150–210	11	82	3625
	5227282	2.2 Turbo (Nippondenso)	150–210	11	82	3625
	5227282	2.5—All	150–210	11	82	3625
1988	5227282	2.2—All	150–220	11	82	3625
	5227282	2.5 (Nippondenso)	150–220	11	82	3625
	5227282	2.5 (Bosch)	150–220	11	85	3700

Troubleshooting Basic Starting System Problems

Problem	Cause	Solution
Starter motor rotates engine slowly	• Battery charge low or battery defective	• Charge or replace battery
	• Defective circuit between battery and starter motor	• Clean and tighten, or replace cables
	• Low load current	• Bench-test starter motor. Inspect for worn brushes and weak brush springs.
	• High load current	• Bench-test starter motor. Check engine for friction, drag or coolant in cylinders. Check ring gear-to-pinion gear clearance.
Starter motor will not rotate engine	• Battery charge low or battery defective	• Charge or replace battery
	• Faulty solenoid	• Check solenoid ground. Repair or replace as necessary.
	• Damage drive pinion gear or ring gear	• Replace damaged gear(s)
	• Starter motor engagement weak	• Bench-test starter motor
	• Starter motor rotates slowly with high load current	• Inspect drive yoke pull-down and point gap, check for worn end bushings, check ring gear clearance
	• Engine seized	• Repair engine
Starter motor drive will not engage (solenoid known to be good)	• Defective contact point assembly	• Repair or replace contact point assembly
	• Inadequate contact point assembly ground	• Repair connection at ground screw
	• Defective hold-in coil	• Replace field winding assembly
Starter motor drive will not disengage	• Starter motor loose on flywheel housing	• Tighten mounting bolts
	• Worn drive end busing	• Replace bushing
	• Damaged ring gear teeth	• Replace ring gear or driveplate
	• Drive yoke return spring broken or missing	• Replace spring
Starter motor drive disengages prematurely	• Weak drive assembly thrust spring	• Replace drive mechanism
	• Hold-in coil defective	• Replace field winding assembly
Low load current	• Worn brushes	• Replace brushes
	• Weak brush springs	• Replace springs

move the clutch stop ring collar. Remove the clutch assembly from the starter.

10. Remove the clutch shift lever bushing. Remove the clutch shift lever. Position a suitable tool which will enable you to pry off the C-clip retainer, and then pry it off.

11. Remove the retaining washer. Remove the sun and the planetary gears from the annulus gear.

12. Inspect all parts carefully. Replace all defective components as required.

13. Reassemble the annulus, sun and planetary gears. Then, install the retaining washer over the clutch gear. Finally, install the C-clip and C-clip retainer.

14. Lock the retaining pins of the clutch shift mechanism into the holes in the shift lever fork. Install the clutch shift lever bushing over the pins in the center of the shift lever. Then, slide the clutch assembly over the clutch drive gear on the end of the armature shaft.

15. Install the snap ring collar, larger end downward (toward the starter motor). Then, work the snap ring down onto the shaft until it locks in the snap ring groove. Finally, work the clutch stop ring collar back up the shaft until it seats against the snap ring, using a battery cable connection puller.

16. Install the duct plate onto the rear of the gear train. Then, assemble the gear train into the drive end housing with the bushing at the center and shift lever facing upward and entering the solenoid housing.

17. Install the rubber water seal into the drive end housing. Then, install the armature shaft into the rear of the drive train assembly so the teeth of the sun gear at its front end will mesh with the tyhree planetary gears inside.

18. Find a socket wrench with an outside diameter approximately the same diameter as the commutator at the rear of the armature. Work the brushes back into the holders against spring pressure and slide the socket into the center of the four brushes to retain them. Position the brush plate behind the armature with the socket aligned with the commutator. Then, slide the brush plate forward and into its normal position so the brushes will rest against the commutator.

19. Put the end shield into position on the starter. Then, install the two through-bolts.

20. Install the end shield bushing seal, flat washer, C-washer, and cap. Then, install the two screws that hold the camp onto the starter.

21. Put the solenoid into position over the clutch shift fork. Then, install the three solenoid mounting screws.

22. Install the field coil washer, terminal and terminal nut.

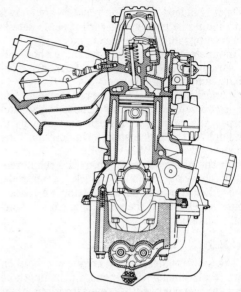

Cross-section of the 2.5 L engine

ENGINE MECHANICAL

Description

A 135 cu. in. (2.2 Liter) engine is standard. A 156 cu. in. (2.6 Liter) engine, manufactured by Mitsubishi, is optional on 1982-86 models. A 153 cu. in. 2.5 L Chrysler built engine is optional on 1987-88 models. It is based on the 2.2 L engine, achieving its increased size through a longer stroke (4.09 vs. 3.62). Also optional on some recent models is a turbocharged version of the 2.2, employing dished pistons which lower the compression ratio to 8.5:1.

The 2.2 Liter engine is a four cylinder overhead camshaft power plant with an aluminum cylinder head. The crankshaft is supported by five main bearings. No vibration damper is used. A sintered iron timing belt sprocket is mounted on the crankshaft. The intake manifold and oil filter base are aluminum.

The 2.6 Liter optional engine is also a four cylinder overhead camshaft power plant with a cast iron block, aluminum head and a silent shaft system. The countershafts (silent shafts) are incorporated in the cylinder block to reduce noise and vibration. Its most distinguishing feature is a jet valve located beside the intake valve of each cylinder. This valve works off the intake valve rocker arm and injects a swirl of air into the combustion chamber to promote more complete combustion.

The 2.5 Liter engine is basically similar to the 2.2, although a different block casting must be used to accomodate the longer stroke. Even though many basic components and dimensions are shared, the 2.5 incorporates one very radical change: a balance shaft system to minimize vibration. These two, counter-rotating shafts are located in a special housing mounted to the underside of the block and under the crankshaft, within the oil pan. The shafts are interconnected by gears and driven (from the crankshaft) through a roller chain to keep them in time.

The intake manifolds on these engines are all aluminum castings. A four-branch fan design is used on all normally aspirated Chrysler-built engines. A log type design is used for Turbo and Turbo II engines. It incorporates machined openings for the fuel injectors as well as a throttle body. The Turbo II uses a two-piece design incorporating an upper plenum and a lower set of four runners. All turbochargers utilize a water cooled turbine housing to aid longevity.

Engine Overhaul Tips

Most engine overhaul procedures are fairly standard. In addition to specific parts replacement procedures and complete specifications for your individual engine, this chapter also is a guide to accept rebuilding procedures. Exam-

ples of standard rebuilding practice are shown and should be used along with specific details concerning your particular engine.

Competent and accurate machine shop services will ensure maximum performance, reliability and engine life.

In most instances it is more profitable for the do-it-yourself mechanic to remove, clean and inspect the component, buy the necessary parts and deliver these to a shop for actual machine work.

On the other hand, much of the rebuilding work (checking crankshaft, block, piston, rods, and other components and fitting new bearings) is well within the scope of the do-it-yourself mechanic.

TOOLS

The tools required for an engine overhaul or parts replacement will depend on the depth of your involvement. With a few exceptions, they will be the tools found in a mechanic's tool kit (see Chapter 1). More in-depth work will require any or all of the following:

- a dial indicator (reading in thousandths) mounted on a universal base
- micrometers and telescope gauges
- jaw and screw-type pullers
- scraper
- valve spring compressor
- ring groove cleaner
- piston ring expander and compressor
- ridge reamer
- cylinder hone or glaze breaker
- Plastigage®
- engine stand

The use of most of these tools is illustrated in this chapter. Many can be rented for a one-time use from a local parts jobber or tool supply house specializing in automotive work.

Occasionally, the use of special tools is called for. See the information on Special Tools and the Safety Notice in the front of this book before substituting another tool.

INSPECTION TECHNIQUES

Procedures and specifications are given in this chapter for inspecting, cleaning and assessing the wear limits of most major components. Other procedures such as Magnaflux® and Zyglo® can be used to locate material flaws and stress cracks. Magnaflux® is a magnetic process applicable only to ferrous materials. The Zyglo® process coats the material with a fluorescent dye penetrant and can be used on any material Check for suspected surface cracks can be more readily made using spot check dye. The dye is sprayed onto the suspected area, wiped off and the area sprayed with a developer. Cracks will show up brightly.

OVERHAUL TIPS

Aluminum has become extremely popular for use in engines, due to its low weight. Observe the following precautions when handling aluminum parts:

- Never hot tank aluminum parts (the caustic hot tank solution will eat the aluminum.
- Remove all aluminum parts (identification tag, etc.) from engine parts prior to the tanking.
- Always coat threads lightly with engine oil or anti-seize compounds before installation, to prevent seizure.
- Never overtorque bolts or spark plugs especially in aluminum threads.

Stripped threads in any component can be repaired using any of several commercial repair kits (Heli-Coil®, Microdot®, Keenserts®, etc.).

When assembling the engine, any parts that will be frictional contact must be prelubed to provide lubrication at initial start-up. Any product specifically formulated for this purpose can be used, but engine oil is not recommended as a prelube, as it will not be retained on the wearing surfaces in sufficient quantities to provide adequate lubrication for new parts.

When semi-permanent (locked, but removable) installation of bolts or nuts is desired, threads should be cleaned and coated with Loctite® or other similar, commercial non-hardening sealant.

REPAIRING DAMAGED THREADS

Several methods of repairing damaged threads are available. Heli-Coil® (shown here), Keenserts® and Microdot® are among the most widely used. All involve basically the same principle – drilling out stripped threads, tapping the hole and installing a prewound insert – making welding, plugging and oversize fasteners unnecessary.

Two types of thread repair inserts are usually supplied: a standard type for most Inch Coarse, Inch Fine, Metric Course and Metric Fine thread sizes and a spark lug type to fit most spark plug port sizes. Consult the individual manufacturer's catalog to determine exact applications. Typical thread repair kits will contain a selection of prewound threaded inserts, a tap (corresponding to the outside diameter threads of the insert) and an installation tool. Spark plug inserts usually differ because they require a tap equipped with pilot threads and a combined reamer/tap section. Most manufacturers also supply blister-packed thread repair inserts separately in addition to a master kit containing a variety of taps and inserts plus installation tools.

Before effecting a repair to a threaded hole, remove any snapped, broken or damaged bolts

Standard Torque Specifications and Fastener Markings

In the absence of specific torques, the following chart can be used as a guide to the maximum safe torque of a particular size/grade of fastener.

- There is no torque difference for fine or coarse threads.
- Torque values are based on clean, dry threads. Reduce the value by 10% if threads are oiled prior to assembly.
- The torque required for aluminum components or fasteners is considerably less.

U.S. Bolts

SAE Grade Number	1 or 2			5			6 or 7		
Number of lines always 2 less than the grade number.									
Bolt Size (Inches)—(Thread)	Maximum Torque			Maximum Torque			Maximum Torque		
	Ft./Lbs.	Kgm	Nm	Ft./Lbs.	Kgm	Nm	Ft./Lbs.	Kgm	Nm
¼—20	5	0.7	6.8	8	1.1	10.8	10	1.4	13.5
—28	6	0.8	8.1	10	1.4	13.6			
5/16—18	11	1.5	14.9	17	2.3	23.0	19	2.6	25.8
—24	13	1.8	17.6	19	2.6	25.7			
3/8—16	18	2.5	24.4	31	4.3	42.0	34	4.7	46.0
—24	20	2.75	27.1	35	4.8	47.5			
7/16—14	28	3.8	37.0	49	6.8	66.4	55	7.6	74.5
—20	30	4.2	40.7	55	7.6	74.5			
½—13	39	5.4	52.8	75	10.4	101.7	85	11.75	115.2
—20	41	5.7	55.6	85	11.7	115.2			
9/16—12	51	7.0	69.2	110	15.2	149.1	120	16.6	162.7
—18	55	7.6	74.5	120	16.6	162.7			
5/8—11	83	11.5	112.5	150	20.7	203.3	167	23.0	226.5
—18	95	13.1	128.8	170	23.5	230.5			
¾—10	105	14.5	142.3	270	37.3	366.0	280	38.7	379.6
—16	115	15.9	155.9	295	40.8	400.0			
7/8—9	160	22.1	216.9	395	54.6	535.5	440	60.9	596.5
—14	175	24.2	237.2	435	60.1	589.7			
1—8	236	32.5	318.6	590	81.6	799.9	660	91.3	894.8
—14	250	34.6	338.9	660	91.3	849.8			

Metric Bolts

Relative Strength Marking	4.6, 4.8			8.8		
Bolt Markings						
Bolt Size Thread Size x Pitch (mm)	Maximum Torque			Maximum Torque		
	Ft./Lbs.	Kgm	Nm	Ft./Lbs.	Kgm	Nm
6 x 1.0	2–3	.2–.4	3–4	3–6	.4–.8	5–8
8 x 1.25	6–8	.8–1	8–12	9–14	1.2–1.9	13–19
10 x 1.25	12–17	1.5–2.3	16–23	20–29	2.7–4.0	27–39
12 x 1.25	21–32	2.9–4.4	29–43	35–53	4.8–7.3	47–72
14 x 1.5	35–52	4.8–7.1	48–70	57–85	7.8–11.7	77–110
16 x 1.5	51–77	7.0–10.6	67–100	90–120	12.4–16.5	130–160
18 x 1.5	74–110	10.2–15.1	100–150	130–170	17.9–23.4	180–230
20 x 1.5	110–140	15.1–19.3	150–190	190–240	26.2–46.9	160–320
22 x 1.5	150–190	22.0–26.2	200–260	250–320	34.5–44.1	340–430
24 x 1.5	190–240	26.2–46.9	260–320	310–410	42.7–56.5	420–550

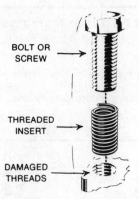

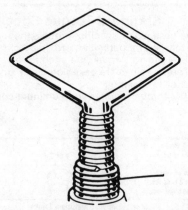

Damaged bolt holes can be repaired with thread repair inserts

Screw the threaded insert onto the installation tool until the tang engages the slot. Screw the insert into the tapped hole until it is ¼–½ turn below the top surface. After installation break off the tang with a hammer and punch

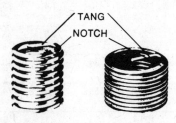

Standard thread repair insert (left) and spark plug thread insert (right)

thread can be repaired, as shown in the series of accompanying illustrations.

Checking Engine Compression

A noticeable lack of engine power, excessive oil consumption and/or poor fuel mileage measured over an extended period are all indicators of internal engine wear. Worn piston rings, scored or worn cylinder bores, blown head gaskets, sticking or burnt valves and worn valve seats are all possible culprits here. A check of each cylinder's compression will help you locate the problems.

As mentioned in the Tools and Equipment section of Chapter 1, a screw-in type compression gauge is more accurate that the type you simply hold against the spark plug hole, although it takes slightly longer to use. It's worth it to obtain a more accurate reading. Follow the procedures below.

1. Warm up the engine to normal operating temperature.

Drill out the damaged threads with specified drill. Drill completely through the hole or to the bottom of a blind hole

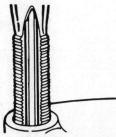

With the tap supplied, tap the hole to receive the thread insert. Keep the tap well oiled and back it out frequently to avoid clogging the threads

or studs. Penetrating oil can be used to free frozen threads. The offending item can be removed with locking pliers or with a screw or stud extractor. After the hole is clear, the

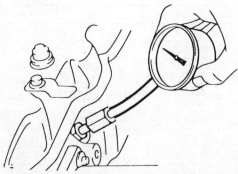

The screw-in type compression gauge is more accurate

2. Remove all the spark plugs.

3. Disconnect the high tension lead from the ignition coil.

4. Fully open the throttle either by operating the carburetor throttle linkage by hand or by having an assistant floor the accelerator pedal.

5. Screw the compression gauge into the no.1 spark plug hole until the fitting is snug.

WARNING: *Be careful not to crossthread the plug hole. On aluminum cylinder heads use extra care, as the threads in these heads are easily ruined.*

6. Ask an assistant to depress the accelerator pedal fully on both carbureted and fuel injected vehicles. Then, while you read the compression gauge, ask the assistant to crank the engine two or three times in short bursts using the ignition switch.

7. Read the compression gauge at the end of each series of cranks, and record the highest of these readings. Repeat this procedure for each of the engine's cylinders. Compare the highest reading of each cylinder to the compression pressure specification in the Tune-Up Specifications chart in Chapter 2. The specs in this chart are maximum values.

A cylinder's compression pressure is acceptable on these cars if it is not less than 75% of maximum. The minimum pressure for these engines is 100 psi.

General Engine Specifications

Year	Engine Displacement Cu. In. (L)	Fuel/Induction System Type	Advertised Horsepower @ rpm	Advertised Torque @ rpm (ft. lbs.)	Bore x Stroke (in.)	Compression Ratio	Oil Pressure
1981	135 (2.2)	2 bbl	84 @ 4800	111 @ 2800	3.44 x 3.62	8.5:1	50
	156 (2.6)	2 bbl	92 @ 4500	131 @ 2500	3.59 x 3.86	8.2:1	57
1982	135 (2.2)	2 bbl	84 @ 4800	111 @ 2800	3.44 x 3.62	8.5:1	50
	156 (2.6)	2 bbl	92 @ 4500	131 @ 2500	3.59 x 3.86	8.2:1	57
1983	135 (2.2)	2 bbl	94 @ 4800	158 @ 2800	3.44 x 3.62	9.0:1	50
	156 (2.6)	2 bbl	93 @ 4500	179 @ 2500	3.59 x 3.86	8.2:1	56.5
1984	135 (2.2)	2 bbl	96 @ 5200	119 @ 3200	3.44 x 3.62	9.0:1	50
	135 (2.2)	EFI	99 @ 5600	121 @ 3200	3.44 x 3.62	9.0:1	50
	135 (2.2)	EFI Turbo	142 @ 5600	160 @ 3600	3.44 x 3.62	8.1:1	50
	156 (2.6)	2 bbl	101 @ 4800	140 @ 2800	3.59 x 3.86	8.7:1	85
1985	135 (2.2)	2 bbl	96 @ 5200	119 @ 3200	3.44 x 3.62	9.0:1	50
	135 (2.2)	EFI	99 @ 5600	121 @ 3200	3.44 x 3.62	9.0:1	50
	135 (2.2)	EFI Turbo	146 @ 5200	168 @ 3600	3.44 x 3.62	8.1:1	50
	156 (2.6)	2 bbl	101 @ 4800	140 @ 2800	3.59 x 3.86	8.7:1	85
1986	135 (2.2)	2 bbl	96 @ 5200	119 @ 3200	3.44 x 3.62	9.5:1	50
	135 (2.2)	EFI	99 @ 5600	121 @ 3200	3.44 x 3.62	9.5:1	50
	135 (2.2)	EFI Turbo	146 @ 5200	170 @ 3600	3.44 x 3.62	8.5:1	50
	153 (2.5)	EFI	100 @ 4800	133 @ 2800	3.44 x 4.09	9.0:1	50
1987	135 (2.2)	2 bbl	96 @ 5200	119 @ 3200	3.44 x 3.62	9.5:1	50
	135 (2.2)	EFI	99 @ 5600	121 @ 3200	3.44 x 3.62	9.5:1	50
	135 (2.2)	EFI Turbo	146 @ 5200	170 @ 3600	3.44 x 3.62	8.0:1	50
	153 (2.5)	EFI	100 @ 4800	133 @ 2800	3.44 x 4.09	9.0:1	80
1988	135 (2.2)	EFI	97 @ 5200	122 @ 3200	3.44 x 3.62	9.5:1	52.5
	135 (2.2)	EFI Turbo	146 @ 5200	171 @ 3600	3.44 x 3.62	8.1:1	52.5
	135 (2.2)	EFI Turbo ②	—	—	3.44 x 3.62	8.1:1	52.5
	153 (2.5)	EFI	100 @ 4800	136 @ 2800	3.44 x 4.09	9.0:1	52.5

EFI—Electronic Fuel Injection
① 10:1—Shelby and Hi-Performance Models
② Turbo with intercooling

8. If a cylinder is unusually low, pour a tablespoon of clean engine oil into the cylinder through the spark plug hole and repeat the compression test. If the compression comes up after adding the oil, it appears that the cylinder's piston rings or bore are damaged or worn. If the pressure remains low, the valves may not be seating properly (a valve job is needed), or the head gasket may be blown near that cylinder. If compression in any two adjacent cylinders is low, and if the addition of oil doesn't help the compression, there is leakage past the head gasket. Oil and coolant water in the combustion chamber can result from this problem. There may be evidence of water droplets in the oil film on the engine dipstick when a head gasket has blown.

Engine

REMOVAL AND INSTALLATION

Manual Transmission

NOTE: *There are three ways of handling this job. The engine and transmission can be removed together; the transmission can be completely removed from the car first; or the transmission can be disconnected from the engine and left in the car. In the third case, the transmission must be supported securely* by a holding fixture or floor jack arrangement of some sort. The following is for engine removal leaving the transmission in the car.

1. Disconnect the battery.
2. Mark the hood hinge outline and remove the hood.
3. Drain the cooling system.

CAUTION: *When draining the coolant, keep in mind that cats and dogs are attracted by the ethylene glycol antifreeze, and are quite likely to drink any that is left in an uncovered container or in puddles on the ground. This will prove fatal in sufficient quantity. Always drain the coolant into a sealable container. Coolant should be reused unless it is contaminated or several years old.*

4. Remove the radiator hoses and remove the radiator, fan and shroud assembly.
5. Remove the air cleaner and hoses.
6. The air conditioning compressor does not have to be disconnected.

Remove it from its bracket and position it out of the way. Securing it with wire is the best method.

NOTE: *On A/C cars, do not disconnect any hoses from the A/C system. Disconnect compressor with hoses attached. If the car has power steering, remove the power steering pump mounting bolts and set the pump aside without disconnecting any hoses.*

7. Disconnect all wiring from the engine, alternator and carburetor.

Valve Specifications

Year	Engine Displacement Cu. In.	Seat Angle (deg)	Face Angle (deg)	Spring Test Pressure (lbs. @ in.)	Spring Installed Height (in.)	Stem to Guide Clearance (in.)		Stem Diameter (in.)	
						Intake	Exhaust	Intake	Exhaust
1981	135	45	45.5	175 @ 1.22	1.65	.001—.003	.002–.004	.312–.313	.311–.312
	156	43.75	45.25	34.1 @ 1.18	1.59	.001–.002	.002–.003	.315	.315
1982	135	45	45.5	175 @ 1.22	1.65	.001–.003	.002–.004	.312–.313	.311–.312
	156	43.75	45.22	34.1 @ 1.18	1.59	.001–.002	.002–.003	.315	.315
1983–84	135	45	45	175 @ 1.22	1.65	.0009–.0026	.0030–.0047	.3124	.3103
	156	45	45	61 @ 1.59	1.59	.0012–.0024	.0020–.0035	.315	.315
1985	135	45	45	150 @ 1.22	1.65	.0009–.0026	.0030–.0047	.3124	.3103
	135 Turbo	45	45	175 @ 1.22	1.65	.0009–.0026	.0030–.0047	.3124	.3103
	156	45	45	61 @ 1.59	1.59	.0012–.0024	.0020–.0035	.315	.315
1986–87	135	45	45	150 @ 1.22	1.65	.0009–.0026	.0030–.0047	.3124	.3103
	135 Turbo	45	45	175 @ 1.22	1.65	.0009–.0026	.0030–.0047	.3124	.3103
	153	45	45	150 @ 1.22	1.65	.0009–.0026	.0030–.0047	.3124	.3103
1988	135	45	45	202 @ 1.22	1.65	.0009–.0026	.0030–.0047	.3124	.3103
	135 Turbo	45	45	202 @ 1.22	1.65	.0009–.0026	.0030–.0047	.3124	.3103
	153	45	45	202 @ 1.22	1.65	.0009–.0026	.0030–.0047	.3124	.3103

8. Disconnect the fuel line, heater hoses and accelerator linkage.

9. Disconnect the air pump lines.

10. Remove the alternator. Remove the oil filter.

11. Disconnect the clutch and speedometer cables.

12. Raise the vehicle and support it on jackstands.

13. Remove the starter.

14. Disconnect the exhaust pipe.

15. Remove the air pump. Remove the right inner splash shield.

16. Disconnect the transmission linkage.

17. Lower the vehicle.

18. Attach a lifting fixture and shop crane to the engine. Support the transmission securely. Remove the engine ground strap. Remove the bolt that passes through the insulator on the right side engine mount. Remove the bolts fastening the transmission case to the cylinder block. Remove the transmission case lower cover. Make sure the clutch cable has been disconnected. Remove the front engine mount screw and nut. Remove the transmission anti roll strut on 1983 and later models. On 1984 and later models, remove the insulator through-bolt from inside the wheel house. Remove the engine from the vehicle.

19. Lower the engine into place and loosely install all the engine mounting bolts. When all are installed, torque to 40 ft.lb. Install the transmission case to cylinder block mounting screws and torque to 70 ft.lb.

20. Remove the lifting fixture and raise the vehicle, supporting it on jackstands.

21. Install the right inner splash shield. Install the starter. Connect the ground strap.

22. Connect the transmission linakge, install the air pump, connect the exhaust pipe and lower the vehicle.

23. Connect the clutch and speedometer cables.

24. Install the alternator. Install the oil filter.

Crankshaft and Connecting Rod Specifications

All measurements are given in inches

Year	Engine Displacement Cu. In.	Crankshaft				Connecting Rod		
		Main Brg Journal Dia	Main Brg Oil Clearance	Shaft End-Play	Thrust on No.	Journal Diameter	Oil Clearance	Side Clearance
1981	135	2.362–2.363	.0004–.0026	.002–.007	3	1.968–1.969	.0004–.0026	.005–.013
	156	2.3622	.0008–.0028	.002–.007	3	2.0866	.0008–.0028	.004–.010
1982	135	2.362–2.363	.0004–.0026	.002–.007	3	1.968–1.969	.0004–.0026	.005–.013
	156	2.3622	.0008–.0028	.002–.007	3	2.0866	.0004–.0026	.005–.013
1983–85	135	2.362–2.363	.0003–.0031	.002–.007	3	1.968–1.969	.0008–.0034	.005–.013
	135 Turbo	2.362–2.363	.0004–.0023	.002–.007	3	1.968–1.969	.0008–.0031	.005–.013
	156	2.3622	.0008–.0028	.002–.007	3	2.0866	.0008–.0028	.004–.010
1986–87	135	2.362–2.363	.0003–.0031	.002–.007	3	1.968–1.969	.0008–.0034	.005–.013
	135 Turbo	2.3622–2.3627	.0004–.0023	.002–.007	3	1.968–1.969	.0008–.0031	.005–.013
	153	2.362–2.363	.0003–.0031	.002–.007	3	1.968–1.969	.0008–.0034	.005–.013
1988	135	2.362–2.363	.0004–.0028	.002–.007	3	1.968–1.969	.0008–.0034	.005–.013
	135 Turbo	2.362–2.363	.0004–.0028	.002–.007	3	1.968–1.969	.0008–.0031	.005–.013
	153	2.362–2.363	.0004–.0028	.002–.007	3	1.968–1.969	.0008–.0034	.005–.013

Ring Gap

All measurements are given in inches

Year	Engine No. Cyl Displacement (cu. in.)	Top Compression	Bottom Compression	Oil Control
1981	135	.011–.021	.011–.021	.015–.055
	156	.011–.018	.011–.018	.0078–.035
1982	135	.011–.021	.011–.021	.015–.055
	156	.011–.018	.011–.018	.0078–.035
1983–85	135	.011–.021	.011–.021	.015–.055
	135 Turbo	.010–.020	.009–.018	.015–.055
	156	.010–.018	.010–.018	.0078–.035
1986–88	135	.011–.021	.011–.021	.015–.055
	135 Turbo	.010–.020	.009–.019	.015–.055
	153	.011–.021	.011–.021	.015–.055

Ring Side Clearance

All measurements are given in inches

Year	Engine	Top Compression	Bottom Compression	Oil Control
1981	135	.0015–.0031	.0015–.0037	Snug
	156	.0024–.0039	.0008–.0024	Snug
1982	135	.0015–.0031	.0015–.0037	Snug
	156	.0024–.0039	.0008–.0024	Snug
1983–85	135	.0015–.0031	.0015–.0037	Snug
	156	.0024–.0039	.0008–.0024	Snug
1986–88	135, 153	.0015–.0031	.0015–.0037	.008

Piston Clearance

Year	Engine No. Cyl. Displacement (cu. in.)	Piston to Bore Clearance (in.)
1981	135	.0005–.0240
	156	.0005–.0240
1982	135	.0005–.0240
	156	.0005–.0240
1983–85	135	.0005
	156	.0008–.0016
1986	135, 153	.0005–.0015
	135 Turbo	.0015–.0025
1987–88	135, 153	.0005–.0015
	135 Turbo	.0015–.0026

25. Install the air pump lines.
26. Connect the fuel line, heater hoses and accelerator linkage.
27. Connect all wiring.
28. Mount the air conditioning compressor.
29. Install the air cleaner.
30. Install the radiator and hoses.
31. Fill the cooling system.
32. Install the hood.
33. Connect the battery.
34. Start the engine and run it to normal operating temperature.
35. Check the timing and adjust if necessary. Adjust the carburetor idle speed and mixture, and the transmission linkage.

Automatic Transmission

The engine is removed without the transmission.

1. Disconnect the battery.
2. Scribe the outline of the hood hinges and remove the hood.
3. Drain the cooling system.
CAUTION: *When draining the coolant, keep in mind that cats and dogs are attracted by the ethylene glycol antifreeze, and are quite likely to drink any that is left in an uncovered container or in puddles on the ground. This will prove fatal in sufficient quantity. Always drain the coolant into a sealable container. Coolant should be reused unless it is contaminated or several years old.*
4. Disconnect the hoses from the radiator and engine.
5. Remove the air cleaner and hoses.
6. Disconnect the air conditioning compres-

sor and set it aside, with refrigerant lines attached.

CAUTION: *Do not disconnect any of the refrigerant lines.*

7. Disconnect and tag all electrical connections from the engine.

8. Disconnect the fuel line, accelerator cable and heater hoses. Plug the lines to prevent leakage.

9. Remove the diverter valve and lines from the air pump.

10. Remove the alternator.

11. Remove the upper bell housing bolts.

12. Raise and support the vehicle.

13. Remove the wheels and right and left splash shields.

14. Remove the power steering pump and set it aside. Do not disconnect the lines.

15. Remove the water pump and crankshaft pulleys.

16. Remove the front engine mounting bolt.

17. Remove the inspection cover from the transmission and remove the bolts from the flex plate. Mark the flex plate for installation in the same position. Install a C-clamp to hold the torque converter in position.

18. Remove the starter.

19. Remove the remaining lower bell housing bolts.

20. Lower the vehicle and support the transmission with a jack.

21. Remove the oil filter and the oil pan drain plug and drain the oil.

CAUTION: *The EPA warns that prolonged contact with used engine oil may cause a number of skin disorders, including cancer! You should make every effort to minimize your exposure to used engine oil. Protective gloves should be worn when changing the oil. Wash your hands and any other exposed skin areas as soon as possible after exposure to used engine oil. Soap and water, or waterless hand cleaner should be used.*

22. Attach a lifting fixture to the engine and remove the engine.

23. To install the engine , hoist it into the engine compartment. Align the engine mounts and the boltholes for the transaxle bell housing and corresponding thread holes in the block. Then install the mounting bolts *without tightening any of them*. Finally, torque them to 40 ft. lbs.

24. Install the bolts fastening the transmission bell housing to the engine and torque them to 70 ft. lbs.

25. Mount the engine ground strap. Install the right/inner splash shield.

26. Reconnect the starter electrical connections.

27. Reconnect the exhaust pipe to the exhaust manifold. Use a new sealing ring and torque the nuts/bolts to 250 inch lbs.

28. Remove the C-clamp from the torque converter housing. Align the flex plate to the torque converter according to the matchmarks mae above; then, install the mounting bolts and torque them to 40 ft. lbs.

29. Install the power steering pump and reconnect and adjust the belt.

30. Install the alternator and reconnect and

Torque Specifications
All readings in ft. lbs.

Year	Engine Displacement Cu In.	Cylinder Head Bolts	Rod Bearing Bolts	Main Bearing Bolts	Crankshaft Pulley Bolt	Flywheel-to Crankshaft Bolts	Manifolds Intake	Manifolds Exhaust	Camshaft Cap Bolts
1981	135	45①	40②	30②	50	NA	17	17	14
	156	69③	34	58	87	97	13	13	13
1982–85	135	45①	40②	30②	50	65	200④	200④	165④
	156	69③	34	58	87	—	150④	150④	160④
1986–87	135	65⑤	40②	30②	50	70	200④	200④	165④
	153	65⑤	40②	30②	50	70	200④	200④	165④
1988	135	65⑤	40②	30②	50	70	200④	200④	215
	153	65⑤	40②	30②	50	70	200④	200④	215

① Torque Sequence 30—45—45 plus ¼ turn
② Plus ¼ turn
③ Cold engine; Hot engine 76 ft. lbs.
④ Readings in inch pounds
NA—not available
⑤ Torque Sequence—45—65—65 plus ¼ turn

adjust the belt. Reconnect the electrical connectors according to markings made during removal.

31. Connect the fuel line(s), heater hoses, and accelerator cable.

32. Connect all the electrical connections at the carburetor, fuel injection system, and ignition system.

33. Install the oil filter and oil pan drain plug and fill the pan with the required amount of the specified oil.

34. Remount the air conditioner compressor.

35. Install the air cleaner and hoses.

36. Install the radiator and shroud. Reconnect the hoses and clamp snugly. Reconnect the electrical connector for the electric fan. Fill the cooling system with 50/50 anti-freeze/water mix.

37. Install the hood and connect the battery.

38. Be sure to check that all lines, hoses and wires are properly connected. Start the engine and check for leaks. Bleed the cooling system as described later in this chapter and then refill it. If the transmission does not perform properly, ajust the linkage.

Valve Cover

REMOVAL AND INSTALLATION

1. On carbureted engines, disconnect the PCV line from the module, depress the retaining clip, and turn the module counterclockwise to unlock it from the valve cover. Then, remove it.

2. Remove/disconnect any other lines or hoses that run across the cam cover.

3. Loosen the 10 cover installation bolts and remove them. Gently rock the cover to free it from the gasket or sealer and remove it.

4. On 1986-88 models with TBI, remove the air/oil separating curtain located on top of the head just under the valve cover. Be careful to keep the rubber bumpers located at the top of the curtain in place.

5. On 1981-87 covers, replace the two end seals, forcing the locating tabs into the matching holes in the cover.

6. To install, first, if the engine has the air/oil separating curtain, install it as described below (otherwise, proceed to the next step):

   a. Position the curtain manifold side first with the upper surface contacting the cylinder head and the cutouts over the cam towers. The cutouts must face the manifold.

   b. Press the distributor side of the curtain into position below the cylinder head rail.

   c. Make sure both rubber bumpers are in place at the top.

7. On 1981-87 engines, form a gasket on the sealing surface of the head. It is necessary to

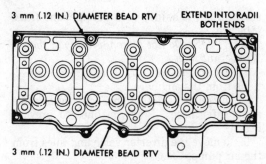

3 mm (.12 IN.) DIAMETER BEAD RTV   EXTEND INTO RADII BOTH ENDS

3 mm (.12 IN.) DIAMETER BEAD RTV

Applying RTV sealer to the cylinder head to seal the cam cover

use an RTV silicone aerobic gasket material (Chrysler Part No. 4318025 or equivalent).

8. On 1988 engines, install the gasket onto the cam cover (on normally aspirated engines with Throttle Body Injection, fasten the gasket in place by forcing the tabs through the holes in the cover).

9. On 1981-87 engines, install the reinforcements over both sides. Install the mounting bolts and torque them alternately and evenly to 105 in. lbs.

Rocker Shafts

REMOVAL AND INSTALLATION

The only engine covered by this manual that has rocker shafts is the 2.6L engine. Refer to "Camshaft and Bearings Removal and Installation" later in this chapter for rocker arm and shaft removal procedures for that engine.

Rocker Arms

REMOVAL AND INSTALLATION

2.2L and 2.5L Engines

The rocker arms may be removed very easily after camshaft removal. In case they are to be removed as a group for inspection or to proceed further with disassembly, mark each as to location for installation in the same position.

If the rockers are to be removed in order to gain access to a valve or lifter, you will need a special tool designed to hook over the camshaft and depress the applicable valve. Use Chrysler Tool No. 4682 or an equivalent tool purchased in the aftermarket. To remove a rocker:

1. Mark the rocker as to its location, unless you expect to remove only one, or one at a time.

2. Turn the engine over, using a wrench on the crankshaft pulley, until the cam that actuates the rocker you want to remove it pointing straight up.

3. Install the tool so that the jaws on its fulcrum fit on either side of the valve cap. Then, clip the hook at its forward end over the adja-

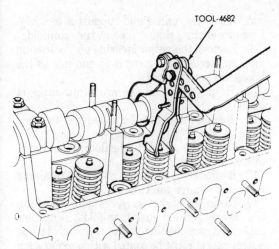

TOOL-4682

Depressing a valve with the special tool in order to remove its rocker lever

cent thin section of the camshaft (a part not incorporating either a cam or a bearing journal).

4. Lift the rocker gently at the lash adjuster end (the end opposite the tool). Pull downward gently on the outer end of the tool lever just until the rocker can be disengaged from the lifter. Pull it out from between the valve and camshaft.

5. Install the new rocker or reinstall the old one in reverse. That is, depress the valve just far enough to slide the lever in between the top of the valve stem and the camshaft and still clear the lifter. When the rocker is located on the valve stem and lifter, gradually release the tension on the tool.

6. Repeat the procedure until all the necessary rockers have been replaced.

Thermostat

REMOVAL AND INSTALLATION

The thermostat on the 2.2 and 2.5 Liter engines is located in the thermostat housing on the cylinder head. 2.6 Liter engines have the thermostat housing near the intake manifold.

1. Drain the cooling system to a level below the thermostat.

CAUTION: *When draining the coolant, keep in mind that cats and dogs are attracted by the ethylene glycol antifreeze, and are quite likely to drink any that is left in an uncovered container or in puddles on the ground. This will prove fatal in sufficient quantity. Always drain the coolant into a sealable container. Coolant should be reused unless it is contaminated or several years old.*

2. Remove the hose clamp and then disconnect the hose from the thermostat housing.

3. Remove the two mounting bolts and then remove the thermostat housing.

4. Remove the thermostat and discard the gasket. Clean both gasket surfaces thoroughly.

5. Dip the new gasket in water and then install it. Position the thermostat in the water box, making sure it is properly seated by centering it in the water box, on top of the gasket. Install the housing and install the two bolts.

6. Reconnect the hose and install and tighten the hose clamp.

7. Refill the cooling system, start the engine, and check for leaks. After the engine has reached operating temperature, allow it to cool. Then, recheck coolant level in the radiator, refilling as necessary.

Intake Manifold

REMOVAL AND INSTALLATION

2.6L Engines

1. Disconnect the battery negative cable. Drain the cooling system.

CAUTION: *When draining the coolant, keep in mind that cats and dogs are attracted by the ethylene glycol antifreeze, and are quite likely to drink any that is left in an uncovered container or in puddles on the ground. This will prove fatal in sufficient quantity. Always drain the coolant into a sealable container. Coolant should be reused unless it is contaminated or several years old.*

2. Disconnect the coolant hose running from the water pump to the intake manifold.

3. Disconnect the carburetor air intake hose and move it out of the way.

4. Label and then disconnect all vacuum hoses connected to the intake manifold and carburetor.

5. Disconnect the throttle linkage at the carburetor and move it out of the way.

6. Disconnect the inlet line at the fuel filter, collecting gasoline that spills out in a metal cup. Then, remove the fuel filter and pump and move them to one side.

7. Remove the mounting nuts and accompanying washers from the manifold attaching studs, and remove the manifold from the engine.

8. Clean all gasket surfaces and install the intake manifold using new gaskets. Torque the bolts in three stages to the specified torque.

9. Reinstall the fuel pump and fuel filter. Connect the inlet line and clamp it securely.

10. Reconnect the throttle linkage to the carburetor and adjust it to eliminate excessive play.

11. Reconnect all the vacuum hoses to the intake manifold and carburetor, according to labels made earlier.

12. Connect the carburetor air intake hose to the carburetor and clamp it securely.

13. Connect the coolant hose running from the water pump to the intake manifold.

14. Refill the cooling system with 50/50 ethylene glycol and water mix. Connect the battery. Start the engine, and operate it, checking for leaks. After the engine reaches operating temperature, shut it off. When it has cooled, refill the cooling system.

Intake and Exhaust Manifolds

REMOVAL AND INSTALLATION

2.2 Normally Aspirated and 2.5L Engines

NOTE: *These engines use a combined intake/exhaust manifold gasket. Therefore, the manifolds must always be removed and replaced together.*

1. Disconnect the negative battery cable. Drain the cooling system.

CAUTION: *When draining the coolant, keep in mind that cats and dogs are attracted by the ethylene glycol antifreeze, and are quite likely to drink any that is left in an uncovered container or in puddles on the ground. This will prove fatal in sufficient quantity. Always drain the coolant into a sealable container. Coolant should be reused unless it is contaminated or several years old.*

2. Remove the air cleaner and hoses.

3. If the engine is fuel injected, depressurize the fuel system, as described in Chapter 1. Remove all wiring and any hoses connected to the carburetor or injection throttle body and the manifold.

4. Disconnect the accelerator linkage.

5. Loosen the power steering pump mounting bolts and remove the belt. Disconnect the power brake vacuum hose at the manifold.

6. On Canadian cars only: Remove the coupling hose connecting the diverter valve and the exhaust manifold air injection tube.

7. Disconnect the water hose from the water crossover.

Intake and exhaust manifold bolt pattern for carbureted 2.2 L and 2.6 L engines

8. Raise the vehicle and support it securely. Disconnect the exhaust pipe at the manifold.

9. Remove the power steering pump, leaving lines connected, and hang it to one side so the hoses are not stressed.

10. Remove the intake manifold support bracket.

11. Remove the intake manifold-to-head bolts.

12. Lower the vehicle to the floor. Remove the intake manifold.

13. Remove the exhaust manifold retaining nuts and remove the exhaust manifold.

14. Clean all gasket surfaces and reposition the intake and exhaust manifolds using new gaskets. A composition gasket is installed as-is; a steel gasket must be coated with a sealer such as Chrysler Part No. 3419115 or equivalent.

15. Put the exhaust manifold into position and install the retaining nuts just finger-tight. Put the intake manifold into position and install all accessible bolts. Raise the car and support it securely.

16. Install all the manifold-to-head bolts finger-tight. Install the intake manifold support bracket. Install the power steering pump, bolting it into position with bolts just finger-tight. Connect the exhaust pipe at the manifold, using a new seal, and torque the bolts and nuts to 250 inch lbs.

17. Lower the car to the floor. Torque the manifold nuts and bolts in three stages, starting at the center and progressing outward, to the specified torque.

18. Connect the power brake vacuum hose to the manifold. Connect the water hose to the water crossover.

19. On Canadian cars only: Install the coupling hose connecting the diverter valve and the exhaust manifold air injection tube.

20. Install the power steering pump belt and adjust tension.

21. Connect the accelerator linkage. Install the air cleaner and hoses.

22. Install all wiring and any hoses disconnected from the carburetor or injection throttle body and the manifold. Refill the cooling system, reconnect the battery, start the engine and run it to check for leaks. Refill the cooling system after the engine has reached operating temperature (air has been bled out) and it has cooled off again.

Exhaust Manifold

REMOVAL AND INSTALLATION

2.6L Engines

1. Remove air cleaner.

2. Remove the heat shield from the exhaust

manifold. Remove the EGR lines and reed valve, if equipped.

3. Unbolt the exhaust flange connection.

4. Remove the nuts holding manifold to the cylinder head.

5. Remove the manifold.

6. Installation is the reverse of removal. Tighten flange connection bolts to 11-18 ft.lb. Tighten manifold bolts to 11-14 ft.lb.

Turbocharger

REMOVAL AND INSTALLATION

1984-85 Vehicles

1. Disconnect the battery and drain coolant. CAUTION: *When draining the coolant, keep in mind that cats and dogs are attracted by the ethylene glycol antifreeze, and are quite likely to drink any that is left in an uncovered container or in puddles on the ground. This will prove fatal in sufficient quantity. Always drain the coolant into a sealable container. Coolant should be reused unless it is contaminated or several years old.*

2. From under the car:

  a. Disconnect the exhaust pipe at the articulated joint and disconnect the O_2 sensor electrical connections.

  b. Remove the turbocharger-to-block support bracket.

  c. Loosen the clamps for the oil drain-back tube and then move the tube downward onto the block fitting so it no longer connects with the turbocharger.

  d. Disconnect the turbocharger coolant supply tube at the block outlet below the power steering pump bracket and at the tube support bracket.

3. Disconnect and remove the air cleaner complete with the throttle body adaptor, hose, and air cleaner box and support bracket.

4. Loosen the throttle body to turbocharger inlet hose clamps. Then, remove the three throttle body-to-intake manifold attaching screws and remove the throttle body.

5. Loosen the turbocharger discharge hose end clamps, leaving the center band in place to retain the de-swirler.

6. Pull the fuel rail out of the way after removing the hose retaining bracket screw, four bracket screws from the intake manifold, and two bracket-to-heat shield retaining clips. The rail, injectors, wiring harness, and fuel lines will be moved as an assembly.

7. Disconnect the oil feed line at the turbocharger bearing housing.

8. Remove the three screws attaching the heat shield to the intake manifold and remove the shield.

9. Disconnect the coolant return tube and hose assembly at the turbocharger and water box. Remove the tube support bracket from the cylinder head and remove the assembly.

10. Remove the four nuts attaching the turbocharger to the exhaust manifold. Then, remove the turbocharger by lifting it off the exhaust manifold studs, tilting it downward toward the passenger side of the car, and then pulling it up and out of the car, and out of the engine compartment.

  a. When repositioning the turbo on the mounting studs, make sure the discharge tube goes in position so it's properly connected to both the intake manifold and turbocharger. Apply an anti-seize compound such as Loctite® 771-64 or equivalent to the threads. Torque the nuts to 30 ft.lb.

  b. Observe the following torques:
- Oil feed line nuts: 125 in.lb.
- Heat shield to intake manifold screws: 105 ft.lb.
- Coolant tube nuts: 30 ft.lb.
- Fuel rail bracket-to-intake manifold retaining screws: 250 in.lb.
- Discharge tube hose clamp: 35 in.lb.
- Throttle body-to-intake manifold screws: 250 in.lb.
- Throttle body hose clamps: 35 in.lb.
- Hose adapter-to-throttle body screws: 55 in.lb.
- Air cleaner box support bracket screws: 40 ft.lb.
- Coolant tube nut-to-block connector: 30 ft.lb.

  c. When installing the turbocharger-to-block support bracket, first install screws finger tight. Tighten the block screw first (to 40 ft.lb.), and then tighten the screw going into the turbocharger housing (to 20 ft.lb.). Tighten the articulated ball joint shoulder bolts to 250 in. lbs.

  d. Make sure to fill the cooling system back up before starting the engine, recheck the level after the coolant begins circulating through the radiator, and check for leaks after you install the pressure cap. Check the turbocharger carefully for any oil leaks and correct if necessary.

1986-88 Vehicles

1. Disconnect the battery and drain the cooling system. Disconnect the air cleaner hoses and remove the air cleaner assembly.

CAUTION: *When draining the coolant, keep in mind that cats and dogs are attracted by the ethylene glycol antifreeze, and are quite likely to drink any that is left in an uncovered container or in puddles on the ground. This will prove fatal in sufficient quantity. Always drain the coolant into a sealable container. Coolant should be reused unless it is contaminated or several years old.*

2. Separate the throttle body from the intake manifold. Disconnect the PCV valve, vacuum vapor harness, power brake vacuum hose and accelerator linkage. On the Turbo II models only, disconnect the charge temperature sensor.

3. Refer to Chapter 5 under Fuel Injector Removal and Installation and remove the fuel rail.

4. Refer to the engine removal procedure earlier in this chapter and remove the front engine mount through bolt. Rotate the top of the engine forward and away from the firewall.

5. Unfasten the coolant line where it runs along the water box and turbo housing. Disconnect it at the turbocharger housing; remove the fitting from the turbocharger as well.

6. Disconnect the oil feed line at the turbo housing.

7. Remove the waste gate rod-to-gate retaining clip.

8. Remove the two upper and one lower (driver's side) nuts that retain the turbocharger to the manifold. Disconnect the oxygen sensor electrical lead and vacuum lines.

9. Raise the car and support it securely. Remove the right front wheel and tire for access.

10. Remove the right side driveshaft as described in Chapter 7.

11. Remove the turbocharger-to-block support bracket. Then, separate the oil drainback tube fitting from the turbo housing and remove the fitting and associated hose.

12. Remove the one remaining nut retaining the turbo to the manifold.

13. Disconnect the articulated exhaust pipe joint at the turbocharger turbine housing outlet.

14. Remove the lower coolant line and the inlet fitting through which coolant passes into the housing.

15. Lift the turbo off the manifold mounting studs and lower it down and out of the vehicle.

16. If you need to remove the intake manifold, now remove the 8 bolts and washers and remove it. The same basic procedure can be followed to remove the exhaust manifold.

17. Clean the manifold surfaces of all gasket materials. Inspect gasket surfaces for flatness--warping must not exceed 0.006″ per foot. Inspect the manifolds for cracks or distortion and replace as necessary.

18. Install a new two-sided grafoil or equivalent type gasket onto the block without sealer; then install the intake manifold. Put the intake manifold into position and install the bolts. Start torquing at the center and torque outward, tightening to 200 in. lbs. When all the bolts are torqued, repeat the process, torquing an additional 200 in. lbs. Repeat this process until the specified torque is reached.

19. Install the exhaust manifold the same way.

20. Position the turbocharger onto the exhaust manifold. Apply an anti-seize compound such as Loctite 771-64® or equivalent to the threads and install one lower retaining nut on the passenger side, torquing to 40 ft.lb.

21. Apply a thread sealant to the lower coolant inlet line fitting and install the fitting into the turbocharger housing. Connect the lower coolant line.

22. Install a new gasket and install the oil drain-back tube fitting into the turbocharger housing. Connect the coolant line to the fitting.

23. Install the turbocharger-to-block support bracket and install the attaching screws finger tight. First, torque the block screw to 40 ft.lb. and then torque the screw attaching the bracket to the turbocharger housing to 20 ft.lb.

24. Reposition the exhaust pipe and connect it to the turbo housing outlet. Torque the attaching bolts to 250 in. lbs. of torque.

25. Install the right side driveshaft. Lower the car to the ground.

26. Install the remaining three turbocharger-to-intake manifold nuts, torquing them to 40 ft.lb.

27. Perform the remaining steps of the procedure in reverse order. Bear these points in mind:

a. The oil feed line to the turbo bearing housing is torqued to 125 in. lbs.

b. Apply thread sealer to turbo coolant line fittings and torque them to 30 ft.lb.

c. In reassembling the front engine mount, align the mount in the crossmember bracket, install the bolt, and torque it to 40 ft.lb.

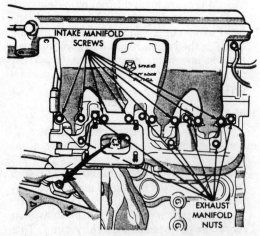

Turbo I and Turbo II intake/exhaust manifolds

Air Conditioner Compressor

WARNING: *If the compressor must be completely removed from the car for repairs, and the compressor refrigerant lines must be disconnected, refer to Chapter 1 for safe discharging procedures for the refrigerant. The system must be discharged before attempting to disconnect the lines. Also note that you will need caps or another positive method to tightly seal the refrigerant lines immediately after you open them.*

1. Disconnect the negative battery cable. Discharge the system as described in Chapter 1. Disconnect the clutch electrical connector.

2. Once the system has been discharged, unbolt the connections at the compressor and plug all four openings.

3. Loosen the A/C compressor belt idler pulley tensioning bracket mounting and pivot bolts. Remove the tension from the compressor drive belt and then remove the belt.

4. Support the compressor. Remove the two mounting bolts from the lower side of the compressor and the two mounting nuts from above it. Remove the compressor.

5. Install the compressor in reverse order, noting these points:

    a. Torque the attaching nuts and bolts to 40 ft.lb.

    b. Make sure sealing surfaces are clean and free of scratches and replace gaskets. Gaskets are specific to suction and discharge fittings, so fit them according to the number of pilots on the fitting/number of holes in the gasket. Make the connections, install the bolts, and torque them to 170-230 in. lbs.

    c. Have the system thoroughly evacuated at a repair shop and then have it recharged, or recharge it according to the procedures given in Chapter 1.

Radiator
REMOVAL AND INSTALLATION

1. Move the temperature selector to full on.
2. Open the radiator drain cock.

CAUTION: *When draining the coolant, keep in mind that cats and dogs are attracted by the ethylene glycol antifreeze, and are quite likely to drink any that is left in an uncovered container or in puddles on the ground. This will prove fatal in sufficient quantity. Always drain the coolant into a sealable container. Coolant should be reused unless it is contaminated or several years old.*

3. When the coolant reserve tank is empty, remove the radiator cap.
4. Remove the hoses.
5. If equipped with automatic transmission, disconnect and plug the fluid cooler lines.

6. Disconnect the fan electrical connector.
7. Remove the fan shroud/motor attaching bolts. *Being careful not to damage the fan blades,* remove the shroud by pulling it upward and out of the attachment clips at the bottom.
8. Remove the upper and lower mounting brackets. Remove the top radiator attaching bolts.
9. Remove the bottom radiator attaching bolts 1981-85 models only).
10. Lift the radiator from the engine compartment.
11. Installation is the reverse of removal. On 1987-88 models without rubber grommets at the top, preload the upper mounting brackets with 10 lbs. force downward. Tighten all mounting bolts to 105 in. lbs. Make sure the hoses are fully installed onto the fittings and that clamps are properly tightened. Refill the cooling system with 50/50 water/antifreeze mix by filling the radiator to the top and the overflow tank to the fill line. If there is no overflow tank, recheck the coolant level after the system has reached operating temperature and has then cooled.

Air Conditioning Condenser
REMOVAL AND INSTALLATION

CAUTION: *The air conditioning system in filled with refrigerant under high pressure. The refrigerant must be discharged before you can safely work on any of the components.*

1. Have the air conditioning system discharged by a professional or discharge it yourself as described in Chapter 1. Remove the radiator as described above.
2. Remove the refrigerant line attaching nut and separate the lines at the condenser sealing plate. Immediately cap the ends with a plastic cap designed for this purpose or with plastic sheeting and tape.
3. Remove the two mounting bolts located near the top of the condenser. These attach the condenser to the radiator core support.
4. Lift the condenser out of the engine compartment, being careful not to damage fins or piping.
5. Install the condenser in reverse order. Replace all gaskets and O-rings. O-rings must be coated with refrigerant oil drawn from an unopened container prior to installation.
6. If the condenser used is a new one, make sure to have oil added to the system to replace that which was removed with the old compressor. This requires specialized service knowledge. A 500 SUS viscosity, wax-free oil must be used. The compressor holds 7-7.25 oz.

Water Pump

REMOVAL AND INSTALLATION

2.2 and 2.5L Engines

1. Disconnect the battery negative cable. Drain the cooling system.

CAUTION: *When draining the coolant, keep in mind that cats and dogs are attracted by the ethylene glycol antifreeze, and are quite likely to drink any that is left in an uncovered container or in puddles on the ground. This will prove fatal in sufficient quantity. Always drain the coolant into a sealable container. Coolant should be reused unless it is contaminated or several years old.*

2. Remove the upper radiator hose.
3. Remove the alternator.

WARNING: *Do not disconnect the air conditioner compressor lines in the next step. The compressor can be moved far enough out of the way to remove the water pump without disturbing the refrigerant-filled lines.*

4. Unbolt the air conditioning compressor brackets from the water pump and secure the compressor out of the way. Support the compressor so it will not put stress on the lines.
5. Disconnect the bypass hose, heater return hose, and lower radiator hose.
6. Unbolt and remove the water pump assembly. Disassemble the pump as follows:

a. Remove the three bolts fastening the drive pulley to the water pump.

b. Remove the 9 bolts fastening the water pump body to the housing. Then, use a chisel to gently break the bond between the pump and housing.

c. Clean the gasket surfaces on the pump body and housing. Remove the O-ring gasket and discard it. Clean the O-ring groove.

d. Apply RTV sealer to the sealing surface of the water pump body. The bead should be ⅛" in diameter and should encircle all bolt holes. Assemble the pump body to the housing, install the 9 bolts, and torque them to 105 in. lbs. Make sure the gasketing material has set (as per package instructions) before actually filling the system.

e. Position a new O-ring in the O-ring groove. Then, put the pulley on the pump, install the 3 attaching bolts, and torque them to 105 in. lbs.

7. Installation is the reverse of removal. Torque the top 3 water pump bolts to 250 in. lbs. and the lower bolt to 50 ft.lb. Make sure to refill the system with 50/50 antifreeze/water mix.

2.6L Engines

1. Disconnect the negative battery cable. Drain the cooling system.

CAUTION: *When draining the coolant, keep in mind that cats and dogs are attracted by the ethylene glycol antifreeze, and are quite likely to drink any that is left in an uncovered container or in puddles on the ground. This will prove fatal in sufficient quantity. Always drain the coolant into a sealable container. Coolant should be reused unless it is contaminated or several years old.*

2. Disconnect the radiator hose, bypass hose, and heater hose at the pump.
3. Remove the two mounting bolts and remove the drive pulley shield.
4. Remove the lock screw and the two pivot screws. Then, separate the pump from the drive belt and remove it.
5. Remove the bolts attaching the water pump housing to the pump body and separate the pump from the body.
6. Discard the gasket and clean the gasket surfaces. Remove the O-ring, replace it, and clean the O-ring groove.
7. Install a new gasket on the pump body, put the new pump into position onto it, and then install the bolts, torquing them to 80 in. lbs. Put a new O-ring into the O-ring groove.
8. Position the pump on the engine, connect the drive belt, and install the pivot and locking screws loosely. Tension the drive belt and then final-tighten all three mounting bolts.
9. The remaining steps are the reverse of the removal procedure. Make sure to refill the cooling system with 50/50 antifreeze/water mix.

CYLINDER HEAD

REMOVAL AND INSTALLATION

2.2 and 2.5L Engines

1. Disconnect the negative battery terminal. Make sure the engine is cold.
2. Drain the cooling system. If the dipstick

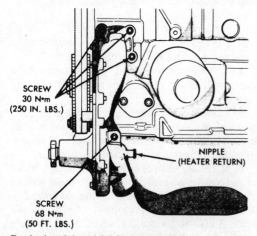

SCREW
30 N·m
(250 IN. LBS.)

NIPPLE
(HEATER RETURN)

SCREW
68 N·m
(50 FT. LBS.)

Replacing 2.2 and 2.5 L water pump

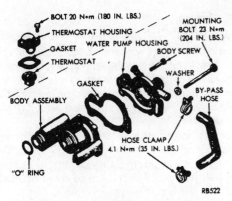

Thermostat Housing and Water Pump— 2.6L Engine

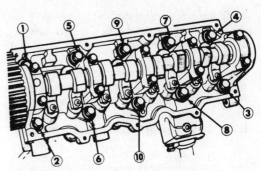

Cylinder head bolt removal sequence—2.2 and 2.6 L engines

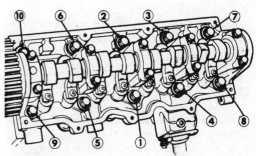

Cylinder head bolt tightening sequence—2.2 and 2.6 L engines

bracket attaches to the thermostat housing, disconnect the it from the thermostat housing and rotate the dipstick bracket away from the mounting stud to disconnect it without bending it.

CAUTION: *When draining the coolant, keep in mind that cats and dogs are attracted by the ethylene glycol antifreeze, and are quite likely to drink any that is left in an uncovered container or in puddles on the ground. This will prove fatal in sufficient quantity. Always drain the coolant into a sealable container. Coolant should be reused unless it is contaminated or several years old.*

3. Remove the air cleaner assembly.

4. Label and then disconnect all lines, hoses and wires from the head, manifold and carburetor. Before disconnecting the fuel lines on fuel injected engines, be sure to depressurize the system as described in Chapter 1.

5. Disconnect the accelerator linkage.

6. Remove the distributor cap.

7. Disconnect the exhaust pipe.

8. Remove the carburetor on engines so-equipped.

9. Remove the intake and exhaust manifolds as described earlier. On turbo engines, remove the turbo and then remove the manifolds.

10. Remove the front cover.

11. Turn the engine by hand until all gear timing marks are aligned.

12. Loosen the drive belt tensioner and slip the timing belt off the sprockets.

13. If equipped with air conditioning, remove the compressor from the mounting brackets and support it out of the way with wires. Remove the mounting bracket from the head. Then, if the engine is equipped with the solid mount attached to block and head:

 a. Remove the alternator pivot bolt and remove the alternator.

 b. Remove the A/C belt idler.

 c. If the car has a turbo, remove the right

engine mount yoke bolt, which secures the isolator support bracket to the engine mount bracket.

 d. Now, remove all 5 side mounting bolts—those facing the radiator.

 e. Remove the front mounting nut and bolt (both face the fender well). Coolant will leak from the bolthole.

 f. Now, rotate the bracket away from the engine and slide it on the stud until it is free.

 g. Now, reinstall the front mounting bolt into the hole to stop the leakage of coolant.

14. Remove the valve cover, gaskets and seals as described above.

15. Remove head bolts in the order shown.

16. Lift off the head and discard the gasket.

17. Inspect the cylinder head and block surfaces with a straightedge and feeler gauge to make sure it is flat within 0.004″. If not, the cylinder head or block deck must be machined. Clean both gasket surfaces thoroughly.

18. Make certain all gasket surfaces are thoroughly cleaned and are free of deep nicks or scratches. Always use new gaskets and seals. Never reuse a gasket or seal, even if it looks good.

19. Position the head on the block, and then insert bolts 8 and 10 (see illustration) to align the head, gasket and block.

NOTE: *With the 1986 model year, the 10mm*

bolts have been replaced with 11mm bolts marked "11" on the head. Tighten bolts in the order shown to specifications. This is a four step procedure.

On 1981-86 models: first torque the bolts in the order shown to 30 ft.lb.; then, torque them in the order shown to 45 ft.lb.; again, in the order shown, torque them to 45 ft. lbs; then, turn each bolt ¼ turn tighter, again in the order shown.

On 1986-88 models: first torque the bolts in the order shown to 45 ft.lb.; then, torque them in the order shown to 65 ft.lb.; again, in the order shown, torque them to 65 ft. lbs; then, turn each bolt ¼ turn tighter, again in the order shown.

Note that on the 1986-88 models using the 11mm bolts, torque must reach 90 ft.lb.; otherwise, replace the bolt.

20. Install the valve cover, gaskets and seals as described above.

21. If the car is equipped with air conditioning:

a. Remove the front mounting bolt for the compressor installed to stop coolant leakage.

b. Install the A/C compressor bracket by rotating it into place in reverse of the removal procedure. Install the front mounting nut and bolt and all 5 side mounting bolts.

c. On turbo cars the right engine mount yoke bolt was removed. Reinstall it to secure the isolator support bracket to the engine mounting bracket. Torque it to 75 ft. lbs.

d. Install the A/C belt idler.

e. Install the alternator, including the alternator pivot bolt.

22. Make sure all timing marks are aligned. Install the timing belt and tension it as described later. The drive belt is correctly tensioned when it can be twisted 90 degrees with the thumb and index finger midway between the camshaft and the intermediate shaft. Check to make sure tension is correct.

23. Install the front cover. Install the intake and exhaust manifolds (with turbo, if so equipped), as described below in this chapter. Reconnect the exhaust pipe, using a new seal, and torque the nuts/bolts to 250 inch lbs.

24. Install the distributor cap. Connect the accelerator linkage.

25. Reconnect all electrical wiring, fuel and vacuum hoses, and other wiring.

26. Install the air cleaner and reconnect all air and vacuum hoses.

27. Fill the cooling system. Reconnect the battery negative cable. Start the engine and run it until it reaches operating temperature, checking for leaks. After the engine has cooled, refill the cooling system.

2.6L Engines

WARNING: *Do not perform this operation on a warm engine. Remove the head bolts in the sequence shown in several steps. Loosen the head bolts evenly, not one at a time. Do not attempt to slide the cylinder head off the block, as it is located with dowel pins. Lift the head straight up and off the block.*

1. Disconnect the battery. Remove the air cleaner and duct. Remove the PCV hose. Remove the water pump pulley cover and remove the fuel pump and carb-to-head cover bracket. Remove the water pump drive belt.

2. Remove the two bolts that retain it and remove the cylinder head cover.

3. Drain the cooling system. Disconnect the upper radiator hose and heater hoses.

CAUTION: *When draining the coolant, keep in mind that cats and dogs are attracted by the ethylene glycol antifreeze, and are quite likely to drink any that is left in an uncovered container or in puddles on the ground. This will prove fatal in sufficient quantity. Always drain the coolant into a sealable container. Coolant should be reused unless it is contaminated or several years old.*

4. Turn the crankshaft until No. 1 piston is at the top of its compression stroke (both No. 1 cylinder valves closed and timing marks at Top Center). Remove the distributor cap and matchmark the distributor body with the rotor and the cylinder head. Also matchmark the timing gear and chain.

5. Mark the spark plug wires and disconnect them. Remove the mounting bolt and remove the distributor.

6. Disconnect power brake and any other vacuum hoses that are in the way. Disconnect all wiring that is in the way. Disconnect the carburetor linkage.

7. Remove the camshaft sprocket bolt and sprocket, without disturbing timing chain timing. Remove the distributor drive gear. Disconnect the air feeder hoses from underneath the vehicle.

8. If the car has power steering, unbolt the pump and move aside without disconnecting hoses.

9. Remove the ground wire and dipstick tube. Remove the exhaust manifold heat shield and separate the exhaust manifold from the catalytic converter.

10. Remove the cylinder head bolts in several stages, using the sequence illustrated. Then, pull the cylinder head off the engine.

11. Install the new gasket without sealer and in a position that causes all bolt holes and the outer border to line up with the bolt holes and outer edge of the block. Lightly oil all the bolts

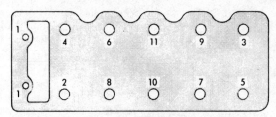

2.6.1. engine cylinder head bolt loosening sequence

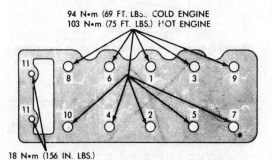

2.6L cylinder head bolt tightening sequence

and install them finger tight. Then, torque the bolts to 35 ft.lb. in the sequence shown. Now, torque the bolts to 69 ft.lb. in the sequence shown. Torque the cylinder head to timing chain cover bolts to 156 in. lbs.

12. Connect the exhaust manifold to the catalytic converter. Install the ground wire and dipstick tube.

13. Install the power steering pump and belt and adjust the belt tension.

14. Connect the air feeder hoses from underneath the vehicle.

15. Install the camshaft sprocket and bolt and the distributor drive gear. Check the timing chain timing and ensure that it is correct.

16. Reconnect the throttle linkage.

17. Reconnect all wiring.

18. Connect the power brake and any other vacuum hoses that were disconnected.

19. Install the distributor and spark plug wires, according to the markings made at removal.

20. Connect the upper radiator hose and heater hoses. Install the cylinder head cover.

21. Install the fuel pump cover bracket and water pump pulley cover.

22. Reconnect the PCV hose.

23. Install the air cleaner and reconnect all ducting and vacuum hoses securely.

24. Connect the battery. Refill the cooling system. Start the engine and check for leaks. When the engine has reached operating temperature, set the ignition timing. When the engine has cooled back off, refill the cooling system.

CYLINDER HEAD INSPECTION AND RESURFACING

1. With the valves installed to protect the valve seats, remove deposits from the combustion chambers and valve heads with a scraper and a wire brush. Be careful not to damage the cylinder head gasket surface. After the valves are removed, clean the valve guide bores with a valve guide cleaning tool. Using cleaning solvent to remove dirt, grease and other deposits, clean all bolts holes; be sure the oil passage is clean (V6 engines).

2. Remove all deposits from the valves with a fine wire brush or buffing wheel.

3. Inspect the cylinder heads for cracks or excessively burned areas in the exhaust outlet ports.

4. Check the cylinder head for cracks and inspect the gasket surface for burrs and nicks. Replace the head if it is cracked.

5. On cylinder heads that incorporate valve seat inserts, check the inserts for excessive wear, cracks, or looseness.

RESURFACING

Cylinder Head Flatness

When the cylinder head is removed, check the flatness of the cylinder head gasket surfaces.

1. Place a straightedge across the gasket surface of the cylinder head. Using feeler gauges, determine the clearance at the center of the straightedge.

2. If warpage exceeds 0.003″ (0.076mm) in a 6″ (152mm) span, or 0.006″ (0.152mm) over the total length, the cylinder head must be resurfaced.

3. If it is necessary to refinish the cylinder head gasket surface, do not plane or grind off more than 0.254mm (0.010″) from the original gasket surface.

NOTE: *When milling the cylinder heads of V6 engines, the intake manifold mounting*

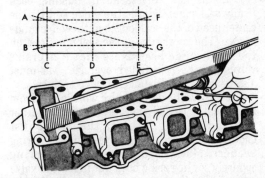

Inspect the cylinder head for flatness in every direction illustrated

position is altered, and must be corrected by milling the manifold flange a proportionate amount. Consult an experienced machinist about this.

Valves

REMOVAL AND INSTALLATION

2.2L and 2.5L Engines

1. Remove the cylinder head described above. Mark all valves and rockers for reinstallation in the same positions.

2. Situate the head so the valves will be free to move downward. You'll need a valve spring compressor tool such as Chrysler No. 4682. This tool hooks around the thinnest diameter sections of the camshaft and pushes downward on either side of each valve spring retainer. Rotate the camshaft so the first rocker arm is under the base circle of the cam. Then, depress the valve spring with the special tool just until the rocker arm can be slid out.

3. Repeat this procedure for each of the rest of the rockers.

4. Remove all the hydraulic lash adjusters, keeping them in order. Support each valve from underneath as you work on it and then depress each valve spring retainer with the special tool. Remove the keepers from either side of the valve stem and then slowly release spring pressure. Remove the spring.

5. Remove the stem seal by gently prying it side-to-side with a screwdriver blade. Work the seal off the guide post and remove it. Repeat Steps 4 and 5 for each valve. Inspect each valve's stem lock grooves for burrs and remove them prior to removing the valve; otherwise, *valve guides may be damaged.* Then, the valves may be removed from the head from underneath.

6. To install, first coat the valve stems with clean engine oil, and then insert each valve into the guide from the lower side of the head.

7. Install new valve seals by pushing each firmly and squarely over the guide so that the center bead of the seal lodges in the valve guide groove. The lower edge of the seal must rest on the valve guide boss. Note that if oversize valves have been installed, oversize seals must also be installed. Install the valve springs.

8. Support the valve you're working on from underneath. Install the valve spring retainer over each spring, depress the spring just enough to expose the grooves for the spring keepers. Make sure to depress the spring squarely so the spring does not touch the valve stem. Install the keepers securely and raise the retainer slowly, making sure the keepers stay in position. Repeat these steps for all eight valves.

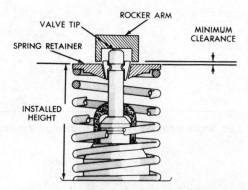

Checking clearance between the valve rocker ears and spring retainers on the 2.2 and 2.5 L engines

9. Install each of the hydraulic lash adjusters in its proper position.

10. Check the valve spring installed height. It must be 1.62-1.68″. If it exceeds specifications, valve spring tension will not be adequate. If necessary, install a spring seat under each spring whose height is too great to make it meet specification.

11. Support the head so that the valves will be free to move downward. Install the rockers, each in its original position, in reverse of the removal procedure. Depress the valve spring retainers only enough to install the rockers, and make sure the keepers stay in place. Check the clearance between the ears of the rocker arm and the spring retainer for each valve with the lash adjuster dry of oil and fully collapsed. If the minimum clearance of 0.020″ is not met, the rocker will have to be machined to create it. After clearance specifications are met, remove the rockers and adjusters, immerse adjusters in clean engine oil and pump them to prime them with oil. Finally, reinstall the adjusters and rockers. Make sure, if you're working with the head on the engine, you don't turn the camshaft until lifters have had at least 10 minutes to leak down.

2.6L Engine

1. Remove the cylinder head as described above. Remove the camshaft bearing caps and rocker shafts as an assembly (see the procedure for camshaft removal). Leave the bolts in the front and rear caps.

2. Using a spring compressor designed for use on overhead cam engines with inclined valves, depress each valve spring, remove keepers, and then remove each valve from underneath. Support each valve while doing this so you won't have to depress the spring unnecessarily.

3. Remove each jet valve by unscrewing it with a special socket wrench designed for this

purpose. Pull out valve stems seals with a pair of pliers.

4. Valve stems should be coated with oil before each valve is installed. Assemble the springs, retainers, and keepers, making sure you do not depress retainers unnecessarily. Check installed height and compare it with specification. If installed height is excessive, install a thicker spring seat until specifications are met. Disassamble valves, springs, and retainers.

5. Install new valve seals onto the cylinder head by tapping them lightly via a special installer such as Chrysler part No. MD998005. Now, springs, retainers, and keepers may be installed.

6. Install jet valves by screwing them in. Torque to 168 in. lbs. The jet valves themselves have springs, retainers, keepers, and seals. You'll need a special tool No. MD998309 to compress the spring, and another, No. MD998308 to install the seal. Keep all jet valve parts together for each jet valve assembly-do not mix them up. The jet valve stem seal is installed by tapping on the special tool to gently force the seal over the jet body. Also, install a new jet valve O-ring coated with clean engine oil before installing the jet valve back into the head.

7. Make sure in final assembly to set the jet valve clearance after the head bolts are torqued and before setting intake valve clearance. Both must finally be set with the engine hot.

ADJUSTMENT

The 2.2 and 2.5 liter engines have hydraulic lash adjusters. All that is necessary is that they be replaced with some oil inside them after valve work is completed. On the 2.6 liter engine, intake, exhaust, and jet valves must be adjusted as described in Chapter 2.

INSPECTION

2.2 and 2.5 Liter Engines

1. Clean the valves thoroughly and discard burned, warped, or cracked valves.

2. If the valve face is only lightly pitted, the valve may be refaced to an angle of 45 degrees by a qualified machine shop.

3. Measure the valve stem for wear at various points and check it against the specifications shown in the ''Valve Specifications'' chart.

4. Once the valve face has been cleaned up, margin must also be checked. This is the thickness of the valve head below the face. It must be 0.031" on the intake and 0.0469" on the exhaust. Valves must also meet standards as to

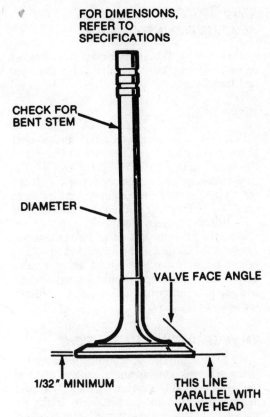

Critical valve dimensions—2.2 and 2.5 L engines

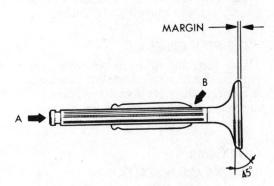

Critical valve dimensions—2.6 liter engine

head diameter and length. These are Intake, 1.60" and 4.425"; Exhaust, 1.39" and 4.425".

2.6 Liter Engine

1. Check the tip of the stem for pitting (A).

2. Check stem to guide clearance (B). It must be 0.004" or less for intake and 0.006" or less for exhaust.

3. Check margin. It must be 0.028" or more for intake and 0.039" or more for exhaust. If reusable, valves should be refaced by a competent automotive machine shop.

Valve Springs
REMOVAL AND INSTALLATION

The valve springs are removed and installed as described just above under Valve Removal and Installation.

INSPECTION

Place the valve spring on a flat surface next to a carpenter's square. Measure the height of the spring, and rotate the spring against the edge of the square to measure distortion. If the spring height varies (by comparison) by more than 1/16″ (1.6mm) or if the distortion exceeds 1/16″ (1.6mm), replace the spring.

Have the valve springs tested for spring pressure at the installed and compressed (installed height minus valve lift) height using a valve spring tester. Springs should be within one pound, plus or minus each other. Replace springs as necessary.

VALVE SPRING INSTALLED HEIGHT

After installing the valve spring, measure the distance between the spring mounting pad and the lower edge of the spring retainer. Compare the measurement to specifications. If the installed height is incorrect, add shim washers between the spring mounting pad and the spring. Use only washers designed for valve springs, available at most parts houses.

VALVE STEM OIL SEALS

When installing valve stem oil seals, ensure that a small amount of oil is able to pass the seal to lubricate the valve stems and guide walls, otherwise, excessive wear will occur.

Valve Seats
REMOVAL AND INSTALLATION

The seats are integral with the aluminum cylinder head on all engines and so can only be machined to specification, not replaced. If a seat is too worn to be brought to specification, the head must be replaced.

CUTTING THE SEATS

Measuring and, if necessary, cutting the valve seat surfaces of the cylinder head are operations requiring precision instruments and machinery. In some cases, if wear is excessive, the cylinder head may have to be replaced, as seats are integral with the head.

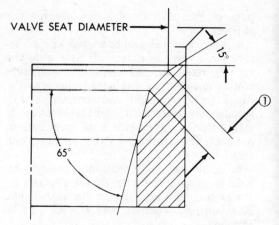

Valve seat dimensions and angles—2.2 liter engine

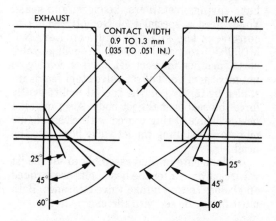

Valve seat dimensions and angles—2.6 liter engine

Valve Guides
REMOVAL AND INSTALLATION
2.2 and 2.5 Liter Engines

Valve guides are replaceable, but it is necessary to first make sure the valve seats can be brought to specification. If the valve seats cannot be refaced, the head must be replaced anyway.

Worn guides should be pressed out from the combustion chamber side and new guides pressed in as far as they will go. In some cases, existing guides can be "knurled" to restore the inside diameter to specifications. All this work must be performed by a competent machine shop, as special skills and extremely sophisticated special equipment are required.

WARNING: *Service valve guides have a shoulder. Once the guide is seated, do not use more than 1 ton pressure or the guide shoulder could break.*

STEM-TO-GUIDE CLEARANCE

Valve stem-to-guide clearance should be checked upon assembling the cylinder head, and is especially necessary if the valve guides have been reamed or knurled, or if oversize valve have been installed. Excessive oil consumption often is a result of too much clearance between the valve guide and valve stem.

1. Clean the valve stem with lacquer thinner or a similar solvent to remove all gum and varnish. Clean the valve guides using solvent and an expanding wire-type valve guide cleaner (a rifle cleaning brush works well here).

2. Mount a dial indicator so that the stem is 90° to the valve stem and as close to the valve guide as possible.

3. Move the valve off its seat, and measure the valve guide-to-stem clearance by rocking the stem back and forth to actuate the dial indicator. Measure the valve stems using a micrometer and compare to specifications, to determine whether stem or guide wear is responsible for excessive clearance.

VALVE LAPPING

The valve must be lapped into their seats after resurfacing, to ensure proper sealing. Even if the valve have not been refaced, they should be lapped into the head before reassembly.

Set the cylinder head on the workbench, combustion chamber side up. Rest the head on wooden blocks on either end, so there are 2-3" (51-76mm) between the tops of the valve guides and the bench.

1. Lightly lube the valve stem with clean engine oil. Coat the valve seat completely with valve grinding compound. Use just enough compound so that the full width and circumference of the seat are covered.

2. Install the valve in its proper location in the head. Attach the suction cup end of the valve lapping tool to the valve head. It usually helps to put a small amount of saliva into the suction cup to aid it sticking to the valve.

3. Rotate the tool between the palms, changing position and lifting the tool often to prevent grooving. Lap the valve in until a smooth, evenly polished seat and valve face are evident.

4. Remove the valve from the head. Wipe away all traces of grinding compound from the valve face and seat. Wipe out the port with a solvent soaked rag, and swab out the valve guide with a piece of solvent soaked rag to make sure there are no traces of compound grit inside the guide. This cleaning is very important, as the engine will ingest any grit remaining when started.

5. Proceed through the remaining valves, one at a time. Make sure the valve faces, sets, cylinder ports and valve guides are clean before reassembling the valve train.

Oil Pan
REMOVAL AND INSTALLATION

1. Drain the engine oil.
CAUTION: *The EPA warns that prolonged contact with used engine oil may cause a number of skin disorders, including cancer! You should make every effort to minimize your exposure to used engine oil. Protective gloves should be worn when changing the oil. Wash your hands and any other exposed skin areas as soon as possible after exposure to used engine oil. Soap and water, or waterless hand cleaner should be used.*

2. Support the pan and remove the attaching bolts.

3. Lower the pan and remove the gasket, if it has one.

4. Clean all gasket surfaces thoroughly. Install the 2.6L pan using gasket sealer and a new gasket.
NOTE: *The 2.2 and 2.5 Liter engine uses a form-in-place type gasket. Chrysler Part Number 4205918 or its equivalent RTV gasket material must be used.*

5. On all 2.2 and 2.5L engines from 1981-87, use new end seals and apply a 1.2" bead of sealer to the rest of the pan. Make sure to apply sealer where the end seals meet the block. On 1988 2.5L engines, replace the end seals and the side gaskets. Apply RTV to the parting lines between end and side seals on these engines. If necessary, use grease or RTV to hold the side seals in place.

6. Torque the pan bolts to 200 in. lbs. (2.2 and 2.5 Liter) and 5 ft.lb. (2.6 Liter).

7. Refill the engine with oil, start the engine, and check for leaks.

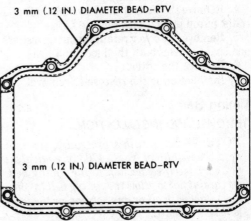

3 mm (.12 IN.) DIAMETER BEAD–RTV

3 mm (.12 IN.) DIAMETER BEAD–RTV

Apply sealer to the oil pan on 2.2 and 2.5 L engines as shown

Oil Pump

REMOVAL AND INSTALLATION

1981-84 2.2L Engine

1. Remove the oil pan.
2. Remove the two pump mounting bolts.
3. Pull the pump down and out of the engine.
4. Installation is the reverse of removal. Make sure the pump body is *fully* seated in the block before installing the mounting bolts. Torque the pump mounting bolts to 200 in. lbs.

1985-89 2.2 and all 2.5L Engines

1. Remove the oil pan as described above.
2. Remove the mounting bolts and remove the pump.
3. Apply a sealer such as Loctite 515® to the pump/block sealing surface.
4. Lubricate the pump rotor, shaft, and drive gear.
5. When installing the pump, rotate the shaft back and forth slightly so the drive mechanism will engage fully and permit the pump to sit squarely against the block.
6. *Holding the pump upward to ensure full seating*, install the mounting bolts. Torque them to 200 in. lbs.

2.6L Engines

See Timing Chain, Cover, Silent Shaft and Tensioner removal and installation procedure.

Timing Belt Cover and Seal

REMOVAL AND INSTALLATION

2.2 and 2.5L Engines

1. Loosen the alternator mounting bolts, pivot the alternator and remove the drive belt.
2. Do the same thing with the air conditioning compressor.
3. Raise the vehicle on a hoist and remove the right inner splash shield.
4. Remove the bolts from the crankshaft and water pump pulleys and remove both.
5. Remove the cover retaining nuts, washers and spacers from both the block and head.
6. Remove the cover.
7. Installation is the reverse of removal.

Timing Belt

REMOVAL AND INSTALLATION

NOTE: *To perform this procedure, you will need a special tool No. C-4703 or equivalent to apply specified tension to the timing belt. Be careful not to allow the timing belt to come in contact with oil or any solvent, or the teeth will be weakened.*

1. Remove the timing belt cover as described above.
2. Place a floor jack under the engine. Spread

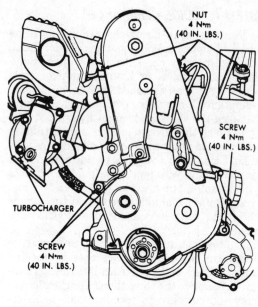

Timing cover attachments—2.2 and 2.5 L engines

the load is such a way that the oil pan will not be damaged. Then, remove the main through bolt from the right engine mount – the one that is situated right near the timing cover.

3. Raise the engine slightly for access to the crankshaft sprocket.
4. Using the larger bolt on the crankshaft pulley, turn the engine until the #1 cylinder is at TDC of the compression stroke. At this point the valves for the #1 cylinder will be closed and the timing mark will be aligned with the pointer on the flywheel housing. Make sure that the dots on the cam sprocket and cylinder head are aligned.

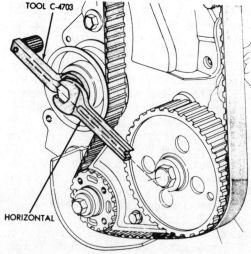

Adjusting timing belt tension—2.2 and 2.5 L engines

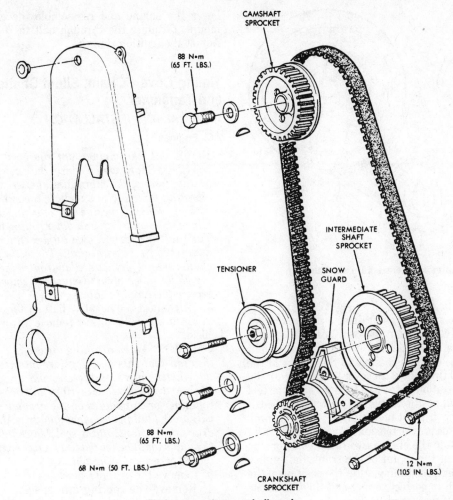

CAMSHAFT
SPROCKET

88 N•m
(65 FT. LBS.)

INTERMEDIATE
SHAFT
SPROCKET

TENSIONER

SNOW
GUARD

88 N•m
(65 FT. LBS.)

68 N•m (50 FT. LBS.)

CRANKSHAFT
SPROCKET

12 N•m
(105 IN. LBS.)

Timing sprockets and oil seals

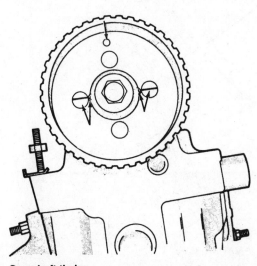

Camshaft timing

5. Loosen the tensioner pulley center nut. Then, rotate the large hex counterclockwise to reduce belt tension. Now, slide the belt off the tensioner pulley, and then the crankshaft, auxiliary shaft and camshaft pulleys.

6. Check that the V-notch or dot on the crankshaft pulley aligns with the dot mark or line on the intermediate shaft. Check also that the arrows on the hub of the camshaft are in line with the No. 1 camshaft cap-to-cylinder head line.

WARNING: *If the timing marks are not perfectly aligned, poor engine performance and probable engine damage will result!*

7. Install the belt on the pulleys with the teeth located so as to perfectly maintain the alignment off all pulleys described just above.

8. Adjust the tensioner by installing special tool C-4703 or equivalent onto the large hex.

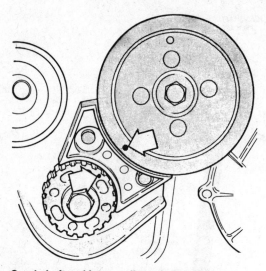

Crankshaft and intermediate shaft timing

Install the tool with the weight hanging away from the auxiliary shaft drive pulley and allow its weight to tension the belt. Position the tool so that after its tension is applied, the weight will be as close as possible to the height of the center of the pulley (the lever is horizontal). Reset the position of the tool to make sure the tool sits in this position after its tension is applied, if necessary. It must be within 15° of horizontal. Finally, torque the tensioner locknut to 32 ft.lb.

9. Rotate the engine two full revolutions by the bolt at the center of the crankshaft pulley and recheck the timing. Alter the position of the belt teeth to correct timing and then reset the tension, if necessary.

10. Install the timing belt cover and pulleys,

lower the engine and reassemble the engine mount, torquing the through bolt to 70 ft.lb. Adjust the ignition timing.

Timing Cover, Chain, Silent Shafts and Tensioner
REMOVAL AND INSTALLATION
2.6L Engines

NOTE: *All 2.6 engines are equipped with two Silent Shafts which cancel the vertical vibrating force of the engine and the secondary vibrating forces, which include the sideways rocking of the engine due to the turning direction of the crankshaft and other rolling parts. The shafts are driven by a duplex chain and are turned by the crankshaft. The silent shaft chain assembly is mounted in front of the timing chain assembly and must be removed to service the timing chain.*

1. Disconnect the negative battery terminal.
2. Drain the radiator and remove it from the vehicle.

CAUTION: *When draining the coolant, keep in mind that cats and dogs are attracted by the ethylene glycol antifreeze, and are quite likely to drink any that is left in an uncovered container or in puddles on the ground. This will prove fatal in sufficient quantity. Always drain the coolant into a sealable container. Coolant should be reused unless it is contaminated or several years old.*

3. Remove the cylinder head.
4. Remove the cooling fan, spacer, water pump pulley and belt.
5. Remove the alternator and water pump.

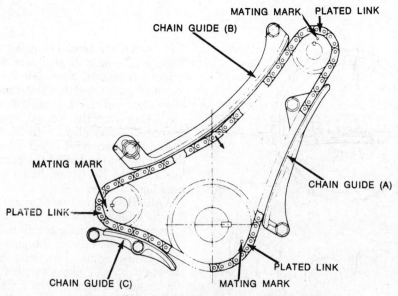

"Silent Shaft" balancing system on 2.6L engines

6. Raise the front of the vehicle and support it on jackstands.

7. Remove the oil pan and screen. Remove the crankshaft pulley.

8. Remove the timing case cover.

9. Remove the chain guides, side (A), top (B), bottom (C), from the **B** chain (outer).

10. Remove the locking bolts from the **B** chain sprockets.

11. Remove the crankshaft sprocket, silent shaft sprocket and the outer chain.

12. Remove the crankshaft and camshaft sprockets and the timing chain.

13. Remove the camshaft sprocket holder and the chain guides, both left and right.

14. Remove the tensioner.

15. Remove the sleeve from the oil pump. Remove the oil pump by first removing the bolt locking the oil pump driven gear and the right silent shaft, then remove the oil pump mounting bolts. Remove the silent shaft from the engine block.

NOTE: *If the bolt locking the oil pump and the silent shaft is hard to loosen, remove the oil pump and the shaft as a unit.*

16. Remove the left silent shaft thrust washer and take the shaft from the engine block.

Installation is performed in the following manner:

1. Install the right silent shaft into the engine block.

2. Install the oil pump assembly. Do not lose the woodruff key from the end of the silent shaft. Torque the oil pump mounting bolts from 6 to 7 ft.lb.

3. Tighten the silent shaft and oil pump driven gear mounting bolt.

NOTE: *The silent shaft and the oil pump can be installed as a unit, if necessary.*

4. Install the left silent shaft into the engine block.

5. Install a new O-ring on the thrust plate and install the unit into the engine block, using a pair of bolts without heads, as alignment guides.

CAUTION: *If the thrust plate is turned to align the bolt holes, the O-ring may be damaged.*

6. Remove the guide bolts and install the regular bolts into the thrust plate and tighten securely.

7. Rotate the crankshaft to bring No. 1 piston to TDC.

8. Install the cylinder head.

9. Install the sprocket holder and the right and left chain guides.

10. Install the tensioner spring and sleeve on the oil pump body.

11. Install the camshaft and crankshaft sprockets on the timing chain, aligning the sprocket punch marks to the plated chain links.

12. While holding the sprocket and chain as a unit, install the crankshaft sprocket over the crankshaft and align it with the keyway.

13. Keeping the dowel pin hole on the camshaft in a vertical position, install the camshaft sprocket and chain on the camshaft.

NOTE: *The sprocket timing mark and the plated chain link should be at the 2 to 3 o'clock position when correctly installed.*

CAUTION: *The chain must be aligned in the right and left chain guides with the tensioner pushing against the chain. The tension for the inner chain is determined by spring tension.*

14. Install the crankshaft sprocket for the outer or "B" chain.

15. Install the two silent shaft sprockets and align the punched mating marks with the plated links of the chain.

16. Holding the two shaft sprockets and chain, install the outer chain in alignment with the mark on the crankshaft sprocket. Install the shaft sprockets on the silent shaft and the oil pump driver gear. Install the lock bolts and recheck the alignment of the punch marks and the plated links.

17. Temporarily install the chain guides, Side (A), Top (B), and Bottom (C).

18. Tighten Side (A) chain guide securely.

19. Tighten Bottom (C) chain guide securely.

20. Adjust the position of the Top (B) chain guide, after shaking the right and left sprockets to collect any chain slack, so that when the chain is moved toward the center, the clearance between the chain guide and the chain links will be approximately $9/64''$. Tighten the Top (B) chain guide bolts.

21. Install the timing chain cover using a new gasket, being careful not to damage the front seal.

22. Install the oil screen and the oil pan, using a new gasket. Torque the bolts to 4.5 to 5.5 ft.lb.

23. Install the crankshaft pulley, alternator and accessory belts, and the distributor.

24. Install the oil pressure switch, if removed, and install the battery ground cable.

25. Install the fan blades, radiator, fill the system with coolant and start the engine.

Timing Sprockets
REMOVAL AND INSTALLATION
2.2 and 2.5L Engines

NOTE: *To hold the camshaft sprocket still while you remove it, it's best to use a special tool such as C-4687 or equivalent and, for 2.5 L engines, an adapter such as C-4687-1.*

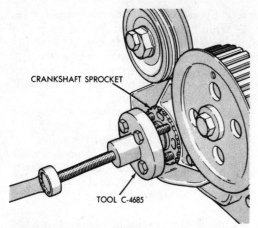

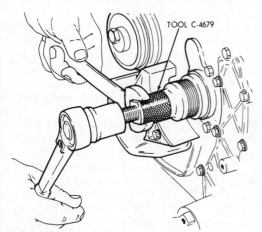

CRANKSHAFT SPROCKET

TOOL C-4685

Crankshaft sprocket removal

TOOL C-4679

Crankshaft, intermediate shaft, camshaft oil seal removal

TOOL C-4687

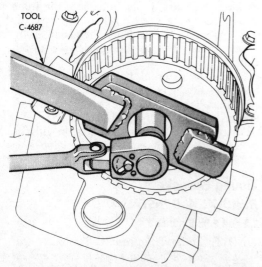

Removing and installing the camshaft and intermediate shaft sprockets

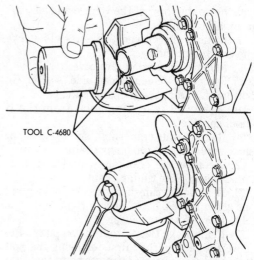

TOOL C-4680

Installing the crankshaft, intermediate shaft and camshaft seal

1. Raise and support the car on jackstands.
2. Remove the right inner splash shield.
3. Remove the crankshaft and water pump pulleys.
4. Unbolt and remove both halves of the timing belt cover.
5. Take up the weight of engine with a jack.
6. Remove the right engine mount bolt and raise the engine slightly.
7. Remove the timing belt tensioner and remove the belt.
8. Remove the crankshaft sprocket bolt, and with a puller, remove the sprocket.
9. Using special tool C-4679 or its equivalent (2.2L) or C-4991 or equivalent (2.5L), remove the crankshaft seal.
10. Unbolt and remove the camshaft and intermediate shaft sprockets. Use the special tool or tool and adapter specified in the note above to hold the camshaft sprocket as you loosen the bolt.
11. To install the crankshaft seal, first polish the shaft with 400 grit emery paper. If the seal has a steel case, lightly coat the OD of the seal with Loctite Stud N' Bearing Mount® or its equivalent. If the seal case is rubber coated, generously apply a soap and water solution to facilitate installation. Install the seal with a seal driver. Use C-4680 or equivalent on the 2.2L engine and C-4992 on the 2.5L.
12. Install the sprockets making sure that the timing marks are aligned as illustrated. When installing the camshaft sprocket, make certain the arrows on the sprocket are in line with the #1 camshaft bearing cap-to-cylinder head line.
13. The small hole in the camshaft sprocket must be at the top and in line with the vertical center line of the engine.

14. Rotate the engine two full revolutions and recheck timing mark positioning.

15. Install the belt.

16. Rotate the engine to the #1 piston TDC position.

17. Install the belt tensioner and place tool C-4703 on the large hex nut with the weight hanging away from the auxiliary shaft pulley.

18. Allow the tool to tension the belt. Then, if necessary, reset the tool position so that the axis of the tool is within 15 degrees of horizontal when its tension is positioning the belt.

19. Turn the engine clockwise two full revolutions to #1 TDC.

20. Torque the tensioner locknut to 32 ft.lb. Other torques are: Timing belt cover bolts, 105 in. lb.

- Camshaft sprocket bolt, 65 ft.lb.
- Crankshaft sprocket bolt, 50 ft.lb.
- Intermediate shaft sprocket bolt, 65 ft.lb.

2.6L Engines

See the procedures under Timing Chain, Cover and Silent Shafts.

Balance Shafts

REMOVAL AND INSTALLATION

NOTE: *To complete this procedure, you will need a Tool C-4916 or equivalent or a shim 0.039" thick and 2.75" long.*

1. Drain and remove the oil pan as described above. Remove the attaching bolts and remove the pickup.

CAUTION: *The EPA warns that prolonged contact with used engine oil may cause a number of skin disorders, including cancer! You should make every effort to minimize*

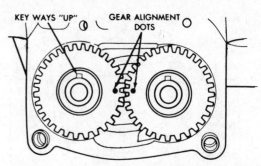

Alignment of timing marks on the balance shaft drive gears

your exposure to used engine oil. Protective gloves should be worn when changing the oil. Wash your hands and any other exposed skin areas as soon as possible after exposure to used engine oil. Soap and water, or waterless hand cleaner should be used.

2. Remove the timing belt cover, belt, and crankshaft sprocket as described above. Remove the front crankshaft oil seal retainer as described above.

3. Remove its three mounting bolts and remove the chain cover.

4. Remove the mounting bolt from the chain guide and remove the guide; remove the mounting bolt from the tensioner, and remove it.

5. Remove the bolts which retain the balance shaft gear and chain sprocket (the chain sprocket is retained by Torx® bolts). Remove both sprockets and the chain as an assembly.

6. Remove the gear cover retaining stud with a deep well socket. Then, remove the gear cover. Remove the gears.

7. Unbolt and remove the carrier rear cover. Then, slide the balance shafts out of the carrier.

8. If it is necessary to remove the balance shaft carrier, remove the six carrier-to-crankcase attaching bolts and remove the carrier.

9. Installation is in reverse order. Start by installing the carrier and torquing the mounting bolts to 40 ft.lb.

10. Lubricate the bearing surfaces with engine oil and reinstall the shafts. Install the rear cover and torque the bolts to 105 in. lbs.

11. Turn both balance shafts until the keyways are parallel to the vertical centerline of the engine and above the shafts. Turn the timing gears so the timing marks align at the center. Install the drive gear with the shorter hub onto the sprocket-driven shaft. Install the gear with the longer hub onto the gear driven shaft.

12. Install the gear cover and torque the stud to 105 in. lbs.

13. Install the crankshaft timing belt sprocket and torque the Torx® bolts to 130 in. lbs. Turn the crankshaft until the timing marks on

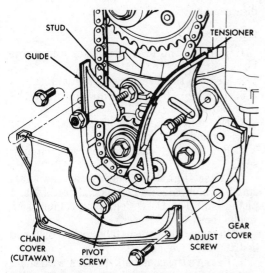

Balance shafts timing chain cover, guide, and tensioner (2.5 L engines)

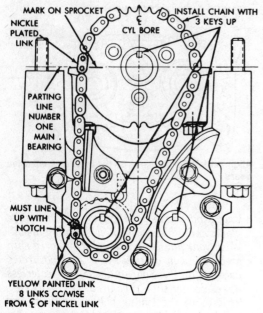

MARK ON SPROCKET
NICKLE PLATED LINK
INSTALL CHAIN WITH 3 KEYS UP
CYL BORE
PARTING LINE NUMBER ONE MAIN BEARING
MUST LINE UP WITH NOTCH
YELLOW PAINTED LINK 8 LINKS CC/WISE FROM ℄ OF NICKEL LINK

Timing of balance shafts

the chain sprocket line up with the parting line on the left side of No. 1 main bearing cap.

14. Place the chain over the crankshaft sprocket in such a way that the nickel plated link of the chain fits over the timing mark on the crankshaft sprocket.

15. Engage the balance shaft sprocket with the timing chain so that the yellow dot on the sprocket mates with the chain link that is painted yellow.

16. With both balance shaft keyways pointing up, slide the balance shaft sprocket onto the nose of the balance shaft. If necessary, push the nose of the balance shaft in slightly to allow the sprocket to clear the chain cover, when it is installed. Now, *the timing marks on the sprocket, the painted link, and the arrow on the side of the gear cover must all line up with their corresponding marks. If not, retime the shafts as necessary, because improper timing will result in severe engine vibration!* If the sprockets are all timed correctly, install the balance shaft bolts. Put a wooden block between the crankcase and a crankshaft counterweight to prevent rotation; then, torque the balance shaft bolts to 250 in. lbs.

18. Install the chain tensioner with bolts just finger tight. Install the special tool or the shim described in the note above between the tensioner and chain. Then, apply pressure to the tensioner directly behind the adjustment slot to push the tensioner and shim up against the chain. The shim must contact the shoe of the tensioner from the bottom almost all the way to the top and all slack must be removed. Hold the

tension and torque the top tensioner bolt, and then the pivot bolt to 105 in. lbs. Remove the shim or tool. Install the chain guide onto the double-ended stud. Make sure the tab on the guide fits into the slot on the gear cover. Install the nut and washer and torque to 105 in. lbs.

19. Install the carrier covers and torque the bolts to 105 in. lbs.

20. Perform the remaining steps of the installation procedure in reverse of removal.

Camshaft and Bearings
REMOVAL AND INSTALLATION
2.2 and 2.5L Engines

1. Remove the timing belt as described above. Remove the cam cover as described above.

2 Mark the rocker arms for installation identification.

3. Loosen the camshaft bearing capnuts several turns each.

4. Using a wooden or rubber mallet, rap the rear of the camshaft a few times to break it loose.

5. Remove the capnuts and caps being very careful that the camshaft does not cock. Cocking the camshaft could cause irreparable damage to the bearings.

6. Check all oil holes for blockage.

7. Install the bearing caps with #1 at the timing belt end and #5 at the transmission end. Caps are numbered and have arrows facing forward. Capnut torque is 14 ft.lb.

8. Apply RTV silicone gasket material to the seal ends.

9. Install the bearing caps BEFORE the seals are installed.

10. The rest of the procedure is the reverse of disassembly.

2.6L Engines

1. Remove the breather hoses and purge hose.

2. Remove the air cleaner and fuel line.

3. Remove the fuel pump. Remove the distributor.

4. Disconnect the spark plug cables.

5. Remove the rocker cover.

6. Remove the breather and semi-circular seal.

7. After slightly loosening the camshaft sprocket bolt, turn the crankshaft until No. 1 piston is at Top Dead Center on compression stroke (both valves closed).

8. Remove the camshaft sprocket bolt and distributor drive gear.

9. Remove the camshaft sprocket with chain and allow it to rest on the camshaft sprocket holder.

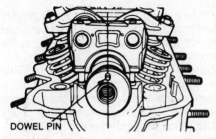

Install the camshaft on 2.6L engines by aligning the dowel pin with the notch in the top of the front bearing cap

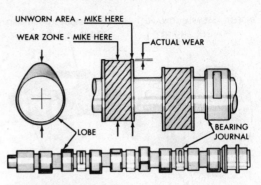

Measuring cam lobe wear

10. Remove the camshaft bearing cap tightening bolts. Do not remove the front and rear bearing cap bolts altogether, but keep them inserted in the bearing caps so that the rocker assembly can be removed as a unit.

11. Remove the rocker arms, rocker shafts and bearing caps as an assembly.

12. Remove the camshaft.

13. Installation is the reverse of removal. Lubricate the camshaft lobes and bearings and fit camshaft lobes and bearings and fit camshaft into head. Install the assembled rocker arm shaft assembly. The camshaft should be positioned so that the dowel pin on the front end of the cam is in the 12 o'clock position and in line with the notch in the top of the front bearing cap.

CAMSHAFT ENDPLAY CHECK

1. Move the camshaft as far forward as possible.

2. Install a dial indicator on the end of the camshaft.

3. Zero the indicator, push the camshaft backward, then forward as far as possible and record the play. Maximum play should be 0.006″.

INSPECTING THE CAMSHAFT

Measure cam lobe height at the nose or thickest point. Measure at the very edge of the

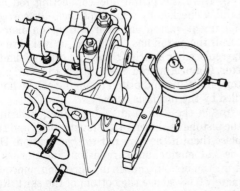

Checking camshaft end play

lobe, where there is no wear, and at the center, where wear is at a maximum. On the 2.2 and 2.5 liter engines, 0.010″ wear is permitted, while on the 2.6, the figure is 0.020″. Replace the camshaft if it is worn excessively.

Pistons and Connecting Rods
IDENTIFICATION

The pistons used in the 2.2 and 2.5 Liter engines have notches in them to indicate the proper installed position. The notch faces the front of the engine, when installed. Connecting rods have markings to indicate proper assembly of the rod to the cap. 2.6 Liter engines have arrows on the pistons. These arrows must face front when installed in the engine. The connecting rods are numbered for easy identification.

REMOVAL AND INSTALLATION
2.2 and 2.5 Liter Engines

1. Follow the instructions under "Cylinder Head" removal and "Timing Belt" or "Timing Chain" removal.

2. Remove the oil pan as described later in this chapter.

3. This procedure is much easier performed with the engine of the car.

4. Pistons should be removed in the order: 1-3-4-2. Turn the crankshaft until the piston to be removed is at the bottom of its stroke.

5. Place a cloth on the head of the piston to be removed and using a ridge reamer, remove the ridge from the upper end of the cylinder bore.

NOTE: *Never remove more than $1/22$″ from the ring travel are when removing the ridges.*

6. Mark all connecting rod bearing caps so that they may be returned to their original locations in the engine. The connecting rod caps are marked with rectangular forge marks which must be mated during assembly and be installed on the intermediate shaft side of the en-

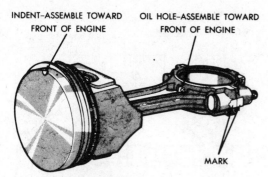

INDENT-ASSEMBLE TOWARD FRONT OF ENGINE

OIL HOLE-ASSEMBLE TOWARD FRONT OF ENGINE

MARK

2.2 L pistons for 1981–85 engines

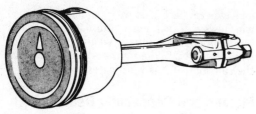

2.6L pistons with connecting rod markings

gine. Mark all pistons so they can be returned to their original cylinders.

WARNING: *Don't score the cylinder walls or the crankshaft journal.*

7. Using an internal micrometer, measure the bores across the thrust faces of the cylinder and parallel to the axis of the crankshaft at a minimum of four equally spaced locations. The bore must not be out-of-round by more than 0.005″ and it must not taper more than 0.010″. Taper is the difference in wear between two bore measurements in any cylinder. See the Engine Rebuilding section for complete details.

8. If the cylinder bore is in satisfactory condition, place each ring in the bore in turn and square it in the bore with the head of the piston.

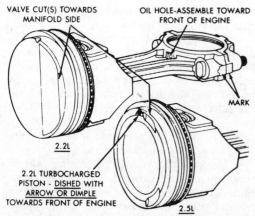

VALVE CUT(S) TOWARDS MANIFOLD SIDE

OIL HOLE-ASSEMBLE TOWARD FRONT OF ENGINE

MARK

2.2L

2.2L TURBOCHARGED PISTON - DISHED WITH ARROW OR DIMPLE TOWARDS FRONT OF ENGINE

2.5L

2.2 L pistons for 1986–88 engines, and 2.5 L pistons

Measure the ring gap. If the ring gap is greater than the limit, get a new ring. If the ring gap is less than the limit, file the end of the ring to obtain the correct gap.

9. Check the ring side clearance by installing rings on the piston, and inserting a feeler gauge of the correct dimension between the ring and the lower land. The gauge should slide freely around the ring circumference without binding. Any wear will form a step on the lower land. Remove any pistons having high steps. Before checking the ring side clearance, be sure that the ring grooves are clean and free of carbon, sludge, or grit.

10. Piston rings should be installed so that their ends are at three equal spacings. Avoid installing the rings with their ends in line with the piston pin bosses and the thrust direction.

11. Install the pistons in their original bores, if you are reusing the same pistons. Install short lengths of rubber hose over the connecting rod bolts to prevent damage to the cylinder walls or rod journal.

12. Install a ring compressor over the rings on the piston. Lower the piston and rod assembly into the bore until the ring compressor contacts the block. Using a wooden hammer handle, push the piston into the bore while guiding the rod onto the journal.

NOTE: *On 2.2L and 2.5L engines, the arrow or notch on the piston should face toward the front (drive belt) of the engine.*

CLEANING AND INSPECTION

1. Use a piston ring expander and remove the rings from the piston.

2. Clean the ring grooves using an appropriate cleaning tool, exercise care to avoid cutting too deeply.

3. Clean all varnish and carbon from the piston with a safe solvent. Do not use a wire brush or caustic solution on the pistons.

4. Inspect the pistons for scuffing, scoring, cracks, pitting or excessive ring groove wear. If wear is evident, the piston must be replaced.

5. Have the piston and connecting rod assembly checked by a machine shop for correct alignment, piston pin wear and piston diameter. If the piston has "collapsed" it will have to be replaced or knurled to restore original diameter. Connecting rod bushing replacement, piston pin fitting and piston changing can be handled by the machine shop.

6. On the 2.2L and 2.5L engines, measure the pistons as shown in the illustrations and replace them if they are not to specification. On the 2.6L engine, measure piston diameter with a micrometer in the thrust direction approximately 0.08″ above the bottom of the skirt. Replace the piston if wear is excessive.

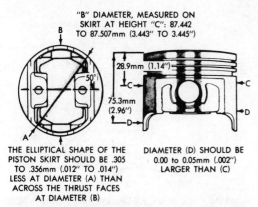

"B" DIAMETER, MEASURED ON SKIRT AT HEIGHT "C": 87.442 TO 87.507mm (3.443" TO 3.445")

28.9mm (1.14")

75.3mm (2.96")

THE ELLIPTICAL SHAPE OF THE PISTON SKIRT SHOULD BE .305 TO .356mm (.012" TO .014") LESS AT DIAMETER (A) THAN ACROSS THE THRUST FACES AT DIAMETER (B)

DIAMETER (D) SHOULD BE 0.00 to 0.05mm (.002") LARGER THAN (C)

Measuring piston wear for 2.2 and 2.5 L engine pistons. Note that the dimension for elliptical wear is as shown for 1981–85 pistons; for 1986–88 pistons, it is 0.30–0.35 mm or 0.0118–0.0138 in.

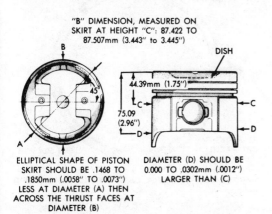

"B" DIMENSION, MEASURED ON SKIRT AT HEIGHT "C": 87.422 TO 87.507mm (3.443" to 3.445")

DISH

44.39mm (1.75")

75.09 (2.96")

ELLIPTICAL SHAPE OF PISTON SKIRT SHOULD BE .1468 TO .1850mm (.0058" TO .0073") LESS AT DIAMETER (A) THEN ACROSS THE THRUST FACES AT DIAMETER (B)

DIAMETER (D) SHOULD BE 0.000 TO .0302mm (.0012") LARGER THAN (C)

Measuring piston wear—turbocharged 2.2 liter engines. Figures are for 1984–85 engines. Figures for 1985–88 are: "B" dimension—3.4416–3.4441 in.; Elliptical shape—0.0074–0.0106 in. less at "A" than at "B"; Diameter at "D" should be 0.000–0.0012 in. larger than diameter "C".

PISTON PIN REPLACEMENT

The pin connecting the piston and connecting rod is press fitted. On the 2.6L engine, the pin bushing in the rod is also press fitted into the top of the rod. You should take the piston/rod assemblies to a machine shop to have pin/bushing wear checked and corrected, if necessary. Installing new rods or pistons requires the use of a press—have the machine shop handle the job for you. The shop should also check the connecting rods for straightness at this time, and replace them, if necessary.

2.6 Liter Engine

Pistons and rods are usually (and most easily) removed as part of a complete engine overhaul. A complete disassembly entails removing the engine from the car and mounting it on a stand, and then removing the cylinder head and

oil pan. The front cover, timing chain, and rear main seal are removed. Then, the connecting rod caps are marked and removed and kept in order. The crankshaft is supported or the engine turned upside down and the caps marked, removed, and kept in order. The crankshaft is removed.

Now, the ridge formed at the top of each cylinder by ring wear is removed with a ridge reamer. This is done to prevent damage to the rings or cylinder as the piston is removed. Protect the wear surfaces from grit formed in the reaming process by covering the piston and nearby areas of the cylinder with a clean rag that will catch all the particles. Once the ridges are reamed out, number and remove the pistons and rods.

If, for some reason the engine has suffered ring and cylinder wear but does not require an entire rebuild, you can remove the pistons and rods with the engine in the car. The cylinder head and oil pan must be removed, and connecting rod caps numbered and removed. Turn the crankshaft so each piston is at bottom center position, ream out the ridge as described above, and then mark and remove each piston rod assembly.

In either case, refer to the appropriate procedures above and below for more detailed information.

All four pistons are installed (in original order) with the arrows facing forward—toward the timing chain. Note the relationship between the arrow and marks on the connecting rod and cap. These marks will end up below the number on the top face of the piston.

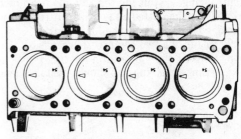

Pistons on the 2 6 liter engine are installed with the arrows facing the timing chain

On the 2.6 liter engine, note the relationship between the arrow on the top of the piston, and numbered marks on both connecting rod and cap

PISTON RING REPLACEMENT

2.2 and 2.5L Engines

1. Remove the rings from the piston with a ring expander. Clean both the piston ring grooves and the rings thoroughly for more accurate measurement of clearances.

2. Inspect the ring grooves on the piston for excessive wear. Install the ring in the groove with a piston ring expander and check side clearance with a feeler gauge. If clearance is excessive, rings will have to be replaced. If new rings cannot restore clearance, replace both the rings and the piston.

3. Take the new piston rings and compress them, one at a time into the cylinder that they will be used in. Press the ring 0.62″ from the bottom of the cylinder they will be used in using an inverted piston.

4. Use a feeler gauge and measure the distance between the ends of the ring, to measure the ring end-gap. Compare the reading to the one called for in the specifications table. File the ends of the ring with a fine file to obtain necessary clearance, if it should be too tight (a rare condition). If ring gap is excessive, the ring must be replaced.

WARNING: *If inadequate ring end-gap is utilized ring breakage will result!*

5. Install new rings on the piston, lower ring first, using a piston ring expander. The "Top" mark on the ring must face upward.

6. When installing oil rings; first, install the ring in the groove. Hold the ends of the ring butted together (they must not overlap) and install the bottom rail (scraper) with the end about one inch away from the butted end of the control ring. Install the top rail about an inch away from the butted end of the control but on the opposite side from the lower rail.

7. Install the two compression rings.

8. Consult the illustration for ring positioning, arrange the rings as shown, install a ring

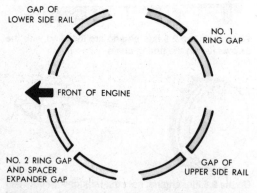

Align the piston ring gaps so they are offset as shown, to prevent ring leakage

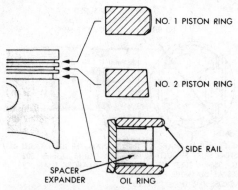

Install the rings on the 2.6 liter engine as shown. Note the difference between No. 1 and No. 2 rings. Markings on the rings should face upward.

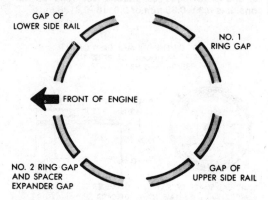

Stagger the rings gaps as shown to prevent ring leakage

compressor and insert the piston and rod assembly into the engine.

2.6L Engine

Piston rings and grooves must be thoroughly cleaned to check side clearance. Remove the rings from each piston with an expander, clean both ring grooves and rings, and reinstall (see below). Measure side clearance with a flat feeler gauge.

The cylinder bores will have to be measured for wear as described below under Cleaning and Inspection. If the bores are satisfactory, and ring side clearance is satisfactory too, each ring must be individually installed in the bottom of its cylinder bore at least 0.63″ from the bottom. Use the piston, inserted part way into the bore, to square the ring's position. Measure end gap with a flat feeler gauge. Excessive dimensions in terms of either side clearance or ring gap require replacement of rings and, if this does not cure excessive side clearance, the rings and piston.

Install the oil ring expander first, and then the upper oil ring rail and, finally the lower oil ring side rail. When installing the side rails, do not use a ring expander, but place one end between the piston and ring groove and the ring expander. Hold the end firmly and work your way around the expander from that point to work it down and into position.

With a ring expander, install first the No. 2 ring and, finally, the No. 1 ring. Finally, stagger the ring gaps as shown in the illustration. The oil ring expander gap must be at least 45 degrees from the side rail gaps but not aligned either with the piston pin or the thrust direction.

Cylinder Bore

INSPECTION

2.2 and 2.5L Engines

Check the cylinder bore for wear using a telescope gauge and a micrometer, measure the cylinder bore diameter perpendicular to the piston pin at a point 2½" below the top of the engine block. Measure the piston skirt perpendicular to the piston pin. The difference between the two measurements is the piston clearance. If the clearance is within specifications, finish honing or glaze breaking is all that is required. If clearance is excessive a slightly oversize piston may be required. If greatly oversize, the engine will have to be bored and 0.010" or larger oversized pistons installed.

2.6L Engine

Measure the cylinder bores with an inside micrometer at top, just below center, and bottom and in both the thrust and piston pin installation directions. Top and bottom measurements should be 0.38" from the extreme top or bottom of the bore. The bore dimension must not exceed 3.5866". Out-of-round or taper must not exceed 0.0008". In other words, the highest and lowest readings must not be more than 0.008" apart. These figures must also produce piston clearance within specifications (piston diameter subtracted from bore dimension).

MEASURING THE OLD PISTONS

Check used piston-to-cylinder bore clearance as follows:

1. Measure the cylinder bore diameter with a telescope gauge.
2. Measure the piston diameter. When measuring the pistons for size or taper, measurements must be made with the piston pin removed.
3. Subtract the piston diameter from the cylinder bore diameter to determine piston-to-bore clearance.
4. Compare the piston-to-bore clearances obtained with those clearances recommended. Determine if the piston-to-bore clearance is in the acceptable range.

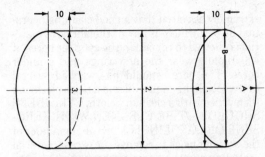

Check cylinder bore wear at these positions on the 2.2 liter engine. Measure at a point 10 mm or ⅜ in. from the top and bottom

5. When measuring taper, the largest reading must be at the bottom of the skirt.

SELECTING NEW PISTONS

1. If the used piston is not acceptable, check the service piston size and determine if a new piston can be selected. (Service pistons are available in standard, high limit and standard oversize.
2. If the cylinder bore must be reconditioned, measure the new piston diameter, then hone the cylinder bore to obtain the preferred clearance.
3. Select a new piston and mark the piston to identify the cylinder for which it was fitted. (On some vehicles, oversize pistons may be found. These pistons will be 0.254mm [0.010"] oversize).

CYLINDER HONING

1. When cylinders are being honed, follow the manufacturer's recommendations for the use of the hone.
2. Occasionally, during the honing operation, the cylinder bore should be thoroughly cleaned and the selected piston checked for correct fit.
3. When finish-honing a cylinder bore, the hone should be moved up and down at a sufficient speed to obtain a very fine uniform surface finish in a cross-hatch pattern of approximately 45-65° included angle. The finish marks should be clean but not sharp, free from imbedded particles and torn or folded metal.
4. Permanently mark the piston for the cylinder to which it has been fitted and proceed to hone the remaining cylinders.

WARNING: *Handle the pistons with care. Do not attempt to force the pistons through the cylinders until the cylinders have been honed to the correct size. Pistons can be distorted through careless handling.*

5. Thoroughly clean the bores with hot water and detergent. Scrub well with a stiff bristle brush and rinse thoroughly with hot water. It is

extremely essential that a good cleaning operation be performed. If any of the abrasive material is allowed to remain in the cylinder bores, it will rapidly wear the new rings and cylinder bores. The bores should be swabbed several times with light engine oil and a clean cloth and then wiped with a clean dry cloth. CYLINDERS SHOULD NOT BE CLEANED WITH KEROSENE OR GASOLINE! Clean the remainder of the cylinder block to remove the excess material spread during the honing operation.

PISTON RING END GAP

Piston ring end gap should be checked while the rings are removed from the pistons. Incorrect end gap indicates that the wrong size rings are being used; ring breakage could occur.

Compress the piston rings to be used in a cylinder, one at a time, into that cylinder. Squirt clean oil into the cylinder, so that the rings and the top 2″ (51mm) of cylinder wall are coated. Using an inverted piston, press the rings approximately 1″ (25mm) below the deck of the block (on diesels, measure ring gap clearance with the ring positioned at the bottom of ring travel in the bore). Measure the ring end gap with the feeler gauge, and compare to the Ring Gap chart in this chapter. Carefully pull the ring out of the cylinder and file the ends squarely with a fine file to obtain the proper clearance.

PISTON RING SIDE CLEARANCE CHECK AND INSTALLATION

Check the pistons to see that the ring grooves and oil return holes have been properly cleaned. Slide a piston ring into its groove, and check the side clearance with a feeler gauge. On gasoline engines, make sure you insert the gauge between the ring and its lower land (lower edge of the groove), because any wear that occurs forms a step at the inner portion of the lower land. On diesels, insert the gauge between the ring and the upper land. If the piston grooves have worn to the extend that relatively high steps exist on the lower land, the piston grooves have worn to the extent that relatively high steps exist on the lower land, the piston should be replaced, because these will interfere with the operation of the new rings and ring clearance will be excessive. Piston rings are not furnished in oversize widths to compensate for ring groove wear.

Install the rings on the piston, lowest ring first, using a piston ring expander. There is a high risk of breaking or distorting the rings, or scratching the piston, if the rings are installed by hand or other means.

Position the rings on the piston as illustrated; spacing of the various piston ring gaps is

crucial to proper oil retention and even cylinder wear. When installing new rings, refer to the installation diagram furnished with the new parts.

ROD BEARING REPLACEMENT

The crankshaft must be miked to ensure that it meets wear specifications. See the section below on Crankshaft and Main Bearings. In addition, assuming that connecting rod bearings do not show signs of excess wear or heat (roughness, grooving, blue color from heat, etc.), the bearing clearance must be checked with Plastigage®. This is done by drying all the surfaces and then inserting a Plastigage® insert in between the crankpin and the bearing surface. Assemble the connecting rod cap to the rod. Oil the bolts and then torque them to: 40 ft.lb. plus ¼ turn on 2.2 and 2.5L engines and 34 ft.lb. on the 2.6L engine. Do not turn the crankshaft.

Then, remove the cap and read the clearance by comparing the width of the groove left on the crankpin to the width of the marks on a scale provided with the insert kit. If the bearing clearance meets specifications, make sure to clean the insert mark off the crankpin and thoroughly lubricate all parts with clean engine oil before final assembly.

In most cases, if wear is excessive, the crankshaft should be machined and undersize bearings installed. This work should be done by a competent machine shop.

You must also check connecting rods for excessive clearance between the side of the rod and the cheek of the crankshaft. Connecting rod clearance between the rod and crankthrow casting is checked with a feeler gauge. Pry the rod carefully to one side as far as possible and measure the distance on the other side of the rod. The clearance must be 0.005-0.013″ for new parts with a wear limit of 0.015″ on 2.2 and 2.5L engines; on the 2.6L, it must be 0.004-0.010″. Check with a flat feeler gauge. Excess clearance must be corrected by replacing the rod or possibly the rod and crankshaft.

Pistons must be installed into their original bores. All parts must be thoroughly lubricated with engine oil. Use a ring compressor to hold the rings in the compressed position as you slip the piston/rod assembly down into the cylinder. The compressor will rest right against the top of the block. If the crankshaft is still in place, make sure the crankpin is in Bottom Dead Center position. Protect the crankpin from contact with connecting rod studs, if necessary by slipping lengths of rubber hose over the studs. Make sure the rod caps face in the right direction and torque the nuts to 34 ft.lb.

Rear Main Oil Seal

REMOVAL AND INSTALLATION

2.2L Engines

The rear main seal is located in a housing on the rear of the block. To replace the seal it is necessary to remove the engine.

1. Remove the transmission and flywheel.

CAUTION: *Before removing the transmission, align the dimple on the flywheel with the pointer on the flywheel housing. The transmission will not mate with the engine during installation unless this alignment is observed.*

2. Very carefully, pry the oil seal out of the support ring. Be careful not to nick or damage the crankshaft flange seal surface or retainer bore.

3. Place special tool #C-4681 or its equivalent on the crankshaft.

4. Lightly coat the outside diameter of the seal with Loctite Stud N' Bearing Mount® or its equivalent. Also coat the inside of the seal with engine oil.

5. Place the seal over tool #C-4681 and gently tap it into place with a plastic hammer.

6. Reinstall the remaining parts in the reverse order of removal.

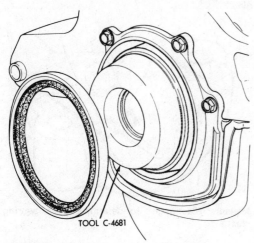

Installing rear oil seal

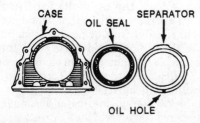

Rear main oil seal on 2.6L engines

2.6L Engines

The rear main oil seal is located in a housing on the rear of the block. To replace the seal, remove the transmission and flywheel or flex plate and do the work from underneath the vehicle or remove the engine and do the work on the bench.

1. Remove the housing from the block.
2. Remove the separator from the housing.
3. Pry out the old seal.
4. Lightly oil the replacement seal. The oil seal should be installed so that the seal plate fits into the inner contact surface of the seal case. Install the separator with the oil holes facing down.

Crankshaft and Main Bearings

REMOVAL AND INSTALLATION

1. Rod bearings can be installed when the pistons have been removed for servicing (rings etc.) or, in most cases, while the engine is still in the car. Rearing replacement, however, is far easier with the engine out of the car and disassembled.

2. For in-car service, remove the oil pan, spark plugs and front cover if necessary. Turn the engine until the connecting rod to be serviced is at the bottom of its travel. Remove the bearing cap, place two pieces of rubber hose over the rod cap bolts and push the piston and rod assembly up the cylinder bore until enough room is gained for bearing insert removal. Take care not to push the rod assembly up too far or the top ring will engage the cylinder ridge or come out of the cylinder and require head removal for reinstallation.

3. Clean the rod journal, the connecting rod end and the bearing cap after removing the old bearing inserts. Install the new inserts in the rod and bearing cap, lubricate them with oil. Position the rod over the crankshaft journal and install the rod caps. Make sure the cap and

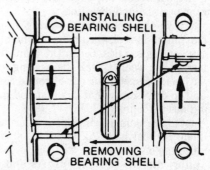

Removing/installing the upper bearing insert with a roll-out pin

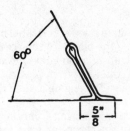

Here's how to make your own roll-out pin

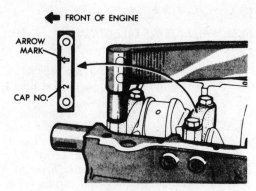

On the 2.6 liter engine, install the caps in numbered order, arrows facing forward

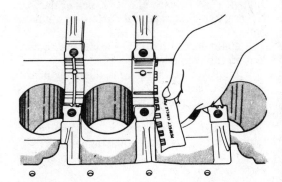

Checking main bearing clearance on the 2.6 liter engine

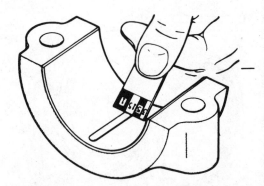

Measure Plastigage® to determine main bearing clearance

rod numbers match, torque the rod nuts to specifications.

4. Main bearings may be replaced while the engine is still in the car by "rolling" them out and in.

5. Special roll-out pins are available from automotive parts houses or can be fabricated from a cotter pin. The roll out pin fits in the oil hole of the main bearing journal. When the crankshaft is rotated opposite the direction of the bearing lock tab, the pin engages the end of the bearing and rolls out the insert.

6. Remove main bearing cap and roll out upper bearing insert. Remove insert from main bearing cap. Clean the inside of the bearing cap and crankshaft journal.

7. Lubricate and roll upper insert into position, make sure the lock tab is anchored and the insert is not cocked. Install the lower bearing insert into the cap; lubricate and install on the engine. Make sure the main bearing cap is installed facing in the correct direction. Make sure the oil holes line up with those in the block and that the upper shell (grooved) on #3 main bearing is located in the block (rather than in the cap) on the 2.2 and 2.5L engines. Torque to specifications.

8. With the engine out of the car. Remove the intake manifold, cylinder head, front cover, timing gears and/or chain, oil pan, oil pump and flywheel.

9. Remove the piston and rod assemblies. Remove the main bearing caps after marking them for position and direction.

10. Remove the crankshaft bearing inserts and rear main oil seal. Clean the engine block and cap bearing saddles. Clean the crankshaft and inspect for wear. Check the bearing journals with a micrometer for out-of-round condition and to determine what size rod and main bearing inserts to install.

11. Install the main bearing upper inserts and rear main oil seal half (2.2 and 2.5L engines only) into the engine block.

12. Lubricate the bearing inserts and the crankshaft journals. Slowly and carefully lower the crankshaft into position.

13. On the 2.2 and 2.5L engines, install the

bearing inserts and rear main seal into the bearing caps, and install the caps from the middle out. Check the cap bolts for "necking down". This is a condition that would prevent the right size nut from being run down until it touches the cap or would cause some threads not to touch a straightedge run along the side of the bolt. Replace if necessary. Torque cap bolts to specifications alternately, in stages.

On the 2.6 liter engine, install the main caps in numbered sequence, No. 1 nearest the timing chain and No. 5 at the transmission end. Make sure the arrows on the caps point toward the timing chain end of the engine. Torque alternately and in three stages to 58 ft.lb.

14. Remove bearing caps, one at a time, and check the oil clearance with Plastigage® (see the procedure just below). Reinstall if clearance is within specifications. Check the crankshaft end-play as described below, and if it is within specifications install connecting rod and piston assemblies with new rod bearing inserts. Check connecting rod bearing oil clearance and rod side play (see the procedure above); if these are correct, assemble the rest of the engine.

BEARING OIL CLEARANCE

1. Remove cap from the bearing to be checked. Using a clean, dry rag, thoroughly clean all oil from crankshaft journal and bearing insert.

NOTE: *Plastigage® is soluble in oil; therefore, oil on the journal or bearing could result in erroneous readings.*

2. Place a piece of Plastigage® along the full width of the insert, reinstall cap, and torque to specifications.

3. Remove bearing cap, and determine clearance by comparing width of Plastigage® to the scale on Plastigage® envelope. Journal taper is determined by comparing width of the Plastigage® strip near its ends. Rotate crankshaft 90 degrees and retest, to determine journal eccentricity.

NOTE: *Do not rotate crankshaft with Plastigage® installed.*

4. If bearing insert and journal appear intact, and are within tolerances, no further main bearing service is required. Just make sure to oil the bearing and crankshaft journal surfaces thoroughly and reassamble caps to specified torque. If bearing or journal appear defective, cause of failure should be determined before replacement.

CRANKSHAFT END-PLAY

Place a pry bar between a main bearing cap and crankshaft casting taking care not to damage any journals. Pry backward or forward and measure the distance between the thrust bearing (center main 3) and crankshaft with a feeler gauge. Compare reading with specifications. If too great a clearance is determined, a larger thrust bearing and crank machining may be required. Check with an automotive machine shop for their advice.

CRANKSHAFT REPAIRS

If a journal is damaged on the crankshaft, repair is possible by having the crankshaft machined, after removal from engine to a standard undersize. Consult the machine shop for their advice.

COMPLETING THE REBUILDING PROCESS

Fill the oil pump with oil, to prevent cavitating (sucking air) on initial engine start up. Install the oil pump and the pick-up tube on the engine. Coat the oil pan gasket as necessary, and install the gasket and the oil pan. Mount the flywheel and the crankshaft vibration damper or pulley on the crankshaft.

NOTE: *Always use new bolts when installing the flywheel. Inspect the clutch shaft pilot bushing in the crankshaft. If the bushing is excessively worn, remove it with an expanding puller and a slide hammer, and tap a new bushing into place.*

Position the engine, cylinder head side up. Lubricate the lifters, and install them into their bores. Install the cylinder head, and torque it as specified. Insert the pushrods (where applicable), and install the rocker shaft(s) (if so equipped) or position the rocker.

Install the intake and exhaust manifolds, the carburetor(s), the distributor and spark plugs. Mount all accessories and install the engine in the car. Fill the radiator with coolant, and the crankcase with high quality engine oil.

BREAK-IN PROCEDURE

Start the engine, and allow it to run at low speed for a few minutes, while checking for leaks. Stop the engine, check the oil level, and fill as necessary. Restart the engine, and fill the cooling system to capacity. Check and adjust the ignition timing. Run the engine at low to medium speed (800-2,500 rpm) for approximately ½ hour, and retorque the cylinder head bolts. Road test the car, and check again for leaks.

NOTE: *Some gasket manufacturers recommend not retorquing the cylinder head(s) due to the composition of the head gasket. Follow the directions in the gasket set.*

Flywheel and Ring Gear
REMOVAL AND INSTALLATION

The flywheel on manual transmission cars serves as the forward clutch engagement surface. It also serves as the ring gear with which the starter pinion engages to crank the engine. The most common reason to replace the flywheel is broken teeth on the starter ring gear. To remove it, remove the transmission as described in Chapter 7. Then, unbolt and remove the clutch and pressure plate. Finally, *support the flywheel in a secure manner* and then remove the eight attaching bolts and remove the flywheel.

On automatic transmission cars, the torque converter actually forms part of the flywheel. It is bolted to a thin flexplate which, in turn, is bolted to the crankshaft. The flex plate also serves as the ring gear with which the starter pinion engages in engine cranking. The flex plate occasionally cracks; the teeth on the ring gear may also break, especially if the starter is often engaged while the pinion is still spinning. The torque converter and flex plate are separated so the converter and transmission can be removed together. Remove the automatic transaxle as described in Chapter 7. Then, remove the attaching bolts and remove the flexplate from the flywheel.

Install the flywheel in reverse order, torquing the flywheel-to-crankshaft mounting bolts as follows:

- All transaxles, 1986-88 – 70 ft.lb.
- Automatic transaxles, 1981-85 – 65 ft.lb.
- Manual transaxles, 1984-86 – 65 ft.lb.
- Manual transaxles, 198183 – 50 ft.lb.

When the flywheel or flexplate is back in position, reinstall the transmission as described in Chapter 7.

Exhaust Pipes, Mufflers, and Tailpipes

For a number of different reasons, exhaust system work can be the most dangerous type of work you can do on your car. *Always observe the following precautions:*

1. Support the car extra securely. Not only will you often be working directly under it, but you'll frequently be using a lot of force – say, heavy hammer blows, to dislodge rusted parts. This can cause a car that's improperly supported to shift and possibly fall.

2. Wear goggles. Exhaust system parts are always rusty. Metal chips can be dislodged, even when you're only turning rusted bolts. Attempting to pry pipes apart with a chisel makes chips fly even more frequently.

3. If you're using a cutting torch, keep it at a great distance from either the fuel tank or lines. Stop what you're doing and feel the temperature of fuel bearing pipes or the tank frequently. Even slight heat can expand or vaporize the fuel, resulting in accumulated vapor or even a liquid leak near your torch.

4. Watch where your hammer blows fall. You could easily tap a brake or fuel line when you hit an exhaust system part with a galncing blow. Inspect all lines and hoses in the area where you've been working before driving the car.

Special Tools

A number of special exhaust system tools can be rented from auto supply houses or local stores that rent special equipment. A common one is a tail pipe expander, designed to enable you to join pipes of identical diameter.

It may also be quite helpful to use solvents designed to loosen rusted bolts or flanges. Soaking rusted parts the night before you do the job can speed the work of freeing rusted parts considerably. Remember that these solvents are often flammable. Apply them only after the parts are cool.

Note that a special flexible coupling is used to connect the exhaust pipe to the exhaust manifold. If this important coupling should develop a leak, be sure to replace the seal ring with a quality part, install it in the proper direction, and torque the bolts to specifications. Check also for any cracks in the exhaust pipe, exhaust manifold, or flanges and replace such parts as necessary.

REMOVAL AND INSTALLATION

1. Support the vehicle securely. Apply penetrating oil to all clamp bolts and nuts you will be working on. Support the vehicle by the body, if

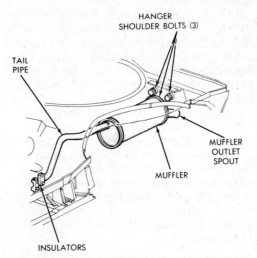

Typical tailpipe and muffler

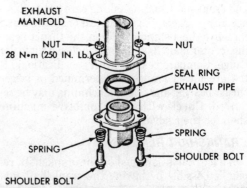

The special exhaust joint coupling is used to allow the engine to move without stressing or cracking exhaust system components

possible, to increase working clearances.

2. If the tailpipe is integral with the muffler, and the muffler must be replaced, cut the tail pipe with a hacksaw right near the front of the muffler. The replacement muffler is then installed using a clamp to attach to the tailpipe.

3. Loosen clamps and supports to permit alignment of all parts, and then retighten. Make sure there is adequate clearance so exhaust parts stay clear of underbody parts.

4. Clean the mating surfaces of pipes or the muffler to ensure a tight seal. Use new insulators, clamps, and supports unless the condition of old parts is very good. Note that the slip joint at the front of the muffler uses a U-clamp. The bolts should be torqued to 270 in. lbs. on cars with normally aspirated engines and to 360 in. lbs. on turbocharged cars.

Emission Controls

EMISSION CONTROL SYSTEMS

Crankcase Ventilation System
OPERATION

The PCV system is used to draw the incompletely burned fuel/air mixture that passes the piston rings and valve guides out of the crankcase and valve cover. This mixture contains a great deal of unburnt hydrocarbons. The PCV system conducts it to the engine's air intake system for burning with the fresh mixture in the combustion chambers. In this way, total emissions of unburnt fuel are greatly reduced.

The system's PCV "Positive Crankcase Ventilation" valve is connected, via a short hose, to the intake manifold on normally aspirated engines, and to the intake side of the turbocharger on turbocharged cars. The PCV valve itself controls total flow to the system so that, regardless of engine intake vacuum, a stable amount of air will enter the system.

The Chrysler system is unique in that it draws fresh air into the PCV circuit without passing it through the engine crankcase. Fresh air is mixed with the blowby being handled by the system at low rpm, when vacuum is high

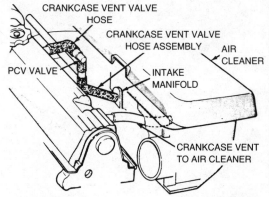

The PCV system used on cars with Throttle Body fuel injection

and blowby minimal. This mixing occurs at the PCV module on carbureted cars. On fuel injected and injected turbo cars, the mixing occurs near the PCV valve or in the top of the valve cover. A filter in the PCV module or air cleaner filters fresh air so that dust will not enter the engine's intake system.

The carburetor or fuel injection system is precisely calibrated to compensate for the extra air the system introduces into the engine's combustion chambers. At the same time, because of the high vacuum the system operates under, the potential exists for it to bleed a great deal of excess air into the system and disturb the mixture. If the engine runs poorly, especially at idle speeds (when vacuum is highest), inspect the PCV system thoroughly for leaks and the PCV valve for clogging or sticking. It may have clogged, failing partly open, so that too much excess air will enter the system causing lean operation.

Since the PCV system removes vapors from the crankcase that, if left there, could condense and contribute significantly to engine wear, effective maintenance can improve both engine

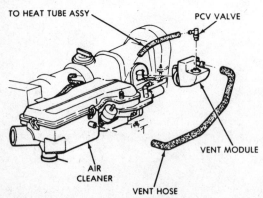

The PCV system used on carbureted cars

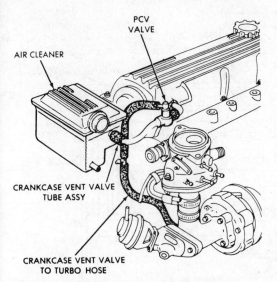

The PCV system used on Turbo I cars

performance and longevity. If there are otherwise unexplained oil leaks through seals or if crankcase vapors are expelled into the engine compartment, check the system for clogged hoses or a PCV valve that is stuck shut or clogged. See Chapter 1 for basic maintenance and PCV valve tests.

Evaporation Control System

This system prevents the release of gasoline vapors from the fuel tank and the carburetor into the atmosphere. It is vacuum operated and draws the fumes into a charcoal canister where they are temporarily held until they are drawn into the intake manifold for burning.

The canister is a sealed, maintenance-free device located in the wheelwell. It is fed from the fuel tank and the carburetor float bowl. When the engine starts, air pump pressure closes off the connection to the carburetor fuel bowl. On

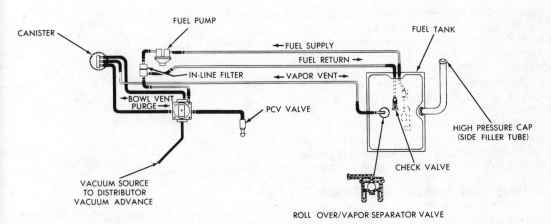

Evaporation control system—2.2L engine

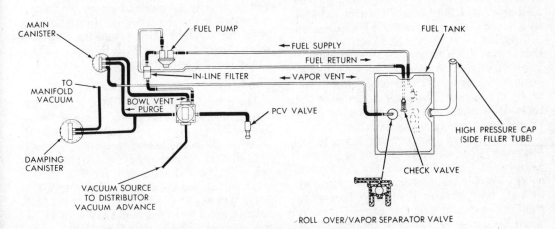

Evaporation control system—2.6L engine

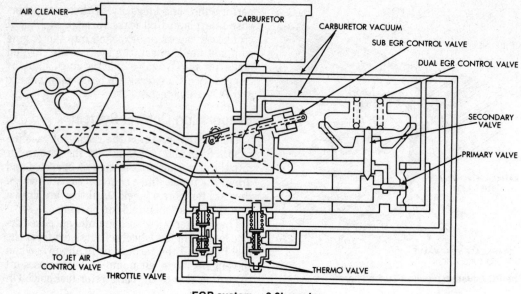

AIR CLEANER

CARBURETOR

CARBURETOR VACUUM

SUB EGR CONTROL VALVE

DUAL EGR CONTROL VALVE

SECONDARY VALVE

PRIMARY VALVE

TO JET AIR CONTROL VALVE

THROTTLE VALVE

THERMO VALVE

EGR system—2.6L engine

most models, an electric solenoid known as a "purge solenoid" opens when the engine temperature exceeds 145°F. This applies manifold vacuum to the canister to draw the stored fuel vapor out of the charcoal element inside.

For proper operation of the system and to prevent gas tank failure, the lines should be cleaned if they should become plugged, and no cap other than the one specified should be used on the fuel tank filler neck. A special fuel-resistant hose is used. If any hoses need replacing, be sure to use hose rated for this type of service.

Exhaust Gas Recirculation System

This system reduces the amount of oxides of nitrogen in the exhaust by allowing a predetermined amount of exhaust gases to recirculate and dilute the incoming fuel/air mixture. The principal components of the system are the EGR valve and the Coolant Control Exhaust Gas Recirculation Valve (CCEGR) used on 1981-86 models or the Coolant Vacuum Switch Cold Closed (CVSCC) used on 1986-88 models. The EGR valve is located in the intake manifold and directly regulates the flow of exhaust gasses into the intake. The latter is located in the thermostat housing and overrides the EGR valve when coolant temperature is below 125°F.

Exhaust system backpressure tends to increase the rate at which the EGR valve flows exhaust gas back into the engine. For this reason, on fuel injected and turbocharged engines, an Exhaust Backpressure Transducer is used to regulate the vacuum that opens the EGR valve. When backpressure increases, the transducer will decrease vacuum in such a way that the

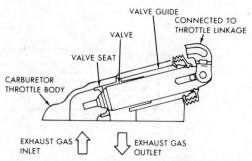

VALVE GUIDE

CONNECTED TO THROTTLE LINKAGE

VALVE

VALVE SEAT

CARBURETOR THROTTLE BODY

EXHAUST GAS INLET

EXHAUST GAS OUTLET

Sub EGR control valve

valve opening will be reduced and gas flow rate will remain correct in spite of that backpressure increase.

2.6 L engines use a Sub EGR Control Valve. This valve is an integral part of the carburetor, and is directly opened and closed by linkage connected to the throttle valve. In conjunction with the standard EGR system the sub EGR more closely modulates EGR flow in response to the throttle valve opening.

TESTING

The symptoms of possible EGR system failure include: spark knock, engine sag or severe hesitation on acceleration, or rough idle or stalling. Check the following items:

1. Start the engine and allow it to idle in neutral with the throttle closed, for over 70 seconds. Abruptly accelerate the engine to 2,000-3,000 rpm as you watch the groove in the EGR valve stem. The stem should move visibly. If not, proceed with the tests that follow.

2. Inspect all vacuum hose connections be-

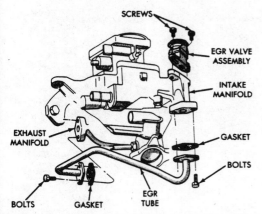

EGR valve mounting for Throttle Body fuel injected engines

REMOVAL AND INSTALLATION
EGR Valve

1. Disconnect the vacuum line going to the EGR valve. Inspect it for cracking, poor seal due to hardness, or other problems and replace if necessary.

2. Remove the two bolts attaching the EGR valve to the intake manifold. Remove the EGR valve.

3. Clean both gasket surfaces and check for cracks. Replace parts as necessary.

4. Install a new gasket and the EGR valve onto the manifold. Install the two attaching bolts and torque to 200 in. lbs. Reconnect the vacuum line.

EGR Tube

1. Remove the four EGR tube attaching bolts from the intake and exhaust manifold connections. Remove the EGR tube.

2. Clean all four gasket surfaces. Inspect gasket surfaces for signs of cracking and replace the EGR tube or manifolds if cracking is found. Discard old gaskets and supply new ones.

3. Assemble the tube and gaskets into place, installing the attaching bolts only loosely.

4. Torque the attaching bolts to 200 in. lbs.

Oxygen Sensor
OPERATION

The oxygen sensor's tip is located in the exhaust stream. When the tip reaches a certain temperature, it reacts with the oxygen in the mixture to produce an output voltage which rises as the oxygen content drops (rich mixture) and drops as the oxygen content increases (lean mixture). This voltage is conducted to the SMEC (Single Module Engine Controller) or SCC (Spark Control Computer). The SMEC or SCC, in turn, influences the mixture being produced by the injection system or carburetor.

If the engine exhibits high hydrocarbon and carbon monoxide emissions in a test required for local licensing, this may indicate that the oxygen sensor is at fault. The sensor may also fail in a lean mode, which would produce low emissions but slightly lean running so that engine operation would be just slightly rough. The sensor should be replaced at 52,500 miles as a matter of routine maintenance. If the sensor may be reinstalled, an anti-seize compound such as Loctite 771-64® will be needed.

REMOVAL AND INSTALLATION

NOTE: *To remove the oxygen sensor, a special removal tool is needed. There are two types of sensors — standard and heated. Heated sensors have a multi-prong electrical ter-*

tween the carburetor/throttle body, intake manifold, and vacuum transducer. All connections and hoses must be leak-free. Replace hoses that are hardened, melted or cracked. Inspect the vacuum passage in the carburetor body or throttle body. If necessary, remove the assembly from the engine and clean it.

3. Connect a hand operated vacuum pump or other confirmed source of vacuum that can be valved to the EGR valve vacuum motor, via rubber hose connections. Tee a vacuum gauge into the line, if you are not using a pump equipped with a vacuum gauge. Have the engine running at normal operating temperature and normal idle speed. Apply vacuum as you read the vacuum gauge. Listen to the engine as you gradually increase vacuum. The engine speed should begin to drop as vacuum reaches 2.0-2.5 in.Hg. The engine may stumble or even stall. This means exhaust gas is flowing through the system the way it is supposed to. If a separate vacuum supply has no effect on engine speed or smoothness, repeat the test, watching the EGR valve stem. If the stem does not move, it will probably be necessary to replace the EGR valve. Unless the stem has been frozen in place by deposits and can be freed up, replace the valve. If the stem moves, but there is no effect on engine operation, clean the EGR system passages — they are clogged.

4. If the EGR system recycles too much exhaust and the system idles roughly, try idling the engine with the EGR valve vacuum line disconnected and plugged. If this has little or no effect, try removing the EGR valve/transducer and inspecting it to make sure the EGR valve poppet is seated. If it will not seat, replace the valve.

5. Check also for an EGR tube-to-manifold leak. On 2.2 and 2.5L engines, torque the EGR tube-to-manifold nut to 300 in. lbs.

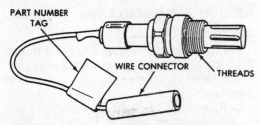

Standard oxygen sensor without terminal boot or heating, used on carbureted or throttle body injected engines without turbocharging

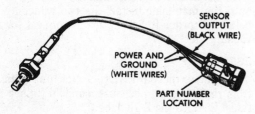

Heated oxygen sensor, which incorporates a three-wire connector

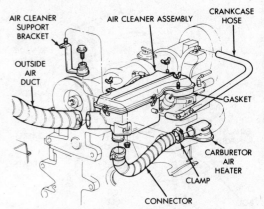

Heated inlet air system—2.2L engine

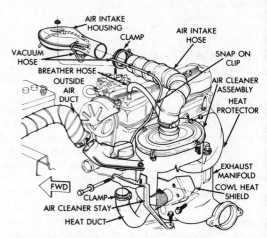

Heated inlet air system—2.6L engine

minal with three wires, and standard sensors have only a single wire connector. For standard sensors, use tool C-4589 or an equivalent from the aftermarket; for heated sensors, use C-4907 or equivalent. It is necessary to be able to adapt this tool to a torque wrench. Also needed is a tap to clean the sensor mounting threads. The dimensions are: 18mm x 1.5 x 6E.

1. Make sure the engine has been turned off for several hours so all parts will have cooled sufficiently for safe handling. *Pulling on the plug and not the wiring*, disconnect the oxygen sensor electrical lead.

2. Install the special tool and unscrew the sensor from the exhaust manifold.

3. Turn the tap into the sensor threads to chase any corrosion or dirt out.

4. If installing a new sensor, make sure to get the proper replacement parts. Sensors used with turbo cars have a terminal boot not used on other sensors. As previously mentioned, 1988 models use a heated sensor with a multi-prong plug.

5. If the sensor is to be reinstalled, coat the threads with the anti-seize compound. Turn the sensor into the threads and torque it to 20 ft.lb.

6. Reconnect the electrical connector securely.

Heated Air Inlet System
OPERATION

All carbureted and Throttle Body injected engines are equipped with a vacuum device locat-ed in the air cleaner air intake. A small door is operated by a vacuum diaphragm and a thermostatic spring. When the air temperature outside is 65°F or lower on carbureted engines, or 115°F or lower on throttle body injected engines, the door will block off air entering from outside and allow air channeled from the exhaust manifold area to enter the intake. This air is heated by the hot manifold. At 90°F or above on carbureted engines and 140°F or above on TBI engines, the door fully blocks off the heated air. At temperatures in between, the door is operated in intermediate positions. During heavy acceleration the door is controlled by engine vacuum to allow the maximum amount of air to enter the carburetor.

This system is critically important to the operation of carbureted and throttle body injected cars because, when the carburetor or throttle body handles cold air, mixture calibration will become incorrect (too lean). The result will be lean running (misfire and hesitation). Engine performance will deteriorate even more during warmup in cold weather. The carburetor will

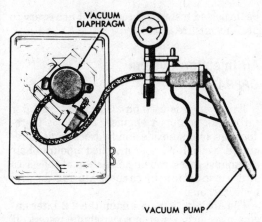

Testing the heated air system vacuum diaphragm

also be more likely to ice up in cool, damp weather. There may also be high emissions of hydrocarbons, as revealed by emissions testing.

TESTING

NOTE: *You'll need a hand vacuum pump or other source of measurable vacuum for this test.*

1. Remove the air cleaner from the engine and allow it to cool to 65°F on carbureted engines and 115°F (or below) on fuel injected engines.

2. Inspect all the vacuum lines associated with the system and replace them if they are cracked or broken or if they do not seal tightly at the connections.

3. Apply 20 in. Hg of vacuum to the inlet side of the temperature sensor, a small round device with two vacuum ports, one of which was connected to the intake manifold. Apply the vacuum to the port that was connected to the manifold. Observe the temperature door—it should close.

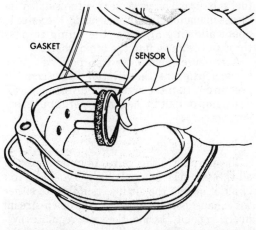

Replacing the air temperature sensor—heated air intake system

4. If the door remains open, connect the vacuum source to the vacuum diaphragm on the temperature door. The door should close and then retest the system.

5. If the door now closes, replace the temperature sensor. If the door still does not close, replace the air cleaner, as the temperature door vacuum diaphragm and door are integral parts of it.

REMOVAL AND INSTALLATION

Temperature Sensor

1. Remove the air cleaner. Note routing and then disconnect both vacuum hoses from the sensor.

2. Pry the retaining clips off the sensor connections and discard them. Pull the sensor and gasket out of the wall of the air cleaner.

3. Install the new sensor and gasket and fasten the sensor in place by forcing the new retaining clips all the way onto the vacuum connectors. Make sure to hold the sensor against the air cleaner by its outside diameter as you install the clips so as to compress the gasket.

4. Reconnect the vacuum hoses securely and reinstall the air cleaner.

Catalytic Converter

OPERATION

Two catalysts are used on each car on model years through 1985. On dual catalyst systems, a small one located just after the exhaust manifold ignites early in the engine warm-up cycle, and a larger one located under the car body completes the clean-up process during warmed-up operation of the car. Catalysts promote complete oxidation of exhaust gases through the effect of a platinum and palladium coated mass in the catalyst shell. Three-way catalysts combine oxidation (normal burning) of the fuel with reduction—the removal of oxygen from Nitrogen Oxides. The platinum and palladium are noble metals which accelerate combustion by providing chemical entities necessary for complete burning after nearly all the energy and chemical activity in the mixture are depleted. After the combustion process is completed, the material returns to the noble metal coating; the catalytic converter has the theoretical potential to last indefinitely. If the unit should be damaged, it must be replaced—no service is possible.

1986-88 models employ a 3-way catalyst. Two converters, working under different fuel/air mixture conditions are used. The first catalyst is fed exhaust from the engine that is at the chemically correct mixture ratio of 14.7:1. At this point, the exhaust gases contain oxygen that has combined with the nitrogen in the air to form nitrogen oxides (a pollutant); and un-

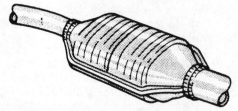

An underfloor catalytic converter. Note that the entire unit is sealed.

burnt (or oxygen-short) hydrocarbons and carbon monoxide (another pollutant). This converter creates conditions which cause the oxygen in the nitrogen oxides to combine with the unburnt material. This is called "reduction" of the nitrogen oxides. Once the nitrogen oxides have been reduced, the air pump adds extra air (and oxygen). The second converter uses this extra oxygen to complete the job of oxidizing the unburnt material.

Two things act to destroy the catalyst: the use of leaded gas and excessive heat. The use of leaded fuel is the most common cause of catalyst destruction. The lead coats the thin layer of platinum and palladium that actually promotes final combustion of the almost completely burned hydrocarbons that enter the catalytic converter. The coating keeps the mixture from actually contacting the noble metals. The lead may also cause the "substrate"—the material that carries the noble metal coating to clog the passages of the converter, causing the car to run at reduced power or even stop altogether.

The catalyst is fed fuel/air mixture in its least potent form—when combustion is almost 100% complete and nearly all energy has been removed. Excessive heat results in the converter when raw fuel and air with a high oxygen content enter the catalytic converter—a device which greatly accelerates the combustion process. This most often occurs when a spark plug wire is disconnected. Excessive heat during misfiring due to poor vehicle maintenance and prolonged testing with the ignition system wires disconnected are two common ways a catalyst may be rendered ineffective. Test procedures should be accomplished as quickly as possible. The car should be shut off whenever misfiring is noted. Misfiring due to extremely lean or extremely rich mixtures will also damage the catalyst.

While the catalyst itself is a maintenance-free item, it should be understood that long life depends completely on proper fueling and good maintenance. The car should be tuned as required, and fuel and air filters and the oxygen sensor should be changed as specified in the maintenance chart in Chapter One. Ignition wires and the distributor cap and rotor should be inspected/tested and replaced if necessary to prevent misfire.

Air Injection System
OPERATION

This system is used on all 1981-87 2.2 Liter carburetor-equipped engines. Its job is to reduce carbon monoxide and hydrocarbons to required levels. It adds a controlled amount of air to exhaust gases, causing oxidation of the gases and a reduction in carbon monoxide and hydrocarbons.

The air injection system on the 2.2 Liter engine also includes an air switching system. It has been designed so that air injection will not interfere with the EGR system to control NOx emissions, and on vehicles equipped with an oxygen sensor, to insure proper air-fuel distribution for maximum fuel economy.

The vehicles produced for sale in the 50 states pump air into the base of the exhaust manifold and into the catalytic converter body. The Canadian system pumps air through the head at the exhaust port.

The air injection system consists of a belt-driven air pump, a diverter valve (Canadian engines only) a switch-relief valve, rubber hoses, and check valve tube assemblies to protect the hoses and other components from high temperature exhaust gases in case the air pump fails.

Diverter Valve

The purpose of the diverter valve is to prevent backfire in the exhaust system during sudden deceleration. Sudden throttle closure at the beginning of deceleration temporarily creates an air-fuel mixture too rich to burn. This mixture becomes burnable when it reaches the exhaust area and combines with injector air. The next firing of the cylinder will ignite this air-fuel mixture. The valve senses the sudden increase in manifold vacuum, causing the valve to open, allowing air from the pump to pass through the valve into the atmosphere.

A pressure relief valve incorporated in the same housing as the diverter valve controls pressure within the system by diverting excessive pump output to the atmosphere at high engine speed.

Switch-Relief Valve

The purpose of this valve, an integral part of all U.S. air injection systems, is two-fold. First of all, it directs the air injection flow to either the exhaust port location or to the down-stream injection point. Second, the valve regulates system pressure by controlling the output of the air pump at high speeds. When the pressure reaches a certain level, some of the output is vented to the atmosphere through the silencer.

Check Valve

A check valve is located in the injection tube assemblies that lead to the exhaust manifold and the catalyst injection points on the 50 state engines and to the exhaust port area, through four hollow bolts on the Canadian engines.

This valve has a one-way diaphragm which prevents hot exhaust gases from backing up into the hose and pump. It also protects the system in the event of pump belt failure, excessively high exhaust system pressure, or air hose ruptures.

DIAGNOSIS AND TESTING

The most common problem with the air pump system is air pump noise. It first must be understood that a small amount of rattling or chirping noise comes from an air pump in perfect mechanical condition. It should also be understood that, if the air pump requires replacement, the new pump will be extra noisy until it has broken in. Operate the new pump for 1,000 miles before condemning it as noisy.

If the air pump belt suddenly becomes noisy, first check that tension is correct. If the belt is slipping, noise will often be the result. Retension the belt or, if it is glazed (with smooth, glassy wear surfaces), replace it, making sure to tension the new belt properly and to readjust it a week or two later.

Check also that the pump rotates freely by removing the belt and turning the pump drive pulley by hand. There is normally some slight roughness and rattling when turning the drive pulley. A frozen pump's pulley will be impossible or extremely hard to turn.

If the car is in generally good tune and mechanical condition, and runs well but exhibits high CO and hydrocarbon emissions, the air pump system may not be supplying air to the catalytic converter (or exhaust manifold on Canadian cars). In this case, the best procedure is to disconnect the outlet hose passing from the switch/relief valve to the converter and check for airflow. If there is no flow at idle speed, and noticeable flow above idle speed, which increases when the engine is accelerated, the air pump system is okay and the problem may be in the oxygen sensor or fuel system. If air does not flow at this point in the system, disconnect the hose at the air pump side of the switch/relief valve and repeat the test. If there is air at this point now, and no vacuum actuating the switch/relief valve, replace it.

Check also that all hoses are free of cracks, breaks and clogs and that they are tightly and fully connected.

AIR PUMP REMOVAL AND INSTALLATION

1. Disconnect the hoses at the air pump and. Disconnect the air and vacuum hoses at the switch/relief valve.

2. Remove the air pump drive pulley shield from the engine.

3. Loosen the air pump pivot and and adjusting bolts and remove the air pump drive belt.

4. Remove the air pump attaching bolts and

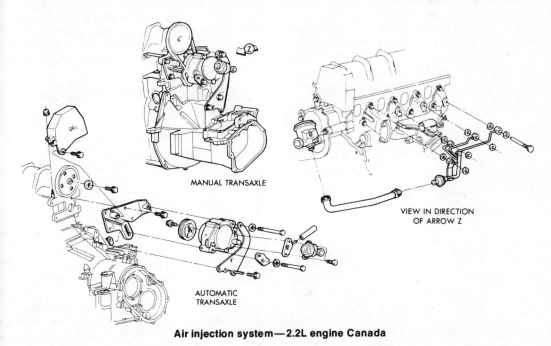

MANUAL TRANSAXLE

VIEW IN DIRECTION
OF ARROW Z

AUTOMATIC
TRANSAXLE

Air injection system—2.2L engine Canada

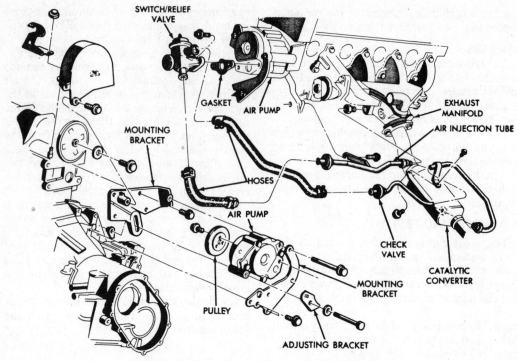

1985–87 air pump arrangement—carbureted 2.2 L engine

remove the pump and switch/relief valve as an assembly.

5. Remove the switch/relief valve and gasket from the pump. Clean both gasket surfaces. Install a new gasket and the relief valve and torque the mounting bolts to 125 in. lbs.

6. Install the drive pulley on the new air pump and torque the mounting bolt to 12 in. lbs. or less.

7. Position the air pump onto the engine and install the mounting bolts loosely. Loosen the bolts attaching the rear air pump bracket to the transmission housing.

8. Install the drive belt onto the air pump drive pulley. Then apply torque with a torque wrench to the adjusting bracket. Use 80-100 ft.lb. to obtain proper tension. *Do not apply force to the pump body!* Hold this figure and tighten the bracket-to-transmission bolts (maximum— 40 ft.lb.).

Pulse Air Feeder System

OPERATION

2.6 Liter Engines

Pulse Air Feeder (PAF) is used for supplying secondary air into the exhaust system between the front and rear catalytic converters, for the purpose of promoting oxidation of exhaust emissions in the rear converter.

The PAF consists of a main reed valve and a sub reed valve. The main reed valve is actuated in response to movement of a diaphragm, which is activated by pressure generated when the piston is in the compression stroke. The sub reed valve is opened on the exhaust stroke.

SYSTEM INSPECTION

To inspect the system, remove the hose connected to the air cleaner and check for vacuum, with the engine running. If vacuum is not present, check the lines for leaks and evidence of oil leaks. Periodic maintenance of this system is not required.

Air Aspiration System

OPERATION

Some 1983-88 cars with the 2.2 and 2.5L engines use an air aspiration system in place of an air pump. This system operates off the pulses generated in the exhaust system when the exhaust valves open and close. Canadian carbureted engines and U.S. 50 States Throttle Body Injection engines are the most common applications.

INSPECTION AND TESTING

The most common part of this system to fail is the aspirator valve. Symptoms of failure are excessive exhaust system noise under the hood at idle speed and hardening of the rubber hose leading from the valve to the air cleaner.

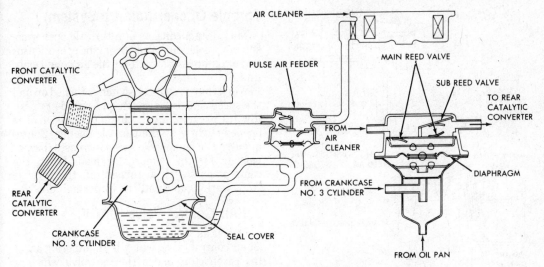

Pulse air feeder system 2.6L engine

To determine whether or not the system has failed, disconnect the aspirator system intake hose from the at the air cleaner. Start the engine and allow it to idle in neutral.

CAUTION: *Hot exhaust gases may be emitted from the system if the valve has failed.*

Cautiously and gradually place your hand near the open end of the aspirator system intake hose. If the valve is operating, the system will be drawing in fresh air, the area around the valve will be cool and you will be able to feel pulses when you touch the open end of the inlet. If the valve has failed, there will be no pulses that can be felt and hot exhaust gas will be emitted.

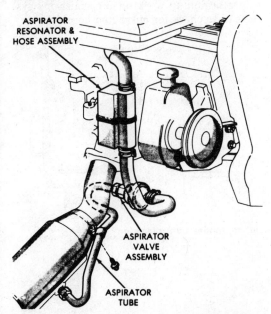

The air aspiration system used with Throttle Body Injection

REMOVAL AND INSTALLATION

The aspirator tube and aspirator valve must be replaced as an assembly. To replace, loosen the hose clamp and disconnect the intake hose at the intake side of the aspirator valve. Then, remove the aspirator tube bracket screw at the converter, unscrew the flared connector collar nut at the converter and remove the assembly.

Install a new tube in reverse order, torquing the flare nut to 40 ft.lb. Tighten all hose clamps securely.

Deceleration Spark Advance System

The deceleration spark advance system consists of a solenoid valve and an engine speed sensor. During vehicle deceleration, ignition timing is advanced by intake manifold vacuum acting on the distributor advance through the solenoid valve. However, when the engine speed sensor detects engine speed at or below 1,300 rpm the vacuum acting on the vacuum advance

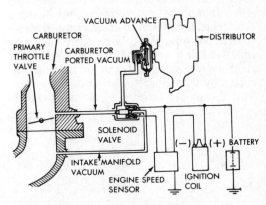

Deceleration spark advance system

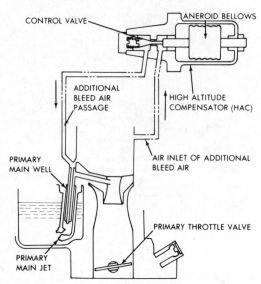

High altitude compensation system

is changed from the intake manifold to carburetor ported vacuum. This is performed by the movement of the Decel Spark Advance System Solenoid Valve in order to maintain smooth vehicle operation.

High Altitude Compensation System

A high altitude compensation system is installed on California vehicles. This modification affects the primary metering system as follows:

A small cylindrical bellows chamber mounted on the body panel in the engine compartment and connected to the carburetor with hoses, is vented to the atmosphere at the top of the carburetor. Atmospheric pressure expands and contracts the bellows.

A small brass tapered-seat valve regulates air flow when it is raised off its seat by expanding the bellows.

If the car travels to a mountainous area, rarefied atmosphere is encountered, producing a rich airfuel mixture. At a predetermined atmospheric pressure, the bellows opens, allowing additional air to enter the main air bleeds. The auxiliary air, along with the air normally inducted by the carburetor provides the system with the proper amount of air necessary to maintain the correct air/fuel mixture.

Throttle Opener (Idle-Up System)

This system consists of a throttle opener assembly, a solenoid valve, an engine speed sensor and a compressor switch for the air conditioner unit.

When the compressor switch is turned on and the speed sensor detects engine speed at or below its present level, the solenoid valve is opened slightly by the throttle opener. Consequently, the engine idle speed increases to compensate for the compressor load. When the compressor switch is turned off, the throttle stops working and returns to normal idle.

Jet Air Control Valve (JACV)

The jet air control valve system consists of a jet air control valve, which is an integral part of the carburetor, and a thermo-valve which is controlled by coolant temperature. Its purpose is to help decrease hydrocarbons and carbon monoxide during engine warm-up while the choke is operating.

Carburetor vacuum opens the valve thereby allowing air to flow into the jet air passage preventing an overly rich air-fuel mixture. There is also a thermo-valve in the system. The function of the thermo-valve is to stop jet valve operation when the coolant temperature is above or below a pre-set value.

Emission Control Hose Routing

Where available, the vacuum hose routing diagrams for the emission systems on your car are reproduced here so that you can study them before beginning work on the emissions systems or to check for misrouted hoses.

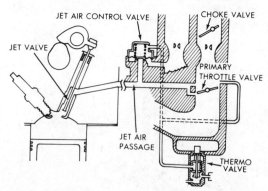

Jet air volume control system

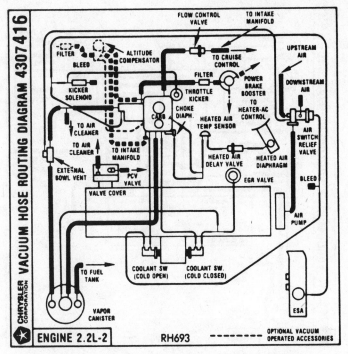

Emissions system hose routing—1984 2.2 L Federal

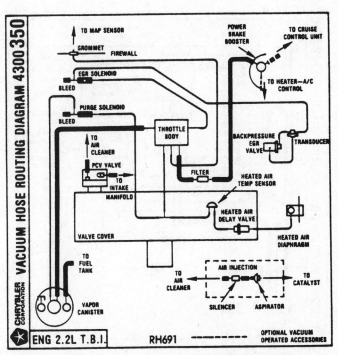

Emissions system hose routing—1984 2.2 L EFI

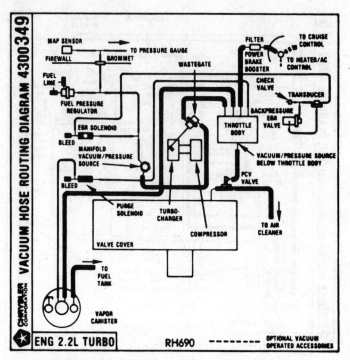

Emissions system hose routing—1984 2.2 L Turbo

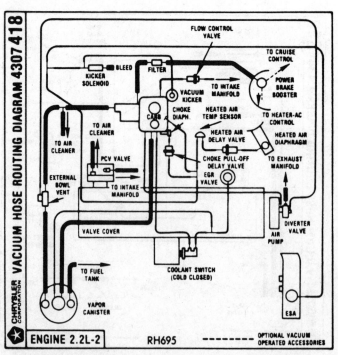

Emissions system hose routing—1984 2.2 L Canada

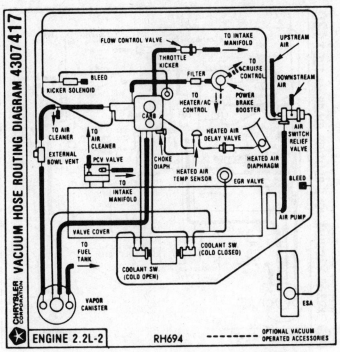

Emissions system hose routing—1984 2.2 L California

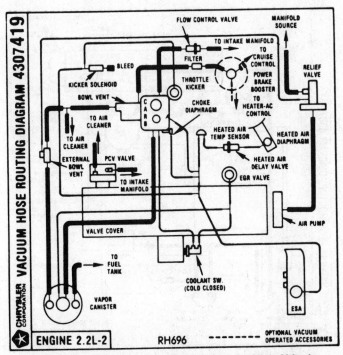

Emissions system hose routing—1984 2.2 L High Altitude

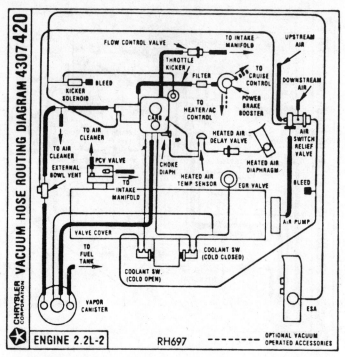

Emissions system hose routing—1984 Z28 Federal and Canada

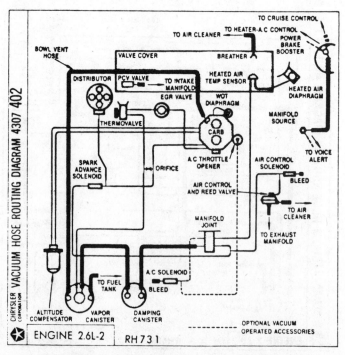

Emissions system hose routing—1984 2.6 L Federal

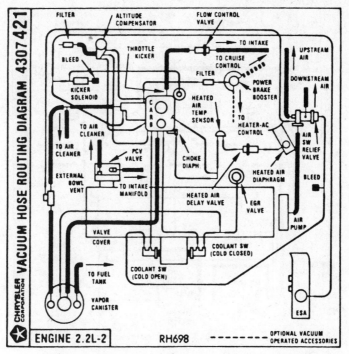

Emissions system hose routing—1984 Z28 California

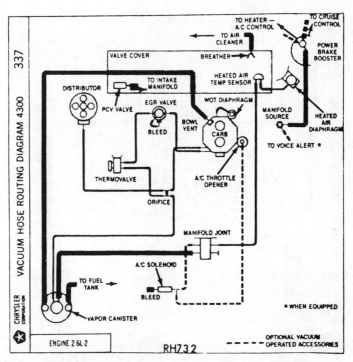

Emissions system hose routing—1984 2.6 L Canada

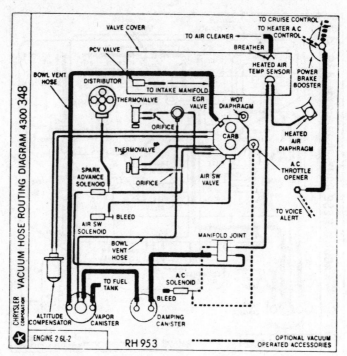

Emissions system hose routing—1984 2.6 L California

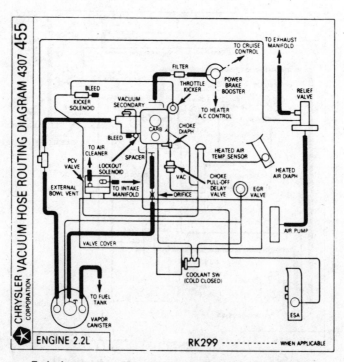

Emissions system hose routing—1985 2.2 L K-car Canada

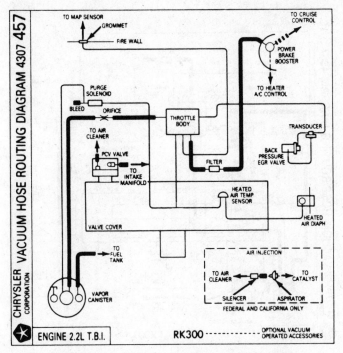

Emissions system hose routing—1985 2.2 L EFI

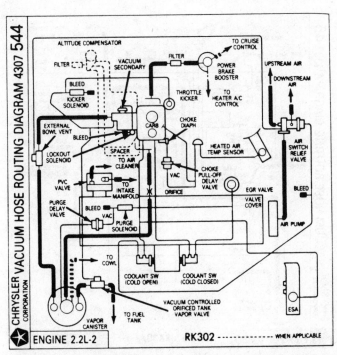

Emissions system hose routing—1985 2.2 L Carbureted Federal

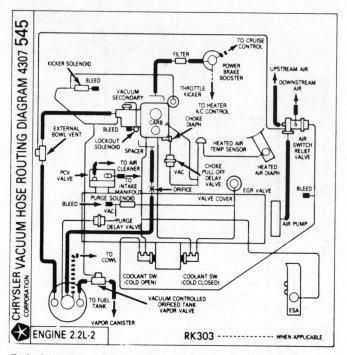

Emissions system hose routing—1985 2.2 L Carbureted California

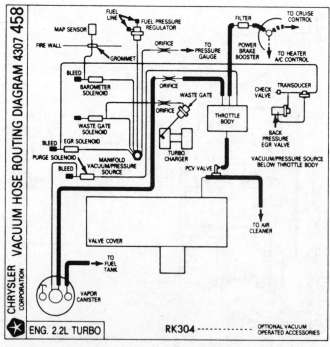

Emissions system hose routing—1985 2.2 L Turbo

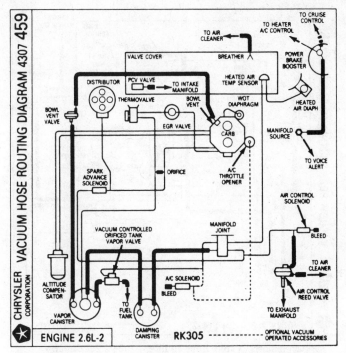

Emissions system hose routing—1985 2.6 L Federal

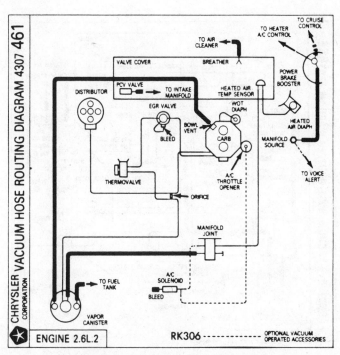

Emissions system hose routing—1985 2.6 L Canada

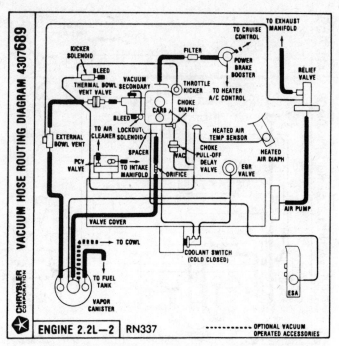

Emissions system hose routing—1986 2.2 L Canada

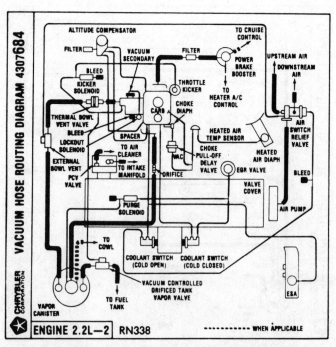

Emissions system hose routing—1986 2.2 L Federal

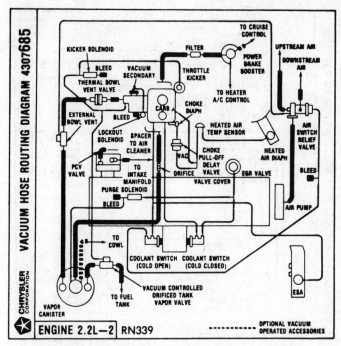

Emissions system hose routing—1986 2.2 L California

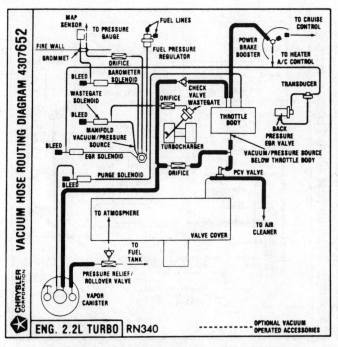

Emissions system hose routing—1986 2.2 L Turbo

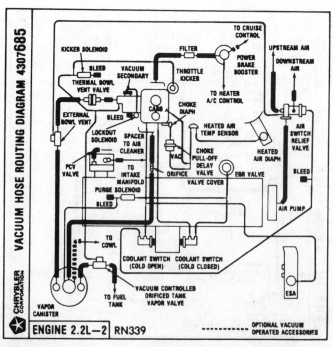

Emissions system hose routing—1986 2.2 L, 2.5 L Throttle Body EFI

Emissions system hose routing—1987 2.2 L Canadian and California engines

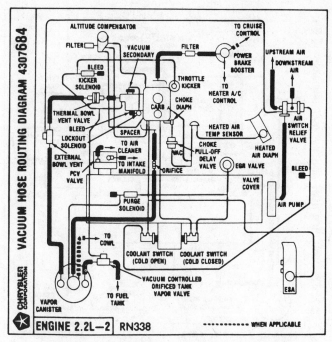

Emissions system hose routing—1987 2.2 L Federal

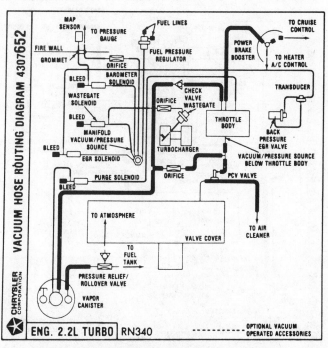

Emissions system hose routing—1987 2.2 L Turbo

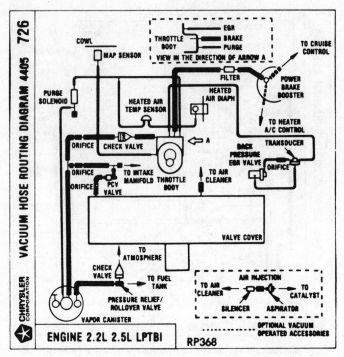

Emissions system hose routing—1987 2.2 and 2.5 L Throttle Body Injected engines

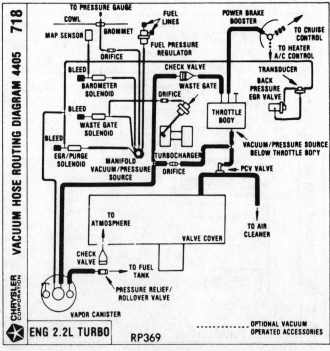

Emissions system hose routing—1987 2.2 L Turbo I

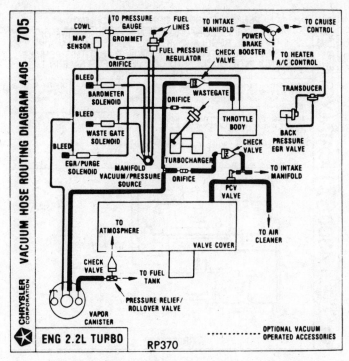

Emissions system hose routing—1987 2.2 L Turbo II

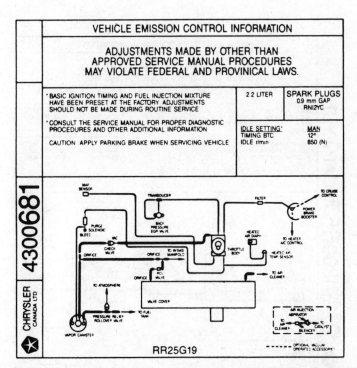

Emissions system hose routing—1988 2.2 and 2.5 L Canadian, Altitude, and Federal Throttle Body fuel injected engines

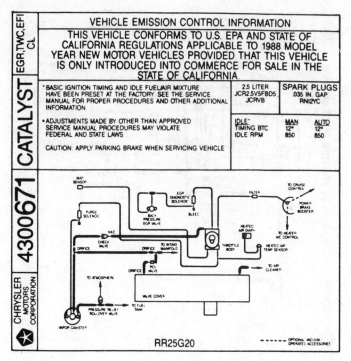

Emissions system hose routing—1988 2.2 and 2.5 L California Throttle Body fuel injected engines

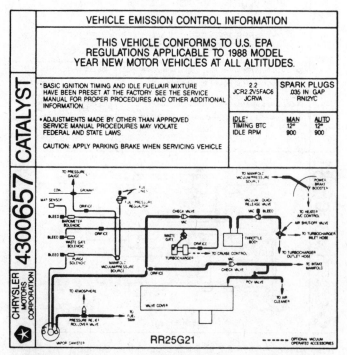

Emissions system hose routing—All 1988 2.2 L Turbo I engines

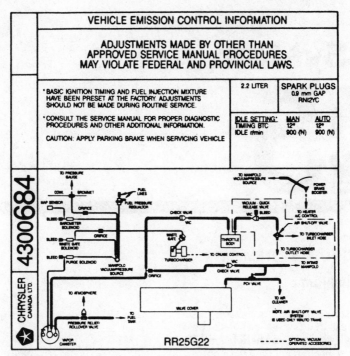

VEHICLE EMISSION CONTROL INFORMATION

**ADJUSTMENTS MADE BY OTHER THAN
APPROVED SERVICE MANUAL PROCEDURES
MAY VIOLATE FEDERAL AND PROVINCIAL LAWS.**

* BASIC IGNITION TIMING AND FUEL INJECTION MIXTURE HAVE BEEN PRESET AT THE FACTORY. ADJUSTMENTS SHOULD NOT BE MADE DURING ROUTINE SERVICE.

* CONSULT THE SERVICE MANUAL FOR PROPER DIAGNOSTIC PROCEDURES AND OTHER ADDITIONAL INFORMATION.

CAUTION: APPLY PARKING BRAKE WHEN SERVICING VEHICLE

2.2 LITER

SPARK PLUGS
0.9 mm GAP
RN12YC

IDLE SETTING*	MAN	AUTO
TIMING BTC	12°	12°
IDLE r/min	900 (N)	900 (N)

4300684

CHRYSLER CANADA LTD.

RR25G22

Emissions system hose routing—All 1988 2.2 L Turbo II engines

Fuel System

CARBURETED FUEL SYSTEM

Mechanical Fuel Pump

OPERATION

The fuel pump used with carburetor-equipped engines is located on the left side of the engine and is a mechanical type with an integral vapor separator for satisfactory hot weather performance. The pump is driven by an eccentric cam that is cast on the accessory driveshaft.

REMOVAL AND INSTALLATION

1. Make sure the battery negative cable is disconnected. Have a metal cup handy to collect any fuel that may spill.
2. Place a drain pan underneath and then remove the oil filter with a strap wrench.
3. Disconnect the fuel and vapor lines, catching fuel that spills. Dispose of fuel safely.
4. Plug the lines to prevent fuel leaks.
5. On 1987 models, remove the fuel pump

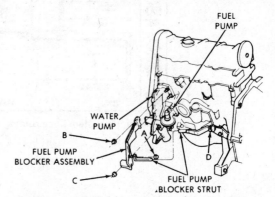

Removing/installing the fuel pump used on carbureted cars

impact blocker strut by removing the three mounting nuts and the bolt.

6. Remove the attaching bolts and remove the fuel pump.

NOTE: *The pump is not repairable. It must be replaced as a complete unit. Always use a new gasket when installing the pump and make certain that the gasket surfaces are clean.*

7. To install the pump, first position a new gasket against the block. Then, put the pump in position over the gasket with bolt holes lined up squarely. Install the bolts and torque them to 250 inch lbs.
8. Connect the fuel lines to the pump and torque the fittings to 175 inch lbs.
9. On models so-equipped, install the impact blocker strut. Install the three nuts and the bolt finger-tight. Then, refer to the illustration and torque the nuts/bolt in the order listed below to the torque listed there:
- B: 250 inch lbs.
- C: 40 ft. lbs.
- D: 75 ft. lbs.
- A: 105 inch lbs.
10. Clean the block surface, check the gasket,

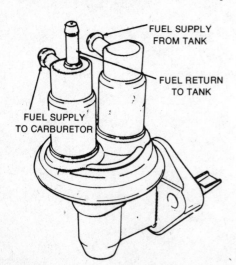

Fuel pump

and then install the oil filter, tightening it by hand only. If the gasket is damaged, replace the filter.

11. Start the engine and check for leaks. Check the crankcase oil level and refill as necessary.

TESTING

The fuel pump may be tested three different ways – for volume, vacuum and pressure. While it is best to test in all three ways, a pressure test will most often reveal a defective pump. Only if pressure meets specifications and there are still fuel supply problems is it necessary to complete all three tests.

NOTE: *To perform these tests, a pressure gauge capable of reading 1-10 psi; a vacuum gauge that will read 0-25 in.Hg; a metal container of just over 1 qt.; several plugs the right diameter for the engine's fuel lines; a watch; and a supply of new fuel hose clamps.*

1. Using a metal cup to collect spilled fuel, disconnect the fuel pump outlet hose at the bottom of the filter and plug it. Connect a pressure gauge into the line.

2. Disconnect the coil-to-distributor high tension wire so the engine won't start. Have a helper crank the engine as you watch the pressure gauge.

3. Read the gauge and compare the pressure to the range shown in the Tune-Up Specifications chart in Chapter 2. If the pressure is either too high or too low, replace the pump. If the pump passes this test and you still have doubts about its performance, proceed with the tests that follow.

4. Remove the pressure gauge from the fuel pump discharge. Disconnect the fuel pump suction line and plug it, collect any spilled fuel, and then connect a vacuum gauge to the suction side of the fuel pump.

5. Again have a helper turn the ignition key on while you watch the gauge. The fuel pump should produce a minimum of 11 in.Hg (readings may go as high as 22 in.Hg).

6. If the pump passes these tests, but there is still some question about its ability to produce adequate flow (poor high rpm full throttle performance in spite of a clean filter), proceed with the volume test.

WARNING: *This test must be performed very carefully! It is necessary to run the engine while checking the volume of flow. The potential for spilling and igniting gasoline is very great. Proceed very carefully or, if you are not sure you can perform the test safely, have it performed professionally.*

7. Make sure both fuel filters are clean.

8. Start the engine and allow it to idle a few seconds to stabilize the fuel supply to the carbu-

retor. Make sure the engine is warmed up and off the choke (at normal idle speed). Stop the engine.

9. Disconnect the fuel line at the inlet of the filter-reservoir on the carburetor. Collect any fuel that drains out and dispose of it safely.

10. Plug this line and position it so it will drain into the 1 qt. container. Start the engine and allow it to run a few seconds to stabilize the fuel supply to the carburetor. Make sure the engine is warmed up and at normal idle speed. Have a watch available so you can time the test.

11. Position the 1 qt. container under the fuel line. Pull the plug out and allow the fuel to drain into the container as the engine continues to idle. Run the engine for about 15 seconds, and then stop the engine (before the carburetor begins to run out of fuel). Connect the line to the fuel filter, start the engine, and run it for 15-20 seconds to restore full fuel level to the carburetor.

12. Then, stop the engine, and repeat Steps 10 and 11. There should be a total of four 15-second cycles in which you idle the engine on the fuel in the carburetor and drain the fuel pump output into the container. After four cycles, if the pump has moved 1 qt. or more into the container, it is okay. Otherwise, replace it, even if pressure and vacuum are satisfactory.

Carburetor

ADJUSTMENTS

Idle Adjustment
Holley 5220/6520

1. Put the transaxle in neutral and set the parking brake securely. Turn off all accessories. Allow the engine to warm up on the lowest step of the fast idle cam. Install a tachometer.

2. Make the following preparations for adjustment, depending on the year:

a. Disconnect and plug the vacuum connector at the CVSCC (Coolant Vacuum Switch Cold Closed) on 1984 and earlier engines so-equipped.

b. Pull the PCV valve out of the vent module and allow it to breathe underhood air.

c. Disconnect the oxygen feedback system test connector located on the left fender shield if working on a 6520 carburetor.

d. Disconnect the wiring from the kicker solenoid located on the left fender shield on 1986-87 models. On 1985 and earlier models so-equipped, ground the carburetor switch with a jumper wire.

3. If the tachometer indicates the rpm is not set to specifications, turn the idle speed screw, located on the top of the idle solenoid, until the correct rpm is achieved. See the underhood

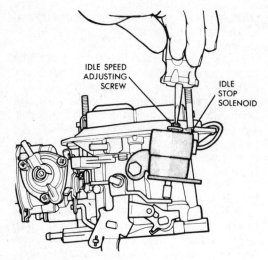

Idle set rpm adjustment

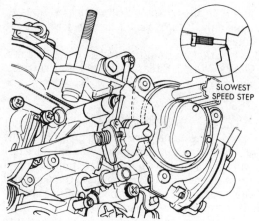

Fast idle speed adjustment

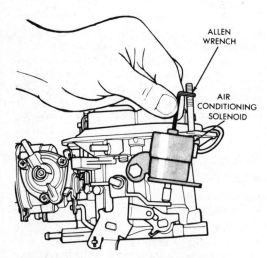

Air conditioning idle speed adjustment

sticker or the tune-up chart in Chapter 2 for correct idle speed.

4. Restore the PCV system and other vacuum and electrical connections.

Air Conditioning Idle Speed Adjustment
Holley 5220/6520

1. Turn the air conditioner on and set the blower on low. Disconnect and plug the EGR valve vacuum hose.

2. Remove the adjusting screw and spring from the top of the air conditioning solenoid.

3. Insert a ⅛" Allen wrench into the solenoid and adjust to obtain the correct idle speed as per the under hood sticker. This adjustment is required on 1981-82 models only. On later models, just verify that the A/C idle speed kicker works.

4. Make sure that the air conditioning clutch is operating during the speed adjustments.

5. Replace the adjusting screw and spring on the solenoid and turn off the air conditioner.

Fast Idle Speed Adjustment
Holley 5220/6520

1. On 1981-82 cars, disconnect the two-way electrical connector at the carburetor (red and tan wires). On all cars, disconnect the jumper wire at the radiator fan and install a jumper wire so the fan will run continuously. On 1983 and later cars: Pull the PCV valve out of the valve cover and allow it to draw underhood air; disconnect the oxygen sensor system connector located on the left fender shield near the shock tower; and ground the carburetor switch with a jumper wire.

2. Open the throttle slightly and place the adjustment screw on the slowest speed step of the fast idle cam. With the choke fully open adjust the fast idle speed to comply with the figure on the under-hood sticker. Return the vehicle to idle, then replace the adjusting screw on the slowest speed step of the fast idle cam to verify fast idle speed. Re-adjust as necessary.

3. Turn the engine off, remove the jumper wire and reconnect the fan. Reinstall the PCV valve and remove the tachometer. On 1983 and later models, reconnect the oxygen sensor system connector, and remove the jumper wire at the carburetor.

Idle Adjustment
Mikuni Carburetor (2.6L Engine)

1. Place the transaxle in neutral, set the parking brake, and turn off all accessories. Disconnect the radiator fan. Run the engine until it reaches operating temperature. On 1983 and earlier models allow the engine to idle for one minute to stabilize RPM.

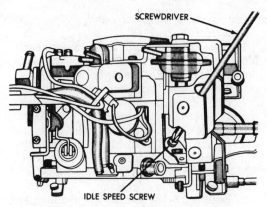

Adjusting idle speed on the Mikuni carburetor (2.6 L engine)

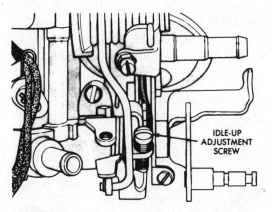

Adjusting the idle-up (air conditioner-on) on the Mikuni carburetor

2. On 1984 models, turn the engine off, and then disconnect the negative battery cable for three seconds and then reconnect it. Disconnect the engine harness lead from the O_2 sensor at the bullet connector. Don't pull on the sensor wire in doing this. Restart the engine. On 1984 and 1985 vehicles, run the engine at 2,500 rpm for 10 seconds. Then, wait two minutes before checking idle speed.

3. Check the idle speed with a tachometer. If not to specifications, on 1984-84 models, discconnect idle switch connector if the idle speed must be adjusted. Now, adjust the idle speed with the idle screw.

4. On A/C models, turn on the air conditioning with the temperature control lever set to the coldest setting. If the RPM is not 900, turn the idle-up screw to obtain this reading.

5. Turn off the engine and reconnect all connectors.

Vacuum Kick Adjustment
Holley 5220/6520

If the vacuum kick is adjusted to open the choke too far, the engine may stall or idle very

roughly just after cold start. If it is adjusted so the choke does not open enough, there may be black smoke in the exhaust.

NOTE: *To perform this procedure, you will need a source of 15 in.Hg or more. The vacuum kick diaphragm may be damaged if you attempt to retract it manually. You will also need a drill or dowel whose diameter is equivalent to the specification for Vacuum Kick in the Carburetor Specifications Chart.*

1. Remove the air cleaner. Open the throttle, close the choke and hold it in the closed position, and then release the throttle to trap the fast idle cam in the choke-closed position.

2. Disconnect the vacuum hose at the choke vacuum kick diaphragm. Connect a vacuum pump and apply 15 in.Hg or more of vacuum.

3. Gently move the choke blade toward closed position just until play is eliminated from the vacuum kick linkage (so the vacuum kick is determining choke blade position).

4. Insert the drill or dowel into the gap between the upper edge of the choke blade and the air horn wall, toward the center of the gap. The dowel or drill should just fit into the gap. If necessary, rotate the allen head screw in the center of the diaphragm housing to create the proper gap and then recheck with the measuring device.

5. Restore all vacuum connections and reinstall the air cleaner.

Mixture Adjustment

Chrysler recommends the use of a propane enrichment procedure to adjust the mixture. The equipment needed for this procedure is not readily available to the general public. The complete procedure is given, for reference purposes, in Chapter 1.

NOTE: *Mixture screws are sealed under tamperproof plugs. The only time mixture adjustments are necessary is during a major carburetor overhaul. Refer to the instructions supplied with the overhaul kit.*

Float Level Adjustment
HOLLEY 5220/6520

1. Invert the air horn and remove the gasket. Insert a gauge or drill of 12mm diameter between the air horn and float. The gauge must lay flat along the gasket surface.

2. If the adjustment is incorrect, bend the tang which actuates the needle valve to correct it. Bend the tang up toward the floats to decrease the measurement and downward to increase it.

3. Check float drop with a float drop gauge or using a ruler and straightedge. Float drop must be 47.5mm. Bend the tang on the outer end of

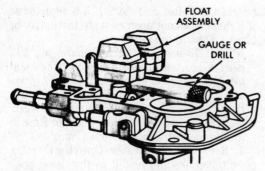

Adjusting float level on the 5220/6520 carburetors

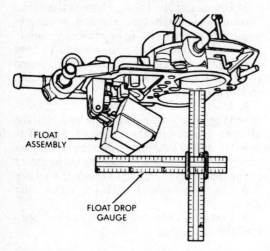

Adjusting float drop on 5220/6520 carburetors

the float hinge outward to increase float drop and inward to decrease it.

MIKUNI CARBURETORS (2.6L ENGINES)

NOTE: *Before attempting to adjust float level, get a shim pack part No. MD606952. These shims are placed under the float needle*

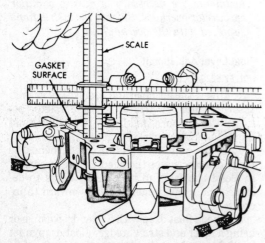

Adjusting float level on Mikuni carburetors

seat to change its position and, therefore, the float level.

1. Invert the air horn. Remove the gasket. Measure the distance from the bottom of the float to the surface of the air horn. The dimension must be 19-21mm.

2. If the dimension is incorrect, disassemble the float, remove the needle and unscrew the float needle seat. Change the shim under the seat or add or subtract shims as necessary. Shims are 0.30mm, 0.40mm and 0.50mm thick. Adding a shim of 0.30mm will lower float level by three times that or 0.90mm.

3. Reassemble the seat, needle and float and recheck the level. Repeat the process until the float level is within the required range.

Throttle Cable

REMOVAL AND INSTALLATION

1. From inside the vehicle, remove the cable housing retainer clip and core wire retaining plug.

2. Remove the core wire from the pedal shaft.

3. From under the hood, pull the housing end-fitting out of the dash panel grommet.

4. Remove the cable clevis from the carburetor lever stud. Now the cable mounting bracket will separate by using wide-jaw pliers to compress the end-fitting tabs.

5. Installation is the reverse of removal.

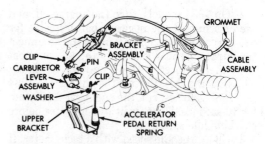

Throttle cable attachment to carburetor 2.6L engine

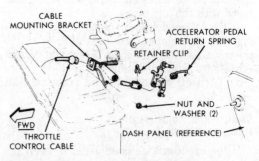

Throttle cable attachment 2.2L engine

Carburetor

REMOVAL AND INSTALLATION

NOTE: *When removing the carburetor on the 2.2 Liter engine, it should not be necessary to disturb the isolator, unless it has been determined that there is a leak in it.*

1. Disconnect the negative battery terminal. Allow the engine to cool thoroughly.

2. Remove the air cleaner.

3. Remove the gas cap.

4. Disconnect the fuel inlet line and all necessary wiring.

NOTE: *It is necessary to drain the coolant on the 2.6 Liter engine before removing the coolant lines at the carburetor.*

5. Disconnect the coolant lines from the carburetor, (2.6 Liter engines only).

6. Disconnect the throttle linkage and all vacuum hoses.

7. Remove the mounting nuts and remove the carburetor. Hold the carburetor level to avoid spilling fuel from the bowl.

8. Installation is the reverse of removal.

Before checking and adjusting any idle speed, check the ignition timing and adjust if neces-

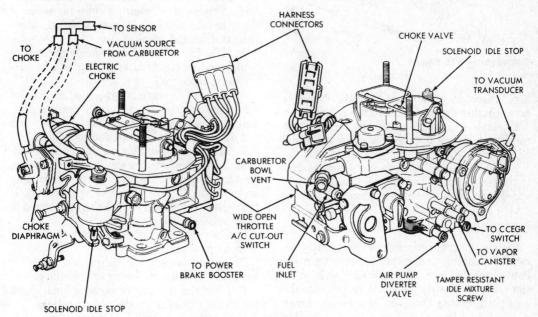

Details of the 2.2L carburetor

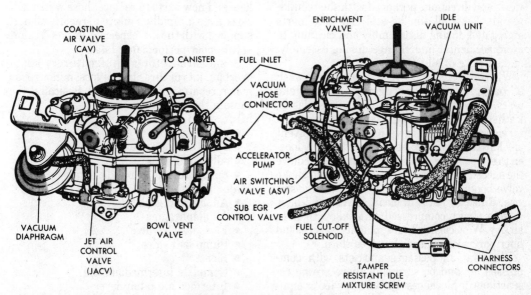

Details of the 2.6L carburetor

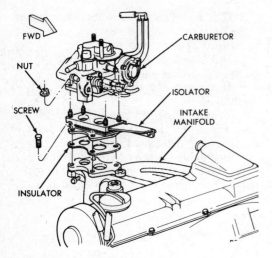

Carburetor—2.2L engine

sary. Disconnect the plug the EGR vacuum hose. Unplug the connector at the radiator fan and install a jumper wire so the fan will run continuously. Remove the PCV valve. Allow the PCV valve to draw under hood air and plug the $3/16''$ diameter hose at the canister. Connect a tachometer and start the engine. Check the idle speed with the air cleaner in place.

OVERHAUL

Efficient carburetion depends greatly on careful cleaning and inspection during overhaul, since dirt, gum, water, or varnish in or on the carburetor parts are often responsible for poor performance. Overhaul your carburetor in a clean, dust-free area. Carefully disassemble the carburetor, referring often to the exploded views and directions packaged with the rebuilding kit. Keep all similar and look-alike parts segregated during disassembly and cleaning to avoid accidental interchange during assembly. Make a note of all jet sizes.

When the carburetor is disassembled, wash all parts (except diaphragms, electric choke units, pump plunger, and any other plastic, leather, fiber, or rubber parts) in clean carburetor solvent. Do not leave parts in the solvent any longer than is necessary to sufficiently loosen the deposits. Excessive cleaning may remove the special finish from the float bowl and choke valve bodies, leaving these parts unfit for service. Rinse all parts in clean solvent and blow them dry with compressed air or allow them to air dry. Wipe clean all cork, plastic, leather, and fiber part with a clean, lint-free cloth.

Blow out all passages and jets with compressed air and be sure that there are no restrictions or blockages. Never use wire or similar tools to clean jets, fuel passages, or air bleeds. Clean all jets and valve separately to avoid accidental interchange.

Check all parts for wear or damage. If wear or damage is found, replace the defective parts. Especially check the following.

1. Check the float needle and seat for wear. If wear is found, replace the complete assembly.

2. Check the float hinge pin for wear and the float(s) for dents or distortion. Replace the float if fuel has leaked into it.

3. Check the throttle and choke shaft bores for wear or an out-of-round condition. Damage or wear to the throttle arm, shaft, or shaft bore will often require replacement of the throttle body. These parts require a close tolerance of fit; wear may allow air leakage, which could affect starting and idling.

NOTE: *Throttle shafts and bushings are not included in overhaul kits. They can be purchased separately.*

4. Inspect the idle mixture adjusting needles for burrs or grooves. Any such condition requires replacement of the needle, since you will not be able to obtain a satisfactory idle.

5. Test the accelerator pump check valves. They should pass air one way but not the other. Test for proper seating by blowing and sucking on the valve. Replace the valve as necessary. If the valve is satisfactory, wash the valve again to remove breath moisture.

6. Check the bowl cover for warped surfaces with a straightedge.

7. Closely inspect the valves and seats for wear and damage, replacing as necessary.

8. After the carburetor is assembled, check the choke valve for freedom of operation.

Carburetor overhaul kits are recommended for each overhaul. These kits contain all gaskets and new parts to replace those which deteriorate most rapidly. Failure to replace all parts supplied with the kit (especially gaskets) can result in poor performance later.

Some carburetor manufacuturers supply overhaul kits of three basic types: minor repair; major repair; and gasket kits. Basically, they contain the following:

Minor Repair Kits:
- All gaskets
- Float needle valve
- All diaphragms
- Spring for the pump diaphragm

Major Repair Kits:
- All jets and gaskets
- All diaphragms
- Float needle valve
- Pump ball valve
- Float
- Complete intermediate rod
- Intermediate pump lever
- Some cover hold-down screws and washers

CHILTON'S
FUEL ECONOMY
& TUNE-UP TIPS

55 WAYS TO IMPROVE FUEL ECONOMY

Tune-up • Spark Plug Diagnosis • Emission Controls

Fuel System • Cooling System • Tires and Wheels

General Maintenance

CHILTON'S FUEL ECONOMY & TUNE-UP TIPS

Fuel economy is important to everyone, no matter what kind of vehicle you drive. The maintenance-minded motorist can save both money and fuel using these tips and the periodic maintenance and tune-up procedures in this Repair and Tune-Up Guide.

There are more than 130,000,000 cars and trucks registered for private use in the United States. Each travels an average of 10-12,000 miles per year, and, and in total they consume close to 70 billion gallons of fuel each year. This represents nearly ⅔ of the oil imported by the United States each year. The Federal government's goal is to reduce consumption 10% by 1985. A variety of methods are either already in use or under serious consideration, and they all affect you driving and the cars you will drive. In addition to "down-sizing", the auto industry is using or investigating the use of electronic fuel delivery, electronic engine controls and alternative engines for use in smaller and lighter vehicles, among other alternatives to meet the federally mandated Corporate Average Fuel Economy (CAFE) of 27.5 mpg by 1985. The government, for its part, is considering rationing, mandatory driving curtailments and tax increases on motor vehicle fuel in an effort to reduce consumption. The government's goal of a 10% reduction could be realized — and further government regulation avoided — if every private vehicle could use just 1 less gallon of fuel per week.

How Much Can You Save?

Tests have proven that almost anyone can make at least a 10% reduction in fuel consumption through regular maintenance and tune-ups. When a major manufacturer of spark plugs sur-

TUNE-UP

1. Check the cylinder compression to be sure the engine will really benefit from a tune-up and that it is capable of producing good fuel economy. A tune-up will be wasted on an engine in poor mechanical condition.

2. Replace spark plugs regularly. New spark plugs alone can increase fuel economy 3%.

3. Be sure the spark plugs are the correct type (heat range) for your vehicle. See the Tune-Up Specifications.

Heat range refers to the spark plug's ability to conduct heat away from the firing end. It must conduct the heat away in an even pattern to avoid becoming a source of pre-ignition, yet it must also operate hot enough to burn off conductive deposits that could cause misfiring.

The heat range is usually indicated by a number on the spark plug, part of the manufacturer's designation for each individual spark plug. The numbers in bold-face indicate the heat range in each manufacturer's identification system.

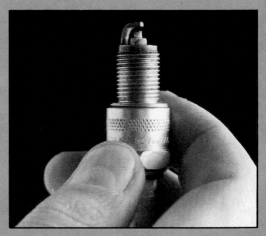

Periodically, check the spark plugs to be sure they are firing efficiently. They are excellent indicators of the internal condition of your engine.

On AC, Bosch (new), Champion, Fram/Autolite, Mopar, Motorcraft and Prestolite, a higher number indicates a hotter plug. On Bosch (old), NGK and Nippondenso, a higher number indicates a colder plug.

4. Make sure the spark plugs are properly gapped. See the Tune-Up Specifications in this book.

5. Be sure the spark plugs are firing efficiently. The illustrations on the next 2 pages show you how to "read" the firing end of the spark plug.

6. Check the ignition timing and set it to specifications. Tests show that almost all cars have incorrect ignition timing by more than 2°.

Manufacturer	Typical Designation
AC	R **45** TS
Bosch (old)	WA **145** T30
Bosch (new)	HR **8** Y
Champion	RBL **15** Y
Fram/Autolite	**415**
Mopar	P-**62** PR
Motorcraft	BRF-**42**
NGK	BP **5** ES-15
Nippondenso	W **16** EP
Prestolite	14GR **5** 2A

veyed over 6,000 cars nationwide, they found that a tune-up, on cars that needed one, increased fuel economy over 11%. Replacing worn plugs alone, accounted for a 3% increase. The same test also revealed that 8 out of every 10 vehicles will have some maintenance deficiency that will directly affect fuel economy, emissions or performance. Most of this mileage-robbing neglect could be prevented with regular maintenance.

Modern engines require that all of the functioning systems operate properly for maximum efficiency. A malfunction anywhere wastes fuel. You can keep your vehicle running as efficiently and economically as possible, by being aware of your vehicle's operating and performance characteristics. If your vehicle suddenly develops performance or fuel economy problems it could be due to one or more of the following:

PROBLEM	POSSIBLE CAUSE
Engine Idles Rough	Ignition timing, idle mixture, vacuum leak or something amiss in the emission control system.
Hesitates on Acceleration	Dirty carburetor or fuel filter, improper accelerator pump setting, ignition timing or fouled spark plugs.
Starts Hard or Fails to Start	Worn spark plugs, improperly set automatic choke, ice (or water) in fuel system.
Stalls Frequently	Automatic choke improperly adjusted and possible dirty air filter or fuel filter.
Performs Sluggishly	Worn spark plugs, dirty fuel or air filter, ignition timing or automatic choke out of adjustment.

Check spark plug wires on conventional point type ignition for cracks by bending them in a loop around your finger.

Be sure that spark plug wires leading to adjacent cylinders do not run too close together. (Photo courtesy Champion Spark Plug Co.)

7. If your vehicle does not have electronic ignition, check the points, rotor and cap as specified.

8. Check the spark plug wires (used with conventional point-type ignitions) for cracks and burned or broken insulation by bending them in a loop around your finger. Cracked wires decrease fuel efficiency by failing to deliver full voltage to the spark plugs. One misfiring spark plug can cost you as much as 2 mpg.

9. Check the routing of the plug wires. Misfiring can be the result of spark plug leads to adjacent cylinders running parallel to each other and too close together. One wire tends to pick up voltage from the other causing it to fire "out of time".

10. Check all electrical and ignition circuits for voltage drop and resistance.

11. Check the distributor mechanical and/or vacuum advance mechanisms for proper functioning. The vacuum advance can be checked by twisting the distributor plate in the opposite direction of rotation. It should spring back when released.

12. Check and adjust the valve clearance on engines with mechanical lifters. The clearance should be slightly loose rather than too tight.

SPARK PLUG DIAGNOSIS

Normal

APPEARANCE: This plug is typical of one operating normally. The insulator nose varies from a light tan to grayish color with slight electrode wear. The presence of slight deposits is normal on used plugs and will have no adverse effect on engine performance. The spark plug heat range is correct for the engine and the engine is running normally.

CAUSE: Properly running engine.

RECOMMENDATION: Before reinstalling this plug, the electrodes should be cleaned and filed square. Set the gap to specifications. If the plug has been in service for more than 10-12,000 miles, the entire set should probably be replaced with a fresh set of the same heat range.

Oil Deposits

APPEARANCE: The firing end of the plug is covered with a wet, oily coating.

CAUSE: The problem is poor oil control. On high mileage engines, oil is leaking past the rings or valve guides into the combustion chamber. A common cause is also a plugged PCV valve, and a ruptured fuel pump diaphragm can also cause this condition. Oil fouled plugs such as these are often found in new or recently overhauled engines, before normal oil control is achieved, and can be cleaned and reinstalled.

RECOMMENDATION: A hotter spark plug may temporarily relieve the problem, but the engine is probably in need of work.

Incorrect Heat Range

APPEARANCE: The effects of high temperature on a spark plug are indicated by clean white, often blistered insulator. This can also be accompanied by excessive wear of the electrode, and the absence of deposits.

CAUSE: Check for the correct spark plug heat range. A plug which is too hot for the engine can result in overheating. A car operated mostly at high speeds can require a colder plug. Also check ignition timing, cooling system level, fuel mixture and leaking intake manifold.

RECOMMENDATION: If all ignition and engine adjustments are known to be correct, and no other malfunction exists, install spark plugs one heat range colder.

Photos Courtesy Fram Corporation

Carbon Deposits

APPEARANCE: Carbon fouling is easily identified by the presence of dry, soft, black, sooty deposits.

CAUSE: Changing the heat range can often lead to carbon fouling, as can prolonged slow, stop-and-start driving. If the heat range is correct, carbon fouling can be attributed to a rich fuel mixture, sticking choke, clogged air cleaner, worn breaker points, retarded timing or low compression. If only one or two plugs are carbon fouled, check for corroded or cracked wires on the affected plugs. Also look for cracks in the distributor cap between the towers of affected cylinders.

RECOMMENDATION: After the problem is corrected, these plugs can be cleaned and reinstalled if not worn severely.

MMT Fouled

APPEARANCE: Spark plugs fouled by MMT (Methycyclopentadienyl Maganese Tricarbonyl) have reddish, rusty appearance on the insulator and side electrode.

CAUSE: MMT is an anti-knock additive in gasoline used to replace lead. During the combustion process, the MMT leaves a reddish deposit on the insulator and side electrode.

RECOMMENDATION: No engine malfunction is indicated and the deposits will not affect plug performance any more than lead deposits (see Ash Deposits). MMT fouled plugs can be cleaned, regapped and reinstalled.

High Speed Glazing

APPEARANCE: Glazing appears as shiny coating on the plug, either yellow or tan in color.

CAUSE: During hard, fast acceleration, plug temperatures rise suddenly. Deposits from normal combustion have no chance to fluff-off; instead, they melt on the insulator forming an electrically conductive coating which causes misfiring.

RECOMMENDATION: Glazed plugs are not easily cleaned. They should be replaced with a fresh set of plugs of the correct heat range. If the condition recurs, using plugs with a heat range one step colder may cure the problem.

Ash (Lead) Deposits

APPEARANCE: Ash deposits are characterized by light brown or white colored deposits crusted on the side or center electrodes. In some cases it may give the plug a rusty appearance.

CAUSE: Ash deposits are normally derived from oil or fuel additives burned during normal combustion. Normally they are harmless, though excessive amounts can cause misfiring. If deposits are excessive in short mileage, the valve guides may be worn.

RECOMMENDATION: Ash-fouled plugs can be cleaned, gapped and reinstalled.

Detonation

APPEARANCE: Detonation is usually characterized by a broken plug insulator.

CAUSE: A portion of the fuel charge will begin to burn spontaneously, from the increased heat following ignition. The explosion that results applies extreme pressure to engine components, frequently damaging spark plugs and pistons.

Detonation can result by over-advanced ignition timing, inferior gasoline (low octane) lean air/fuel mixture, poor carburetion, engine lugging or an increase in compression ratio due to combustion chamber deposits or engine modification.

RECOMMENDATION: Replace the plugs after correcting the problem.

EMISSION CONTROLS

13. Be aware of the general condition of the emission control system. It contributes to reduced pollution and should be serviced regularly to maintain efficient engine operation.

14. Check all vacuum lines for dried, cracked or brittle conditions. Something as simple as a leaking vacuum hose can cause poor performance and loss of economy.

15. Avoid tampering with the emission control system. Attempting to improve fuel econ-

FUEL SYSTEM

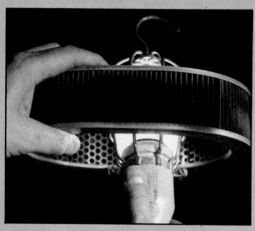

Check the air filter with a light behind it. If you can see light through the filter it can be reused.

Extremely clogged filters should be discarded and replaced with a new one.

18. Replace the air filter regularly. A dirty air filter richens the air/fuel mixture and can increase fuel consumption as much as 10%. Tests show that 1/3 of all vehicles have air filters in need of replacement.

19. Replace the fuel filter at least as often as recommended.

20. Set the idle speed and carburetor mixture to specifications.

21. Check the automatic choke. A sticking or malfunctioning choke wastes gas.

22. During the summer months, adjust the automatic choke for a leaner mixture which will produce faster engine warm-ups.

COOLING SYSTEM

29. Be sure all accessory drive belts are in good condition. Check for cracks or wear.

30. Adjust all accessory drive belts to proper tension.

31. Check all hoses for swollen areas, worn spots, or loose clamps.

32. Check coolant level in the radiator or expansion tank.

33. Be sure the thermostat is operating properly. A stuck thermostat delays engine warm-up and a cold engine uses nearly twice as much fuel as a warm engine.

34. Drain and replace the engine coolant at least as often as recommended. Rust and scale

TIRES & WHEELS

38. Check the tire pressure often with a pencil type gauge. Tests by a major tire manufacturer show that 90% of all vehicles have at least 1 tire improperly inflated. Better mileage can be achieved by over-inflating tires, but never exceed the maximum inflation pressure on the side of the tire.

39. If possible, install radial tires. Radial tires deliver as much as 1/2 mpg more than bias belted tires.

40. Avoid installing super-wide tires. They only create extra rolling resistance and decrease fuel mileage. Stick to the manufacturer's recommendations.

41. Have the wheels properly balanced.

MMT Fouled

APPEARANCE: Spark plugs fouled by MMT (Methycyclopentadienyl Maganese Tricarbonyl) have reddish, rusty appearance on the insulator and side electrode.

CAUSE: MMT is an anti-knock additive in gasoline used to replace lead. During the combustion process, the MMT leaves a reddish deposit on the insulator and side electrode.

RECOMMENDATION: No engine malfunction is indicated and the deposits will not affect plug performance any more than lead deposits (see Ash Deposits). MMT fouled plugs can be cleaned, regapped and reinstalled.

High Speed Glazing

APPEARANCE: Glazing appears as shiny coating on the plug, either yellow or tan in color.

CAUSE: During hard, fast acceleration, plug temperatures rise suddenly. Deposits from normal combustion have no chance to fluff-off; instead, they melt on the insulator forming an electrically conductive coating which causes misfiring.

RECOMMENDATION: Glazed plugs are not easily cleaned. They should be replaced with a fresh set of plugs of the correct heat range. If the condition recurs, using plugs with a heat range one step colder may cure the problem.

Ash (Lead) Deposits

APPEARANCE: Ash deposits are characterized by light brown or white colored deposits crusted on the side or center electrodes. In some cases it may give the plug a rusty appearance.

CAUSE: Ash deposits are normally derived from oil or fuel additives burned during normal combustion. Normally they are harmless, though excessive amounts can cause misfiring. If deposits are excessive in short mileage, the valve guides may be worn.

RECOMMENDATION: Ash-fouled plugs can be cleaned, gapped and reinstalled.

Detonation

APPEARANCE: Detonation is usually characterized by a broken plug insulator.

CAUSE: A portion of the fuel charge will begin to burn spontaneously, from the increased heat following ignition. The explosion that results applies extreme pressure to engine components, frequently damaging spark plugs and pistons.

Detonation can result by over-advanced ignition timing, inferior gasoline (low octane) lean air/fuel mixture, poor carburetion, engine lugging or an increase in compression ratio due to combustion chamber deposits or engine modification.

RECOMMENDATION: Replace the plugs after correcting the problem.

Photos Courtesy Champion Spark Plug Co.

EMISSION CONTROLS

13. Be aware of the general condition of the emission control system. It contributes to reduced pollution and should be serviced regularly to maintain efficient engine operation.

14. Check all vacuum lines for dried, cracked or brittle conditions. Something as simple as a leaking vacuum hose can cause poor performance and loss of economy.

15. Avoid tampering with the emission control system. Attempting to improve fuel econ-

FUEL SYSTEM

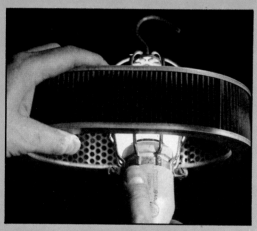

Check the air filter with a light behind it. If you can see light through the filter it can be reused.

Extremely clogged filters should be discarded and replaced with a new one.

18. Replace the air filter regularly. A dirty air filter richens the air/fuel mixture and can increase fuel consumption as much as 10%. Tests show that ⅓ of all vehicles have air filters in need of replacement.

19. Replace the fuel filter at least as often as recommended.

20. Set the idle speed and carburetor mixture to specifications.

21. Check the automatic choke. A sticking or malfunctioning choke wastes gas.

22. During the summer months, adjust the automatic choke for a leaner mixture which will produce faster engine warm-ups.

COOLING SYSTEM

29. Be sure all accessory drive belts are in good condition. Check for cracks or wear.

30. Adjust all accessory drive belts to proper tension.

31. Check all hoses for swollen areas, worn spots, or loose clamps.

32. Check coolant level in the radiator or ex-

pansion tank.

33. Be sure the thermostat is operating properly. A stuck thermostat delays engine warm-up and a cold engine uses nearly twice as much fuel as a warm engine.

34. Drain and replace the engine coolant at least as often as recommended. Rust and scale

TIRES & WHEELS

38. Check the tire pressure often with a pencil type gauge. Tests by a major tire manufacturer show that 90% of all vehicles have at least 1 tire improperly inflated. Better mileage can be achieved by over-inflating tires, but never exceed the maximum inflation pressure on the side of the tire.

39. If possible, install radial tires. Radial tires

deliver as much as ½ mpg more than bias belted tires.

40. Avoid installing super-wide tires. They only create extra rolling resistance and decrease fuel mileage. Stick to the manufacturer's recommendations.

41. Have the wheels properly balanced.

omy by tampering with emission controls is more likely to worsen fuel economy than improve it. Emission control changes on modern engines are not readily reversible.

16. Clean (or replace) the EGR valve and lines as recommended.

17. Be sure that all vacuum lines and hoses are reconnected properly after working under the hood. An unconnected or misrouted vacuum line can wreak havoc with engine performance.

23. Check for fuel leaks at the carburetor, fuel pump, fuel lines and fuel tank. Be sure all lines and connections are tight.

24. Periodically check the tightness of the carburetor and intake manifold attaching nuts and bolts. These are a common place for vacuum leaks to occur.

25. Clean the carburetor periodically and lubricate the linkage.

26. The condition of the tailpipe can be an excellent indicator of proper engine combustion. After a long drive at highway speeds, the inside of the tailpipe should be a light grey in color. Black or soot on the insides indicates an overly rich mixture.

27. Check the fuel pump pressure. The fuel pump may be supplying more fuel than the engine needs.

28. Use the proper grade of gasoline for your engine. Don't try to compensate for knocking or "pinging" by advancing the ignition timing. This practice will only increase plug temperature and the chances of detonation or pre-ignition with relatively little performance gain.

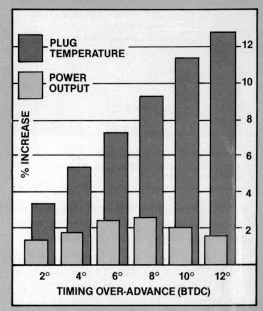

Increasing ignition timing past the specified setting results in a drastic increase in spark plug temperature with increased chance of detonation or preignition. Performance increase is considerably less. (Photo courtesy Champion Spark Plug Co.)

that form in the engine should be flushed out to allow the engine to operate at peak efficiency.

35. Clean the radiator of debris that can decrease cooling efficiency.

36. Install a flex-type or electric cooling fan, if you don't have a clutch type fan. Flex fans use curved plastic blades to push more air at low speeds when more cooling is needed; at high speeds the blades flatten out for less resistance. Electric fans only run when the engine temperature reaches a predetermined level.

37. Check the radiator cap for a worn or cracked gasket. If the cap does not seal properly, the cooling system will not function properly.

42. Be sure the front end is correctly aligned. A misaligned front end actually has wheels going in differed directions. The increased drag can reduce fuel economy by .3 mpg.

43. Correctly adjust the wheel bearings. Wheel bearings that are adjusted too tight increase rolling resistance.

Check tire pressures regularly with a reliable pocket type gauge. Be sure to check the pressure on a cold tire.

GENERAL MAINTENANCE

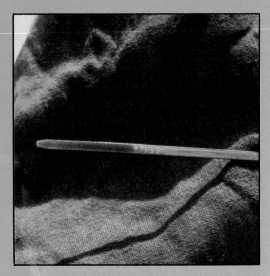

Check the fluid levels (particularly engine oil) on a regular basis. Be sure to check the oil for grit, water or other contamination.

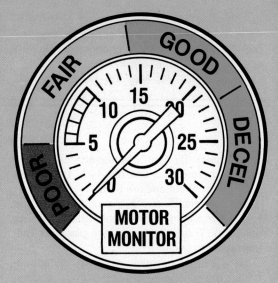

A vacuum gauge is another excellent indicator of internal engine condition and can also be installed in the dash as a mileage indicator.

44. Periodically check the fluid levels in the engine, power steering pump, master cylinder, automatic transmission and drive axle.

45. Change the oil at the recommended interval and change the filter at every oil change. Dirty oil is thick and causes extra friction between moving parts, cutting efficiency and increasing wear. A worn engine requires more frequent tune-ups and gets progressively worse fuel economy. In general, use the lightest viscosity oil for the driving conditions you will encounter.

46. Use the recommended viscosity fluids in the transmission and axle.

47. Be sure the battery is fully charged for fast starts. A slow starting engine wastes fuel.

48. Be sure battery terminals are clean and tight.

49. Check the battery electrolyte level and add distilled water if necessary.

50. Check the exhaust system for crushed pipes, blockages and leaks.

51. Adjust the brakes. Dragging brakes or brakes that are not releasing create increased drag on the engine.

52. Install a vacuum gauge or miles-per-gallon gauge. These gauges visually indicate engine vacuum in the intake manifold. High vacuum = good mileage and low vacuum = poorer mileage. The gauge can also be an excellent indicator of internal engine conditions.

53. Be sure the clutch is properly adjusted. A slipping clutch wastes fuel.

54. Check and periodically lubricate the heat control valve in the exhaust manifold. A sticking or inoperative valve prevents engine warm-up and wastes gas.

55. Keep accurate records to check fuel economy over a period of time. A sudden drop in fuel economy may signal a need for tune-up or other maintenance.

Gasket Kits:
- All gaskets

After cleaning and checking all components, reassemble the carburetor, using new parts and referring to the exploded view. When reassembling, make sure that all screws and jets are tight in their seats, but do not overtighten as the tips will be distorted. Tighten all screws gradually, in rotation. Do not tighten needle valves into their seats; uneven jetting will result. Always use new gaskets. Be sure to adjust the float level when reassembling.

Carburetor Specifications
Holley 5220/6520

Year	Carb. Part No.	Dry Float Setting (in.)	Solenoid Idle Stop (rpm)	Fast Idle Speed (rpm)	Vacuum Kick (in.)
1981	R9060A R9061A	.480	850	1100	.030
	R9125A R9126A	.480	850	1200	.030
	R9052A R9053A	.480	850	1400	.070
	R9054A R9055A	.480	850	1400	.040
	R9602A R9603A	.480	850	1500	.065
	R9604A R9605A	.480	850	1600	.065
1982	R9824A	.480	900	1400	.065
	R9503A R9504A R9750A R9751A	.480	850	1300	.085
	R9822A R9823A	.480	850	1400	.080
	R9505A R9506A R9752A R9753A	.480	900	1600	.100
1983	R-40003A	.480	775	1400	.070
	R-40004A		900	1500	.080
	R-40005A		900	1350	.080
	R-40006A		850	1275	.080
	R-40007A		775	1400	.070
	R-40008A		900	1600	.070
	R-40010A		900	1500	.080
	R-40012A		900	1600	.070
	R-40014A		850	1275	.080
	R-40080A		850	1400	.045
	R-40081A		850	1400	.045
1984	R-40060-1A	.480	see	see	.055
	R-40085-1A				.040
	R-40170A R-40171A	.480			.060

Carburetor Specifications (cont.)
Holley 5220/6520

Year	Carb. Part No.	Dry Float Setting (in.)	Solenoid Idle Stop (rpm)	Fast Idle Speed (rpm)	Vacuum Kick (in.)
1984	R-40067-1A R-40068-1A R-40058-1A	.480	underhood	underhood	.070
	R-40107-1A	.480			.055
	R-40064-1A R-40065-1A R-40081-1A R-40082-1A	.480	sticker	sticker	.080
	R-40071A R-40122A				
1985	R40058A	.480	see	see	.070
	R40060A	.480			.055
	R40116A R40117A	.480	underhood	underhood	.095
	R40134A R40135A R40138A R40139A	.480	sticker	sticker	.075
1986	U.S.	.480	see	see	.075
	Canada	.480	underhood sticker	underhood sticker	.095
1987	All	.480	see underhood sticker	see underhood sticker	.075

THROTTLE BODY FUEL INJECTION SYSTEM

NOTE: *This book contains only basic testing and service procedures for your car's fuel injection system. More comprehensive testing and diagnosis procedures may be found in CHILTON'S GUIDE TO TO FUEL INJECTION AND FEEDBACK CARBURETORS, book part number 7288, available at your local retailer. Note also that whenever replacing any fuel lines, it is necessary to use hoses marked "EFI/EFM" or an equivalent product from the aftermarket. Whenever replacing hose clamps, use clamps incorporating a rolled edge to prevent hose damage, rather than standard aviation type clamps. This will prevent damage to the hoses that could produce dangerous leaks.*

General Information

This electronic fuel injection system is a computer regulated single point fuel injection system that provides precise air/fuel ratio for all driving conditions. At the center of this system is a digital pre-programmed computer known as a logic module that regulates ignition timing, air-fuel ratio, emission control devices and idle speed. This component has the ability to update and revise its programming to meet changing operating conditions.

Various sensors provide the input necessary for the logic module to correctly regulate the fuel flow at the fuel injector. These include the manifold absolute pressure, throttle position, oxygen feedback, coolant temperature, charge temperature and vehicle speed sensors. In addition to the sensors, various switches also provide important information. These include the neutral-safety, heated rear window, air conditioning, air conditioning clutch switches, and an electronic idle switch.

All inputs to the logic module are converted into signals sent to the power module. These signals cause the power module to change either the fuel flow at the injector or ignition timing or both.

The logic module tests many of its own input and output circuits. If a fault is found in a ma-

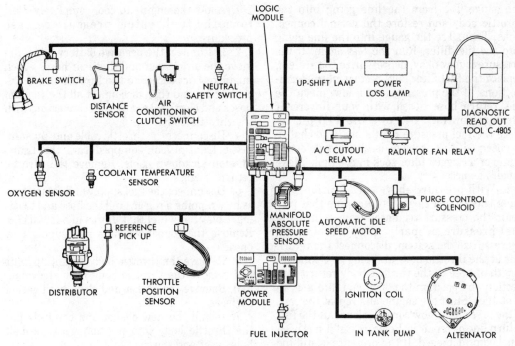

Diagram of the Single-Point EFI system

jor system this information is stored in the logic module. Information on this fault can be displayed to a technician by means of a flashing light emitting diode (LED) or by connecting a diagnostic read out and reading a numbered display code which directly relates to a specific fault.

NOTE: *Experience has shown that many complaints that may occur with EFI can be traced to poor wiring or hose connections. A visual check will help spot these most common faults and save unnecessary test and diagnosis time.*

Electric Fuel Pump
REMOVAL AND INSTALLATION

An electric fuel pump is used with fuel injection systems in order to provide higher and more uniform fuel pressures. It is located in the tank. To remove it, disconnect the battery, and then remove the fuel tank, as described at the end of this chapter. Then, with a hammer and non-metallic punch, tap the fuel pump lock ring counterclockwise to release the pump.

To install the pump, first wipe the seal area of the tank clean and install a new O-ring seal. Replace the filter on the end of the pump if it appears to be damaged. Then position the pump in the tank and install the locking ring. Tighten the ring in the same general way in which you loosened it. Do not overtighten it, as this can cause leakage. Install the tank as described at the end of this chapter.

TESTING

NOTE: *To perform this procedure, you will need a gauge capable of reading 10-20 psi and the extra length of hose, clamps and fittings necessary to Tee the gauge into a $\frac{5}{16}"$ fuel line. Have a metal container handy to collect any fuel that may spill.*

1. Release the fuel system pressure. Disconnect the fuel supply line at the throttle body. Tee in the gauge between the fuel supply line and the fuel supply nipple on the throttle body, connecting the inlet side of the tee to the fuel supply line and the throttle body side of the Tee to the throttle body with a rubber hose and clamps.

WARNING: *At the beginning of the next step, watch carefully for fuel leaks. Shut the engine off immediately at any sign of leakage.*

2. Start the engine and run it at idle. Read the fuel pressure gauge. Pressure should be 14.5 psi. If pressure is correct, the pump is okay and you should depressurize the system, remove the gauge, and restore the normal fuel line connections. If the pressure is low, proceed with the next step to test for filter clogging. If the pressure is too high, proceed with Step 4.

3. Stop the engine and then depressurize the system as described under the procedure for changing the fuel filter in Chapter 1. Remove

the gauge Tee from the line going into the throttle body and restore the normal connections. Then, Tee the gauge into the line going into the fuel filter. Run the test again. If the pressure is now okay, depressurize the system, replace the fuel filter, and restore normal connections. If the pressure is still low, pinch the fuel return hose closed with your fingers. If pressure now increases to above 14.5 psi, replace the fuel pressure regulator. If no change is observed, the problem is either a defective pump or a clogged filter sock in the tank. Make repairs as necessary.

4. With pressure above specification, you must check for a clogged return line that prevents the pressure regulator from controlling fuel pressure properly. Stop the engine, depressurize the system, disconnect the return line at the throttle body and plug it. Connect a length of hose to the throttle body return connection and position the open end into a clean container. Start the engine and repeat the test. If the pressure is now correct, clean out the fuel return line or repair it. Relocate it if it has been pinched or damaged. If the pressure is still too high, replace the pressure regulator.

Throttle Body

REMOVAL AND INSTALLATION

NOTE: *To perform this operation, you'll need a new throttle body-to-manifold gasket and new original equipment-type fuel hose clamps (with rolled edges).*

1. Allow the engine to cool completely. Perform the fuel system pressure release procedure.

2. Disconnect the negative battery cable. Remove the air cleaner and those air hoses which might restrict access to the throttle body.

3. Label and then disconnect all the vacuum hoses and electrical connectors connecting with the throttle body.

4. Disconnect the throttle cable and, on automatic transmission-equipped cars the transmission kickdown cable. Remove the throttle return spring.

5. Disconnect the fuel supply and return hoses by wrapping a rag around the hose and twisting. Collect any fuel that drains in a metal cup. Remove the copper washers and supply new ones.

6. Remove the throttle body mounting bolts and remove the throttle body from the manifold. Remove the gasket and clean both gasket surfaces.

7. Install the new gasket and carefully put the throttle body into position with the bolt holes in it and the manifold lined up.

8. Install the mounting bolts and torque them alternately and evenly to 200 inch lbs.

9. Install the throttle return spring. Reconnect the throttle and, if necessary, transmission cable linkages.

10. Reconnect the wiring connectors and vacuum hoses.

11. Reconnect the fuel supply hose to the supply connection on the throttle body, using a new

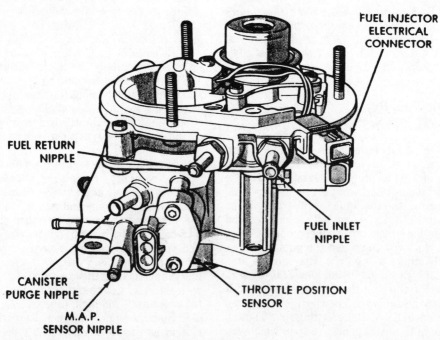

The throttle body used on TBI systems (1988 2.2 L engines without turbocharging and 2.5 L engines)

copper washer. Reconnect the return hose to the return connection with a new copper washer. Use new clamps and torque to 10 inch lbs.

12. Install the air cleaner and hoses. Reconnect the negative battery cable.

13. Start the engine and check for fuel leaks.

Fuel Injector

REMOVAL AND INSTALLATION

NOTE: *A Torx® screwdriver is required to perform this operation. New O-rings for the injector and cap should also be supplied. A set of three will be required to re-use and old injector, while a new injector will be supplied with a new upper O-ring.*

1. Remove the air cleaner and air hoses. Release the fuel system pressure as described in Chapter 1. Then, disconnect the negative battery cable.

2. Remove the Torx® head screw with the right screwdriver. With two appropriate, blunt prying instruments located in the screwdriver slot on either side, gently and evenly pry upward to remove the injector cap.

3. Then, place an appropriate, blunt prying instrument into the screwdriver slot on either side of the electrical connector and gently and evenly pry the injector upward and out of the throttle body unit. Once the injector is removed, check that the lower O-ring has been removed from the throttle body unit.

4. Remove the two O-rings from the injector body and the single O-ring from the cap and replace them. If the injector is being replaced, a new upper O-ring will already be installed.

5. Carefully assemble the injector and cap together with the keyway and key aligned. Then, align the cap and injector so the cap's hole aligns with the bolt hole in the throttle body. Start the injector/cap assembly into the throttle body without applying downward pressure.

6. With the assembly almost seated, rotate the cap as necessary to ensure perfect alignment of the cap and throttle body. Then apply gentle, downward pressure on both sides to seat the injector and cap.

7. Install the Torx® screw and torque it to 30-35 inch lbs.

8. Connect the battery. Start the engine and check for leaks with the air cleaner off. Then, replace the air cleaner and hoses.

Pressure Regulator

REMOVAL AND INSTALLATION

NOTE: *Make sure to have a towel or rag on hand to absorb fuel. Supply a new O-ring and gasket for the pressure regulator.*

1. Remove the air cleaner and air hoses. Release the fuel system pressure as described in Chapter 1. Then, disconnect the negative battery cable.

2. Remove the three screws which attach the pressure regulator to the throttle body. Then, *quickly* place a rag over the fuel inlet chamber to absorb any fuel that remains in the system. When fuel is absorbed, dispose of the rag safely.

3. Pull the pressure regulator from the throttle body. Carefully remove the O-ring and gasket.

4. Carefully install the new O-ring and gasket onto the regulator.

5. Position the pressure regulator onto the throttle body. Press it into place squarely so as to seal the O-ring and gasket.

6. Install the three attaching screws and torque to 40 inch lbs.

7. Connect the battery. Start the engine and check for leaks with the air cleaner off. Then, replace the air cleaner and hoses.

Idle Speed Adjustment

NOTE: *This procedure applies to vehicles built through 1986. Later models require a "Throttle Body Minimum Airflow Check Procedure". This cannot be performed without utilizing an expensive electronic test system. If airflow is incorrect on these models, the throttle body must be replaced.*

1. Before adjusting the idle on an electronic fuel injected vehicle the following items must be checked.

   a. AIS motor has been checked for operation.

   b. Engine has been checked for vacuum or EGR leaks.

   c. Engine timing has been checked and set to specifications.

   d. Coolant temperature sensor has been checked for operation.

2. Connect a tachometer and timing light to engine.

3. Disconnect throttle body 6-way connector. Remove brown with white trace AIS wire from connector and reconnect the connector.

4. Connect one end of a jumper wire to AIS wire and other end to battery positive post for 5 seconds.

5. Connect a jumper to radiator fan so that it will run continuously.

6. Start and run engine for 3 minutes to allow speed to stabilize.

7. Using tool C-4804 or equivalent, turn idle speed adjusting screw to obtain 800 ± 10 rpm Manual; 725 ± 10 rpm (Automatic) with transaxle in neutral.

NOTE: *If idle will not adjust down, check for binding linkage, speed control servo cable adjustments, or throttle shaft binding.*

8. Check that timing is 18° ± 2° BTDC Manual; 12° ± 2° BTDC Automatic.

9. If timing is not to above specifications turn idle speed adjusting screw until correct idle speed and ignition timing are obtained.

10. Turn off engine, disconnect tachometer and timing light, reinstall AIS wire and remove jumper wire.

MULTI-PORT ELECTRONIC FUEL INJECTION

General Information

The turbocharged multi-port Electronic Fuel Injection system combines an electronic fuel and spark advance control system with a turbocharged intake system. At the center of this system is a digital, pre-programmed computer known as a Logic Module that regulates ignition timing, air-fuel ratio, emission control devices and idle speed. This component has the ability to update and revise its programming to meet changing operating conditions.

Various sensors provide the input necessary for the Logic Module to correctly regulate fuel flow at the fuel injectors. These include the Manifold Absolute Pressure, Throttle Position, Oxygen Feedback, Coolant Temperature, Charge Temperature, and Vehicle Speed Sensors. In addition to the sensors, various switches also provide important information. These include the Transmission Neutral-Safety, Heated Rear Window, Air Conditioning, and the Air Conditioning Clutch Switches.

Inputs to the Logic Module are converted into signals sent to the Power Module. These signals cause the Power Module to change either the fuel flow at the injector or ignition timing or both. The Logic Module tests many of its own input and output circuits. If a fault is found in a major circuit, this information is stored in the Logic Module. Information on this fault can be displayed to a technician by means of the instrument panel power loss lamp or by connecting a diagnostic readout and observing a numbered display code which directly relates to a general fault.

NOTE: *Most complaints that may occur with turbocharged muti-point Electronic Fuel Injection can be traced to poor wiring or hose connections. A visual check will help stop these faults and save unnecessary test and diagnosis time.*

Electric Fuel Pump

REMOVAL AND INSTALLATION

An electric fuel pump is used with fuel injection systems in order to provide higher and more uniform fuel pressures. It is located in the tank. To remove it, disconnect the battery, and then remove the fuel tank, as described at the end of this chapter. Then, with a hammer and non-metallic punch, tap the fuel pump lock ring counterclockwise to release the pump.

To install the pump, first wipe the seal area of the tank clean and install a new O-ring seal. Replace the filter on the end of the pump if it appears to be damaged. Then position the pump in the tank and install the locking ring. Tighten the ring in the same general way in which you loosened it. Do not overtighten it, as this can cause leakage. Install the tank as described at the end of this chapter.

TESTING

NOTE: *To perform this test, you will need a pressure gauge capable of reading pressures above 55 psi. The gauge must have a connection that will fit the fuel rail service valve. The gauge will be compatible with Chrysler part No. C-3292 and the connector fitting compatible with C-4805. You may also need a Tee and fittings necessary to Tee the gauge into the fuel supply line at the tank, and a 2 gallon container suitable for collecting fuel.*

1. Release the fuel system pressure as described in Chapter 1. Remove the protective cover from the service valve on the fuel rail.

2. Connect the gauge to the pressure tap on the fuel rail. Hold the gauge and have someone start the engine. Run the engine at idle speed in Neutral (manual transmissions) or Park (automatic transmissions).

3. Read the pressure. It should be 53-57 psi. If it is outside the range, take note of it. Stop the engine, depressurize the system, disconnect the gauge and replace the protective cover. If the pressure is correct, the test is complete. If the pressure is below the range, proceed with the steps following; if it is too high, proceed with Step 7.

WARNING: *In the next step, note that fuel may drain from the lines as you disconnect them. Make sure all surrounding exhaust system parts are cool and that all sources of ignition are removed from the area. Collect fuel and dispose of it safely.*

4. Connect the gauge into the fuel supply line running between the tank and the filter which is located at the rear of the vehicle.

WARNING *Make sure all connections are secure.*

5. Have someone start the engine. Read the pressure gauge. If the pressure has risen more than 5 psi, replace the filter. If the pressure is now within range: allow the engine to cool; remove all sources of ignition; depressurize the

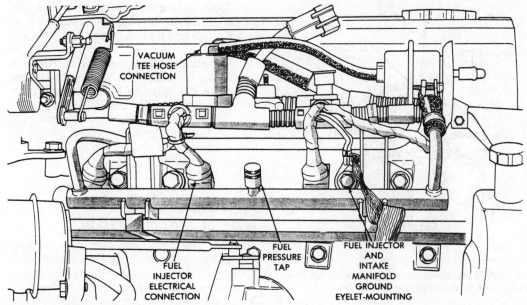

VACUUM
TEE HOSE
CONNECTION

FUEL
PRESSURE
TAP

FUEL INJECTOR
AND
INTAKE
MANIFOLD
GROUND
EYELET-MOUNTING

FUEL
INJECTOR
ELECTRICAL
CONNECTION

To test the fuel pump pressure on turbocharged cars, connect the fuel pressure gauge to the fuel pressure tap shown at center

system; disconnect the gauge from the lines; replace the fuel filter; and restore connections.

6. If the pressure is still too low, gently and gradually pinch the fuel return line closed as you watch the gauge. If the pressure increases, the fuel pressure regulator is at fault. If there is no change, the problem is either clogging of the filter sock mounted on the pump itself or a defective pump.

7. If the pressure is too high, shut off the engine, allow it to cool, depressurize the system and then disconnect the fuel return hose at the chassis, near the fuel tank. Connect a 3 foot length of hose to the open end of the line running along the chassis. Position the open end of the line into a container suitable for collecting fuel. Have a helper start the engine and check the pressure. If it is now correct, check the in-tank fuel return hose for kinking. If the hose is okay, and the system still exhibits excessive pressure with the tank half full or more, the fuel pump reservoir check valve or aspirator jet may be obstructed and the assembly must be replaced.

8. If the pressure is still too high, shut off the engine, and allow it to cool. Depressurize the system and then reconnect the fuel lines at the rear. Disconnect the fuel return hose at the pressure regulator. Collect all fuel that drains. Then, run the open connection into a large metal container. Connect the fuel gauge back into the fuel rail. Start the engine and repeat the test. If the fuel pressure is now correct, clean a clogged return line or replace pinched or kinked

sections of the return line. If no such problems exist, replace the fuel pressure regulator.

Idle Speed Adjustment

NOTE: *This procedure applies to vehicles built through 1986. Later models require a "Throttle Body Minimum Airflow Check Procedure". This cannot be performed without utilizing an expensive electronic test system. If airflow is incorrect on these models, the throttle body must be replaced.*

Before adjusting the idle on an electronic fuel injected vehicle the following items must be checked:

a. AIS motor has been checked for operation.

b. Engine has been checked for vacuum or EGR leaks.

c. Engine timing has been checked and set to specifications.

d. Coolant temperature sensor has been checked for operation.

Once these checks have been made and you know these components are performing satisfactorily:

1. Install a tachometer.

2. Warm up engine to normal operating temperature (accessories off).

3. Shut engine off and disconnect radiator fan.

4. Disconnect Throttle Body 6-way connector. Remove the brown with white tracer AIS

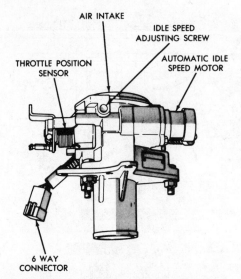

AIR INTAKE

IDLE SPEED
ADJUSTING SCREW

THROTTLE POSITION
SENSOR

AUTOMATIC IDLE
SPEED MOTOR

6 WAY
CONNECTOR

Location of idle speed adjusting screw on the throttle body of the multi-port injection system

wire from the connector and reconnect connector.

5. Start engine with transaxle selector in park or neutral.

6. Apply 12 volts to AIS brown with white tracer wire. This will drive the AIS fully closed and the idle should drop.

7. Disconnect then reconnect coolant temperature sensor.

8. With transaxle in neutral, idle speed should be 775 ± 25 rpm (700 ± 25 rpm green engine).

9. If idle is not to specifications adjust idle air bypass screw.

10. If idle will not adjust down, check for vacuum leaks, AIS motor damage, throttle body damage, or speed control cable adjustment.

Throttle Body

REMOVAL AND INSTALLATION

1. Disconnect the negative battery cable. Remove the nuts attaching the air cleaner adaptor to the throttle body, loosen the hose clamps, and remove the air cleaner adaptor.

2. Remove the three control cables—accelerator, accelerator and, if so-equipped, automatic transmission kickdown and speed control cables. Then remove the throttle cable bracket from the throttle body.

3. Note locations and then disconnect the electrical connectors.

4. Note their locations or, if necessary, label them and then disconnect the vacuum hoses from the throttle body.

5. Remove the throttle body-to-adaptor attaching nuts. Then, remove the throttle body and its gasket.

6. Clean gasket surfaces and install a new gasket. Instal the throttle body-to-adaptor attaching nuts and tighten them alternately and evenly.

7. Reconnect the vacuum hoses, checking the routing and making certain the connections are secure. Reconnect each electrical connector to its connection on the throttle body.

8. Install the throttle and, as necessary, transmission kickdown and speed control cables. Install the air cleaner adaptor. Reconnect the battery.

Fuel Rail and Injectors

REMOVAL AND INSTALLATION

NOTE: *You should have a set of four injector nozzle protective caps and a set of new O-rings before removing the injectors.*

1. Release fuel system pressure as described in Chapter 1. Disconnect the negative battery cable.

2. Loosen the hose clamp on the fuel supply hose at the fuel rail inlet and disconnect it. Collect any fuel that may drain out into a metal cup and dispose of it safely.

3. Disconnect the fuel pressure regulator vacuum hose at the intake manifold vacuum tree.

4. Remove the 2 fuel pressure regulator-to-intake manifold bracket screws.

5. Loosen the clamp at the rail end of the fuel rail-to-pressure regulator hose and then remove the regulator and hose. Collect any fuel that may drain out into a metal cup and dispose of it safely.

6. Remove the bolt from the fuel rail-to-valve cover bracket.

7. Remove the fuel injector head shield clips. Then, remove the four intake manifold-to-rail mounting bolts. Note that one bolt retains a ground strap.

8. Pull the rail away from the manifold in such a way as to pull the injectors straight out of their mounting holes. Pull the injectors out straight so as to avoid damaging their O-rings.

9. To remove individual injectors from the rail, first position the rail on a bench or other surfaces so that the injectors are easily reached. Perform the following for each injector to be removed:

a. Disconnect the wiring connector.

b. Remove the lock ring from the rail and injector.

c. Pull the injector straight out of the injector receiver cup in the fuel rail.

d. Inspect the injector O-rings for damage. Replace it if necessary. If the injector will be re-used and will be off the rail while other

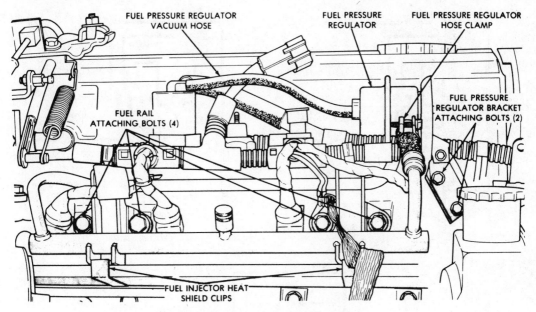

FUEL PRESSURE REGULATOR
VACUUM HOSE

FUEL PRESSURE
REGULATOR

FUEL PRESSURE REGULATOR
HOSE CLAMP

FUEL RAIL
ATTACHING BOLTS (4)

FUEL PRESSURE
REGULATOR BRACKET
ATTACHING BOLTS (2)

FUEL INJECTOR HEAT
SHIELD CLIPS

The fuel rail used with Turbo engines

work is performed, install a protective cap over the nozzle.

e. Lubricate the O-ring that seals the upper end with a drop of clean engine oil. Then, install the inlet end carefully into the fuel rail receiver cup. Proceed slowly and insert the injector straight in to avoid damaging the O-ring.

f. Slide the open end of the injector lock ring down over the injector, and onto the ridge in the receiver cup. The lock ring must lock into the slot on the top of the injector.

10. Remove all protective covers installed over the injector tips. Make sure the bores of the injector mounting holes are clean.

11. Put a drop of clean engine oil on the O-ring at the nozzle end of each injector. Then position the rail with the injectors headed squarely into their mounting holes and gently and evenly slide all four injectors into place.

12. Install the four rail mounting bolts and torque them to 250 inch lbs. Make sure to reconnect the ground strap removed earlier.

13. Connect each plug to its corresponding injector. Install each wiring harness into its clips. Connect the injector wiring harness to the main harness.

14. Install the heat shield clips. Install the bolt fastening the rail mounting bracket to the valve cover.

15. Connect the vacuum line for the fuel pressure regulator to the vacuum tree on the manifold. Then, connect the fuel return hose to the fuel pressure regulator and position and tighten the clamp. Install the bolts fastening the regulator bracket to the intake manifold.

16. Attach the fuel supply hose to the fuel rail and position and tighten the clamp.

17. Recheck all wiring and hose connections for routing and tightness. Then, connect the battery, start the engine, and check for leaks.

FUEL TANK

REMOVAL AND INSTALLATION

1. Release the fuel system pressure as described in Chapter 1 on all models with fuel injection.

2. Disconnect the negative battery terminal.

3. Remove the gas cap to relieve any pressure in the tank.

4. Disconnect the fuel supply line at the right front shock absorber tower, and drain the fuel tank.

5. Remove the bolts that hold the filler tube to the quarter panel.

6. Jack up the vehicle and support it with jackstands. If necessary for access to the filler tube, remove the right rear wheel.

7. Disconnect the wiring from the tank.

8. Remove the screws from the exhaust pipe-to-fuel tank shield, and allow this shield to rest on the exhaust pipe.

9. Support the tank with a jack and remove the tank strap bolts.

10. Lower the tank slightly. If there is a roll-over/separator valve hose connecting into the tank, disconnect it at the valve. Carefully remove the filler tube from the tank.

11. Lower the fuel tank and remove it and the insulator pad.

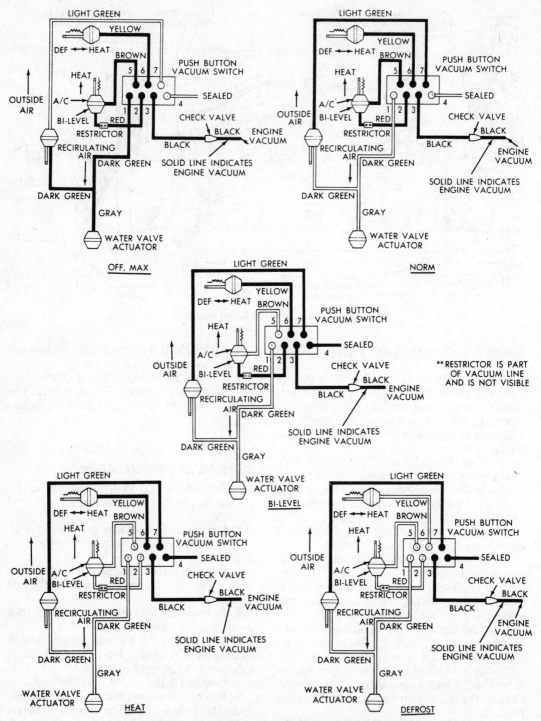

Air conditioner/heater vacuum diagrams for 1984–85 models

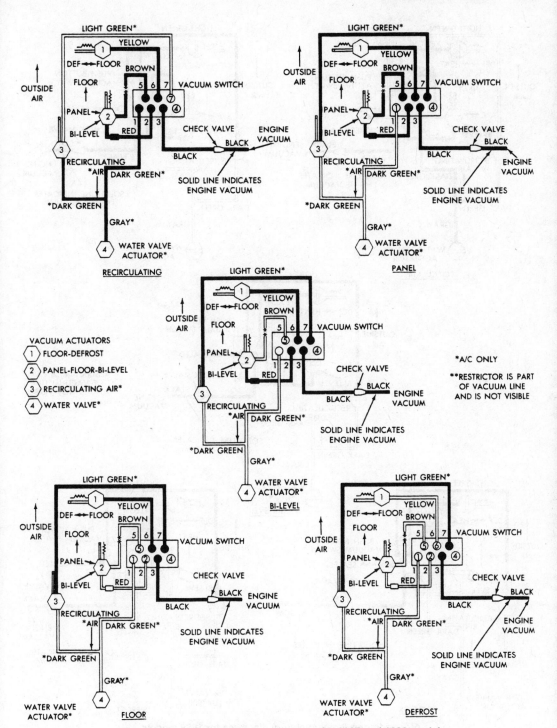

Air conditioner/heater vacuum diagrams for 1987 and 1988 models

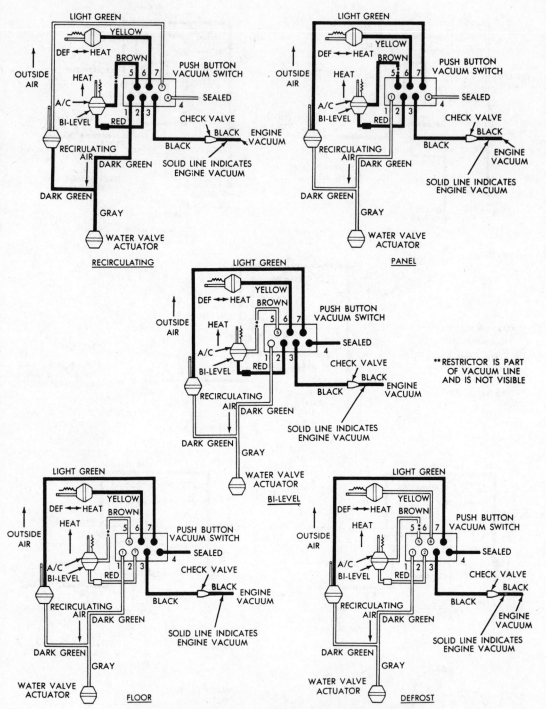

Air conditioner/heater vacuum diagrams for 1986 models

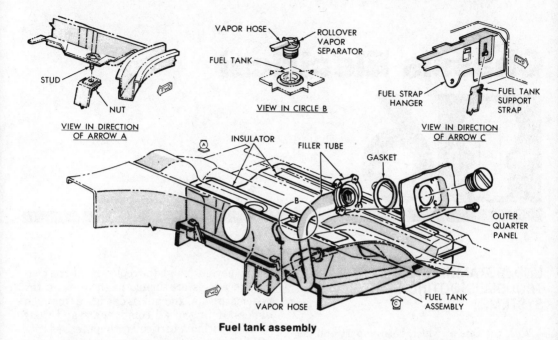

Fuel tank assembly

12. To install the tank, first position the insulator pad on top of the tank and then raise it to within a foot or so of its normal position. Then, connect the filler tube and, if equipped, the rollover/separator valve hose.

13. Raise the tank into its normal position and install the tank strap bolts.

14. Install the exhaust pipe-to-fuel tank shield. Reconnect the gauge and fuel pump wiring (electric pumps only).

15. Install the bolts attaching the filler tube to the quarter panel. Install the right rear wheel, if it was removed previously. Then, lower the car.

16. Reconnect the fuel line at the right front shock absorber tower. Put some fresh, clean fuel in the tank and reinstall the cap. Reconnect the battery. Start the engine and check for leaks. Road test the car to make sure the tank is securely mounted.

Chassis Electrical

6

UNDERSTANDING AND TROUBLESHOOTING ELECTRICAL SYSTEMS

With the rate at which both import and domestic manufacturers are incorporating electronic control systems into their production lines, it won't be long before every new vehicle is equipped with one or more on-board computers. These electronic components (with no moving parts) should theoretically last the life of the vehicle, provided nothing external happens to damage the circuits or memory chips.

While it is true that electronic components should never wear out, in the real world malfunctions do occur. It is also true that any computer-based system is extremely sensitive to electrical voltages and cannot tolerate careless or haphazard testing or service procedures. An inexperienced individual can literally do major damage looking for a minor problem by using the wrong kind of test equipment or connecting test leads or connectors with the ignition switch ON. When selecting test equipment, make sure the manufacturer's instructions state that the tester is compatible with whatever type of electronic control system is being serviced. Read all instructions carefully and double check all test points before installing probes or making any test connections.

The following section outlines basic diagnosis techniques for dealing with computerized automotive control systems. Along with a general explanation of the various types of test equipment available to aid in servicing modern electronic automotive systems, basic repair techniques for wiring harnesses and connectors is given. Read the basic information before attempting any repairs or testing on any computerized system, to provide the background of information necessary to avoid the most common and obvious mistakes that can cost both time and money. Although the replacement and testing procedures are simple in themselves, the systems are not, and unless one has a thorough understanding of all components and their function within a particular computerized control system, the logical test sequence these systems demand cannot be followed. Minor malfunctions can make a big difference, so it is important to know how each component affects the operation of the overall electronic system to find the ultimate cause of a problem without replacing good components unnecessarily. It is not enough to use the correct test equipment; the test equipment must be used correctly.

Safety Precautions

CAUTION: *Whenever working on or around any computer based microprocessor control system, always observe these general precautions to prevent the possibility of personal injury or damage to electronic components.*

• Never install or remove battery cables with the key ON or the engine running. Jumper cables should be connected with the key OFF to avoid power surges that can damage electronic control units. Engines equipped with computer controlled systems should avoid both giving and getting jump starts due to the possibility of serious damage to components from arcing in the engine compartment when connections are made with the ignition ON.

• Always remove the battery cables before charging the battery. Never use a high output charger on an installed battery or attempt to use any type of "hot shot" (24 volt) starting aid.

• Exercise care when inserting test probes into connectors to insure good connections without damaging the connector or spreading the pins. Always probe connectors from the rear (wire) side, NOT the pin side, to avoid accidental shorting of terminals during test procedures.

• Never remove or attach wiring harness connectors with the ignition switch ON, especially to an electronic control unit.

• Do not drop any components during service procedures and never apply 12 volts directly to any component (like a solenoid or relay) unless instructed specifically to do so. Some component electrical windings are designed to safely handle only 4 or 5 volts and can be destroyed in seconds if 12 volts are applied directly to the connector.

• Remove the electronic control unit if the vehicle is to be placed in an environment where temperatures exceed approximately 176°F (80°C), such as a paint spray booth or when arc or gas welding near the control unit location in the car.

ORGANIZED TROUBLESHOOTING

When diagnosing a specific problem, organized troubleshooting is a must. The complexity of a modern automobile demands that you approach any problem in a logical, organized manner. There are certain troubleshooting techniques that are standard:

1. Establish when the problem occurs. Does the problem appear only under certain conditions? Were there any noises, odors, or other unusual symptoms?

2. Isolate the problem area. To do this, make some simple tests and observations; then eliminate the systems that are working properly. Check for obvious problems such as broken wires, dirty connections or split or disconnected vacuum hoses. Always check the obvious before assuming something complicated is the cause.

3. Test for problems systematically to determine the cause once the problem area is isolated. Are all the components functioning properly? Is there power going to electrical switches and motors? Is there vacuum at vacuum switches and/or actuators? Is there a mechanical problem such as bent linkage or loose mounting screws? Doing careful, systematic checks will often turn up most causes on the first inspection without wasting time checking components that have little or no relationship to the problem.

4. Test all repairs after the work is done to make sure that the problem is fixed. Some causes can be traced to more than one component, so a careful verification of repair work is important to pick up additional malfunctions that may cause a problem to reappear or a different problem to arise. A blown fuse, for example, is a simple problem that may require more than another fuse to repair. If you don't look for a problem that caused a fuse to blow, for example, a shorted wire may go undetected.

Experience has shown that most problems tend to be the result of a fairly simple and obvious cause, such as loose or corroded connectors or air leaks in the intake system; making careful inspection of components during testing is essential to quick and accurate troubleshooting. Special, hand held computerized testers designed specifically for diagnosing the system are available from a variety of aftermarket sources, as well as from the vehicle manufacturer, but care should be taken that any test equipment being used is designed to diagnose that particular computer controlled system accurately without damaging the control unit (ECU) or components being tested.

NOTE: *Pinpointing the exact cause of trouble in an electrical system can sometimes only be accomplished by the use of special test equipment. The following describes commonly used test equipment and explains how to put it to best use in diagnosis. In addition to the information covered below, the manufacturer's instructions booklet provided with the tester should be read and clearly understood before attempting any test procedures.*

TEST EQUIPMENT

Jumper Wires

Jumper wires are simple, yet extremely valuable, pieces of test equipment. Jumper wires are merely wires that are used to bypass sections of a circuit. The simplest type of jumper wire is merely a length of multistrand wire with an alligator clip at each end. Jumper wires are usually fabricated from lengths of standard automotive wire and whatever type of connector (alligator clip, spade connector or pin connector) that is required for the particular vehicle being tested. The well equipped tool box will have several different styles of jumper wires in several different lengths. Some jumper wires are made with three or more terminals coming from a common splice for special purpose testing. In cramped, hard-to-reach areas it is advisable to have insulated boots over the jumper wire terminals in order to prevent accidental grounding, sparks, and possible fire, especially when testing fuel system components.

Jumper wires are used primarily to locate open electrical circuits, on either the ground (-) side of the circuit or on the hot (+) side. If an electrical component fails to operate, connect the jumper wire between the component and a good ground. If the component operates only with the jumper installed, the ground circuit is open. If the ground circuit is good, but the component does not operate, the circuit between the power feed and component is open. You can sometimes connect the jumper wire directly from the battery to the hot terminal of the component, but first make sure the component uses

12 volts in operation. Some electrical components, such as fuel injectors, are designed to operate on about 4 volts and running 12 volts directly to the injector terminals can burn out the wiring. By inserting an inline fuseholder between a set of test leads, a fused jumper wire can be used for bypassing open circuits. Use a 5 amp fuse to provide protection against voltage spikes. When in doubt, use a voltmeter to check the voltage input to the component and measure how much voltage is being applied normally. By moving the jumper wire successively back from the lamp toward the power source, you can isolate the area of the circuit where the open is located. When the component stops functioning, or the power is cut off, the open is in the segment of wire between the jumper and the point previously tested.

CAUTION: *Never use jumpers made from wire that is of lighter gauge than used in the circuit under test. If the jumper wire is of too small a gauge, it may overheat and possibly melt. Never use jumpers to bypass high resistance loads (such as motors) in a circuit. Bypassing resistances, in effect, creates a short circuit which may, in turn, cause damage and fire. Never use a jumper for anything other than temporary bypassing of components in a circuit.*

12 Volt Test Light

The 12 volt test light is used to check circuits and components while electrical current is flowing through them. It is used for voltage and ground tests. Twelve volt test lights come in different styles but all have three main parts; a ground clip, a probe, and a light. The most commonly used 12 volt test lights have pick-type probes. To use a 12 volt test light, connect the ground clip to a good ground and probe wherever necessary with the pick. The pick should be sharp so that it can penetrate wire insulation to make contact with the wire without making a large hole in the insulation. The wrap-around light is handy in hard to reach areas or where it is difficult to support a wire to push a probe pick into it. To use the wrap around light, hook the wire so as to be probed with the hook and pull the trigger. A small pick will be forced through the wire insulation into the wire core.

CAUTION: *Do not use a test light to probe electronic ignition spark plug or coil wires. Never use a pick-type test light to probe wiring on computer controlled systems unless specifically instructed to do so. Any wire insulation that is pierced by the test light probe should be taped and sealed with silicone after testing.*

Like the jumper wire, the 12 volt test light is used to isolate opens in circuits. But, whereas the jumper wire is used to bypass the open to operate the load, the 12 volt test light is used to locate the presence of voltage in a circuit. If the test light glows, you know that there is power up to that point; if the 12 volt test light does not glow when its probe is inserted into the wire or connector, you know that there is an open circuit (no power). Move the test light in successive steps back toward the power source until the light in the handle does glow. When it does glow, the open is between the probe and point previously probed.

NOTE: *The test light does not detect that 12 volts (or any particular amount of voltage) is present; it only detects that some voltage is present. It is advisable before using the test light to touch its terminals across the battery posts to make sure the light is operating properly.*

Self-Powered Test Light

The self-powered test light usually contains a 1.5 volt penlight battery. One type of self-powered test light is similar in design to the 12 volt test light. This type has both the battery and the light in the handle and pick-type probe tip. The second type has the light toward the open tip, so that the light illuminates the contact point. The self-powered test light is dual purpose piece of test equipment. It can be used to test for either open or short circuits when power is isolated from the circuit (continuity test). A powered test light should not be used on any computer controlled system or component unless specifically instructed to do so. Many engine sensors can be destroyed by even this small amount of voltage applied directly to the terminals.

Open Circuit Testing

To use the self-powered test light to check for open circuits, first isolate the circuit from the vehicle's 12 volt power source by disconnecting the battery or wiring harness connector. Connect the test light ground clip to a good ground and probe sections of the circuit sequentially with the test light. (start from either end of the circuit). If the light is out, the open is between the probe and the circuit ground. If the light is on, the open is between the probe and end of the circuit toward the power source.

Short Circuit Testing

By isolating the circuit both from power and from ground, and using a self-powered test light, you can check for shorts to ground in the circuit. Isolate the circuit from power and ground. Connect the test light ground clip to a good ground and probe any easy-to-reach test point in the circuit. If the light comes on, there is a short somewhere in the circuit. To isolate the short, probe a test point at either end of the isolated circuit (the light should be on). Leave the test light probe connected and open connectors, switches, remove parts, etc., sequentially, until the light goes out. When the light goes out, the short is between the last circuit component opened and the previous circuit opened.

NOTE: *The 1.5 volt battery in the test light does not provide much current. A weak battery may not provide enough power to illuminate the test light even when a complete circuit is made (especially if there are high resistances in the circuit). Always make sure that the test battery is strong. To check the battery, briefly touch the ground clip to the probe; if the light glows brightly the battery is strong enough for testing. Never use a self-powered test light to perform checks for opens or shorts when power is applied to the electrical system under test. The 12 volt vehicle power will quickly burn out the 1.5 volt light bulb in the test light.*

Voltmeter

A voltmeter is used to measure voltage at any point in a circuit, or to measure the voltage drop across any part of a circuit. It can also be used to check continuity in a wire or circuit by indicating current flow from one end to the other. Voltmeters usually have various scales on the meter dial and a selector switch to allow the selection of different voltages. The voltmeter has a positive and a negative lead. To avoid damage to the meter, always connect the negative lead to the negative (-) side of circuit (to ground or nearest the ground side of the circuit) and connect the positive lead to the positive (+) side of the circuit (to the power source or the nearest power source). Note that the negative voltmeter lead will always be black and that the positive voltmeter will always be some color other than black (usually red). Depending on how the voltmeter is connected into the circuit, it has several uses.

A voltmeter can be connected either in parallel or in series with a circuit and it has a very high resistance to current flow. When connected in parallel, only a small amount of current will flow through the voltmeter current path; the rest will flow through the normal circuit current path and the circuit will work normally. When the voltmeter is connected in series with a circuit, only a small amount of current can flow through the circuit. The circuit will not work properly, but the voltmeter reading will show if the circuit is complete or not.

Available Voltage Measurement

Set the voltmeter selector switch to the 20V position and connect the meter negative lead to the negative post of the battery. Connect the positive meter lead to the positive post of the battery and turn the ignition switch ON to provide a load. Read the voltage on the meter or digital display. A well charged battery should register over 12 volts. If the meter reads below 11.5 volts, the battery power may be insufficient to operate the electrical system properly. This test determines voltage available from the battery and should be the first step in any electrical trouble diagnosis procedure. Many electrical problems, especially on computer controlled systems, can be caused by a low state of charge in the battery. Excessive corrosion at the battery cable terminals can cause a poor contact that will prevent proper charging and full battery current flow.

Normal battery voltage is 12 volts when fully charged. When the battery is supplying current to one or more circuits it is said to be "under load". When everything is off the electrical system is under a "no-load" condition. A fully charged battery may show about 12.5 volts at no load; will drop to 12 volts under medium load; and will drop even lower under heavy load. If the battery is partially discharged the voltage decrease under heavy load may be excessive, even though the battery shows 12 volts or more at no load. When allowed to discharge further, the battery's available voltage under load will decrease more severely. For this reason, it is important that the battery be fully charged during all testing procedures to avoid errors in diagnosis and incorrect test results.

Voltage Drop

When current flows through a resistance, the voltage beyond the resistance is reduced (the larger the current, the greater the reduction in voltage). When no current is flowing, there is no voltage drop because there is no current flow. All points in the circuit which are connected to the power source are at the same voltage as the power source. The total voltage drop always equals the total source voltage. In a long circuit with many connectors, a series of small, unwanted voltage drops due to corrosion at the connectors can add up to a total loss of voltage which impairs the operation of the normal loads in the circuit.

INDIRECT COMPUTATION OF VOLTAGE DROPS

1. Set the voltmeter selector switch to the 20 volt position.
2. Connect the meter negative lead to a good ground.

3. Probe all resistances in the circuit with the positive meter lead.

4. Operate the circuit in all modes and observe the voltage readings.

DIRECT MEASUREMENT OF VOLTAGE DROPS

1. Set the voltmeter switch to the 20 volt position.

2. Connect the voltmeter negative lead to the ground side of the resistance load to be measured.

3. Connect the positive lead to the positive side of the resistance or load to be measured.

4. Read the voltage drop directly on the 20 volt scale.

Too high a voltage indicates too high a resistance. If, for example, a blower motor runs too slowly, you can determine if there is too high a resistance in the resistor pack. By taking voltage drop readings in all parts of the circuit, you can isolate the problem. Too low a voltage drop indicates too low a resistance. If, for example, a blower motor runs too fast in the MED and/or LOW position, the problem can be isolated in the resistor pack by taking voltage drop readings in all parts of the circuit to locate a possibly shorted resistor. The maximum allowable voltage drop under load is critical, especially if there is more than one high resistance problem in a circuit because all voltage drops are cumulative. A small drop is normal due to the resistance of the conductors.

HIGH RESISTANCE TESTING

1. Set the voltmeter selector switch to the 4 volt position.

2. Connect the voltmeter positive lead to the positive post of the battery.

3. Turn on the headlights and heater blower to provide a load.

4. Probe various points in the circuit with the negative voltmeter lead.

5. Read the voltage drop on the 4 volt scale. Some average maximum allowable voltage drops are:

FUSE PANEL — 7 volts
IGNITION SWITCH — 5 volts
HEADLIGHT SWITCH — 7 volts
IGNITION COIL (+) — 5 volts
ANY OTHER LOAD — 1.3 volts
NOTE: *Voltage drops are all measured while a load is operating; without current flow, there will be no voltage drop.*

Ohmmeter

The ohmmeter is designed to read resistance (ohms) in a circuit or component. Although there are several different styles of ohmmeters, all will usually have a selector switch which permits the measurement of different ranges of resistance (usually the selector switch allows the multiplication of the meter reading by 10, 100, 1000, and 10,000). A calibration knob allows the meter to be set at zero for accurate measurement. Since all ohmmeters are powered by an internal battery (usually 9 volts), the ohmmeter can be used as a self-powered test light. When the ohmmeter is connected, current from the ohmmeter flows through the circuit or component being tested. Since the ohmmeter's internal resistance and voltage are known values, the amount of current flow through the meter depends on the resistance of the circuit or component being tested.

The ohmmeter can be used to perform continuity tests for opens or shorts (either by observation of the meter needle or as a self-powered test light), and to read actual resistance in a circuit. It should be noted that the ohmmeter is used to check the resistance of a component or wire while there is no voltage applied to the circuit. Current flow from an outside voltage source (such as the vehicle battery) can damage the ohmmeter, so the circuit or component should be isolated from the vehicle electrical system before any testing is done. Since the ohmmeter uses its own voltage source, either lead can be connected to any test point.

NOTE: *When checking diodes or other solid state components, the ohmmeter leads can only be connected one way in order to measure current flow in a single direction. Make sure the positive (+) and negative (-) terminal connections are as described in the test procedures to verify the one-way diode operation.*

In using the meter for making continuity checks, do not be concerned with the actual resistance readings. Zero resistance, or any resistance readings, indicate continuity in the circuit. Infinite resistance indicates an open in the circuit. A high resistance reading where there should be none indicates a problem in the circuit. Checks for short circuits are made in the same manner as checks for open circuits except that the circuit must be isolated from both power and normal ground. Infinite resistance indicates no continuity to ground, while zero resistance indicates a dead short to ground.

RESISTANCE MEASUREMENT

The batteries in an ohmmeter will weaken with age and temperature, so the ohmmeter must be calibrated or "zeroed" before taking measurements. To zero the meter, place the selector switch in its lowest range and touch the two ohmmeter leads together. Turn the calibration knob until the meter needle is exactly on zero.

NOTE: *All analog (needle) type ohmmeters*

must be zeroed before use, but some digital ohmmeter models are automatically calibrated when the switch is turned on. Self-calibrating digital ohmmeters do not have an adjusting knob, but its a good idea to check for a zero readout before use by touching the leads together. All computer controlled systems require the use of a digital ohmmeter with at least 10 meagohms impedance for testing. Before any test procedures are attempted, make sure the ohmmeter used is compatible with the electrical system or damage to the onboard computer could result.

To measure resistance, first isolate the circuit from the vehicle power source by disconnecting the battery cables or the harness connector. Make sure the key is OFF when disconnecting any components or the battery. Where necessary, also isolate at least one side of the circuit to be checked to avoid reading parallel resistances. Parallel circuit resistances will always give a lower reading than the actual resistance of either of the branches. When measuring the resistance of parallel circuits, the total resistance will always be lower than the smallest resistance in the circuit. Connect the meter leads to both sides of the circuit (wire or component) and read the actual measured ohms on the meter scale. Make sure the selector switch is set to the proper ohm scale for the circuit being tested to avoid misreading the ohmmeter test value.

CAUTION: *Never use an ohmmeter with power applied to the circuit. Like the self-powered test light, the ohmmeter is designed to operate on its own power supply. The normal 12 volt automotive electrical system current could damage the meter.*

Ammeters

An ammeter measures the amount of current flowing through a circuit in units called amperes or amps. Amperes are units of electron flow which indicate how fast the electrons are flowing through the circuit. Since Ohms Law dictates that current flow in a circuit is equal to the circuit voltage divided by the total circuit resistance, increasing voltage also increases the current level (amps). Likewise, any decrease in resistance will increase the amount of amps in a circuit. At normal operating voltage, most circuits have a characteristic amount of amperes, called "current draw" which can be measured using an ammeter. By referring to a specified current draw rating, measuring the amperes, and comparing the two values, one can determine what is happening within the circuit to aid in diagnosis. An open circuit, for example, will not allow any current to flow so the ammeter reading will be zero. More current flows

through a heavily loaded circuit or when the charging system is operating.

An ammeter is always connected in series with the circuit being tested. All of the current that normally flows through the circuit must also flow through the ammeter; if there is any other path for the current to follow, the ammeter reading will not be accurate. The ammeter itself has very little resistance to current flow and therefore will not affect the circuit, but it will measure current draw only when the circuit is closed and electricity is flowing. Excessive current draw can blow fuses and drain the battery, while a reduced current draw can cause motors to run slowly, lights to dim and other components to not operate properly. The ammeter can help diagnose these conditions by locating the cause of the high or low reading.

Multimeters

Different combinations of test meters can be built into a single unit designed for specific tests. Some of the more common combination test devices are known as Volt/Amp testers, Tach/Dwell meters, or Digital Multimeters. The Volt/Amp tester is used for charging system, starting system or battery tests and consists of a voltmeter, an ammeter and a variable resistance carbon pile. The voltmeter will usually have at least two ranges for use with 6, 12 and 24 volt systems. The ammeter also has more than one range for testing various levels of battery loads and starter current draw and the carbon pile can be adjusted to offer different amounts of resistance. The Volt/Amp tester has heavy leads to carry large amounts of current and many later models have an inductive ammeter pickup that clamps around the wire to simplify test connections. On some models, the ammeter also has a zero-center scale to allow testing of charging and starting systems without switching leads or polarity. A digital multimeter is a voltmeter, ammeter and ohmmeter combined in an instrument which gives a digital readout. These are often used when testing solid state circuits because of their high input impedance (usually 10 megohms or more).

The tach/dwell meter combines a tachometer and a dwell (cam angle) meter and is a specialized kind of voltmeter. The tachometer scale is marked to show engine speed in rpm and the dwell scale is marked to show degrees of distributor shaft rotation. In most electronic ignition systems, dwell is determined by the control unit, but the dwell meter can also be used to check the duty cycle (operation) of some electronic engine control systems. Some tach/dwell meters are powered by an internal battery, while others take their power from the car battery in use. The battery powered testers usually require calibration much like an ohmmeter before testing.

Special Test Equipment

A variety of diagnostic tools are available to help troubleshoot and repair computerized engine control systems. The most sophisticated of these devices are the console type engine analyzers that usually occupy a garage service bay, but there are several types of aftermarket electronic testers available that will allow quick circuit tests of the engine control system by plugging directly into a special connector located in the engine compartment or under the dashboard. Several tool and equipment manufacturers offer simple, hand held testers that measure various circuit voltage levels on command to check all system components for proper operation. Although these testers usually cost about $300-$500, consider that the average computer control unit (or ECM) can cost just as much and the money saved by not replacing perfectly good sensors or components in an attempt to correct a problem could justify the purchase price of a special diagnostic tester the first time it's used.

These computerized testers can allow quick and easy test measurements while the engine is operating or while the car is being driven. In addition, the on-board computer memory can be read to access any stored trouble codes; in effect allowing the computer to tell you where it hurts and aid trouble diagnosis by pinpointing exactly which circuit or component is malfunctioning. In the same manner, repairs can be tested to make sure the problem has been corrected. The biggest advantage these special testers have is their relatively easy hookups that minimize or eliminate the chances of making the wrong connections and getting false voltage readings or damaging the computer accidentally.

NOTE: *It should be remembered that these testers check voltage levels in circuits; they don't detect mechanical problems or failed components if the circuit voltage falls within the preprogrammed limits stored in the tester PROM unit. Also, most of the hand held testers are designed to work only on one or two systems made by a specific manufacturer.*

A variety of aftermarket testers are available to help diagnose different computerized control systems. Owatonna Tool Company (OTC), for example, markets a device called the OTC Monitor which plugs directly into the assembly line diagnostic link (ALDL). The OTC tester makes diagnosis a simple matter of pressing the correct buttons and, by changing the internal PROM or inserting a different diagnosis cartridge, it will work on any model from full size to subcompact, over a wide range of years. An adapter is supplied with the tester to allow connection to all types of ALDL links, regardless of the number of pin terminals used. By inserting an updated PROM into the OTC tester, it can be easily updated to diagnose any new modifications of computerized control systems.

Wiring Harnesses

The average automobile contains about ½ mile of wiring, with hundreds of individual connections. To protect the many wires from damage and to keep them from becoming a confusing tangle, they are organized into bundles, enclosed in plastic or taped together and called wire harnesses. Different wiring harnesses serve different parts of the vehicle. Individual wires are color coded to help trace them through a harness where sections are hidden from view.

A loose or corroded connection or a replacement wire that is too small for the circuit will add extra resistance and an additional voltage drop to the circuit. A ten percent voltage drop can result in slow or erratic motor operation, for example, even though the circuit is complete. Automotive wiring or circuit conductors can be in any one of three forms:

1. Single strand wire
2. Multistrand wire
3. Printed circuitry

Single strand wire has a solid metal core and is usually used inside such components as alternators, motors, relays and other devices. Multistrand wire has a core made of many small strands of wire twisted together into a single conductor. Most of the wiring in an automotive electrical system is made up of multistrand wire, either as a single conductor or grouped together in a harness. All wiring is color coded on the insulator, either as a solid color or as a colored wire with an identification stripe. A printed circuit is a thin film of copper or other conductor that is printed on an insulator backing. Occasionally, a printed circuit is sandwiched between two sheets of plastic for more protection and flexibility. A complete printed circuit, consisting of conductors, insulating material and connectors for lamps or other components is called a printed circuit board. Printed circuitry is used in place of individual wires or harnesses in places where space is limited, such as behind instrument panels.

Wire Gauge

Since computer controlled automotive electrical systems are very sensitive to changes in resistance, the selection of properly sized wires is critical when systems are repaired. The wire gauge number is an expression of the cross section area of the conductor. The most common system for expressing wire size is the American Wire Gauge (AWG) system.

Wire cross section area is measured in circular mils. A mil is $\frac{1}{1000}''$ (0.001"); a circular mil is the area of a circle one mil in diameter. For example, a conductor $\frac{1}{4}''$ in diameter is 0.250 in. or 250 mils. The circular mil cross section area of the wire is 250 squared (250^2) or 62,500 circular mils. Imported car models usually use metric wire gauge designations, which is simply the cross section area of the conductor in square millimeters (mm^2).

Gauge numbers are assigned to conductors of various cross section areas. As gauge number increases, area decreases and the conductor becomes smaller. A 5 gauge conductor is smaller than a 1 gauge conductor and a 10 gauge is smaller than a 5 gauge. As the cross section area of a conductor decreases, resistance increases and so does the gauge number. A conductor with a higher gauge number will carry less current than a conductor with a lower gauge number.

NOTE: *Gauge wire size refers to the size of the conductor, not the size of the complete wire. It is possible to have two wires of the same gauge with different diameters because one may have thicker insulation than the other.*

12 volt automotive electrical systems generally use 10, 12, 14, 16 and 18 gauge wire. Main power distribution circuits and larger accessories usually use 10 and 12 gauge wire. Battery cables are usually 4 or 6 gauge, although 1 and 2 gauge wires are occasionally used. Wire length must also be considered when making repairs to a circuit. As conductor length increases, so does resistance. An 18 gauge wire, for example, can carry a 10 amp load for 10 feet without excessive voltage drop; however if a 15 foot wire is required for the same 10 amp load, it must be a 16 gauge wire.

An electrical schematic shows the electrical current paths when a circuit is operating properly. It is essential to understand how a circuit works before trying to figure out why it doesn't. Schematics break the entire electrical system down into individual circuits and show only one particular circuit. In a schematic, no attempt is made to represent wiring and components as they physically appear on the vehicle; switches and other components are shown as simply as possible. Face views of harness connectors show the cavity or terminal locations in all multi-pin connectors to help locate test points.

If you need to backprobe a connector while it is on the component, the order of the terminals must be mentally reversed. The wire color code can help in this situation, as well as a keyway, lock tab or other reference mark.

NOTE: *Wiring diagrams are not included in this book. As trucks have become more complex and available with longer option lists, wiring diagrams have grown in size and complexity. It has become almost impossible to provide a readable reproduction of a wiring diagram in a book this size. Information on ordering wiring diagrams from the vehicle manufacturer can be found in the owner's manual.*

WIRING REPAIR

Soldering is a quick, efficient method of joining metals permanently. Everyone who has the occasion to make wiring repairs should know how to solder. Electrical connections that are soldered are far less likely to come apart and will conduct electricity much better than connections that are only "pig-tailed" together. The most popular (and preferred) method of soldering is with an electrical soldering gun. Soldering irons are available in many sizes and wattage ratings. Irons with higher wattage ratings deliver higher temperatures and recover lost heat faster. A small soldering iron rated for no more than 50 watts is recommended, especially on electrical systems where excess heat can damage the components being soldered.

There are three ingredients necessary for successful soldering; proper flux, good solder and sufficient heat. A soldering flux is necessary to clean the metal of tarnish, prepare it for soldering and to enable the solder to spread into tiny crevices. When soldering, always use a resin flux or resin core solder which is non-corrosive and will not attract moisture once the job is finished. Other types of flux (acid core) will leave a residue that will attract moisture and cause the wires to corrode. Tin is a unique metal with a low melting point. In a molten state, it dissolves and alloys easily with many metals. Solder is made by mixing tin with lead. The most common proportions are 40/60, 50/50 and 60/40, with the percentage of tin listed first. Low priced solders usually contain less tin, making them very difficult for a beginner to use because more heat is required to melt the solder. A common solder is 40/60 which is well suited for all-around general use, but 60/40 melts easier, has more tin for a better joint and is preferred for electrical work.

Soldering Techniques

Successful soldering requires that the metals to be joined be heated to a temperature that will melt the solder – usually 360-460°F (182-238°C). Contrary to popular belief, the purpose of the soldering iron is not to melt the solder itself, but to heat the parts being soldered to a temperature high enough to melt the solder when it is touched to the work. Melting flux-cored solder on the soldering iron will usually destroy the effectiveness of the flux.

NOTE: *Soldering tips are made of copper for good heat conductivity, but must be "tinned" regularly for quick transference of heat to the project and to prevent the solder from sticking to the iron. To "tin" the iron, simply heat it and touch the flux-cored solder to the tip; the solder will flow over the hot tip. Wipe the excess off with a clean rag, but be careful as the iron will be hot.*

After some use, the tip may become pitted. If so, simply dress the tip smooth with a smooth file and "tin" the tip again. An old saying holds that "metals well cleaned are half soldered." Flux-cored solder will remove oxides but rust, bits of insulation and oil or grease must be removed with a wire brush or emery cloth. For maximum strength in soldered parts, the joint must start off clean and tight. Weak joints will result in gaps too wide for the solder to bridge.

If a separate soldering flux is used, it should be brushed or swabbed on only those areas that are to be soldered. Most solders contain a core of flux and separate fluxing is unnecessary. Hold the work to be soldered firmly. It is best to solder on a wooden board, because a metal vise will only rob the piece to be soldered of heat and make it difficult to melt the solder. Hold the soldering tip with the broadest face against the work to be soldered. Apply solder under the tip close to the work, using enough solder to give a heavy film between the iron and the piece being soldered, while moving slowly and making sure the solder melts properly. Keep the work level or the solder will run to the lowest part and favor the thicker parts, because these require more heat to melt the solder. If the soldering tip overheats (the solder coating on the face of the tip burns up), it should be retinned. Once the soldering is completed, let the soldered joint stand until cool. Tape and seal all soldered wire splices after the repair has cooled.

Wire Harness and Connectors

The on-board computer (ECM) wire harness electrically connects the control unit to the various solenoids, switches and sensors used by the control system. Most connectors in the engine compartment or otherwise exposed to the elements are protected against moisture and dirt which could create oxidation and deposits on the terminals. This protection is important because of the very low voltage and current levels used by the computer and sensors. All connectors have a lock which secures the male and female terminals together, with a secondary lock holding the seal and terminal into the connec-

tor. Both terminal locks must be released when disconnecting ECM connectors.

These special connectors are weather-proof and all repairs require the use of a special terminal and the tool required to service it. This tool is used to remove the pin and sleeve terminals. If removal is attempted with an ordinary pick, there is a good chance that the terminal will be bent or deformed. Unlike standard blade type terminals, these terminals cannot be straightened once they are bent. Make certain that the connectors are properly seated and all of the sealing rings in place when connecting leads. On some models, a hinge-type flap provides a backup or secondary locking feature for the terminals. Most secondary locks are used to improve the connector reliability by retaining the terminals if the small terminal lock tangs are not positioned properly.

Molded-on connectors require complete replacement of the connection. This means splicing a new connector assembly into the harness. All splices in on-board computer systems should be soldered to insure proper contact. Use care when probing the connections or replacing terminals in them as it is possible to short between opposite terminals. If this happens to the wrong terminal pair, it is possible to damage certain components. Always use jumper wires between connectors for circuit checking and never probe through weather-proof seals.

Open circuits are often difficult to locate by sight because corrosion or terminal misalignment are hidden by the connectors. Merely wiggling a connector on a sensor or in the wiring harness may correct the open circuit condition. This should always be considered when an open circuit or a failed sensor is indicated. Intermittent problems may also be caused by oxidized or loose connections. When using a circuit tester for diagnosis, always probe connections from the wire side. Be careful not to damage sealed connectors with test probes.

All wiring harnesses should be replaced with identical parts, using the same gauge wire and connectors. When signal wires are spliced into a harness, use wire with high temperature insulation only. With the low voltage and current levels found in the system, it is important that the best possible connection at all wire splices be made by soldering the splices together. It is seldom necessary to replace a complete harness. If replacement is necessary, pay close attention to insure proper harness routing. Secure the harness with suitable plastic wire clamps to prevent vibrations from causing the harness to wear in spots or contact any hot components.

NOTE: *Weatherproof connectors cannot be*

replaced with standard connectors. Instructions are provided with replacement connector and terminal packages. Some wire harnesses have mounting indicators (usually pieces of colored tape) to mark where the harness is to be secured.

In making wiring repairs, it's important that you always replace damaged wires with wires that are the same gauge as the wire being replaced. The heavier the wire, the smaller the gauge number. Wires are color-coded to aid in identification and whenever possible the same color coded wire should be used for replacement. A wire stripping and crimping tool is necessary to install solderless terminal connectors. Test all crimps by pulling on the wires; it should not be possible to pull the wires out of a good crimp.

Wires which are open, exposed or otherwise damaged are repaired by simple splicing. Where possible, if the wiring harness is accessible and the damaged place in the wire can be located, it is best to open the harness and check for all possible damage. In an inaccessible harness, the wire must be bypassed with a new insert, usually taped to the outside of the old harness.

When replacing fusible links, be sure to use fusible link wire, NOT ordinary automotive wire. Make sure the fusible segment is of the same gauge and construction as the one being replaced and double the stripped end when crimping the terminal connector for a good contact. The melted (open) fusible link segment of the wiring harness should be cut off as close to the harness as possible, then a new segment spliced in as described. In the case of a damaged fusible link that feeds two harness wires, the harness connections should be replaced with two fusible link wires so that each circuit will have its own separate protection.

NOTE: *Most of the problems caused in the wiring harness are due to bad ground connections. Always check all vehicle ground connections for corrosion or looseness before performing any power feed checks to eliminate the chance of a bad ground affecting the circuit.*

Repairing Hard Shell Connectors

Unlike molded connectors, the terminal contacts in hard shell connectors can be replaced. Weatherproof hard-shell connectors with the leads molded into the shell have non-replaceable terminal ends. Replacement usually involves the use of a special terminal removal tool that depress the locking tangs (barbs) on the connector terminal and allow the connector to be removed from the rear of the shell. The connector shell should be replaced if it shows any evidence of burning, melting, cracks, or breaks. Replace individual terminals that are burnt, corroded, distorted or loose.

NOTE: *The insulation crimp must be tight to prevent the insulation from sliding back on the wire when the wire is pulled. The insulation must be visibly compressed under the crimp tabs, and the ends of the crimp should be turned in for a firm grip on the insulation.*

The wire crimp must be made with all wire strands inside the crimp. The terminal must be fully compressed on the wire strands with the ends of the crimp tabs turned in to make a firm grip on the wire. Check all connections with an ohmmeter to insure a good contact. There should be no measurable resistance between the wire and the terminal when connected.

Mechanical Test Equipment

Vacuum Gauge

Most gauges are graduated in inches of mercury (in.Hg), although a device called a manometer reads vacuum in inches of water (in. H_2O). The normal vacuum reading usually varies between 18 and 22 in.Hg at sea level. To test engine vacuum, the vacuum gauge must be connected to a source of manifold vacuum. Many engines have a plug in the intake manifold which can be removed and replaced with an adapter fitting. Connect the vacuum gauge to the fitting with a suitable rubber hose or, if no manifold plug is available, connect the vacuum gauge to any device using manifold vacuum, such as EGR valves, etc. The vacuum gauge can be used to determine if enough vacuum is reaching a component to allow its actuation.

Hand Vacuum Pump

Small, hand-held vacuum pumps come in a variety of designs. Most have a built-in vacuum gauge and allow the component to be tested without removing it from the vehicle. Operate the pump lever or plunger to apply the correct amount of vacuum required for the test specified in the diagnosis routines. The level of vacuum in inches of Mercury (in.Hg) is indicated on the pump gauge. For some testing, an additional vacuum gauge may be necessary.

Intake manifold vacuum is used to operate various systems and devices on late model vehicles. To correctly diagnose and solve problems in vacuum control systems, a vacuum source is necessary for testing. In some cases, vacuum can be taken from the intake manifold when the engine is running, but vacuum is normally provided by a hand vacuum pump. These hand vacuum pumps have a built-in vacuum gauge that allow testing while the device is still attached to the component. For some tests, an additional vacuum gauge may be necessary.

HEATING AND AIR CONDITIONING

Heater Blower Motor

REMOVAL AND INSTALLATION

1981-86 models

The blower motor is located under the instrument panel on the left side of the heater assembly.

1. Disconnect the negative battery terminal.
2. Disconnect the motor wiring.
3. Remove the two attaching screws and remove the left outlet duct.
4. Remove the motor retaining screws and the motor.
5. Installation is the reverse of removal.

Heater and Air Conditioning Blower Motor

REMOVAL AND INSTALLATION

1981-86 Models

1. Disconnect the negative battery terminal.
2. Remove the three screws securing the glovebox to the instrument panel.
3. Disconnect the wiring from the blower and case.
4. Remove the blower vent tube from the case.
5. Loosen the recirculating door from its bracket and remove the actuator from the housing. Leave the vacuum lines attached.
6. Remove the seven screws attaching the recirculating housing to the air conditioning unit and remove the housing.
7. Remove the three mounting flange nuts and washers.
8. Remove the blower motor from the unit.

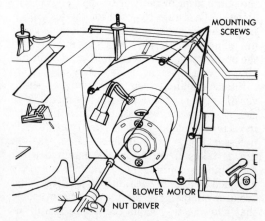

Removing blower motor

9. Installation is the reverse of removal. Replace any damaged sealer.

1987-88 Models

1. Remove the glovebox. If the car has a trim cover on the lower right side of the dash, remove it.
2. Remove the right cowl panel trim cover.
3. Disconnect the blower motor ground lead at the right cowl panel. Unplug the motor electrical connector.
4. The blower motor has an air cooling tube that links the motor with the heater/air conditioning housing. Remove this tube by disconnecting it at both the housing and at the motor.
5. On air conditioned models, remove the recirculation air door actuator and position it so the recircuation air door housing can be removed. Then, remove the 5 recirculation air door housing attaching screws located on the rear face of the housing and the 2 located on the top. Finally, allow the housing to drop downward and remove it from the vehicle.
6. Remove the center spring clamp that secures the blower wheel (you can use a pair of pliers to do this). Pull the blower wheel evenly away from the motor to slide it off the shaft.
7. Remove the 3 blower motor attaching screws and pull the motor off of the air conditioning housing.
8. To install the blower motor, first slide the motor into position and install the attaching screws. Then, position the wheel squarely at the end of the shaft and apply even pressure at two positions to slide it on. Install the center spring clamp.
9. Put the motor into position on the housing and install the attaching screws.
10. Install the recirculation air door housing and its 7 attaching screws.
11. Install the recirculation air door actuator. Install the blower motor air cooling tube.
12. Reconnect the blower motor electrical connector and ground.
13. Install the right cowl panel trim cover.
14. If the car has a trim cover on the lower right side of the dash which was removed, install it.
15. Install the glovebox.

Heater Core

REMOVAL AND INSTALLATION

1981-84 Models Without Air Conditioning

1. Remove the heater assembly.
2. Remove the padding from around the heater core outlets and remove the upper core mounting screws.
3. Pry loose the retaining snaps from around the outer edge of the housing cover.

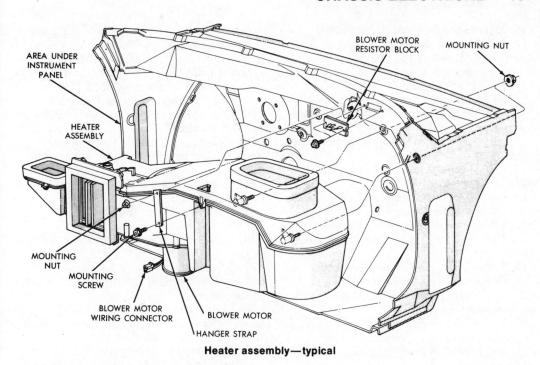

Heater assembly—typical

NOTE: *If a retaining snap should break, the housing cover has provisions for mounting screws.*

4. Remove the housing top cover.

5. Remove the bottom heater core mounting screw.

6. Slide the heater core out of the housing.

7. Installation is the reverse of removal.

Heater Assembly

REMOVAL AND INSTALLATION

1981-85 Cars Without Air Conditioning

1. Disconnect the negative battery cable and drain the radiator.

2. Disconnect the blower motor wiring connector.

3. Reach under the unit, depress the tab on the mode door and temperature control cables, pull the flags from the receivers, and remove the self-adjust clip from the crank arm.

4. Remove the glove box assembly.

5. Disconnect the heater hoses to the unit on the engine side and seal the heater core tube openings and hoses.

6. Through the glove box opening, remove the screw attaching the hanger strap to the heater assembly.

7. Remove the nut attaching the hanger strap to the dash panel and remove the hanger strap.

8. Remove the two nuts attaching the heater assembly to the dash panel. The nuts are on the engine side.

9. Pull out the bottom of the instrument panel and slide out the heater assembly.

10. Installation is the reverse of removal.

1981-84 Air Conditioned Cars

Removal of the Heater-Evaporator Unit is required for core removal. Two people will be required to perform the operation. Discharge, evacuation and recharge and leak testing of the refrigerant system is necessary. This work should either be performed by a trained technician, or handled using the procedures in Chapter 1. Just make sure the system is discharged before attempting removal. During installation, a small can of refrigerant oil will be necessary.

1. Disconnect the battery ground.

2. Drain the coolant.

3. Disconnect the temperature door cable from the heater-evaporator unit.

4. Disconnect the temperature door cable from the retaining clips.

5. Remove the glovebox.

6. Disconnect the vacuum harness from the control head.

7. Disconnect the blower motor lead and anti-diesel relay wire.

8. Remove the seven screws fastening the right trim bezel to the instrument panel. Starting at the right side, swing the bezel clear and remove it.

9. Remove the three screws on the bottom of the center distribution duct cover and slide the cover rearward and remove it.

10. Remove the center distribution duct.

11. Remove the defroster duct adaptor.

12. Remove the H-type expansion valve, located on the right side of the firewall:

    a. Remove the ⅝″ bolt in the center of the plumbing sealing plate.

    b. Carefully pull the refrigerant lines toward the front of the car, taking care to avoid scratching the valve sealing surfaces.

    c. Remove the two Allenhead capscrews and remove the valve.

13. Cap the pipe openings at once. Wrap the valve in a plastic bag.

14. Disconnect the hoses from the core tubes.

15. Disconnect the vacuum lines at the intake manifold and water valve.

16. Remove the unit-to-firewall retaining nuts.

17. Remove the panel support bracket.

18. Remove the right cowl lower panel.

19. Remove the instrument panel pivot bracket screw from the right side.

20. Remove the screws securing the lower instrument panel at the steering column.

21. Pull back the carpet from under the unit as far as possible.

22. Remove the nut from the evaporator-heater unit-to-plenum mounting brace and blower motor ground cable. While supporting the unit, remove the brace from its stud.

23. Lift the unit, pulling it rearward to allow clearance. These operations may require two people.

24. Slowly lower the unit taking care to keep the studs from hanging-up on the insulation.

25. When the unit reaches the floor, slide it rearward until it is out from under the instrument panel.

26. Remove the unit from the car.

27. Place the unit on a workbench. On the inside-the-car-side, remove the nut from the mode door actuator on the top cover and the two retaining clips from the front edge of the cover. To remove the mode door actuator, remove the two screws securing it to the cover.

28. Remove the screws attaching the cover to the assembly and lift off the cover. Lift the mode door out of the unit.

29. Remove the screw from the core retaining bracket and lift out the core.

To install:

30. Place the core in the unit and install the bracket.

31. Install the actuator arm.

CAUTION: *When installing the unit in the car, care must be taken that the vacuum lines to the engine compartment do not hang-up on the accelerator or become trapped between the unit and the firewall. If this happens, kinked lines will result and the unit will have to be removed to free them. Proper routing of these lines will require two people. The portion of the vacuum harness which is routed through the steering column support MUST be positioned BEFORE the distribution housing is installed. The harness MUST be routed ABOVE the temperature control cable.*

32. Place the unit on the floor as far under the panel as possible.

33. Raise the unit carefully, at the same time pull the lower instrument panel rearward as far as possible.

34. Position the unit in place and attach the brace to the stud.

35. Install the lower ground cable and attach the nut.

36. Install and tighten the unit-to-firewall nuts.

37. Reposition the carpet and install, but do not tighten the right instrument panel pivot bracket screw.

38. Place a piece of sheet metal or thin cardboard against the evaporator-heater assembly to center the assembly duct seal.

39. Position the center distributor duct in place making sure that the upper left tab comes in through thel left center air conditioning outlet opening and that each air take-off is properly inserted in its respective outlet.

NOTE: *Make sure that the radio wiring connector does not interfere with the duct.*

40. Install and tighten the screw securing the upper left tab of the center air distribution duct to the instrument panel.

41. Remove the sheet metal or cardboard from between the unit and the duct.

NOTE: *Make sure that the unit seal is properly aligned with the duct opening.*

42. Install and tighten the two lower screws fastening the center distribution duct to the instrument panel.

43. Install and tighten the screws securing the lower instrument panel at the steering column.

44. Install and tighten the nut securing the instrument panel to the support bracket.

45. Make sure that the seal on the unit is properly aligned and seated against the distribution duct assembly.

46. Tighten the instrument panel pivot bracket screw and install the right cowl lower trim.

47. Slide the distributor duct cover assembly onto the center distribution duct so that the notches lock into the tabs and the tabs slide over the rear and side ledges of the center duct assembly.

48. Install the three screws securing the ducting.

49. Install the right trim bezel.

50. Connect the vacuum harness to the control head.

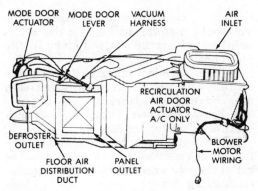

The heater or A/C/heater housing used on 1987–88 models

51. Connect the blower lead and the anti-diesel wire.
52. Install the glovebox.
53. Connect the temperature door cable.
54. Install new O-rings on the evaporator plate and the plumbing plate. Coat the new O-rings with clean refrigerant oil.
55. Place the H-valve against the evaporator sealing plate surface and install the two throughbolts. Torque to 6-10 ft. lb.
56. Carefully hold the refrigerant line connector against the valve and install the bolt. Torque to 14-20 ft. lb.
57. Install the heater hoses at the core tubes.
58. Connect the vacuum lines at the manifold and water valve.
59. Install the condensate drain tube.
60. Have the system evacuated, charged and leak tested by a trained technician, or perform this work yourself using the procedures in Chapter 1.

All 1985-86 Models

1. Discharge the air conditioning system, utilizing the procedures in Chapter 1, or by having the work performed by a professional mechanic.
2. Drain the engine cooling system. Then, disconnnect the heater hoses at the core and plug the core openings with a cork or cap.
3. Mark and then disconnect the vacuum

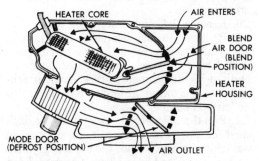

Blend air heater system—typical

lines for the heater/air conditioning system at the intake manifold and water valve.
4. Remove the right side scuff plate and the cowl side trim panel.
5. Remove the glovebox.
6. Remove the air conditioning control head as described below.
7. If the car has a console, remove it.
8. Remove the two bolts and two screws which fasten the forward console mounting bracket to the body and remove it.
9. Remove the center distribution duct.
10. Remove the side window demister adapter on those models so-equipped. Pull the defroster adapter from the bottom of the defroster duct.
11. Remove its clamp and remove the L-shaped condensate drain tube. Disconnect the heater/air conditioning unit from the wiring harness at the connector.
12. Disconnect the control cable at the receiver, located near the evaporator assembly. To do this, depress the tab on the red flag and pull the flag out of the receiver.
13. Remove the right side cowl-to-plenum brace. Pull the carpet out from under the unit and fold it back.
14. Remove the screw holding the hanger strap to the unit. Then, remove the 4 mounting nuts for the unit which are located on the engine compartment side of the cowl. Finally, pull the unit toward the rear of the car until the studs clear the dash liner. Allow it to drop down until it rests on the catalytic converter tunnel.
15. Turn the unit so as to clear the lower instrument panel reinforcement without moving it too far to either side. Then, remove the unit from the car and place it on a workbench, standing behind it just as a front seat passenger would.
16. Disconnect the actuator arm at the mounting shaft by squeezing it with a pair of pliers to release it. *Be careful to avoid prying the mounting clips as you do this, as they will probably be broken.* When the arm is free, remove the retaining clips from the front edge of the cover.
17. Remove the two screws mounting the mode door actuator to the cover and remove it.
18. Remove the 15 screws attaching the cover to the housing and remove it. Then, lift the mode door out.
19. Remove the screw from the heater core tube retaining bracket and lift the core out of the unit.
20. To install, slide the new core into position and then instal the screw into the retaining bracket.
21. Install the mode door. Install the cover to the heater/air conditioning housing and install the 15 attaching screws.

22. Install the mode door actuator and its two attaching screws.

23. Reconnect the actuator arm at the mounting shaft by squeezing it with a pair of pliers to permit it to be installed over the shaft (again be careful not to squeeze the mounting clips). Install the retaining clips on the front edge of the cover.

24. Install the unit back into the car, working it around the instrument panel reinforcement. Raise it until the mounting studs line up with the holes in the cowl and position it so the studs pass through the cowl. Install the four mounting nuts from the engine compartment side.

25. Install the screw attaching the hanger strap to the unit. Work the carpet back into position under the unit. Install the right side cowl-to-plenum brace.

26. Reconnect the control cable at the receiver. Install the L-shaped condensate drain tube. Connect the heater/air conditioning unit wiring harness connector.

27. Install the defroster adapter onto the bottom of the defroster duct. Install the side window demister adapter on those models so-equipped.

28. Install the center distribution duct.

29. Install the forward console mounting bracket. Install the console.

30. Install the air conditioning control head as described below.

31. Install the glovebox. Install the right side scuff plate and the cowl side trim panel.

32. Connect the vacuum lines for the heater/air conditioning system at the manifold and water valve. Remove the plugs and reconnect the heater hoses at the core. Refill the cooling system.

33. Charge the air conditioning system, utilizing the procedures in Chapter 1, or by having the work performed by a professional mechanic. Start the engine and check for leaks. Refill the cooling system after the engine has reached operating temperature and then cooled back off.

1987 Models

NOTE: *To complete this procedure, make sure to have suitable caps or plastic sheeting and tape to cover and seal open refrigerant lines. Also needed are caps or plugs for the heater core tubes.*

1. Discharge the air conditioning system, utilizing the procedures in Chapter 1, or by having the work performed by a professional mechanic. Disconnect the battery negative cable.

2. Drain the engine cooling system. Remove the right side cowl cover. Remove the trim panel from the door opening scuff plate.

3. There is a roll down bolt located behind the instrument panel to the right of the glovebox. Loosen this bolt so that the instrument panel can be shifted later in the procedure.

4. Remove the four instrument cluster center bezel attaching screws, open the glovebox door and remove the bezel.

5. Remove the lower instrument panel module cover, if the car has one.

6. Remove the center console assembly. Position the accessory wiring harness so it will be out of the way when removing the heater/air conditioning unit.

7. Remove the instrument panel center support braces and brackets.

8. Remove the radio as described later in this section.

9. Remove the ash tray and then remove its mounting bracket.

10. Remove the cigarette lighter and socket. Remove the glovebox.

11. Remove the heater/air conditioning control as described later in this chapter. Disconnect the temperature cable attaching flag and vacuum harness from the control assembly.

12. Remove the two attaching screws and remove the center air duct.

13. Disconnect the blower motor relay module and wiring lead from the harness and position both so the heater/air conditioning unit can be removed later.

14. The defroster duct adapter is located between the heater/air conditioning unit and the defroster duct. Pull it downward from its installed position and remove it.

15. Remove the attaching nut and 4 screws from the heater/air conditioning unit support bracket and remove it.

16. Remove the 3 attaching screws from the heat outlet duct (located under the unit) and remove the duct.

17. Slide the front passenger's seat as far to the rear as it will go. Then, roll the carpet out from under the unit.

18. Disconnect the lines from the refrigerant expansion "H" valve, and immediately and tightly cover the openings.

19. Disconnect both heater hoses and plug the core tubes.

20. Remove the condensate drain tube.

21. Remove the four heater/air conditioning unit attaching nuts from the engine compartment side of the cowl. Remove the heater/air conditioning unit support brace lower attaching bolt. Then, swing the brace out of the way to the left and behind the dash panel.

22. Pull the unit directly away from the dash panel (do not twist or turn it, so as to avoid damaging the seals). Once the studs clear both the dash panel and liner, allow it to drop down until it rests on the floor tunnel.

23. Remove the demister adapter duct from the top of the unit to provide working clearance.

24. Then, keeping the unit upright, slide it from under the instrument panel and out the right side door opening.

25. Place the unit on a workbench or in some similar spot where you can work on it effectively. Remove the retaining nut from the blend-air door pivot shaft. Then, position a pair of pliers so that the upper jaw rests against the top of the pivot shaft and the lower jaw will tend to pry the crank lever upward. Gently pry the crank lever off the pivot shaft.

26. Disconnect the vacuum lines from the defrost mode and panel mode vacuum actuators and position them out of the way.

27. Remove the two heater/air conditioning unit cover attaching screws located above the cover in the air inlet plenum. Remove the 11 heater/air conditioning unit cover attaching screws located downward from the cover in the housing. Lift the cover off the heater/air conditioning unit.

28. Remove the heater core-to-dash panel seal from the tubes of the core. Then, pull the core out of the unit.

29. To install, slide the core into the unit and install the seal. Then install the unit cover and all 13 attaching screws.

30. Reconnect the vacuum lines going to the defrost and panel vacuum actuators. Reinstall the blend air door crank lever onto the pivot shaft.

31. Put the unit back into the car. Install the demister adapter duct. Then, raise the unit until the mounting studs are lined up with the holes in the cowl and work the studs through the holes. Install the support brace and attaching bolt. Install the mounting nuts from the other side of the cowl.

32. Install the condensate drain tube. Reconnect the heater hoses.

33. Reinstall the expansion "H" valve. Uncap the openings and immediately reconnect the refrigerant lines.

34. Install the carpet back under the unit. Then, install the heat outlet duct and the 3 attaching screws.

35. Put the heater/air conditioning unit support bracket into position and then install the attaching nut and 4 screws.

36. Put the defroster duct adapter into position between the heater/air conditioning unit and the defroster duct.

37. Connect the blower motor relay module and wiring lead to the harness.

38. Install the center air duct and install the two attaching screws.

39. Connect the temperature cable attaching flag and vacuum harness to the control assembly. Install the heater/air conditioning control as described later in this chapter.

40. Install the glovebox. Install the cigarette lighter and socket.

41. Install the ash tray and its mounting bracket. Install the radio as described later in this section.

42. Install the instrument panel center support braces and brackets.

43. Reposition the accessory wiring harness to its original location. Install the center console assembly.

44. Install the lower instrument panel module cover, if the car has one.

45. Install the instrument cluster bezel and its four attaching screws.

46. Tighten the roll down bolt located behind the instrument panel to the right of the glovebox.

47. Install the trim panel onto the door opening scuff plate. Install the right side cowl cover. Refill the engine cooling system.

48. Reconnect the battery negative cable. Charge the air conditioning system, utilizing the procedures in Chapter 1, or by having the work performed by a professional mechanic. Operate the engine and check for leaks. After the engine has reached operating temperature and then has cooled back off, bring the coolant level back up to where it belongs.

1988 Models

NOTE: *To complete this procedure, make sure to have suitable caps or plastic sheeting and tape to cover and seal open refrigerant lines. Also needed are caps or plugs for the heater core tubes.*

1. Discharge the air conditioning system, utilizing the procedures in Chapter 1, or by having the work performed by a professional mechanic. Disconnect the battery negative cable.

2. Drain the engine cooling system. Disconnect the heater hoses at the core and plug the openings.

3. Remove the air conditioner condensate drain. Label and then disconnect the vacuum lines running from the car body to various components on the heater/air conditioning unit.

4. Disconnect/remove the following items, according to the body style of the car:

    a. On LeBaron, remove the right upper and lower underpanel silencers.

    b. On LeBaron with passive restraints, remove the right side underdash lower trim panel.

    c. On Sundance and Shadow, remove the steering column cover.

    d. On Daytona and LeBaron, with passive restraints, remove the inner steering column cover.

5. Put the bench seat or right individual seat all the way to the rear. Then, on the Sundance, remove the right pillar trim. On all cars, remove the right cowl side trim (note that on the LeBaron, this requires pulling the lower end of the right side A-pillar trim outward).

6. Remove the glovebox. Then, perform each of the following procedures on the model indicated:

a. On Daytona, LeBaron and New Yorker with passive restraints, and on Lancer and LeBaron GTS, remove the right instrument panel reinforcement.

b. On Sundance and Shadow, Caravelle, 600 and New Yorker Turbo, remove the right instrument panel roll-up screw.

c. On Daytona, LeBaron and New Yorker, remove the forward console bezel, side trim, and lower carpet panels. Then, loosen the floor console and move it to the rear. Remove the forward console. If the car has passive restraints, remove the instrument panel-to-floor reinforcement.

d. On the Sundance and Shadow, remove the center dashboard bezel, lower center module cover, floor console, and instrument support brace (this brace runs from the steering column opening to the right cowl side at the bottom of the instrument panel). Remove also the bracket linking the instrument panel and its support, located under the glovebox. Remove the ashtray. Remove the radio as described later. Remove the instrument panel top cover. Finally, remove the 3 right side panel-to-lower windshield panel attaching screws.

e. On the Caravelle, 600 and New Yorker Turbo, remove the forward console and its mounting bracket.

f. On the Aries, Reliant, LeBaron, New Yorker, and Town & Country, remove the floor console.

g. On the Lancer, remove both front and rear consoles.

h. On the Sundance and Shadow, Aries, Reliant, LeBaron, New Yorker, Town & Country, Caravelle, 600, and New Yorker Turbo pull the right lower side of the instrument panel to the rear.

7. On all models, remove the center distribution and defroster adapter ducts. Then, perform each of the following procedures on the model indicated:

a. On the Sundance and Shadow and Lancer, remove and disconnect the relay module.

b. On the Sundance and Shadow, remove the bracket linking the air conditioning unit and instrument panel. Then, on these models, remove the lower air distribution duct.

c. On the Aries, Reliant, LeBaron, New

Yorker, Town & Country, Caravelle, 600 and New Yorker Turbo, remove the audible message center. Then, on these models, remove the right side cowl-to-plenum brace.

8. On all models, disconnect the blower motor wire connector. Then, disconnect the demister hoses at the top of the heater/air conditioning unit.

9. If the car has manual control rather than Automatic Temperature Control:

a. Disconnect the temperature control cable flag from the bottom of the heater/air conditioning unit and unclip the cable from the left side of the heat distribution duct. Then, swing the cable out of the way and to the left.

b. Label and then disconnect the vacuum lines at the unit.

On cars with Automatic Temperature Control: Disconnect the instrument panel wiring from the rear face of the ATC unit.

10. On Lancers, disconnect the right side 25-way connector bracket and fuse block from the panel.

11. Remove the antenna cable from the clip on the top or rear face of the unit, where it is so-routed.

12. Except on Lancers, fold the carpeting back on the right side.

13. Remove the four attaching nuts for the unit from the engine compartment side of the cowl.

14. Remove the lower screw from the unit's hanging strap and then rotate the strap out of the way.

15. Pull the unit to the rear until its studs clear the cowl and liner and then lower it. On the Sundance and Shadow, remove the demister adapter from the top of the unit. Then, on these models, pull the lower right section of the instrument panel rearward and hold it for clearance as you slide the unit out of the

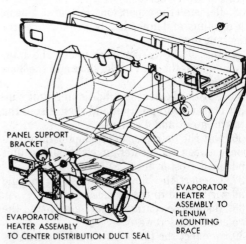

PANEL SUPPORT BRACKET

EVAPORATOR HEATER ASSEMBLY TO PLENUM MOUNTING BRACE

EVAPORATOR HEATER ASSEMBLY TO CENTER DISTRIBUTION DUCT SEAL

Mounting of the heater/A/C unit—1988 models

car in an upright position. On the other models, rotate the unit as necessary for clearance as you pull it out from under the instrument panel.

16. To install the unit, first reverse the step above to get it into position under the dash. On the Sundance and Shadow, install the demister adapter. Then, raise it, line up the four mounting studs with the holes in the cowl, and work the studs through the cowl.

17. Install the four retaining nuts from the engine compartment side of the cowl.

18. Rotate the hanging strap back into position and install the attaching bolt.

19. Reposition the carpeting if it was moved.

20. Reclip the antenna cable, if it is clipped to the heater/air conditioning unit.

21. On Lancers, reconnect the right side 25-way connector bracket and fuse block to the panel.

22. If the car has automatic temperature control, reconnect the instrument panel wiring. Otherwise, reconnect the vacuum lines according to the labels and then reconnect and remount the temperature control cable.

23. Reconnect the demister hoses and the blower motor wiring connector.

24. On the Aries, Reliant, LeBaron, New Yorker, Town & Country, Caravelle, 600 and New Yorker Turbo, install the right side cowl-to-plenum brace. Then install the audible message center.

On the Sundance and Shadow and Lancer, connect the relay module.

On the Sundance and Shadow, install the lower air distribution duct. Then, on these models, install the bracket linking the air conditioning unit and instrument panel.

On the Aries, Reliant, LeBaron, New Yorker, Town & Country, Caravelle, 600 and New Yorker Turbo, install the right side cowl-to-plenum brace. Then, on these models, remove the audible message center.

25. On all models, install the center distribution and defroster adapter ducts.

26. Perform each of the following procedures on the model indicated:

a. On Daytona, LeBaron and New Yorker with passive restraints, and on Lancer and LeBaron GTS, remove the right instrument panel reinforcement.

b. On Sundance and Shadow, Caravelle, 600 and New Yorker Turbo, remove the right instrument panel roll-up screw.

c. On Daytona, LeBaron and New Yorker, remove the forward console bezel, side trim, and lower carpet panels. Then, loosen the floor console and move it to the rear. Remove the forward console. If the car has passive restraints, remove the instrument panel-to-floor reinforcement.

d. On the Sundance and Shadow, install

the 3 right side panel-to-lower windshield panel attaching screws. Install the instrument panel top cover. Install the radio as described later. Install the ashtray. Install the bracket linking the instrument panel and its support, located under the glovebox. Install the instrument panel support brace, floor console, lower center module cover, and center dashboard bezel.

e. On the Caravelle, 600 and New Yorker Turbo, install the forward console and its mounting bracket.

f. On the Aries, Reliant, LeBaron, New Yorker, and Town & Country, install the floor console.

g. On the Lancer, install both front and rear consoles.

h. On the Sundance and Shadow, Aries, Reliant, LeBaron, New Yorker, Town & Country, Caravelle, 600, and New Yorker Turbo push the right lower side of the instrument panel forward and back into its normal position.

27. Install the glovebox. Install the right pillar trim on the Sundance and right side cowl side trim on all cars.

28. Install/connect the following, according to the model of the car:

a. On LeBaron, install the right upper and lower underpanel silencers.

b. On LeBaron with passive restraints, install the right side underdash lower trim panel.

c. On Sundance and Shadow, install the steering column cover.

d. On Daytona and LeBaron, with passive restraints, install the inner steering column cover.

29. Connect the vacuum lines running from the car body to various components on the heater/air conditioning unit, according to the labeling done during removal. Install the air conditioner condensate drain.

30. Unplug the heater core openings and connect the heater hoses at the core. Refill the cooling system.

31. Charge the air conditioning system, utilizing the procedures in Chapter 1, or by having the work performed by a professional mechanic. Operate the engine and check for leaks. After the engine has reached operating temperature and then has cooled back off, bring the coolant level back up to where it belongs.

Air Conditioning Control Head
REMOVAL AND INSTALLATION

1. Disconnect the battery negative cable. Remove the headlight switch knob/shaft assembly by reaching under the instrument panel and de-

pressing the button on the bottom of the switch as you pull outward on the knob.

2. Remove the left instrument panel bezel attaching screws. Remove the left bezel.

3. Remove the two control head mounting screws (upper left and lower right) and slide the control rearward until it is possible to gain access to the rear of the unit.

4. Note locations or label the various cables, the wiring, and vacuum hoses. Then disconnect all of them. Remove the control.

5. Install the control in reverse order. Make sure all cables, electrical connectors and vacuum hoses are securely connected.

6. Install the bezel in reverse order. Install the headlight switch knob and shaft by sliding the shaft into the switch until it locks into place.

Evaporator Core
REMOVAL AND INSTALLATION

The evaporator core can be removed only after the entire heater/air conditioning unit is removed from the car.

1981-84 Air Conditioned Cars

Two people will be required to perform the operation. Discharge, evacuation and recharge and leak testing of the refrigerant system is necessary. This work should either be performed by a trained technician, or handled using the procedures in Chapter 1. Just make sure the system is discharged before attempting removal. During installation, a small can of refrigerant oil will be necessary.

1. Disconnect the battery ground.

2. Drain the coolant.

3. Disconnect the temperature door cable from the heater-evaporator unit.

4. Disconnect the temperature door cable from the retaining clips.

5. Remove the glovebox.

6. Disconnect the vacuum harness from the control head.

7. Disconnect the blower motor lead and anti-diesel relay wire.

8. Remove the seven screws fastening the right trim bezel to the instrument panel. Starting at the right side, swing the bezel clear and remove it.

9. Remove the three screws on the bottom of the center distribution duct cover and slide the cover rearward and remove it.

10. Remove the center distribution duct.

11. Remove the defroster duct adaptor.

12. Remove the H-type expansion valve, located on the right side of the firewall:

a. Remove the ⅝" bolt in the center of the plumbing sealing plate.

b. Carefully pull the refrigerant lines toward the front of the car, taking care to avoid scratching the valve sealing surfaces.

c. Remove the two Allenhead capscrews and remove the valve.

13. Cap the pipe openings at once. Wrap the valve in a plastic bag.

14. Disconnect the hoses from the core tubes.

15. Disconnect the vacuum lines at the intake manifold and water valve.

16. Remove the unit-to-firewall retaining nuts.

17. Remove the panel support bracket.

18. Remove the right cowl lower panel.

19. Remove the instrument panel pivot bracket screw from the right side.

20. Remove the screws securing the lower instrument panel at the steering column.

21. Pull back the carpet from under the unit as far as possible.

22. Remove the nut from the evaporator-heater unit-to-plenum mounting brace and blower motor ground cable. While supporting the unit, remove the brace from its stud.

23. Lift the unit, pulling it rearward to allow clearance. These operations may require two people.

24. Slowly lower the unit taking care to keep the studs from hanging-up on the insulation.

25. When the unit reaches the floor, slide it rearward until it is out from under the instrument panel.

26. Remove the unit from the car.

27. Place the unit on a workbench. On the inside-the-car-side, remove the nut from the mode door actuator on the top cover and the two retaining clips from the front edge of the cover. To remove the mode door actuator, remove the two screws securing it to the cover.

28. Remove the screws attaching the cover to the assembly and lift off the cover. Lift the mode door out of the unit.

29. Remove the screw from the core retaining bracket and lift out the core.

To install:

30. Place the core in the unit and install the bracket.

31. Install the actuator arm.

CAUTION: *When installing the unit in the car, care must be taken that the vacuum lines to the engine compartment do not hang-up on the accelerator or become trapped between the unit and the firewall. If this happens, kinked lines will result and the unit will have to be removed to free them. Proper routing of these lines will require two people. The portion of the vacuum harness which is routed through the steering column support MUST be posi-*

tioned BEFORE the distribution housing is installed. The harness MUST be routed ABOVE the temperature control cable.

32. Place the unit on the floor as far under the panel as possible.

33. Raise the unit carefully, at the same time pull the lower instrument panel rearward as far as possible.

34. Position the unit in place and attach the brace to the stud.

35. Install the lower ground cable and attach the nut.

36. Install and tighten the unit-to-firewall nuts.

37. Reposition the carpet and install, but do not tighten the right instrument panel pivot bracket screw.

38. Place a piece of sheet metal or thin cardboard against the evaporator-heater assembly to center the assembly duct seal.

39. Position the center distributor duct in place making sure that the upper left tab comes in through thel left center air conditioning outlet opening and that each air take-off is properly inserted in its respective outlet.

NOTE: *Make sure that the radio wiring connector does not interfere with the duct.*

40. Install and tighten the screw securing the upper left tab of the center air distribution duct to the instrument panel.

41. Remove the sheet metal or cardboard from between the unit and the duct.

NOTE: *Make sure that the unit seal is properly aligned with the duct opening.*

42. Install and tighten the two lower screws fastening the center distribution duct to the instrument panel.

43. Install and tighten the screws securing the lower instrument panel at the steering column.

44. Install and tighten the nut securing the instrument panel to the support bracket.

45. Make sure that the seal on the unit is properly aligned and seated against the distribution duct assembly.

46. Tighten the instrument panel pivot bracket screw and install the right cowl lower trim.

47. Slide the distributor duct cover assembly onto the center distribution duct so that the notches lock into the tabs and the tabs slide over the rear and side ledges of the center duct assembly.

48. Install the three screws securing the ducting.

49. Install the right trim bezel.

50. Connect the vacuum harness to the control head.

51. Connect the blower lead and the anti-diesel wire.

52. Install the glovebox.

53. Connect the temperature door cable.

54. Install new O-rings on the evaporator plate and the plumbing plate. Coat the new O-rings with clean refrigerant oil.

55. Place the H-valve against the evaporator sealing plate surface and install the two throughbolts. Torque to 6-10 ft. lb.

56. Carefully hold the refrigerant line connector against the valve and install the bolt. Torque to 14-20 ft. lb.

57. Install the heater hoses at the core tubes.

58. Connect the vacuum lines at the manifold and water valve.

59. Install the condensate drain tube.

60. Have the system evacuated, charged and leak tested by a trained technician, or perform this work yourself using the procedures in Chapter 1.

All 1985-86 Models

1. Discharge the air conditioning system, utilizing the procedures in Chapter 1, or by having the work performed by a professional mechanic.

2. Drain the engine cooling system. Then, disconnnect the heater hoses at the core and plug the core openings with a cork or cap.

3. Mark and then disconnect the vacuum lines for the heater/air conditioning system at the intake manifold and water valve.

4. Remove the right side scuff plate and the cowl side trim panel.

5. Remove the glovebox.

6. Remove the air conditioning control head as described below.

7. If the car has a console, remove it.

8. Remove the two bolts and two screws which fasten the forward console mounting bracket to the body and remove it.

9. Remove the center distribution duct.

10. Remove the side window demister adapter on those models so-equipped. Pull the defroster adapter from the bottom of the defroster duct.

11. Remove its clamp and remove the L-shaped condensate drain tube. Disconnect the heater/air conditioning unit from the wiring harness at the connector.

12. Disconnect the control cable at the receiver, located near the evaporator assembly. To do this, depress the tab on the red flag and pull the flag out of the receiver.

13. Remove the right side cowl-to-plenum brace. Pull the carpet out from under the unit and fold it back.

14. Remove the screw holding the hanger strap to the unit. Then, remove the 4 mounting nuts for the unit which are located on the engine compartment side of the cowl. Finally, pull the unit toward the rear of the car until the studs clear the dash liner. Allow it to drop down

until it rests on the catalytic converter tunnel.

15. Turn the unit so as to clear the lower instrument panel reinforcement without moving it too far to either side. Then, remove the unit from the car and place it on a workbench, standing behind it just as a front seat passenger would.

16. Disconnect the actuator arm at the mounting shaft by squeezing it with a pair of pliers to release it. *Be careful to avoid prying the mounting clips as you do this, as they will probably be broken.* When the arm is free, remove the retaining clips from the front edge of the cover.

17. Remove the two screws mounting the mode door actuator to the cover and remove it.

18. Remove the 15 screws attaching the cover to the housing and remove it. Then, lift the mode door out.

19. Remove the screw from the heater core tube retaining bracket and lift the core out of the unit.

20. To install, slide the new core into position and then instal the screw into the retaining bracket.

21. Install the mode door. Install the cover to the heater/air conditioning housing and install the 15 attaching screws.

22. Install the mode door actuator and its two attaching screws.

23. Reconnect the actuator arm at the mounting shaft by squeezing it with a pair of pliers to permit it to be installed over the shaft (again be careful not to squeeze the mounting clips). Install the retaining clips on the front edge of the cover.

24. Install the unit back into the car, working it around the instrument panel reinforcement. Raise it until the mounting studs line up with the holes in the cowl and position it so the studs pass through the cowl. Install the four mounting nuts from the engine compartment side.

25. Install the screw attaching the hanger strap to the unit. Work the carpet back into position under the unit. Install the right side cowl-to-plenum brace.

26. Reconnect the control cable at the receiver. Install the L-shaped condensate drain tube. Connect the heater/air conditioning unit wiring harness connector.

27. Install the defroster adapter onto the bottom of the defroster duct. Install the side window demister adapter on those models so-equipped.

28. Install the center distribution duct.

29. Install the forward console mounting bracket. Install the console.

30. Install the air conditioning control head as described below.

31. Install the glovebox. Install the right side scuff plate and the cowl side trim panel.

32. Connect the vacuum lines for the heater/air conditioning system at the manifold and water valve. Remove the plugs and reconnect the heater hoses at the core. Refill the cooling system.

33. Charge the air conditioning system, utilizing the procedures in Chapter 1, or by having the work performed by a professional mechanic. Start the engine and check for leaks. Refill the cooling system after the engine has reached operating temperature and then cooled back off.

1987 Models

NOTE: *To complete this procedure, make sure to have suitable caps or plastic sheeting and tape to cover and seal open refrigerant lines. Also needed are caps or plugs for the heater core tubes.*

1. Discharge the air conditioning system, utilizing the procedures in Chapter 1, or by having the work performed by a professional mechanic. Disconnect the battery negative cable.

2. Drain the engine cooling system. Remove the right side cowl cover. Remove the trim panel from the door opening scuff plate.

3. There is a roll down bolt located behind the instrument panel to the right of the glovebox. Loosen this bolt so that the instrument panel can be shifted later in the procedure.

4. Remove the four instrument cluster center bezel attaching screws, open the glovebox door and remove the bezel.

5. Remove the lower instrument panel module cover, if the car has one.

6. Remove the center console assembly. Position the accessory wiring harness so it will be out of the way when removing the heater/air conditioning unit.

7. Remove the instrument panel center support braces and brackets.

8. Remove the radio as described later in this section.

9. Remove the ash tray and then remove its mounting bracket.

10. Remove the cigarette lighter and socket. Remove the glovebox.

11. Remove the heater/air conditioning control as described later in this chapter. Disconnect the temperature cable attaching flag and vacuum harness from the control assembly.

12. Remove the two attaching screws and remove the center air duct.

13. Disconnect the blower motor relay module and wiring lead from the harness and posi-

tion both so the heater/air conditioning unit can be removed later.

14. The defroster duct adapter is located between the heater/air conditioning unit and the defroster duct. Pull it downward from its installed position and remove it.

15. Remove the attaching nut and 4 screws from the heater/air conditioning unit support bracket and remove it.

16. Remove the 3 attaching screws from the heat outlet duct (located under the unit) and remove the duct.

17. Slide the front passenger's seat as far to the rear as it will go. Then, roll the carpet out from under the unit.

18. Disconnect the lines from the refrigerant expansion "H" valve, and immediately and tightly cover the openings.

19. Disconnect both heater hoses and plug the core tubes.

20. Remove the condensate drain tube.

21. Remove the four heater/air conditioning unit attaching nuts from the engine compartment side of the cowl. Remove the heater/air conditioning unit support brace lower attaching bolt. Then, swing the brace out of the way to the left and behind the dash panel.

22. Pull the unit directly away from the dash panel (do not twist or turn it, so as to avoid damaging the seals). Once the studs clear both the dash panel and liner, allow it to drop down until it rests on the floor tunnel.

23. Remove the demister adapter duct from the top of the unit to provide working clearance.

24. Then, keeping the unit upright, slide it from under the instrument panel and out the right side door opening.

25. Place the unit on a workbench or in some similar spot where you can work on it effectively. Remove the retaining nut from the blend-air door pivot shaft. Then, position a pair of pliers so that the upper jaw rests against the top of the pivot shaft and the lower jaw will tend to pry the crank lever upward. Gently pry the crank lever off the pivot shaft.

26. Disconnect the vacuum lines from the defrost mode and panel mode vacuum actuators and position them out of the way.

27. Remove the two heater/air conditioning unit cover attaching screws located above the cover in the air inlet plenum. Remove the 11 heater/air conditioning unit cover attaching screws located downward from the cover in the housing. Lift the cover off the heater/air conditioning unit.

28. Remove the heater core-to-dash panel seal from the tubes of the core. Then, pull the core out of the unit.

29. To install, slide the core into the unit and install the seal. Then install the unit cover and all 13 attaching screws.

30. Reconnect the vacuum lines going to the defrost and panel vacuum actuators. Reinstall the blend air door crank lever onto the pivot shaft.

31. Put the unit back into the car. Install the demister adapter duct. Then, raise the unit until the mounting studs are lined up with the holes in the cowl and work the studs through the holes. Install the support brace and attaching bolt. Install the mounting nuts from the other side of the cowl.

32. Install the condensate drain tube. Reconnect the heater hoses.

33. Reinstall the expansion "H" valve. Uncap the openings and immediately reconnect the refrigerant lines.

34. Install the carpet back under the unit. Then, install the heat outlet duct and the 3 attaching screws.

35. Put the heater/air conditioning unit support bracket into position and then install the attaching nut and 4 screws.

36. Put the defroster duct adapter into position between the heater/air conditioning unit and the defroster duct.

37. Connect the blower motor relay module and wiring lead to the harness.

38. Install the center air duct and install the two attaching screws.

39. Connect the temperature cable attaching flag and vacuum harness to the control assembly. Install the heater/air conditioning control as described later in this chapter.

40. Install the glovebox. Install the cigarette lighter and socket.

41. Install the ash tray and its mounting bracket. Install the radio as described later in this section.

42. Install the instrument panel center support braces and brackets.

43. Reposition the accessory wiring harness to its original location. Install the center console assembly.

44. Install the lower instrument panel module cover, if the car has one.

45. Install the instrument cluster bezel and its four attaching screws.

46. Tighten the roll down bolt located behind the instrument panel to the right of the glovebox.

47. Install the trim panel onto the door opening scuff plate. Install the right side cowl cover. Refill the engine cooling system.

48. Reconnect the battery negative cable. Charge the air conditioning system, utilizing the procedures in Chapter 1, or by having the

work performed by a professional mechanic. Operate the engine and check for leaks. After the engine has reached operating temperature and then has cooled back off, bring the coolant level back up to where it belongs.

1988 Models

NOTE: *To complete this procedure, make sure to have suitable caps or plastic sheeting and tape to cover and seal open refrigerant lines. Also needed are caps or plugs for the heater core tubes.*

1. Discharge the air conditioning system, utilizing the procedures in Chapter 1, or by having the work performed by a professional mechanic. Disconnect the battery negative cable.

2. Drain the engine cooling system. Disconnect the heater hoses at the core and plug the openings.

3. Remove the air conditioner condensate drain. Label and then disconnect the vacuum lines running from the car body to various components on the heater/air conditioning unit.

4. Disconnect/remove the following items, according to the body style of the car:

    a. On LeBaron, remove the right upper and lower underpanel silencers.

    b. On LeBaron with passive restraints, remove the right side underdash lower trim panel.

    c. On Sundance and Shadow, remove the steering column cover.

    d. On Daytona and LeBaron, with passive restraints, remove the inner steering column cover.

5. Put the bench seat or right individual seat all the way to the rear. Then, on the Sundance, remove the right pillar trim. On all cars, remove the right cowl side trim (note that on the LeBaron, this requires pulling the lower end of the right side A-pillar trim outward).

6. Remove the glovebox. Then, perform each of the following procedures on the model indicated:

    a. On Daytona, LeBaron and New Yorker with passive restraints, and on Lancer and LeBaron GTS, remove the right instrument panel reinforcement.

    b. On Sundance and Shadow, Caravelle, 600 and New Yorker Turbo, remove the right instrument panel roll-up screw.

    c. On Daytona, LeBaron and New Yorker, remove the forward console bezel, side trim, and lower carpet panels. Then, loosen the floor console and move it to the rear. Remove the forward console. If the car has passive restraints, remove the instrument panel-to-floor reinforcement.

    d. On the Sundance and Shadow, remove the center dashboard bezel, lower center module cover, floor console, and instrument support brace (this brace runs from the steering column opening to the right cowl side at the bottom of the instrument panel). Remove also the bracket linking the instrument panel and its support, located under the glovebox. Remove the ashtray. Remove the radio as described later. Remove the instrument panel top cover. Finally, remove the 3 right side panel-to-lower windshield panel attaching screws.

    e. On the Caravelle, 600 and New Yorker Turbo, remove the forward console and its mounting bracket.

    f. On the Aries, Reliant, LeBaron, New Yorker, and Town & Country, remove the floor console.

    g. On the Lancer, remove both front and rear consoles.

    h. On the Sundance and Shadow, Aries, Reliant, LeBaron, New Yorker, Town & Country, Caravelle, 600, and New Yorker Turbo pull the right lower side of the instrument panel to the rear.

7. On all models, remove the center distribution and defroster adapter ducts. Then, perform each of the following procedures on the model indicated:

    a. On the Sundance and Shadow and Lancer, remove and disconnect the relay module.

    b. On the Sundance and Shadow, remove the bracket linking the air conditioning unit and instrument panel. Then, on these models, remove the lower air distribution duct.

    c. On the Aries, Reliant, LeBaron, New Yorker, Town & Country, Caravelle, 600 and New Yorker Turbo, remove the audible message center. Then, on these models, remove the right side cowl-to-plenum brace.

8. On all models, disconnect the blower motor wire connector. Then, disconnect the demister hoses at the top of the heater/air conditioning unit.

9. If the car has manual control rather than Automatic Temperature Control:

    a. Disconnect the temperature control cable flag from the bottom of the heater/air conditioning unit and unclip the cable from the left side of the heat distribution duct. Then, swing the cable out of the way and to the left.

    b. Label and then disconnect the vacuum lines at the unit.

On cars with Automatic Temperature Control: Disconnect the instrument panel wiring from the rear face of the ATC unit.

10. On Lancers, disconnect the right side 25-way connector bracket and fuse block from the panel.

11. Remove the antenna cable from the clip on the top or rear face of the unit, where it is so-routed.

12. Except on Lancers, fold the carpeting back on the right side.

13. Remove the four attaching nuts for the unit from the engine compartment side of the cowl.

14. Remove the lower screw from the unit's hanging strap and then rotate the strap out of the way.

15. Pull the unit to the rear until its studs clear the cowl and liner and then lower it. On the Sundance and Shadow, remove the demister adapter from the top of the unit. Then, on these models, pull the lower right section of the instrument panel rearward and hold it for clearance as you slide the unit out of the car in an upright position. On the other models, rotate the unit as necessary for clearance as you pull it out from under the instrument panel.

16. To install the unit, first reverse the step above to get it into position under the dash. On the Sundance and Shadow, install the demister adapter. Then, raise it, line up the four mounting studs with the holes in the cowl, and work the studs through the cowl.

17. Install the four retaining nuts from the engine compartment side of the cowl.

18. Rotate the hanging strap back into position and install the attaching bolt.

19. Reposition the carpeting if it was moved.

20. Reclip the antenna cable, if it is clipped to the heater/air conditioning unit.

21. On Lancers, reconnect the right side 25-way connector bracket and fuse block to the panel.

22. If the car has automatic temperature control, reconnect the instrument panel wiring. Otherwise, reconnect the vacuum lines according to the labels and then reconnect and remount the temperature control cable.

23. Reconnect the demister hoses and the blower motor wiring connector.

24. On the Aries, Reliant, LeBaron, New Yorker, Town & Country, Caravelle, 600 and New Yorker Turbo, install the right side cowl-to-plenum brace. Then install the audible message center.

On the Sundance and Shadow and Lancer, connect the relay module.

On the Sundance and Shadow, install the lower air distribution duct. Then, on these models, install the bracket linking the air conditioning unit and instrument panel.

On the Aries, Reliant, LeBaron, New Yorker, Town & Country, Caravelle, 600 and New Yorker Turbo, install the right side cowl-to-plenum brace. Then, on these models, remove the audible message center.

25. On all models, install the center distribution and defroster adapter ducts.

26. Perform each of the following procedures on the model indicated:

a. On Daytona, LeBaron and New Yorker with passive restraints, and on Lancer and LeBaron GTS, remove the right instrument panel reinforcement.

b. On Sundance and Shadow, Caravelle, 600 and New Yorker Turbo, remove the right instrument panel roll-up screw.

c. On Daytona, LeBaron and New Yorker, remove the forward console bezel, side trim, and lower carpet panels. Then, loosen the floor console and move it to the rear. Remove the forward console. If the car has passive restraints, remove the instrument panel-to-floor reinforcement.

d. On the Sundance and Shadow, install the 3 right side panel-to-lower windshield panel attaching screws. Install the instrument panel top cover. Install the radio as described later. Install the ashtray. Install the bracket linking the instrument panel and its support, located under the glovebox. Install the instrument panel support brace, floor console, lower center module cover, and center dashboard bezel.

e. On the Caravelle, 600 and New Yorker Turbo, install the forward console and its mounting bracket.

f. On the Aries, Reliant, LeBaron, New Yorker, and Town & Country, install the floor console.

g. On the Lancer, install both front and rear consoles.

h. On the Sundance and Shadow, Aries, Reliant, LeBaron, New Yorker, Town & Country, Caravelle, 600, and New Yorker Turbo push the right lower side of the instrument panel forward and back into its normal position.

27. Install the glovebox. Install the right pillar trim on the Sundance and right side cowl side trim on all cars.

28. Install/connect the following, according to the model of the car:

a. On LeBaron, install the right upper and lower underpanel silencers.

b. On LeBaron with passive restraints, install the right side underdash lower trim panel.

c. On Sundance and Shadow, install the steering column cover.

d. On Daytona and LeBaron, with passive restraints, install the inner steering column cover.

29. Connect the vacuum lines running from the car body to various components on the heater/air conditioning unit, according to the label-

ing done during removal. Install the air conditioner condensate drain.

30. Unplug the heater core openings and connect the heater hoses at the core. Refill the cooling system.

31. Charge the air conditioning system, utilizing the procedures in Chapter 1, or by having the work performed by a professional mechanic. Operate the engine and check for leaks. After the engine has reached operating temperature and then has cooled back off, bring the coolant level back up to where it belongs.

RADIO

AM, AM/FM monaural, or AM/FM stero multiplex units are available. All radios are trimmed at the factory and should require no further adjustment. However, after repair or if the antenna trim is to be verified, proceed as follows:

1. Turn radio on.
2. Manually tune the radio to a weak station between 1400 and 1600 KHz on AM.
3. Increase the volume and set the tone control to full treble (clockwise).
4. Viewing the radio from the front, the trimmer control is a slot-head located at the rear of the right side. Adust it carefully by turning it back and forth with a screwdriver until maximum loudness is achieved.

REMOVAL AND INSTALLATION

Airies and Reliant

1. Remove the bezel.
2. If equipped with a mono (single) speaker, remove the instrument panel top cover, speaker, and disconnect the wires from the radio.
3. Remove the two screws attaching the radio to the base panel.
4. Pull the radio thru the front of the base, then disconnect the wiring harness, antenna lead and ground strap.
5. Installation is the reverse of removal.

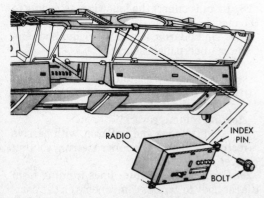

RADIO   INDEX PIN

BOLT

Radio assembly

Daytona and LeBaron

1. Remove the two screws from the bottom of the console trim bezel. Then, lift the bezel out of the console.
2. Remove the two attaching screws fastening the radio to the console.
3. Pull the radio through the front face of the console far enough for access to the wiring. Then, disconnect the wiring harness, antenna lead, and ground strap. Remove the radio.
4. Installation is the reverse of removal.

Lancer

1. Remove the instrument cluster bezel. Then, remove the two radio attaching screws.
2. Disconnect the wiring connectors and antenna cable.
3. Remove the ground strap attaching screw. Remove the radio.
4. Installation is the reverse of removal.

Sundance and Shadow

1. Remove the center module bezel.
2. If the car has a short console, remove the lower center module cover. If the car has a full-length console, remove the right console sidewall.
3. Remove the two radio mounting screws and pull it out of the dash far enough to reach the wiring. Disconnect the power wiring and the antenna cable. Disconnect the ground strap and remove the radio.
4. Installation is the reverse of removal.

WINDSHIELD WIPERS

The windshield wipers can be operated with the wiper switch only when the ignition switch is in the Accessory or Ignition position. A circuit breaker, integral with the wiper switch, protects the circuitry of the wiper system and the vehicle.

Blade and Arm

REMOVAL AND INSTALLATION

Wiper Blade Replacement

1. Lift the wiper arm away from the glass.
2. Depress the release lever on the bridge and remove the blade assembly from the arm.
3. Lift the tab and pinch the end bridge to release it from the center bridge.
4. Slide the end bridge from the blade element and the element from the opposite end bridge.
5. Assembly is the reverse of removal. Make sure that the element locking tabs are securely locked in position.

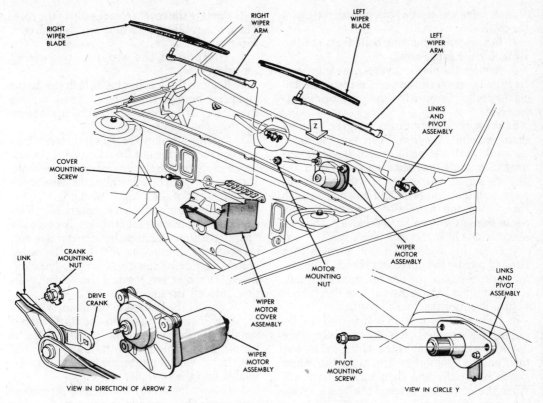

Windshield wiper motor and linkage

Wiper Arm Removal and Installation

FRONT

1. Lift the arm so that the latch can be pulled out to the holding position and then release the arm. The arm will remain off the windshield in this position.

2. Remove the arm off the pivot using a rocking motion.

3. When installing, the motor should be in the park position and the tips of the blades 1½ in. above the bottom of the windshield moulding.

REAR

NOTE: *To remove the rear wiper arm assembly the use of special tool C–3982 or equivalent is necessary. The use of a screwdriver is not recommended as it will distort and damage the arm.*

1. With the tool installed on the arm, lift the arm then remove it from the output shaft.

2. To install, the wiper motor should be in the park position.

3. Install the arm so that the tip of the blade is about 1.3 inches above the lower liftgate gasket.

Windshield Wiper Motor

REMOVAL AND INSTALLATION

1981-85 Front

1. Disconnect the negative battery terminal.

2. Disconnect the linkage from the motor crank arm.

3. Remove the wiper motor plastic cover.

4. Disconnect the wiring harness from the motor.

5. Remove the three mounting bolts from the motor mounting bracket and remove the motor.

6. Installation is the reverse of removal.

1986-88 Aries, Reliant, Caravelle, New Yorker and New Yorker Turbo, Daytona and LeBaron with Passive Restraint System

1. With the ignition switch on, turn the wiper switch on until the wipers have run halfway across the windshield and then turn the switch off. Leave the ignition switch on until the wipers are fully parked and then turn it off.

2. Remove the wiper arms and blades as described above. On the Daytona, disconnect the washer fluid reservoir hose at the tee connector.

3. Remove the plastic screen from the top of the cowl.

4. Remove the mounting bolts from the two pivots for the wiper arms.

5. Remove the plastic cover for the wiper motor from the cowl. Disconnect the motor electrical connector. Remove the three motor mounting nuts.

6. Push the pivots down into the plenum chamber behind the cowl. Then, pull the motor outward, past the point where it clears the mounting studs, and then as far toward the driver's side of the car as it will go. At this point, pull the right pivot and link out through the opening, and then shift the motor to the opposite side of the opening to remove it, the passenger's side link, and that side's pivot.

7. Carefully clamp the motor bracket in a vise and remove the nut from the end of the motor shaft. Separate the linkage from the shaft. If the motor is to be reinstalled, be careful not to turn it out of the "park" position.

8. If the motor's position is disturbed or if installing a new motor that is obviously not in the "park" position: Connect the wiring connector, turn on the ignition switch, turn the wiper switch on briefly and then turn it back off. When the motor has reached the "park" position, turn off the ignition switch.

9. Connect the linkage to the motor with the crank by installing the crank so its D-shaped slot fits over the motor shaft. Install the attaching nut and torque it to 95 ft. lbs.

10. Maneuver the left pivot and its link into the chamber behind the cowl. Slide the assembly all the way to the left (toward the driver's side of the car) until the motor clears the mounting studs and the crank is positioned behind the sheet metal. Push the right pivot and link through the opening in the cowl; then, maneuver the assembly to the right until the motor is lined up with the mounting studs and install it over those studs.

11. Install the 3 motor mounting nuts and torque to 55 inch lbs.

12. Position the pivots and install the pivot mounting bolts, torquing them to 55 inch lbs. Connect the motor wiring connector.

13. Install the plastic motor cover onto the cowl. On Daytona with passive restraints, connect the washer fluid reservoir hose to the Tee connector. Note that the hoses passes through a special hole in the cowl screen. Then, mount the screen to the cowl, on these cars.

14. Install the wiper arms and connect their washer hoses to the Tee connectors.

1986-88 Lancer, LeBaron GTS

1. Remove the wiper arms as described above. Open the hood.

2. Remove the cover from the top of the cowl. Then, remove the 3 attaching screws from each wiper pivot.

3. Disconnect the wiper motor wiring connector.

4. Remove the 3 bolts that attach the motor mounting bracket to the body. Then, remove the motor, its bracket, and the linkage assembly from the cowl plenum.

5. Carefully clamp the motor bracket in a vise and remove the nut from the end of the motor shaft. Separate the linkage from the shaft. If the motor is to be reinstalled, be careful not to turn it out of the "park" position.

6. If the motor's position is disturbed or if installing a new motor that is obviously not in the "park" position: Connect the wiring connector, turn on the ignition switch, turn the wiper switch on briefly and then turn it back off. When the motor has reached the "park" position, turn off the ignition switch.

7. Connect the linkage to the motor with the crank by installing the crank so its D-shaped slot fits over the motor shaft. Install the attaching nut and torque it to 95 ft. lbs.

8. Install the motor, bracket and linkage assembly into the cowl plenum.

9. Loosely install the 3 attaching screws for each pivot. Then, install the 3 motor mounting bracket attaching bolts. Finally, tighten the pivot attaching screws.

10. Connect the motor electrical connector. Install the cowl cover. Install and adjust the wiper arms as described above.

1986-88 Sundance and Shadow

1. Remove the wiper arms as described above. Open the hood.

2. Remove the cowl cover. Remove the 2 retaining nuts from each wiper pivot.

3. Disconnect the wiper motor wiring connector.

4. Remove the 3 bolts that attach the motor mounting bracket to the body and remove the motor, bracket, and linkage from the cowl plenum.

5. Carefully clamp the motor bracket in a vise and remove the nut from the end of the motor shaft. Separate the linkage from the shaft. If the motor is to be reinstalled, be careful not to turn it out of the "park" position.

6. If the motor's position is disturbed or if installing a new motor that is obviously not in the "park" position: Connect the wiring connector, turn on the ignition switch, turn the wiper switch on briefly and then turn it back off. When the motor has reached the "park" position, turn off the ignition switch.

7. Connect the linkage to the motor with the crank by installing the crank so its D-shaped

slot fits over the motor shaft. Install the attaching nut and torque it to 95 ft. lbs.

8. Install the motor, bracket and linkage into the cowl plenum. Position the pivots so the mounting studs pass through the cowl and loosely install the pivot mounting nuts. Then, install and tighten the three motor mounting bolts.

9. Tighten the pivot mounting nuts. Install the cowl cover.

10. Install the wiper arm assemblies as described above.

Rear Wiper Motor
REMOVAL AND INSTALLATION
1981-85

1. Disconnect the negative battery terminal.
2. Remove the blade and arm assembly.
3. Open the liftgate.
4. Remove the motor cover and disconnect the wiring connector.
5. Remove the four bracket retaining screws and remove the motor.
6. Installation is the reverse of removal.

1986-88 Aries, Sundance and Shadow

1. Open the liftgate.
2. Remove the arm and blade as described above. Remove the trim panel from the inside of the liftgate.
3. Disconnect the four screws that mount the motor mounting bracket to the liftgate. Then, remove the motor.
4. Installation is the reverse of removal.

1986-88 Daytona

1. Remove the wiper arm/blade assembly as described above. Remove the grommet from the motor driveshaft.
2. Open the liftgate. Remove the trim panel from inside the liftgate.
3. Disconnect the motor electrical connector.
4. Remove the two screws that mount the

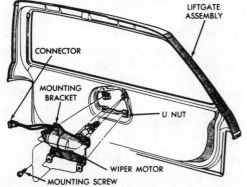

Rear wiper motor installation—1986–88 Aries, Sundance and Shadow

motor bracket onto the liftgate and remove the motor and bracket.

5. Installation is the reverse of removal.

1986-88 Lancer, LeBaron GTS

1. Remove the wiper arm/blade assembly as described above. Remove the grommet and escutcheon from the motor driveshaft.
2. Open the liftgate. Remove the trim panel from inside the liftgate.
3. Disconnect the motor wiring connector. Then, remove the four screws attaching the motor bracket and the motor to the liftgate. Remove the motor.
4. Installation is the reverse of removal.

Wiper Linkage
REMOVAL AND INSTALLATION
1981-85 Models

1. Put the windshield wipers in the park position.
2. Raise the hood and disconnect the negative battery terminal.
3. Remove the wiper arms and blades as previously described.
4. Disconnect the hoses from the tee connector.
5. Remove the pivot screws.
6. Remove the wiper motor plastic cover, and disconnect the wiring harness.
7. Remove the plastic screen from the cowl.
8. Remove the three motor mounting bolts.
9. Push the pivots down into the plenum chamber. Pull the motor out until it clears the mounting studs and then move it to the driver's side as far as it will go. Pull the right pivot and link out through the openin, then shift the motor to the right and remove the motor, the left link and pivot.

NOTE: *Do not rotate the motor output shaft from the park position.*

10. Installation is the reverse of removal.

1986-88 Models

On all these cars, the linkage is removed along with the front windshield wiper motor, using an identical procedure. Refer to the appropriate procedure above.

INSTRUMENTS AND SWITCHES

Instrument Cluster
REMOVAL AND INSTALLATION
1981-85 Conventional Cluster

1. Disconnect the negative battery terminal.
2. Apply the parking brake and block the wheels. Place the gearshift lever in position **1**.

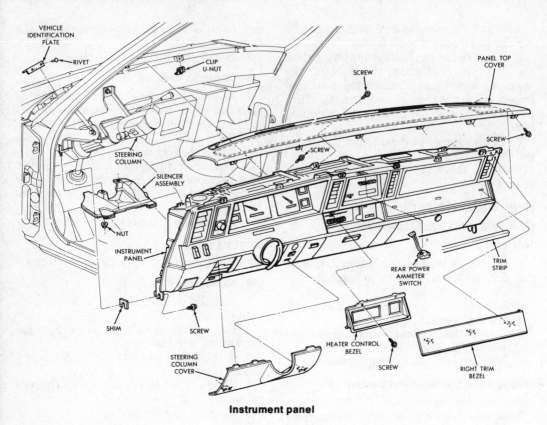

Instrument panel

3. Remove the instrument panel trim strip.

4. Remove the left upper and lower cluster bezel screws.

5. Remove the right lower cluster bezel screw and retaining clip.

6. Remove the instrument cluster bezel by snapping the bezel off of the five retaining clips.

7. Remove the seven retaining screws and remove the upper right bezel.

8. Remove the four rear instrument panel top cover mounting screws.

9. Lift the rear edge of the panel top cover and remove the two screws attaching the upper trim strip retainer and cluster housing to the base panel.

10. Remove the trim strip retainer.

11. Remove the two screws attaching the cluster housing to the base panel of the lower cluster.

12. Lift the rearward edge of the panel top cover and slide the cluster housing rearward.

13. Disconnect the right printed circuit board connector from behind the cluster housing.

14. Disconnect the speedometer cable connector.

15. Disconnect the left printed circuit connector.

16. Remove the cluster assembly.

17. Installation is the reverse of removal.

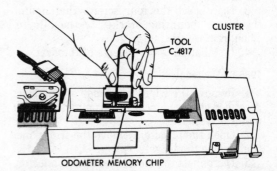

Removing/installing the odometer memory chip in the electronic instrument cluster

1981-85 Electronic Cluster

The electronic cluster is removed in the same manner as the conventional cluster, except for that there is no speedometer cable. When replacing the electronic cluster, the odometer memory chip can be removed from the old cluster and placed in the new one. To remove the chip, special tool C–4817 must be used.

1986-88 Conventional Cluster except Daytona and LeBaron

1. Disconnect the negative battery cable. Apply the parking brake and block the wheels. If

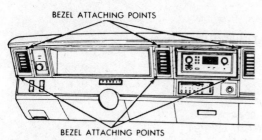

BEZEL ATTACHING POINTS

BEZEL ATTACHING POINTS

Bezel attaching points on the 1986–88 conventional instrument cluster

the car has an automatic transmission with column shift, put the gearshift lever in "1" position.

2. Remove the 6 screws from the cluster bezel. Then, remove the bezel by snapping it off all 5 retaining clips.

3. Remove the rear-facing screws from the instrument panel upper pad. Then, lift the rearward edge of the pad and, holding it up, remove the 2 screws from the top of the cluster.

4. Remove the 2 screws from the bottom of the cluster (these attach it to the dash panel). Lift the rear edge of the pad on top of the dash and hold it upward as you pull the cluster out far enough to reach the wiring.

5. Unscrew the speedometer outer cable retaining collar and then pull the inner cable out of the rear of the speedometer. If necessary, mark the wiring connectors. Then, disconnect all of them.

6. Remove the cluster.

7. To install the cluster, first position it in front of the dash. Then, reconnect the wiring connectors to their original locations. Insert the square end of the speedometer cable into the rear of the speedometer, turning it slightly to line it up, if necessary. Install and tighten the speedometer cable collar nut.

8. Lift the rear edge of the dash pad and hold it upward as you slide the cluster back into position.

9. Install the 4 cluster attaching screws (2 at the bottom and 2 at the top, under the pad). Install the rear-facing screws into the instrument panel upper pad.

10. Install the bezel so all the retaining clips lock. Then, install the 6 bezel attaching screws. Return the gearshift lever to "Park" and reconnect the battery cable.

Electronic Cluster

The electronic cluster is removed in the same manner as the conventional cluster, except for that there is no speedometer cable. When replacing the electronic cluster, the odometer memory chip can be removed from the old cluster and placed in the new one. To remove the chip, special tool C–4817 must be used.

1986-88 Daytona and LeBaron

1. Disconnect the battery negative cable. Remove the 5 screws attaching the top of the cluster bezel to the instrument panel.

2. Pull the bezel to the rear to disengage the 3 clips on its bottom surface and then remove it.

3. Remove the four screws attaching the cluster housing to the dash panel. Pull the cluster assembly to the rear to gain clearance to the wiring. Then, reach underneath it to disconnect the wiring harness. Remove the cluster.

4. To install, connect the wiring harness. Then, put the cluster in position and install the four mounting screws.

5. Install the cluster bezel, first engaging the 3 clips on its bottom surface. Install the 5 screws at the top of the bezel. Reconnect the battery.

Windshield Wiper Switch
REMOVAL AND INSTALLATION

The front wiper switch on these cars is part of the combination turn signal/cruise control/wiper switch. Refer to the appropriate procedure in Chapter 8.

Rear Window Wiper Switch
REMOVAL AND INSTALLATION
Conventional Cluster except Daytona and LeBaron

1. On 1985-88 models, remove the instrument cluster bezel (you can refer to "Instrument Cluster Removal and Installation" above, for attaching screw locations). on 1981-84 models, remove the pull the bottom of the steering column cover to the rear and snap it off the column.

2. Remove the left lower trim bezel by pull-

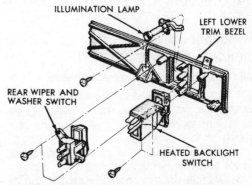

ILLUMINATION LAMP

LEFT LOWER TRIM BEZEL

REAR WIPER AND WASHER SWITCH

HEATED BACKLIGHT SWITCH

Removing the rear wiper switch from the bezel on all models except Daytona and LeBaron

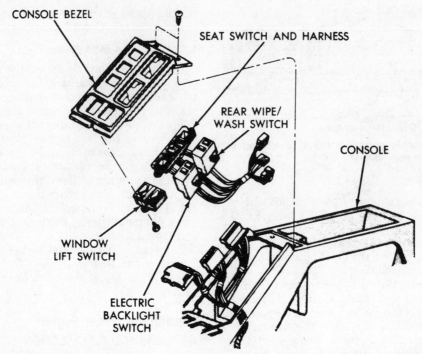

CONSOLE BEZEL

SEAT SWITCH AND HARNESS

REAR WIPE/
WASH SWITCH

CONSOLE

WINDOW
LIFT SWITCH

ELECTRIC
BACKLIGHT
SWITCH

Removing the rear wiper switch from the console bezel on Dayton and LeBaron models

ing it off the two attaching clips. Pull it out of the dash just far enough to reach the wiring connectors. Then, noting which is which for easy installation, disconnect the connectors.

3. Remove the 2 screws attaching the wiper switch to the bezel assembly and pull it off.

4. Installation is the reverse of removal.

Daytona and LeBaron

1. Lift the console lid. Remove the 2 screws from the console bezel and then lift the bezel assembly out of the console.

2. Disconnect the rear wiper/wash switch connectors. Remove the 2 switch-to-bezel mounting screws and remove the switch from the bezel.

3. Installation is the reverse of removal.

Headlight Switch
REMOVAL AND INSTALLATION
All Models Except Sundance and Shadow

1. On 1986-88 models, remove the cluster bezel. Remove the three screws securing the headlamp switch mounting plate to the base panel.

2. Pull the switch and plate rearward and disconnect the wiring connector.

3. Depress the button on the switch and remove the knob and stem.

4. Snap out the escutcheon, then remove the

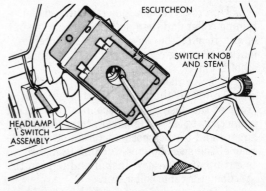

ESCUTCHEON

SWITCH KNOB
AND STEM

HEADLAMP
SWITCH
ASSEMBLY

Headlight switch knob and stem

nut that attaches the switch to the mounting plate.

5. Installation is the reverse of removal.

Sundance and Shadow

1. Remove the headlamp switch bezel from the instrument panel by unsnapping the attaching tangs.

2. Remove the 3 screws securing the switch mounting plate to the instrument panel. Then, pull the switch and mounting plate rearward and out of the instrument panel opening.

3. Disconnect the electrical connector at the switch. Press the release button on the bottom of the switch and then pull the knob and shaft out of the switch.

4. Detach the headlamp switch escutcheon from the mounting plate by unsnapping the attaching tangs and removing it. Then, unscrew the switch-to-mounting plate retaining nut and pull the switch off the mounting plate.

5. To install, first position the switch onto the mounting plate and install the retaining nut. Then, snap the headlamp switch escutcheon back into position.

6. Slide the knob shaft into the switch until it locks. Reconnect the switch electrical connector.

7. Install the mounting plate onto the instrument panel. Install the 3 attaching screws.

8. Snap the headlamp switch bezel back into position.

Clock
REMOVAL AND INSTALLATION
1981-84 Models

1. Remove the 2 attaching screws and remove the heater control bezel. Then, remove the 2 screws attaching the clock to the base panel.

2. Pull the clock to the rear to gain clearance to reach the electrical connector. Then, disconnect the electrical connector and remove the clock.

3. Installation is the reverse of removal.

1985-88 Models

All 1985 and later models use digital clocks only. Digital clocks are part of the radio unit. For removal, refer to the "Radio Removal and Installation" procedure above.

Back-up Light Switch
REMOVAL AND INSTALLATION

On both manual and automatic cars, this switch is mounted on the transaxle. Refer to the appropriate procedure in Chapter 7.

Speedometer Cable
REMOVAL AND INSTALLATION

1. Reach under the instrument panel and depress the spring clip retaining the cable to the speedometer head. Pull the cable back and away from the head.

2. If the core is broken, raise and support the vehicle and remove the cable retaining screw from the cable bracket. Carefully slide the cable out of the transaxle.

3. Coat the new core sparingly with speedometer cable lubricant and insert it in the cable. Install the cable at the transaxle, lower the car and install the cable at the speedometer head.

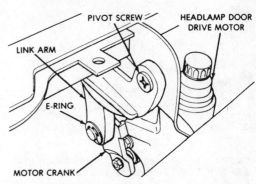

The power headlamp drive mechanism. Note the location of the manual actuating wheel on top of the drive motor.

LIGHTING

Headlights
REMOVAL AND INSTALLATION

1. Remove the headlight bezel.
2. Unhook the spring from the headlight retaining ring if so equipped.
3. Unscrew the retaining ring and remove it. NOTE: *Do not disturb the two long aiming screws.*
4. Unplug the old sealed beam.
5. Connect the replacement bulb and install into the receptacle.
6. Install the retaining ring and connect the spring.
7. Install the headlight bezel.

MANUAL OPERATION OF POWER HEAD-LAMP DOORS

A manual over-ride hand wheel permits the power headlamp doors to be opened in case of motor failure or to service the headlamps. The wheel is located on the top of the headlamp door drive motor. To gain access to the wheel, open the hood and go in through the flap located in the sight shield behind the bumper fascia. The wheel must be turned a number of turns to remove play and then open the doors.

Signal and Marker Lights
REMOVAL AND INSTALLATION
Front Turn Signal and Parking Lights

The marker lights are universally replaced by removing the lamp assembly from the bumper or quarter panel, twisting and pulling the socket out of the assembly, and then twisting the lamp to release it from the socket.

Where the lamp is located in an assembly separate from the headlamp, remove the screws from the lens and pull the assembly out of the bumper fascia.

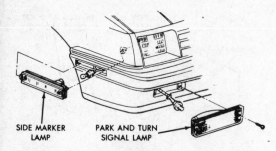

SIDE MARKER LAMP   PARK AND TURN SIGNAL LAMP

Removing the turn signal/parking and side marker lights on the 1988 Sundance and Shadow

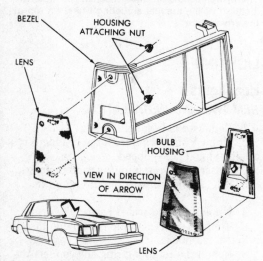

BEZEL

HOUSING ATTACHING NUT

LENS

BULB HOUSING

VIEW IN DIRECTION OF ARROW

LENS

Removing the side marker/turn signal lamp on 1982 Aries and Reliant

Where the lamp is located in the side of the headlamp bezel, remove the two nuts from the rear of the turn signal/parking light assembly. These are located in the wall of the bezel, directly in front of the headlight and will also release the lens (catch it and remove it to a safe place to keep it from being damaged).

Remove the lamp by turning it to release it from the socket. Install the new lamp by inserting it into the socket so the prongs line up with the internal grooves, permitting it to be turned and locked easily. If the lamp cannot be fully inserted and turned readily, turn it 180° and try again. Insert the socket into the assembly and turn it tight to lock it. Then, install the lamp assembly. On separate designs, install the mounting screws. On intergral designs, install the lens and then turn the nuts over the threaded studs on the back of the lens.

Side Marker Lights

The side marker lights are located in a socket locked into the back of the lamp assembly. Reach in behind the bumper, grasp the socket, turn it to release, and pull it from the lamp.

Remove the lamp by turning it to release it from the socket. Install the new lamp by inserting it into the socket so the prongs line up with the internal grooves, permitting it to be turned and locked easily. If the lamp cannot be fully inserted and turned readily, turn it 180° and try again. Insert the socket into the lamp assembly and turn it tight to lock it.

Rear Turn Signal, Brake, and Parking Lights

On sedans: Remove the luggage compartment rear trim cover. Then, loosen the quarter panel silencer and shift it out of the way. Grasp the appropriate socket and rotate it counterclockwise; then pull it out of the lamp. Rotate the bulb counterclockwise and remove it from the socket.

Install the new lamp by inserting it into the socket so the prongs line up with the internal grooves, permitting it to be turned and locked easily. If the lamp cannot be fully inserted and turned readily, turn it 180° and try again. Insert the socket into the lamp assembly and turn it tight to lock it.

On wagons: Depress the flexible bumper fascia and use a socket wrench and extension to remove the two lower attaching nuts for the lamp assembly. Open the hatch to gain access to the two upper nuts and use the same tool to remove them. Pull the lamp assembly off the mounting studs.

Grasp the appropriate socket and rotate it counterclockwise; then pull it out of the lamp. Rotate the bulb counterclockwise and remove it from the socket.

Install the new lamp by inserting it into the socket so the prongs line up with the internal grooves, permitting it to be turned and locked easily. If the lamp cannot be fully inserted and turned readily, turn it 180° and try again. Insert the socket into the lamp assembly and turn it tight to lock it.

TRAILER WIRING

Wiring the car for towing is fairly easy. There are a number of good wiring kits available and these should be used, rather than trying to design your own. All trailers will need brake lights and turn signals as well as tail lights and side marker lights. Most states require extra marker lights for overly wide trailers. Also, most states have recently required back-up lights for trailers, and most trailer manufacturers have been building trailers with back-up lights for several years.

Additionally, some Class I, most Class II and just about all Class III trailers will have electric brakes.

Add to this number an accessories wire, to operate trailer internal equipment or to charge the trailer's battery, and you can have as many as seven wires in the harness.

Determine the equipment on your trailer and buy the wiring kit necessary. The kit will contain all the wires needed, plus a plug adapter set which included the female plug, mounted on the bumper or hitch, and the male plug, wired into, or plugged into the trailer harness.

When installing the kit, follow the manufacturer's instructions. The color coding of the wires is standard throughout the industry.

One point to note, some domestic vehicles, and most imported vehicles, have separate turn signals. On most domestic vehicles, the brake lights and rear turn signals operate with the same bulb. For those vehicles with separate turn signals, you can purchase an isolation unit so that the brake lights won't blink whenever the turn signals are operated, or, you can go to your local electronics supply house and buy four diodes to wire in series with the brake and turn signal bulbs. Diodes will isolate the brake and turn signals. The choice is yours. The isolation units are simple and quick to install, but far more expensive than the diodes. The diodes, however, require more work to install properly, since they require the cutting of each bulb's wire and soldering in place of the diode.

One final point, the best kits are those with a spring loaded cover on the vehicle mounted socket. This cover prevents dirt and moisture from corroding the terminals. Never let the vehicle socket hang loosely. Always mount it securely to the bumper or hitch.

CIRCUIT PROTECTION

Fuses

The fuse box is located behind an access panel in the glovebox on 1981-85 models and under the steering column in 1986-88 models. Remove the panel by unsnapping the clips at the bottom (pulling out hard). Then, slide the retaining tabs out at the top. On earlier models, a special fuse removal tool is located on the back of the access panel. On the later models, slide the fuse block to the left and off the retaining bracket to remove it for easy access to the fuses.

The later models use blade type fuses. Standard fuses have the amperage rating stamped on the silver connector at either end. Blade fuses have the amperage printed on the outer edge and are also color coded according to amperage rating.*Make sure to note the amperage rating before discarding a blown fuse! Always replace the fuse with one of exactly the same rating, as use of a rating even slightly higher than*

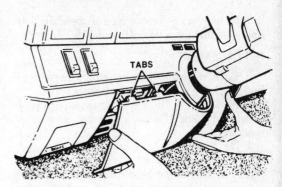
Removing the fuse access panel on 1986 and later models

standard could result in a dangerous vehicle fire.

If a circuit continues to blow a fuse of the proper rating, leave the fuse out and check the circuit or the accessories it runs for an electrical short or mechanical overload.

Remember, in replacing the access panel, to insert the tabs at the top first and then to snap the locking tabs at the bottom into place.

Fusible Links

CAUTION: *Do not replace blown fusible links with standard wire. Only fusible type wire with hypalon insulation can be used, or damage to the electrical system will occur.*

When a fusible link blows it is very important to find out why. They are placed in the electrical system for protection against dead shorts to ground, which can be caused by electrical component failure or various wiring failures.

CAUTION: *Do not just replace the fusible link to correct a problem.*

When replacing all fusible links, they are to

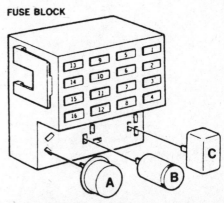
The fuse and flasher block used on 1985 Reliant. "A" is the turn signal flasher, "B" the ignition time delay relay, and "C" the horn relay.

be replaced with the same type of prefabricated link available from your Chyrsler dealer.

REPLACEMENT

1. Cut the fusible link including the connection insulator from the main harness wire.

2. Remove 1 in. of insulation from both new fusible link, and the main harness, and wrap together.

3. Heat the splice with a soldering gun, and apply rosin type solder.

NOTE: *Do not use acid core solder.*

4. Allow the connection to cool, and wrap the new splice with at least 3 layers of electrical tape.

Flashers

Flashers are located either on the bottom of the fuse block or on a module under the dash. They are replaced by simply pulling them straight out. Note that the prongs are arranged in such a way that the flasher must be properly oriented before attempting to install it. Turn the flasher until the orientation of the prongs is correct and simply push it firmly in until the prongs are fully engaged.

UNDERSTANDING THE MANUAL TRANSAXLE

Because of the way an internal combustion engine breathes, it can produce torque, or twisting force, only within a narrow speed range. Most modern engines must turn 2,500 rpm or faster to produce their peak torque. By 4,500-5,500 rpm they are producing so little torque that continued increases in engine speed produce no power increases.

The manual transmission and clutch are employed to vary the relationship between engine speed and the speed of the wheels so that adequate engine power can be produced under all circumstances. The clutch allows engine torque to be applied to the transmission input shaft gradually, due to mechanical slippage. The car can, consequently, be started smoothly from a full stop.

The transmission changes the ratio between the rotating speeds of the engine and the wheels by the use of gears. 4-speed or 5-speed transmissions are most common. The lower gears allow full engine power to be applied to the wheels during acceleration at low speeds.

The clutch drive plate is a thin disc, the center of which is splined to the transmission input shaft. Both sides of the disc are covered with a layer of material which is similar to brake lining and which is capable of allowing slippage without roughness or excessive noise.

The clutch cover is bolted to the engine flywheel and incorporates a diaphragm spring which provides the pressure to engage the clutch. The cover also houses the pressure plate. The driven disc is sandwiched between the pressure plate and the smooth surface of the flywheel when the clutch pedal is released, thus forcing it to turn at the same speed as the engine crankshaft.

The transmission contains a mainshaft which passes all the way through the transmis-sion, from the clutch to the halfshafts. This shaft is separated at one point, so that front and rear portions can turn at different speeds.

Power is transmitted by a countershaft in the lower gears and reverse. The gears of the countershaft mesh with gears on the mainshaft, allowing power to be carried from one to the other. All the countershaft gears are integral with that shaft, while several of the mainshaft gears can either rotate independently of the shaft or be locked to it. Shifting from one gear to the next causes one of the gears to be freed from rotating with the shaft and locks another to it. Gears are locked and unlocked by internal dog clutches which slide between the center of the gear and the shaft. The forward gears usually employ synchronizers; friction members which smoothly bring gear and shaft to the same speed before the toothed dog clutches are engaged.

The clutch is operating properly if:

1. It will stall the engine when released with the vehicle held stationary.

2. The shift lever can be moved freely between 1st and reverse gears when the vehicle is stationary and the clutch disengaged.

A clutch pedal free-play adjustment is incorporated in the linkage. If there is about 25-50mm of motion before the pedal begins to release the clutch, it is adjusted properly. Inadequate free-play wears all parts of the clutch releasing mechanisms and may cause slippage. Excessive free-play may cause inadequate release and hard shifting of gears.

Some clutches use a hydraulic system in place of mechanical linkage. If the clutch fails to release, fill the clutch master cylinder with fluid to the proper level and pump the clutch pedal to fill the system with fluid. Bleed the system in the same way as a brake system. If leaks are located, tighten loose connections or overhaul the master or slave cylinder as necessary.

Front wheel drive cars do not have conventional rear axles or driveshafts. Instead, power is transmitted from the engine to a transaxle, or a combination of transmission and drive axle, in one unit. Both the transmission and drive axle accomplish the same function as their counterparts in a front engine/rear drive axle design. The difference is in the location of the components.

In place of a conventional driveshaft, a front wheel drive design uses two driveshafts, sometimes called halfshafts, which couple the drive axle portion of the transaxle to the wheels. Universal joints or constant velocity joints are used just as they would in a rear wheel drive design.

MANUAL TRANSAXLE

Identification

The Transaxle Identification Number is stamped on a boss located on the upper part of the transaxle housing. Every transaxle also carries an assembly part number, which is also required for parts ordering purposes. On the A-412 manual transaxle, it is located on the top of the housing, between the timing window and the differential.

On the manual transaxles except the A-520 and A-555, this number is located on a metal tag attached to the front of the transaxle. On the A-520 and A-555, the tag is attached to the top of the unit.

Adjustments

SHIFTER ADJUSTMENT

Model A-412

1. Place the transmission in neutral at the 3-4 position.
2. Loosen the shift tube clamp.
3. Place a 16mm spacer between the slider and blocker bracket.
4. Tighten the shift tube clamp and remove the spacer.

A-460, 465, 525 with Shift Rod

1. From the left side of the car, remove the lockpin from the transaxle selector shaft housing.
2. Reverse the lockpin and insert it in the same threaded hole while pushing the selector shaft into the selector housing. A hole in the selector shaft will align with the lockpin, allowing the lockpin to be screwed into the housing. This will lock the selector shaft in the 1-2 neutral position.
3. Raise and support the vehicle on jackstands.
4. Loosen the clamp bolt that secures the gearshift tube to the gearshift connector.

5. Make sure that the gearshift connector slides and turns freely in the gearshift tube.
6. Position the shifter mechanism connector assembly so that the isolator is contacting the standing flange and the rib on the isolator is aligned front and back with the hole in the block-out bracket. Hold the connector in this position while tightening the clamp bolt on the gearshift tube to 14 ft. lb.
7. Lower the car.
8. Remove the lockpin from the selector shaft housing and install it the original way in the housing.
9. Tighten the lockpin to 105 in. lbs.
10. Check the shifter action.

A-525, A-555 with Shift Cable

NOTE: *To adjust the shift cable, two 140mm lengths of rod (except Daytona and K-body LeBarons) and an inch-pound torque wrench are required. The rod stock should be 5mm diameter for Aries, Reliant, LeBaron, Town & Country, Sundance and Shadow; for Lancer and LeBaron GTS, it should be 4mm.*

1. Work over the left front fender and remove the lockpin from the transaxle selector shaft housing.
2. Turn the lockpin so the long end faces downward. Gently attempt to insert it into the same threaded hole while you gradually push the selector shaft into the selector housing. When the pin fits into the selector shaft, stop sliding the shaft into the housing and screw the pin into the housing. If done correctly, this will lock the selector shaft into the Neutral fore and aft position and into the 1-2 shift plane. Make sure that these conditions are met.
3. Unscrew and remove the gearshift knob. Then coat the shift shaft with a soap and water solution and pull the shift boot up and over the pull-up ring.
4. Remove the console as follows:
    a. Remove its two attaching screws and remove the forward console bezel.
    b. Remove the two attaching screws from the inside of the console storage area. Remove the two attaching screws from underneath the forward section of the console.
    c. Disconnect all the console electrical connectors.
    d. Remove the console.
5. The selector (fore and aft) and crossover (side-to-side) shift cables, located on either side of the shifter, each have slotted slides. A bolt locks the position of the slide to the gear lever mechanism. Loosen *both* bolts enough so that the slides can move freely.
6. On all but Daytonas and K-body LeBarons, bend the end of each of the two lengths of rod so the longer portion is just

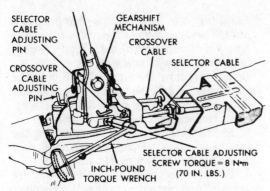

Adjusting the selector cable with the two adjusting pins installed

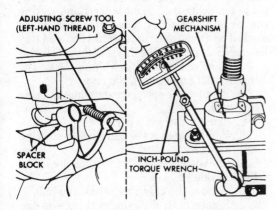

Adjusting the selector cable with the adjusting screw tool installed

127mm long. On Daytonas and K-Body LeBarons, pull the adjusting screw tool off the shifter support bracket (it's taped there).

7. On all but Daytonas and K-body LeBarons, move the gearshift in the fore and aft plane while attempting to insert the rod into the side of the shifter support bracket until it locks the gearshift in place. Repeat the operation in the side-to-side plane, attempting to insert the other rod into the rear of the shifter support bracket. On Daytonas and K-Body LeBarons, pass the bolt portion of the adjusting screw tool through the spacer block and then insert the tool through the shifter support bracket. Move the gearshift until you can turn the bolt and thread it into the shifter, locking it in place. Torque the bolt to 20 in. lbs.

8. Once the shifter is properly locked in place, torque both the lockbolts for the shift cable slides to 70 in. lbs. Then, remove the fabricated rod pins or the adjusting screw tool. Unscrew the adjusting screw tool and tape it back where it was.

9. Unscrew and remove the lock pin from the transaxle, turn it around, and reinstall it, torquing again to 105 in. lbs. Check to make sure the transmission shifts smoothly and effectively into 1st and reverse. Make sure reverse is properly blocked out until the shift ring is raised.

10. Install the gearshift knob and boot. Install the console as follows:

a. Connect all the matching electrical connectors and then put the console into position.

b. Install the four console attaching screws.

c. Install the forward console bezel and its attaching screws.

Back-Up Light Switch

REMOVAL AND INSTALLATION

The back-up light switch is located on the top of the transmission. Disconnect the electrical connector and then unscrew the switch by engaging the flats with an open-end wrench. Install in reverse order, being especially careful to start the switch into the threaded bore of the transaxle without forcing it, to prevent cross-threading.

Manual Transaxle

REMOVAL AND INSTALLATION

A-412

NOTE: *Any time the differential cover is removed, a new gasket must be formed from RTV sealant. See Chapter 1.*

1. Remove the engine timing mark access plug.
2. Rotate the engine to align the drilled mark on the flywheel with the pointer on the engine.
3. Disconnect the battery ground.
4. Disconnect the shift linkage rods.
5. Disconnect the starter and ground wires.
6. Disconnect the backup light switch wire.
7. Remove the starter.
8. Disconnect the clutch cable.
9. Disconnect the speedometer cable.

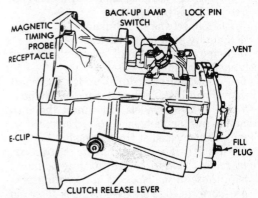

Location of the back-up lamp switch

10. Support the weight of the engine from above, preferably with a shop hoist or the fabricated holding fixture.

11. Raise and support the vehicle.

12. Disconnect the driveshafts and support them out of the way.

13. Remove the left splash shield.

14. Drain the transaxle.

15. Unbolt the left engine mount.

16. Remove the transaxle-to-engine bolts.

17. Slide the transaxle to the left until the mainshaft clears, then, carefully lower it from the car.

18. To install the transaxle, position it so the mainshaft will slide straight into the center of the clutch. Turn the transaxle slightly, if necessary, and change the angle until the mainshaft engages, and then slide the transaxle to the right until the bell housing boltholes line up with the corresponding bores in the block.

19. Install the transaxle-to-engine bolts. Reinstall the through bolt for the left engine mount.

20. Install the left side splash shield.

21. Install the driveshafts back into the transaxle (see "Halfshafts Removal and Installation" below).

22. Lower the vehicle to the ground. Remove the engine support system.

23. Reconnect the speedometer and clutch cables.

24. Install the starter. Connect the backup light switch wire.

25. Reconnect the shift rods. Reconnect the battery. Install the engine timing mark access plug.

26. Adjust the clutch cable and the shift linkage.

27. Fill the transaxle with the recommended fluid (See Chapter 1).

1981-88 A-465, A-525, A-555

1. Disconnect the battery.

2. Install a shop crane and lifting eye under the #4 cylinder exhaust manifold bolt to securely support the engine.

3. Disconnect the shift linkage.

4. Remove both front wheels.

5. Remove the left front splash shield, and left engine mount.

6. Follow the procedures under Halfshaft Removal and Installation later in this chapter.

7. On 1987-88 models, disconnect the anti-rotation link or damper *at the crossmember*, leaving it connected at the transaxle.

NOTE: *It will be easier to locate the transaxle, so as to align the bell housing boltholes with those in the block, if two locating pins are fabricated and are used in place of the top two locating bolts. To fabricate the pins: Buy two extra bolts. Hacksaw the heads off the bolts. Then, cut slots in the ends of the bolts for a flat-bladed screwdriver. Finally, remove all burrs with a grinding wheel.*

Before installing the transmission onto the engine block, install the two locating pins into the top two engine block holes. Refer to the automatic transaxle procedure for specifics.

8. Install a positive means of supporting the engine, such as a support fixture that runs across between the two front fenders.

9. Remove the upper bolts—those that are accessible from above from the bell housing.

10. For 1986 and later vehicles, refer to the appropriate procedure earlier in this chapter to remove or install the driveshafts. This will include removing both front wheels and raising the car and supporting it securely so it can be worked on from underneath. On 1985 and earlier vehicles, remove the driveshafts as follows:

a. Remove the left splash shield. Drain the differential and remove the cover.

b. Remove the speedometer adapter, cable and gear.

c. Remove the sway bar.

d. Remove both lower ball joint-to-steering knuckle bolts.

e. Pry the lower ball joint from the steering knuckle.

f. Remove the driveshaft from the hub.

g. Rotate both driveshafts to expose the circlip ends. Note the flat surface on the inner ends of both axle tripod shafts. Pry the circlip out.

h. Remove both driveshafts.

11. On 1986 and later vehicles, remove the left side splash shield.

12. Disconnect the plug for the neutral safety/backup light switch.

13. Remove the engine mount bracket from the front crossmember.

14. Support the transmission from underneath.

15. Remove the front mount insulator through-bolts.

16. Remove the long through-bolt from the left hand engine mount.

17. Remove the starter. Then, remove any bell housing bolts that are still in position.

18. Slide the transaxle directly away from the engine so the transmission input shaft will slide smoothly out of the bearing in the flywheel and the clutch disc. Lower the transaxle and remove it from the engine compartment.

19. To install the transaxle, first support the unit securely and raise it into precise alignment with the engine block. Then, move it toward the block, inserting the transmission input shaft into the clutch disc. Turn the input shaft slightly, if necessary, to get the splines to engage.

20. Install the lower bell housing bolts and the starter. Bell housing bolts are torqued to 70 ft. lbs.

21. Install the long through-bolt into the left hand engine mount.

22. Install the front mount insulator through-bolts.

23. Remove the jack supporting the transmission. Then, install the engine mount bracket onto the front crossmember.

24. Reconnect the electrical connector for the backup light/neutral safety switch.

25. Install the driveshafts by reversing the removal procedure. Install the left side splash shield.

26. With the wheels remounted and the car back on the floor, install the remaining bell housing bolts and torque them to 105 in. lbs.

27. Remove the engine support fixture.

28. Connect the anti-rotation strut. Torque the bolts to 70 ft. lbs.

29. Connect the shift linkage. Always use new self-locking nuts on the shift linkage. Observe the following torques:

- Shift housing-to-case: 21 ft.lb.
- Strut-to-case: 70 ft.lb.
- Flywheel-to-crankshaft: 65 ft.lb.

OVERHAUL

A-412

TRANSAXLE CASE DISASSEMBLY

NOTE: *Final mainshaft adjustment requires a measurement made with a special tool. Check Step 16 of the assembly procedure before disassembly.*

1. Remove the clutch pushrod, being careful not to bend it.

2. Unscrew the selector shaft plug from the case. Remove the detent spring assembly and rubber boot, then tap out the selector shaft and pry out the oil seal.

3. Using a small pry bar, pry out the two mainshaft bearing retaining nut rubber plugs.

4. Remove the four bolts and the clutch release bearing end cover. Hold the clutch release lever upwards while removing the cover to avoid loading or damage to the case threads. Take out the release bearing and plastic sleeve.

5. Using two small pry bars, push the circlip off the clutch torque shaft. Pull the torque shaft out of the case, then remove the pedal return spring and release lever. Pry out the torque shaft oil seal.

6. Remove the three mainshaft bearing retainer nuts; two were under the rubber covers removed earlier and the 3rd is inside the clutch release housing. The three studs and clips will drop into the case. Remove the Reverse idler set screw (bolt) and the backup light switch.

7. Remove the ten case bolts and the four stud nuts, then the transmission case.

NOTE: *The factory uses a special tool to do this; it pushes against the end of the mainshaft. Make sure to tag the shims for reuse.*

8. Remove the two bolts, the Reverse shift fork and the supports.

9. Remove the snapring from the end of the pinion shaft.

10. Pull off the bearing and the 4th gear from the end of the mainshaft. Remove the 4th gear needle bearing needle bearing.

11. Using a small pry bar, pry off the shift rail E-clips, then remove the shift forks assembly.

12. Remove the mainshaft assembly; it can be disassembled by removing the snaprings and the components. The clutch pushrod seal and bushing assembly can be driven out of the shaft with a 9½mm diameter brass rod. Replace it by driving it with a plastic hammer.

13. Remove the pinion shaft snapring and the 3rd gear, then the 2nd gear and its needle bearing.

14. Pry or pull out the Reverse idler gear shaft.

15. Using a puller, remove the 1st gear and the 1st/2nd synchronizer assembly from the pinion shaft.

NOTE: *The inner sleeve for the 2nd and the 1st gear are removed together.*

16. Remove the 1st gear needle bearing and scribe a mark across the 1st/2nd synchronizer for reassembly.

17. Remove the pinion shaft bolts, the retainer, the thrust washer (the flat side goes up) and the pinion shaft.

ASSEMBLY

1. Place a 0.65mm shim in the bearing housing and press the small bearing cup into the clutch housing, then move the pinion up and down, measuring the end play with a dial indicator.

NOTE: *Do not rotate the shaft while moving it up and down.*

2. The correct preload is determined by adding 0.20mm to the reading obtained from the dial indicator in Step 1, along with the shim thickness, 0.65mm. For example: if the measurement is 0.30mm, the correct shim to use is 1.15mm (0.65 + 0.03 + 0.20 = 1.15). Remove the pinion shaft ball bearing retainer and the pinion shaft. Remove the small bearing cup and the 0.65mm shim and install the correct shim.

3. If new bearings are installed on the pinion shaft, lubricate them with transmission oil, install the shaft and check the shaft turning torque with a torque wrench; it should be 4.4-13.1 in. lbs., if not, reset the preload.

4. Install the pinion shaft and place the 1st gear thrust washer over the shaft, with the flat side up facing the gear. Install the pinion shaft retainer and torque the bolts to 29 ft. lbs.

5. Install the needle bearing, the 1st gear and the 1st gear synchronizer stop ring over the shaft.

NOTE: *The wear limit for spacing between the synchronzier teeth on the 1st gear and those on the stop ring is 0.005mm. There is one tooth missing from the 1st gear stop ring on early models. The 1st gear will grind, if this ring isn't used. Later models have three teeth missing in three places, 120° apart.*

6. Align the marks on the 1st/2nd synchronizer hub and the sleeve, made on disassembly. Install the synchronizer, driving it into place.

7. Drive the 2nd gear needle bearing inner race into place over the shaft.

8. Drive the Reverse idler gear shaft into place.

NOTE: *Make sure that the threaded hole in the top of the shaft is centered, pointing out between the two nearest case edge bolt holes.*

9. Place the 2nd gear needle bearing over the pinion shaft, then the 2nd gear stop ring, the 2nd gear and the 3rd gear onto the shaft; make sure that the 3rd gear has the thrust face down.

10. Install the 3rd gear sanp ring. Measure the end play between 3rd gear and the snapring with a feeler gauge; it should be 0-0.010mm. The snaprings are available in thicknesses from 2.5-3.0mm for adjustment. Replace the snapring with the one selected.

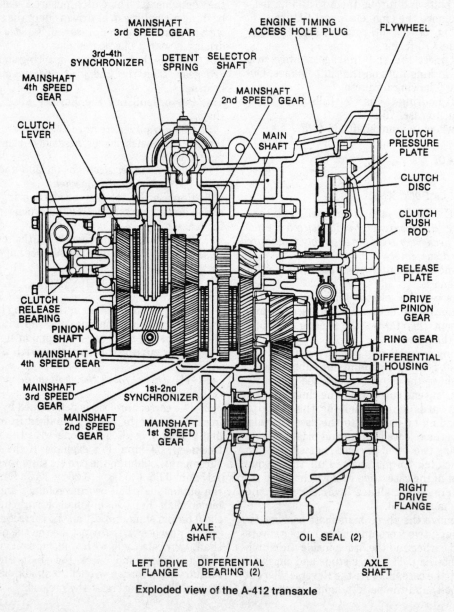

Exploded view of the A-412 transaxle

11. Install the mainshaft assembly.

12. Install the shift fork assemblies and the E-clips.

13. Install the 4th gear needle bearing over the mainshaft and place the 4th gear synchronizer stop ring in place. Install the 4th gear and the snapring.

14. Install the Reverse shift fork and the support brackets, then torque the bolts to 105 in. lbs.

15. Using a feeler gauge, measure the clearance between the top of the pinion shaft 2nd gear and the bottom of the mainshaft 3rd gear.

NOTE: *The ideal clearance is adjusted by forcing the mainshaft up or down in relation to the clutch case. The factory has a special tool to do this from the clutch end.*

16. The next step is to determine the thickness of the shim or shims to be placed between the mainshaft roller bearing and the transmission case. The factory does this by inserting a special tool of the same thickness as the bearing in the case, installing the case, then measuring the up and down movement of the special tool with a dial indicator. Shims are available in 0.30mm and 0.60mm sizes.

17. After the selected shim is installed behind the bearing, torque the bearing retainer clamp bolts to 13 ft. lbs. Install the transmission case-to-clutch housing bolts, using the guide pin for alignment, and torque the nuts and bolts to 20 ft. lbs.

A-465, A-525, A-555

The Chrysler designed and built A-465 (1983-84) and the A-525 (1985-88) fully synchronized 5 speed manual transaxles combine gear reduction, ratio selection and differential functions in one unit housed in a die cast aluminum case. The A-525 has a close ratio gearset with different 2nd, 3rd and 4th gear ratios than the A-465, to provide better performance through the gears, while the 1st and the 5th gear ratios are the same as the A-465 to maintain the same launch and top gear characteristics. A special high torque version known as the A-555 has been made available for the Turbo II models only. It is almost identical with the A-525 except for changes in the differential section.

TRANSAXLE CASE DISASSEMBLY 1984-85 MODELS

1. With the transaxle removed from the vehicle, remove the differential cover bolts and the stud nuts, then remove the cover.

2. Remove the differential bearing retainer bolts.

3. Using tool No. L-4435, rotate the differential bearing retainer to remove it.

4. Remove the extension housing bolts, then the differential assembly and extension housing.

5. Remove the selector shaft housing bolts, then the selector shaft housing.

6. Remove the stud nuts and the bolts from the rear end cover, then using a small pry bar, pry off the rear end cover.

7. On 5-speeds, remove the 5th speed synchronizer strut retainer snapring, strut retainer plate, 5th speed synchronizer, shift fork with rail, intermediate shaft 5th speed gear, input shaft 5th gear snapring and 5th gear. Then, use a puller such as C-4693 with legs C-4621-1 to remove the 5th speed synchronizer hub. On 4-speeds, remove the large snapring from the intermediate shaft rear ball bearing.

8. Remove the bearing retainer plate by tapping it with a plastic hammer.

9. Remove the 3rd/4th shift fork rail.

10. Remove the Reverse idler gear shaft and gear.

11. Remove the input shaft gear assembly and the intermediate shaft gear assembly.

12. To remove the clutch release bearing, remove the E-clips from the clutch release shaft, then disassemble the clutch shaft components.

13. Remove the three input shaft seal retainer bolts, the seal, the retainer assembly and the select shim.

14. Using tools No. C-4171, C-4656 and an arbor press, press the input shaft front bearing cup from the transaxle case.

15. Using tool No. C-4660, remove the two bearing retainer strap bolts, then the intermediate shaft front bearing.

16. Remove the 5th speed shifter pin, the 5th speed detent ball and the spring.

17. Remove the 5th speed synchronizer strut retainer plate snapring and the 5th speed synchronizer strut retainer plate.

18. Remove the 5th speed synchronizer assembly and shift fork with shift rail.

19. Remove the intermediate shaft 5th speed gear, the input shaft 5th speed gear snapring and the 5th speed gear.

20. Remove the bearing support plate bolts and pry off the bearing support plate.

TRANSAXLE CASE DISASSEMBLY 1986-88 MODELS

1. With the transaxle removed from the vehicle, remove the eight differential cover bolts and the two stud nuts and remove the cover.

2. Remove the eight differential bearing retainer bolts.

3. Using the L-4435 or equivalent spanner wrench, rotate the differential bearing retainer to remove it.

4. Remove the four extension housing bolts, then remove the differential assembly and extension housing.

5. Remove the six selector shaft housing assembly bolts and remove the selector shaft housing assembly.

6. Remove the 10 rear end cover bolts and remove the rear end cover. Clean the bead of RTV sealer off the rear end cover.

7. Using snapring pliers, remove the snapring from the 5th speed synchronizer strut retainer plate.

8. Using an Allen wrench, unscrew and then remove the 5th speed shift fork set screw. Then, lift the 5th speed synchronizer sleeve and shift fork off the synchronizer hub. Retrieve the (3) winged struts and top synchronizer spring.

9. Use a puller such as C-4693 with legs C-4621-1 to remove the 5th speed synchronizer hub. Retrieve the remaining synchronizer spring.

10. Slide the 5th speed gear off the intermedi-

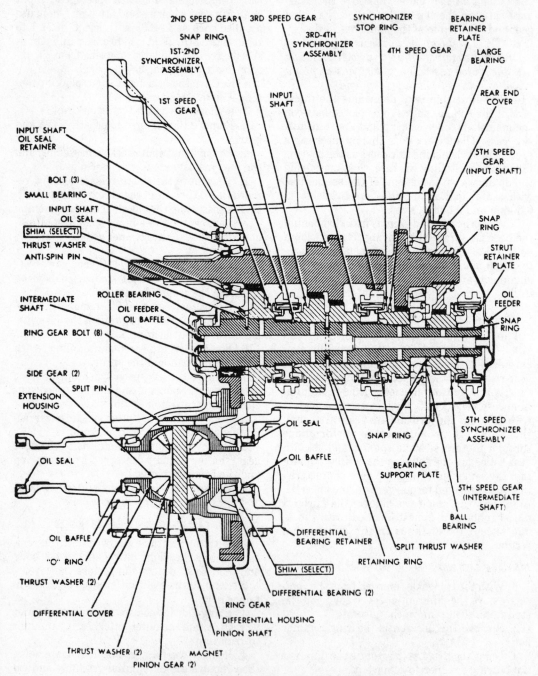

Exploded view of the A-465, A-525 and A-555 transaxle

ate shaft. With snapring pliers, remove the copper colored snapring retaining the 5th speed gear to the input shaft. Then, using a pulley puller such as C-4333, pull the 5th speed gear off the input shaft.

11. Remove the two remaining bearing support plate bolts. Then, use a screwdriver to gently pry off the bearing support plate.

12. With snapring pliers, remove the large snapring from the intermediate shaft rear ball bearing. Then, gently tap the lower surface of the bearing retainer plate with a plastic hammer to free it and lift it off the transaxle case. Clean the RTV sealer from both surfaces.

13. With a socket wrench, unscrew the 5th speed shifter guide pin. Then, remove it. Do the same with the 1st/2nd shift fork setscrew. Then, slide out the 1st/2nd, 3rd/4th shift fork rail.

14. Slide out the reverse idler gear shaft, gear, and plastic stop.

15. Rotate the 3rd/4th shift fork to the left, and the 5th gear shifter to the right. Pull out the 5th speed shift rail. Then, pull out the input shaft assembly. Finally, pull out the intermediate shaft assembly.

16. Now, remove the 1st/2nd, 3rd/4th, and 5th speed shift forks.

17. Proceed with Steps 12-20 of the procedure for 1984-85 models, which are identical with this transaxle for the remaining steps.

ASSEMBLY

The assembly of the transaxle is the reverse of disassembly; however, please note the following:

1. Using tools No. C-4657, C-4171 and an arbor press, press the front bearing onto the intermediate shaft; the input shaft front bearing cup is installed with the same tools used for removal.

2. Determine the shim thickness for the correct bearing end play only if any of the following parts are replaced:
   a. The transaxle case.
   b. The input shaft seal retainer.
   c. The bearing retainer plate.
   d. The rear end cover.
   e. The input shaft or bearings.

3. To determine proper shim thickness, refer to the Input Shaft Bearing End Play Adjustment at the end of this section.

4. Using tool No. C-4674 and a plastic hammer, install the input shaft oil seal.

5. Using a 1.6mm bead of RTV sealant, place it around the edge of the input shaft seal retainer and making sure the drain hole of the retainer is facing downward.

6. The differential bearing retainer is in-stalled with the same special tool used for removal.

NOTE: *The rear end cover, the selector shaft housing and the differential cover are sealed with RTV sealant.*

INTERMEDIATE SHAFT DISASSEMBLY

NOTE: *The 1st/2nd, the 3rd/4th shift forks and the synchronizer stop rings are interchangeable. However, if parts are to be reused reassemble in the original position.*

1. Remove the intermediate shaft rear bearing snapring.

2. Using the puller tool No. C-4693, remove the intermediate shaft rear bearing.

3. Using snapring pliers, remove the 3rd/4th synchronizer hub snapring.

4. Using the puller tool No. L-4534, remove the 3rd/4th synchronizer hub and the 3rd speed gear.

5. Remove the retaining ring, the split thrust washer, the 2nd speed gear and the synchronizer stop ring.

6. Using snapring pliers, remove the 1st/2nd synchronizer hub snapring.

7. Remove the 1st speed gear, the stop ring and the 1st/2nd synchronizer assembly.

8. Remove the 1st speed gear thrust washer and the anti-spin pin.

ASSEMBLY

The assembly of the intermediate shaft is the Reverse of the disassembly; however, please note the following: When assembling the intermediate shaft, make sure the speed gears turn freely and have a minimum of 0.076mm end play. When installing the 1st speed gear thrust washer make sure the chamfered edge is facing the pinion gear. When installing the 1st/2nd synchronizer make sure the relief faces the 2nd speed gear. Use an arbor press to install the intermediate shaft rear bearing, the 3rd/4th synchronizer hub and the 3rd speed gear.

INPUT SHAFT BEARING END PLAY ADJUSTMENT

1. Using special tool No. L-4656 with handle C-4171, press the input shaft front bearing cup slightly forward in the case. Then, using tool No. L-4655 with handle C-4171, press the bearing cup back into the case, from the front, to the properly position the bearing cup before checking the input shaft endplay.

NOTE: *This step is not necessary if the special tool No. L-4655 was previously used to install the input shaft front bearing cup in the case and no input shaft select shim has been installed since pressing the cup into the case.*

2. Select a gauging shim which will give 0.025-0.254mm end play.

NOTE: *Measure the original shim from the*

input shaft seal retainer and select a shim 0.254mm thinner than the original for the gauging shim.

3. Install the gauging shim on the bearing cup and the input shaft seal retainer.

4. Alternately tighten the input shaft seal retainer bolts until the retainer is bottomed against the case, then torque the bolts to 21 ft. lbs.

NOTE: *The input shaft seal retainer is used to draw the input shaft front bearing cup the proper distance into the case bore.*

Halfshafts

IDENTIFICATION

The driveshaft assemblies are three-piece units. Each driveshaft has an inner sliding constant velocity (Tripod) joint and an outer constant velocity (Rzeppa) joint with a stub shaft splined into the hub. On 2.2 L engines with turbocharging, the shafts are of equal length and both are short and of solid construction. With this setup, there is a short, intermediate shaft with a bearing and bracket on the outer side and a Cardan (U-joint) on the inner side.

On vehicles with the normally aspirated (unturbocharged) 2.2 and 2.5 L engines, the connecting shafts for the CV-joints are unequal in length and construction. The left side is a short solid shaft and the right is longer and tubular.

It is impossible to classify driveshaft type according to model and year designations. However, each type of shaft is clearly identifiable according to the design features pointed out on the enclosed illustrations. Use these to classify the joint according to brand and type so that if parts are to be replaced, you can order by manufacturer name as well as the year and model of the car.

REMOVAL AND INSTALLATION

1981-85 A-412 Manual Transmission

1. With the vehicle on the floor and the brakes applied, loosen the hub nut.

NOTE: *The hub and driveshaft are splined together and retained by the hub nut which is torqued to at least 180 ft.lbs.*

2. Raise and support the vehicle and remove the hub nut and washer.

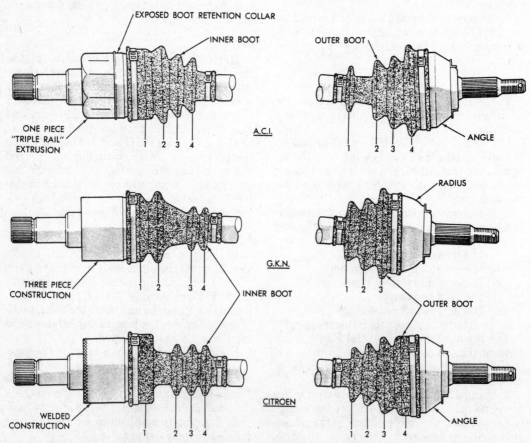

Driveshaft identification for 1981–85 models. Note that the A.C.I. driveshaft is not used on 1981–82 models.

NOTE: *Always support both ends of the driveshaft during removal.*

3. Disconnect the lower control arm ball joint stud nut from the steering knuckle.

4. Remove the six 1.6mm Allen head screws which secure the CV-joint to the transmission flange.

5. Holding the CV-joint housing, push the outer joint and knuckle assembly outward while disengaging the inner housing from the flange face. Quickly turn the open end of the joint upward to retain as much lubricant as possible, then carefully pull the outer joint spline out of the hub. Cover the joint with a clean towel to prevent dirt contamination.

NOTE: *The outer joint and shaft must be supported during disengagement of the inner joint.*

6. Before installation, make sure that any lost lubricant is replaced. The only lubricant specified is Chrysler part number 4131389. No other lubricant of any type is to be used, as premature failure of the joint will result.

7. Clean the joint body and mating flange face.

8. Install the outer joint splined shaft into the hub. Do not secure with thw nut and washer.

9. Early production vehicles were built with a cover plate between the hub and flange face. This cover is not necessary and should be discarded.

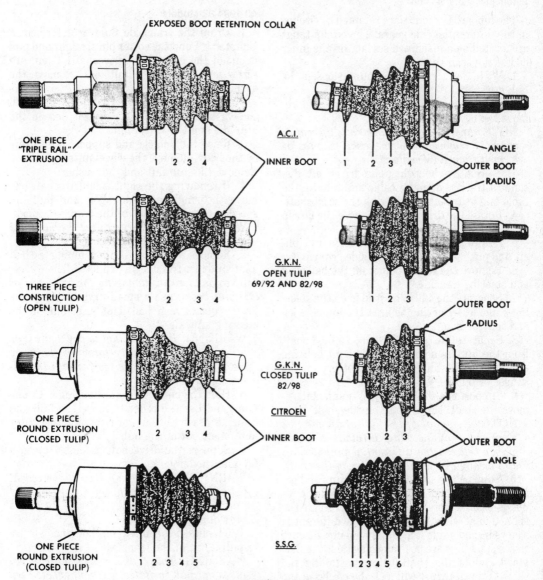

Driveshaft identification for 1986–88 models

10. Position the inner joint in the transmission drive flange and secure it with six new screws. Torque the screws to 37-40 ft.lb.

11. Connect the lower control arm to the knuckle.

12. Install the outer joint and secure it with a new nut and washer. Torque the nut with the car on the ground and the brake set. Torque is 180 ft.lbs. Reinstall the cotter pin.

13. After attaching the driveshaft, if the inboard boot appears to be collapsed or deformed, vent the inner boot by inserting a round-tipped, small diameter rod between the boot and the shaft. As venting occurs, boot will return to its original shape.

1981-83 A460, 465, 525 Manual Transmission and Automatic Transmission

The inboard CV-joints are retained by circlips in the differential side gears. The circlip tangs are located on a machined surface on the inner end of the stub shaft.

1. With the car on the ground, loosen the hub nut.

2. Drain the transaxle differential and remove the cover.

NOTE: *Any time the transaxle differential cover is removed, a new gasket should be formed from RTV sealant.*

3. To remove the right hand driveshaft, disconnect the speedometer cable and remove the cable and gear before removing the driveshaft.

4. Rotate the driveshaft to expose the circlip tangs.

5. Compress the circlip with needle nose pliers and push the shaft into the side gear cavity.

6. Remove the clamp bolt from the ball stud and steering knuckle.

7. Separate the ball joint stud from the steering knuckle, by prying against the knuckle leg and control arm.

8. Separate the outer CV-joint splined shaft from the hub by holding the CV-joint housing and moving the hub away. Do not pry on the slinger or outer CV-joint.

9. Support the shaft at the CV-joints and remove the shaft. Do not pull on the shaft.

NOTE: *Removal of the left shaft may be made easier by inserting the blade of a thin prybar between the differential pinion shaft and prying against the end face of the shaft.*

10. Support the shaft at the CV-joints and position the shaft for reinstallation. Hold the inner joint assembly at the housing. Align the splined joint with the splines in the differential side gear, and guide it into the housing. Be sure the circlip tangs are positioned against the flattened end of the shaft before installing the shaft. A quick thrust will lock the circlip in the groove.

11. Push the hub and knuckle assembly outward and insert the outer splined CV-joint shaft into the hub. Then, insert the ball joint stud into the knuckle assembly. Install the clamp bolt and nut and torque to 70 ft. lbs.

12. If it has been removed, insert the speedometer pinion back into the transaxle with the bolthole in the retaining collar aligned with the threaded hole in the transaxle. Install the retaining bolt.

13. Install the specified lubricant into the transaxle.

14. Install the wheel and wheel nuts. Lower the car to the floor. Clean the hub nut threads, located at the outer end of the shaft. Install the washer and then install the nub nut. Torque the hub nut to 180 ft. lbs.

All 1984-88 Models

1. Drain the transaxle fluid as described in Chapter 1. Bend the cotter pin straight and pull it out of the end of the driveshaft. Then, unscrew and remove the nut lock. Remove the spring washer.

2. Have someone apply the brakes and, with the car still resting on the wheels, loosen the hub nut and the wheel nuts.

3. Raise the vehicle and support it securely by the body. Remove the wheel nuts and wheel. Remove the hub nut and the washer.

4. If removing the right side driveshaft, remove the single attaching bolt and pull the speedometer pinion out of the transaxle case.

WARNING: *Do not pry against the ball joint or CV-joint boots in the next step.*

5. Remove the nut and bolt clamping the ball joint stud into the steering knuckle. Then, carefully *so as to avoid damaging the ball joint or CV-joint boots*, use a small prybar to pry the lower control arm ball joint stud out of the steering knuckle.

WARNING: *Be careful not to pry against or otherwise use excessive force on the wear sleeve of the CV-joint as you perform the following step.*

6. Hold the outer CV-joint housing with one hand and use the other to move the hub and knuckle assembly outward to pull the outer joint shaft out of the hub.

7. Support the driveshaft assembly at both CV-joint housings.

WARNING: *The axle must be supported at both CV-joints during this operation to avoid pulling on the shaft. Any stretching forces may damage the U-joints!*

Then, pull on the inner joint housing in order to pull it out of the transaxle.

WARNING: *Note that the driveshaft, when in its normal, installed position, acts to keep the hub/bearing assembly in place. If the vehi-*

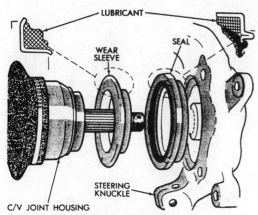

Lubricating the seal and wear sleeve on the outboard end of the driveshaft

cle is to be supported by its wheels or moved on them while the driveshaft is out of the car, install a bolt through the hub to ensure the hub bearing assembly cannot loosen.

8. Thoroughly clean the seal located between the outer end of the driveshaft and the steering knuckle with a safe solvent. Make sure solvent does not get onto the driveshaft boot. Apply a bead of a lubricant such as Mopar Multipurpose Lubricant Part No. 4318063 or the equivalent. Apply it to the full circumference and make the bead ¼ in. wide. Fill the lip-to-housing cavity on the seal around its complete circumference; wet the seal lip with the lubricant, as well.

9. To install the driveshaft, first inspect units on turbocharged cars to make sure the rubber washer seal is in place on the right inner joint. Relocate the seal, if necessary.

10. Support the driveshaft by both CV-joints. Hold the inner joint assembly at the housing. Align the splined joint with the splines in the differential side gear, guide it into the housing, and insert it until it locks.

CAUTION: *If installing an A.C.I. brand shaft, make sure the tripod joint engages in the housing and is not twisted.*

11. If necessary, remove the bolt installed through the hub earlier. Push the hub and knuckle assembly outward and insert the outer splined CV-joint shaft into the hub. Then, insert the ball joint stud into the knuckle assembly. Install the clamp bolt and nut and torque to 70 ft. lbs. *Note that, if replacing the the clamp bolt, it is a prevailing torque type and must be replaced with an equivalent part.*

12. If it has been removed, insert the speedometer pinion back into the transaxle with the bolthole in the retaining collar aligned with the threaded hole in the transaxle. Install the retaining bolt.

13. Install the specified lubricant into the transaxle.

14. Install the wheel and wheel nuts. Lower the car to the floor. Clean the hub nut threads, located at the outer end of the shaft. Install the washer and then install the nub nut. Torque the hub nut to 180 ft. lbs.

15. Install the lock finger tight. Then, back it off until the cotter pin slot aligns with the hole in the end of the driveshaft. Install the cotter pin until it is pulled all the way through. Bend the prongs tightly around the outer end of the nut lock. Make sure the prongs wrap tightly. Torque the wheel nuts to 95 ft. lbs.

16. If the boot on the transaxle end of the shaft is deformed (collapsed), it must be vented and restored to its normal shape. To do so, first remove and discard the clamp on the shaft side (if the shaft has one); then, insert a round, small diameter rod between the boot and the shaft to vent it; then, work the boot back into its normal shape, being careful to keep dirt from getting in or grease from getting out. When the boot has reached its normal shape, remove the rod and install a new service clamp.

HALFSHAFT OVERHAUL

1. With the driveshaft assembly removed from the vehicle, remove the clamps and boot.

2. Depending on the unit separate the tripod assembly from the housing as follows:

Citroen

Since the trunion ball rollers are not retained on bearing studs a retaining ring is used to prevent accidental tripod/housing separation, which would allow roller and needle bearings to fall away.

In the case of the spring loaded inner CV-joints, if it weren't for the retaining ring, the spring would automatically force the tripod out of the housing whenever the shaft was not installed in the vehicle.

Separate the tripod from the housing by slightly deforming the retaining ring in 3 places, with a suitable tool. The retainer ring can be carefully cut from the housing, if necessary. The retention spring will push the housing off the tripod.

CAUTION: *Secure the rollers to the studs, during separation. With the tripod out of the housing, secure the assembly with tape.*

New retainer rings are supplied with the overhaul kits. They are installed by using a hammer and dull punch to roll an edge into the machined groove in the housing. If the slinger used on turbocharged vehicles is bent or damaged, it should be removed during disassembly.

1981-83 G.K.N.

The non-spring loaded G.K.N. inboard joint tripods will slide right out of the housing. There

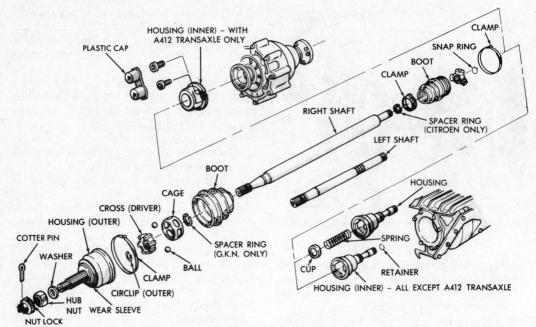

Driveshaft components

is no retaining ring to prevent their removal. Spring loaded G.K.N. inboard CV-joints have tabs on the can cover that prevent the spring from forcing the tripod out of the housing. These tabs must be bent back with a pair of pliers before the tripod can be removed. Under normal conditions it is not necessary to secure the G.K.N. rollers to their studs during separation due to the presence of a retainer ring on the end of each stud. This retention force can easily be overcome if the rollers are pulled or impacted. It is also possible to pull the rollers off by removing or installing the tripod with the connecting shaft at too high an angle, relative to the housing.

Remove the snapring from the shaft end groove then remove the tripod with a brass punch.

1984-88 G.K.N.

The retaining tabs are an integral part of the housing cover. Hold the housing by the inner end and compress the CV-joint retention spring as you use a pair of pliers to bend the tabs back. Make sure to support the housing as the retention spring pushes it out of the tripod. In this way, the housing will not turn too much and the tripod rollers will not be pulled off their studs.

A.C.I.

These units have tripod retaining tabs which are integral with the staked boot retaining collar. Hold the housing in one hand as you slightly compress the CV-joint retention spring At the same time, bend back the retaining tabs with a pair of pliers. Make sure to support the housing as the retaining spring pushes it off the tripod. It is important to do this so that the housing will not turn at too sharp an angle, which would cause the rollers to be pulled off the studs.

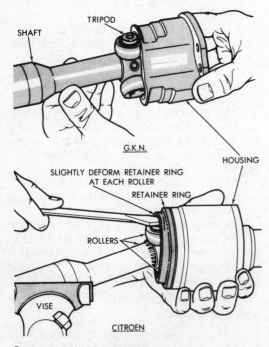

Separate tripod from housing

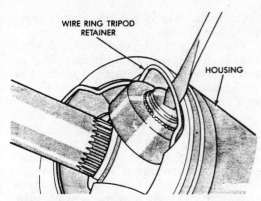

Separating the tripod from the housing—S.S.G. CV-joints

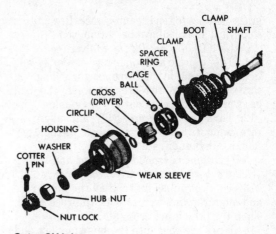

Outer CV joint

S.S.G.

This design uses a wire ring retainer for the tripod rollers. The wire retainer expands into a groove which runs around the top of the housing. Being careful not to damage the delicate retainer, use a thin, flat object to pry it out of the groove and slide the tripod out of the housing.

Remove the snapring from the shaft end groove. Remove the tripod by hand or by lightly tapping the body with a light hammer and brass punch.

DISASSEMBLY

1. Remove the boot clamps and discard them.
2. Wipe away the grease to expose the joint.
3. Support the shaft in a vice. Hold the outer joint, and using a plastic hammer, give a sharp tap to the top of the joint body to dislodge it from the internal circlip.
4. If the shaft is bent, carefully pry the wear sleeve from the CV-joint machined ledge.
5. Remove the circlip from the shaft and discard it.

NOTE: *Replacement boot kits will contain this circlip.*

6. Unless the shaft is damaged do not remove the heavy spacer ring from the shaft.

NOTE: *If the shaft must be replaced, care must be taken that the new shaft is of the proper construction, depending on whether the inner joint is spring loaded or not.*

If the CV-joint was operating satisfactorily, and the grease does not appear contaminated, just replace the boot. If the outer joint is noisy or badly worn, replace the entire unit. The repair kit will include boot, clamps, retaining ring (circlip) and lubricant.

7. Wipe off the grease and mark the position of the inner cross, cage and housing with a dab of paint.
8. Hold the joint vertically in a vise. Do not crush the splines on the shaft.
9. Press down on one side of the inner race to tilt the cage and remove the balls from the opposite side.
10. If the joint is tight, use a hammer and

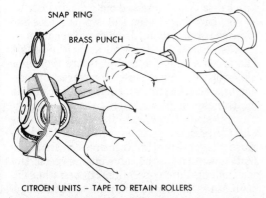

CITROEN UNITS – TAPE TO RETAIN ROLLERS

Remove snapring—then tripod

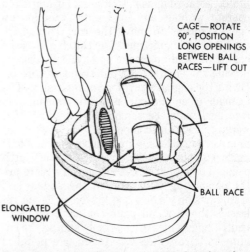

CAGE—ROTATE 90°, POSITION LONG OPENINGS BETWEEN BALL RACES—LIFT OUT

Removing cage and cross assembly from housing

brass drift pin to tap the inner race. Repeat this step until all balls have been removed.

CAUTION: *Do not hit the inner cage.*

11. Tilt the cage and inner race assembly vertically and position the two opposing, elongated cage windows in the area between the ball grooves. Pull the cage out of the housing.

12. Turn the inner cross 90° and align the race lands with an elongated hole in the cage. Remove the inner race.

NOTE: *Spring loaded parts and non-spring loaded parts are not interchangeable.*

13. To reassemble, first install the inner race and align the inner cross with the race lands. Then turn the inner cross 90°.

14. Work the cage into the housing. Tilt and turn the cage and inner race assembly so as to realign the parts.

15. Work the balls back into the assembly and into the ball grooves one by one.

16. Make sure the inner cross, cage, and housing are aligned.

17. If necessary, install the heavy spacer ring on the shaft. Install the new circlip.

18. If it was removed, carefully install the wear sleeve onto the CV-joint machined ledge.

19. Engage the joint body with the internal circlip.

20. Thoroughly pack the joint with grease. Install the boot and boot circlips.

CLUTCH

Understanding the Clutch

The purpose of the clutch is to disconnect and connect engine power from the transmission. A car at rest requires a lot of engine torque to get all that weight moving. An internal combustion engine does not develop a high starting torque (unlike steam engines), so it must be allowed to operate without any load until it builds up enough torque to move the car. Torque increases with engine rpm. The clutch allows the engine to build up torque by physically disconnecting the engine from the transmission, relieving the engine of any load or resistance. The transfer of engine power to the transmission (the load) must be smooth and gradual; if it weren't, drive line components would wear out or break quickly. This gradual power transfer is made possible by gradually releasing the clutch pedal. The clutch disc and pressure plate are the connecting link between the engine and transmission. When the clutch pedal is released, the disc and plate contact each other (clutch engagement), physically joining the engine and transmission. When the pedal is pushed in, the disc and plate separate (the

clutch is disengaged), disconnecting the engine from the transmission.

The clutch assembly consists of the flywheel, the clutch disc, the clutch pressure plate, the throwout bearing and fork, the actuating linkage and the pedal. The flywheel and clutch pressure plate (driving members) are connected to the engine crankshaft and rotate with it. The clutch disc is located between the flywheel and pressure plate, and splined to the transmission shaft. A driving member is one that is attached to the engine and transfers engine power to a driven member (clutch disc) on the transmission shaft. A driving member (pressure plate) rotates (drives) a driven member (clutch disc) on contact and, in so doing, turns the transmission shaft. There is a circular diaphragm spring within the pressure plate cover (transmission side). In a relaxed state (when the clutch pedal is fully released), this spring is convex; that it, it is dished outward toward the transmission. Pushing in the clutch pedal actuates an attached linkage rod. Connected to the other end of this rod is the throwout bearing fork. The throwout bearing is attached to the fork. When the clutch pedal is depressed, the clutch linkage pushes the fork and bearing forward to contact the diaphragm spring of the pressure plate. The outer edges of the spring are secured to the pressure plate and are pivoted on rings so that when the center of the spring is compressed by the throwout bearing, the outer edges bow outward and, by so doing, pull the pressure plate in the same direction - away from the clutch disc. This action separates the disc from the plate, disengaging the clutch and allowing the transmission to be shifted into another gear. A coil type clutch return spring attached to the clutch pedal arm permits full release of the pedal. Releasing the pedal pulls the throwout bearing away from the diaphragm spring resulting in a reversal of spring position. As bearing pressure is gradually released from the spring center, the outer edges of the spring bow outward, pushing the pressure plate into closer contact with the clutch disc. As the disc and plate move closer together, friction between the two increases and slippage is reduced until, when full spring pressure is applied (by fully releasing the pedal), The speed of the disc and plate are the same. This stops all slipping, creating a direct connection between the plate and disc which results in the transfer of power from the engine to the transmission. The clutch disc is now rotating with the pressure plate at engine speed and, because it is splined to the transmission shaft, the shaft now turns at the same engine speed. Understanding clutch operation can be rather difficult at first; if you're still confused after reading this, consider the following analogy. The ac-

Troubleshooting Basic Clutch Problems

Problem	Cause
Excessive clutch noise	Throwout bearing noises are more audible at the lower end of pedal travel. The usual causes are: • Riding the clutch • Too little pedal free-play • Lack of bearing lubrication A bad clutch shaft pilot bearing will make a high pitched squeal, when the clutch is disengaged and the transmission is in gear or within the first 2″ of pedal travel. The bearing must be replaced. Noise from the clutch linkage is a clicking or snapping that can be heard or felt as the pedal is moved completely up or down. This usually requires lubrication. Transmitted engine noises are amplified by the clutch housing and heard in the passenger compartment. They are usually the result of insufficient pedal free-play and can be changed by manipulating the clutch pedal.
Clutch slips (the car does not move as it should when the clutch is engaged)	This is usually most noticeable when pulling away from a standing start. A severe test is to start the engine, apply the brakes, shift into high gear and SLOWLY release the clutch pedal. A healthy clutch will stall the engine. If it slips it may be due to: • A worn pressure plate or clutch plate • Oil soaked clutch plate • Insufficient pedal free-play
Clutch drags or fails to release	The clutch disc and some transmission gears spin briefly after clutch disengagement. Under normal conditions in average temperatures, 3 seconds is maximum spin-time. Failure to release properly can be caused by: • Too light transmission lubricant or low lubricant level • Improperly adjusted clutch linkage
Low clutch life	Low clutch life is usually a result of poor driving habits or heavy duty use. Riding the clutch, pulling heavy loads, holding the car on a grade with the clutch instead of the brakes and rapid clutch engagement all contribute to low clutch life.

tion of the diaphragm spring can be compared to that of an oil can bottom. The bottom of an oil can is shaped very much like the clutch diaphragm spring and pushing in on the can bottom and then releasing it produces a similar effect. As mentioned earlier, the clutch pedal return spring permits full release of the pedal and reduces linkage slack due to wear. As the linkage wears, clutch free-pedal travel will increase and free-travel will decrease as the clutch wears. Free-travel is actually throwout bearing lash.

The diaphragm spring type clutches used are available in two different designs: flat diaphragm springs or bent spring. The bent fingers are bent back to create a centrifugal boost ensuring quick re-engagement at higher engine speeds. This design enables pressure plate load to increase as the clutch disc wears and makes low pedal effort possible even with a heavy-duty clutch. The throwout bearing used with the bent finger design is 1¼″ long and is shorter than the bearing used with the flat finger design. These bearings are not interchangeable. If the longer bearing is used with the bent finger

clutch, free-pedal travel will not exist. This results in clutch slippage and rapid wear.

The transmission varies the gear ratio between the engine and rear wheels. It can be shifted to change engine speed as driving conditions and loads change. The transmission allows disengaging and reversing power from the engine to the wheels.

The clutch is a dry disc unit, with no adjustment for wear provided in the clutch itself. Adjustment is made through an adjustable sleeve in the pedal linkage.

CAUTION: *The clutch driven disc contains asbestos, which has been determined to be a cancer-causing agent. Never clean clutch surfaces with compressed air! Avoid inhaling any dust emitted from any clutch surface! When cleaning clutch surfaces, use a commercially available brake cleaning fluid.*

Adjustments

The clutch cable requires no adjustment for clutch disc wear on the A-460, 465 and 525 transaxles. Unless improperly installed, the

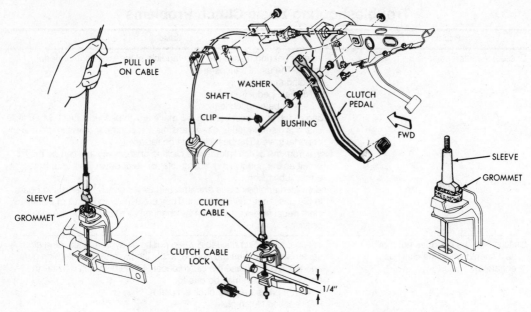

Adjusting clutch free play—A-412 manual transaxle

spring in the clutch pedal holds the cable in the proper position.

A-412 Transaxle

1. Pull up on the clutch cable.
2. While holding the cable up, rotate the adjusting sleeve downward until a snug contact is made against the grommet.
3. Rotate the sleeve slightly to allow the end of the sleeve to seat in the rectangular hole in the grommet.

Driven Disc and Pressure Plate
REMOVAL AND INSTALLATION

A-412 Transaxle

NOTE: *Chrysler recommends the use of special tool L-4533 for disc alignment.*

1. Remove the transaxle as described earlier in this chapter.
2. Loosen the flywheel-to-pressure plate bolts diagonally, one or two turns at a time to avoid warpage.
3. Remove the flywheel and clutch disc from the pressure plate.
4. Remove the retaining ring and release plate.
5. Diagonally loosen the pressure plate-to-crankshaft bolts. Mark all parts for reassembly.
6. Remove the bolts, spacer and pressure plate.
7. The flywheel and pressure plate surfaces should be cleaned thoroughly with fine sandpaper.
8. Align marks and install the pressure plate,

spacer, and bolts. Coat the bolts with thread compound and torque them to 55 ft. lbs.
9. Install the release plate and retaining ring.
10. Using special tool L-4533 or its equivalent, install the clutch disc and flywheel on the pressure plate.
    CAUTION: *Make certain that the drilled mark on the flywheel is at the top, so that the two dowels on the flywheel align with the proper holes in the pressure plate.*
11. Install the six flywheel bolts and tighten them to 15 ft. lbs.
12. Remove the aligning tool.
13. Install the transmission.
14. Adjust the freeplay as described above.

A-460, 465, 525, 555 Transaxle

NOTE: *Chrysler recommends the use of special tool #C-4676 for disc alignment.*

1. Remove the transaxle as described earlier in this chapter.
2. Matchmark the clutch cover and flywheel for installation in the same positions.
3. Insert special tool C-4676 or its equivalent to hold the clutch disc in place.
4. Loosen the cover attaching bolts. Do this procedure in a diagonal manner, a few turns at a time to prevent warping the cover.
5. Remove the cover assembly and disc from the flywheel. Be careful to keep any dirt or other contamination off the friction surfaces.
6. Remove the clutch release shaft and slide the release bearing off the input shaft seal retainer.

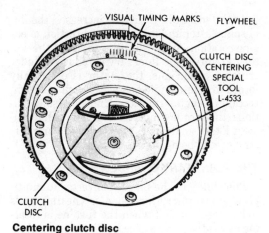

Centering clutch disc

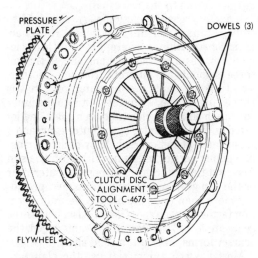

A-460 manual transaxle clutch disc aligning tool

7. Remove the fork from the release bearing thrust plate.

8. Inspect the rear main seal for leakage. Repair the seal at this point, if there is leakage.

9. Make sure the friction surfaces of both the flywheel and the pressure plate are uniform in appearance. If there is evidence of heavy contact at one point and very light contact 180° away, the flywheel or pressure plate may be improperly mounted (torqued) or sprung due to mechanical damage. If there is evidence that the flywheel may not be true, it should be checked with a dial indicator. The indicator must be mounted so that its plunger is in contact with the flywheel wear circle. In a full turn, the indicator should read no more than 0.076mm. Make sure to push forward on the flywheel before you begin taking the reading and zeroing the indicator and press forward on it continuously as you turn to keep any crankshaft endplay out of the reading.

10. With a straightedge, check the pressure plate for flatness. The inner surface of the pressure plate should be straight within 0.5mm. It should also be free of discoloration, cracks, grooves, or ridges. Otherwise, replace it.

11. Spin the clutch bearing to make sure it turns freely and smoothly.

12. Install the fork, release bearing, and clutch release shaft in the reverse order of the removal procedure.

13. Install the clutch assembly onto the flywheel, carefully aligning the dowels on the flywheel with the holes in the assembly. Make sure the alignment marks made earlier also align. Then, apply pressure to the clutch alignment tool to precisely center it as you snug the clutch attaching bolts sufficiently to hold the clutch disc in the proper position.

14. Tighten the clutch cover bolts alternately and evenly until they all are seated. Then, torque to 21 ft. lbs. Remove the disc alignment tool.

AUTOMATIC TRANSAXLE

Understanding Automatic Transmissions

The automatic transmission allows engine torque and power to be transmitted to the rear wheels within a narrow range of engine operating speeds. The transmission will allow the engine to turn fast enough to produce plenty of power and torque at very low speeds, while keeping it at a sensible rpm at high vehicle speeds. The transmission performs this job entirely without driver assistance. The transmission uses a light fluid as the medium for the transmission of power. This fluid also works in the operation of various hydraulic control circuits and as a lubricant. Because the transmission fluid performs all of these three functions, trouble within the unit can easily travel from one part to another. For this reason, and because of the complexity and unusual operating principles of the transmission, a very sound understanding of the basic principles of operation will simplify troubleshooting.

THE TORQUE CONVERTER

The torque converter replaces the conventional clutch. It has three functions:

1. It allows the engine to idle with the vehicle at a standstill, even with the transmission in gear.

2. It allows the transmission to shift from range to range smoothly, without requiring that the driver close the throttle during the shift.

3. It multiplies engine torque to an increas-

ing extent as vehicle speed drops and throttle opening is increased. This has the effect of making the transmission more responsive and reduces the amount of shifting required.

The torque converter is a metal case which is shaped like a sphere that has been flattened on opposite sides. It is bolted to the rear end of the engine's crankshaft. Generally, the entire metal case rotates at engine speed and serves as the engine's flywheel.

The case contains three sets of blades. One set is attached directly to the case. This set forms the torus or pump. Another set is directly connected to the output shaft, and forms the turbine. The third set is mounted on a hub which, in turn, is mounted on a stationary shaft through a one-way clutch. This third set is known as the stator.

A pump, which is driven by the converter hub at engine speed, keeps the torque converter full of transmission fluid at all times. Fluid flows continuously through the unit to provide cooling.

Under low speed acceleration, the torque converter functions as follows:

The torus is turning faster than the turbine. It picks up fluid at the center of the converter and, through centrifugal force, slings it outward. Since the outer edge of the converter moves faster than the portions at the center, the fluid picks up speed.

The fluid then enters the outer edge of the turbine blades. It then travels back toward the center of the converter case along the turbine blades. In impinging upon the turbine blades, the fluid loses the energy picked up in the torus.

If the fluid were now to immediately be returned directly into the torus, both halves of the converter would have to turn at approximately the same speed at all times, and torque input and output would both be the same.

In flowing through the torus and turbine, the fluid picks up two types of flow, or flow in two separate directions. It flows through the turbine blades, and it spins with the engine. The stator, whose blades are stationary when the vehicle is being accelerated at low speeds, converts one type of flow into another. Instead of allowing the fluid to flow straight back into the torus, the stator's curved blades turn the fluid almost 90° toward the direction of rotation of the engine. Thus the fluid does not flow as fast toward the torus, but is already spinning when the torus picks it up. This has the effect of allowing the torus to turn much faster than the turbine. This difference in speed may be compared to the difference in speed between the smaller and larger gears in any gear train. The result is that engine power output is higher, and engine torque is multiplied.

As the speed of the turbine increases, the fluid spins faster and faster in the direction of engine rotation. As a result, the ability of the stator to redirect the fluid flow is reduced. Under cruising conditions, the stator is eventually forced to rotate on its one-way clutch in the direction of engine rotation. Under these conditions, the torque converter begins to behave almost like a solid shaft, with the torus and turbine speeds being almost equal.

THE PLANETARY GEARBOX

The ability of the torque converter to multiply engine torque is limited. Also, the unit tends to be more efficient when the turbine is rotating at relatively high speeds. Therefore, a planetary gearbox is used to carry the power output of the turbine to the driveshaft.

Planetary gears function very similarly to conventional transmission gears. However, their construction is different in that three elements make up one gear system, and, in that all three elements are different from one another. The three elements are: an outer gear that is shaped like a hoop, with teeth cut into the inner surface; a sun gear, mounted on a shaft and located at the very center of the outer gear; and a set of three planet gears, held by pins in a ring-like planet carrier, meshing with both the sun gear and the outer gear. Either the outer gear or the sun gear may be held stationary, providing more than one possible torque multiplication factor for each set of gears. Also, if all three gears are forced to rotate at the same speed, the gearset forms, in effect, a solid shaft.

Most modern automatics use the planetary gears to provide either a single reduction ratio of about 1.8:1, or two reduction gears: a low of about 2.5:1, and an intermediate of about 1.5:1. Bands and clutches are used to hold various portions of the gearsets to the transmission case or to the shaft on which they are mounted. Shifting is accomplished, then, by changing the portion of each planetary gearset which is held to the transmission case or to the shaft.

THE SERVOS AND ACCUMULATORS

The servos are hydraulic pistons and cylinders. They resemble the hydraulic actuators used on many familiar machines, such as bulldozers. Hydraulic fluid enters the cylinder, under pressure, and forces the piston to move to engage the band or clutches.

The accumulators are used to cushion the engagement of the servos. The transmission fluid must pass through the accumulator on the way to the servo. The accumulator housing contains a thin piston which is sprung away from the discharge passage of the accumulator. When fluid passes through the accumulator on the way to the servo, it must move the piston against spring pressure, and this action smooths out the action of the servo.

THE HYDRAULIC CONTROL SYSTEM

The hydraulic pressure used to operate the servos comes from the main transmission oil pump. This fluid is channeled to the various servos through the shift valves. There is generally a manual shift valve which is operated by the transmission selector lever and an automatic shift valve for each automatic upshift the transmission provides: i.e., 2-speed automatics have a low/high shift valve, while 3-speeds have a 1–2 valve, and a 2–3 valve.

There are two pressures which effect the operation of these valves. One is the governor pressure which is affected by vehicle speed. The other is the modulator pressure which is affected by intake manifold vacuum or throttle position. Governor pressure rises with an increase in vehicle speed, and modulator pressure rises as the throttle is opened wider. By responding to these two pressures, the shift valves cause the upshift points to be delayed with increased throttle opening to make the best use of the engine's power output.

Most transmissions also make use of an auxiliary circuit for downshifting. This circuit may be actuated by the throttle linkage or the vacuum line which actuates the modulator, or by a cable or solenoid. It applies pressure to a special downshift surface on the shift valve or valves.

The transmission modulator also governs the line pressure, used to actuate the servos. In this way, the clutches and bands will be actuated with a force matching the torque output of the engine.

The transaxle combines a torque converter, a fully automatic 3 speed transmission, final drive gearing and a differential, into a compact front wheel drive system. For 1987 models, all vehicles with a 2.5 L engine are equippped with a lockup torque converter. For 1988, all vehicles without a turbocharger have this feature. The converter lockup is activated by the engine electronics to carry the drive directly through the converter without hydraulic action. This saves fuel and slightly reduces engine rpm under conditions when the converter would not contribute to vehicle performance.

Identification

Transaxle operation requirements are different for each vehicle and engine combination. Some internal parts will be different to provide for this. When you order replacement parts, refer to the seven digit part number stamped on the rear of the transmission oil pan flange.

Fluid Pan

REMOVAL AND INSTALLATION AND FILTER SERVICE

1. Jack up the vehicle and support it with jackstands.
2. Place a drain pan under the transmission.
3. Loosen the pan bolts. Gently tap the pan at one corner to loosen it, thereby, allowing the fluid to drain.
4. Remove the pan and the oil filter.
5. Install a new filter and tighten the filter bolts to 40 in. lbs.
6. Clean both gasket surfaces of all gasketing material if a gasket is used. If RTV sealer is used, clean all sealer from both surfaces.
7. Reinstall the pan with a new gasket or a new bead of RTV sealant.and tighten the bolts to 14 ft. lbs.
8. Put 4 quarts of Dexron II® transmission fluid in the transaxle.
9. Start the engine and allow it to run for at least 2 minutes. While the engine is running, hold your foot on the service brake, apply the emergency brake and shift the transmission through all gears.
10. Check the fluid in the neutral or park position, and add more if necessary. Recheck the

SERIAL NUMBER LOCATION

Automatic transaxle

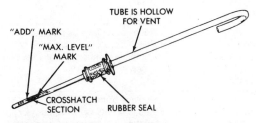

TUBE IS HOLLOW FOR VENT

"ADD" MARK

"MAX. LEVEL" MARK

CROSSHATCH SECTION   RUBBER SEAL

Dipstick and transmission vent

Troubleshooting Basic Automatic Transmission Problems

Problem	Cause	Solution
Fluid leakage	• Defective pan gasket	• Replace gasket or tighten pan bolts
	• Loose filler tube	• Tighten tube nut
	• Loose extension housing to transmission case	• Tighten bolts
	• Converter housing area leakage	• Have transmission checked professionally
Fluid flows out the oil filler tube	• High fluid level	• Check and correct fluid level
	• Breather vent clogged	• Open breather vent
	• Clogged oil filter or screen	• Replace filter or clean screen (change fluid also)
	• Internal fluid leakage	• Have transmission checked professionally
Transmission overheats (this is usually accompanied by a strong burned odor to the fluid)	• Low fluid level	• Check and correct fluid level
	• Fluid cooler lines clogged	• Drain and refill transmission. If this doesn't cure the problem, have cooler lines cleared or replaced.
	• Heavy pulling or hauling with insufficient cooling	• Install a transmission oil cooler
	• Faulty oil pump, internal slippage	• Have transmission checked professionally
Buzzing or whining noise	• Low fluid level	• Check and correct fluid level
	• Defective torque converter, scored gears	• Have transmission checked professionally
No forward or reverse gears or slippage in one or more gears	• Low fluid level	• Check and correct fluid level
	• Defective vacuum or linkage controls, internal clutch or band failure	• Have unit checked professionally
Delayed or erratic shift	• Low fluid level	• Check and correct fluid level
	• Broken vacuum lines	• Repair or replace lines
	• Internal malfunction	• Have transmission checked professionally

Lockup Torque Converter Service Diagnosis

Problem	Cause	Solution
No lockup	• Faulty oil pump	• Replace oil pump
	• Sticking governor valve	• Repair or replace as necessary
	• Valve body malfunction	• Repair or replace valve body or its internal components as necessary
	(a) Stuck switch valve	
	(b) Stuck lockup valve	
	(c) Stuck fail-safe valve	
	• Failed locking clutch	• Replace torque converter
	• Leaking turbine hub seal	• Replace torque converter
	• Faulty input shaft or seal ring	• Repair or replace as necessary
Will not unlock	• Sticking governor valve	• Repair or replace as necessary
	• Valve body malfunction	• Repair or replace valve body or its internal components as necessary
	(a) Stuck switch valve	
	(b) Stuck lockup valve	
	(c) Stuck fail-safe valve	
Stays locked up at too low a speed in direct	• Sticking governor valve	• Repair or replace as necessary
	• Valve body malfunction	• Repair or replace valve body or its internal components as necessary
	(a) Stuck switch valve	
	(b) Stuck lockup valve	
	(c) Stuck fail-safe valve	
Locks up or drags in low or second	• Faulty oil pump	• Replace oil pump
	• Valve body malfunction	• Repair or replace valve body or its internal components as necessary
	(a) Stuck switch valve	
	(b) Stuck fail-safe valve	

Lockup Torque Converter Service Diagnosis *(cont.)*

Problem	Cause	Solution

Sluggish or stalls in reverse	• Faulty oil pump
	• Plugged cooler, cooler lines or fittings
	• Valve body malfunction
	  (a) Stuck switch valve
	  (b) Faulty input shaft or seal ring
		• Replace oil pump as necessary
		• Flush or replace cooler and flush lines and fittings
		• Repair or replace valve body or its internal components as necessary

Loud chatter during lockup engagement (cold)	• Faulty torque converter • Failed locking clutch • Leaking turbine hub seal	• Replace torque converter • Replace torque converter • Replace torque converter
Vibration or shudder during lockup engagement	• Faulty oil pump • Valve body malfunction • Faulty torque converter • Engine needs tune-up	• Repair or replace oil pump as necessary • Repair or replace valve body or its internal components as necessary • Replace torque converter • Tune engine
Vibration after lockup engagement	• Faulty torque converter • Exhaust system strikes underbody • Engine needs tune-up • Throttle linkage misadjusted	• Replace torque converter • Align exhaust system • Tune engine • Adjust throttle linkage
Vibration when revved in neutral Overheating: oil blows out of dip stick tube or pump seal	• Torque converter out of balance • Plugged cooler, cooler lines or fittings • Stuck switch valve	• Replace torque converter • Flush or replace cooler and flush lines and fittings • Repair switch valve in valve body or replace valve body
Shudder after lockup engagement	• Faulty oil pump • Plugged cooler, cooler lines or fittings • Valve body malfunction • Faulty torque converter • Fail locking clutch • Exhaust system strikes underbody • Engine needs tune-up • Throttle linkage misadjusted	• Replace oil pump • Flush or replace cooler and flush lines and fittings • Repair or replace valve body or its internal components as necessary • Replace torque converter • Replace torque converter • Align exhaust system • Tune engine • Adjust throttle linkage

Transmission Fluid Indications

The appearance and odor of the transmission fluid can give valuable clues to the overall condition of the transmission. Always note the appearance of the fluid when you check the fluid level or change the fluid. Rub a small amount of fluid between your fingers to feel for grit and smell the fluid on the dipstick.

If the fluid appears:	It indicates:
Clear and red colored	• Normal operation
Discolored (extremely dark red or brownish) or smells burned	• Band or clutch pack failure, usually caused by an overheated transmission. Hauling very heavy loads with insufficient power or failure to change the fluid, often result in overheating. Do not confuse this appearance with newer fluids that have a darker red color and a strong odor (though not a burned odor).
Foamy or aerated (light in color and full of bubbles)	• The level is too high (gear train is churning oil) • An internal air leak (air is mixing with the fluid). Have the transmission checked professionally.
Solid residue in the fluid	• Defective bands, clutch pack or bearings. Bits of band material or metal abrasives are clinging to the dipstick. Have the transmission checked professionally.
Varnish coating on the dipstick	• The transmission fluid is overheating

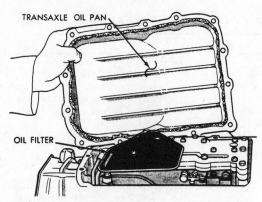

Changing transmission fluid. On those engines using RTV sealer rather than a pan gasket, apply the sealer as shown.

fluid after it has reached normal operating temperature. The fluid level should be between the "Max" and "Add" lines on the dipstick.

Adjustments

NEUTRAL SAFETY/BACK-UP LIGHT SWITCH ADJUSTMENT

The neutral safety switch is the center terminal of the three terminal switch, located on the transaxle. The back-up light switch uses the two outside terminals. The center terminal provides a ground for the starter solenoid circuit through the selector lever in the Park and Neutral positions only.

1. Disconnect the negative battery terminal.
2. Unscrew the switch from the transaxle, and allow the fluid to drain into a pan.
3. Move the selector lever to see that the switch operating lever fingers are centered in the switch opening.
4. Install the new switch and seal. Tighten the switch to 24 ft. lbs.

SHIFT LINKAGE ADJUSTMENT

1981-83

NOTE: *When it is necessary to disassembly the linkage cable from the lever, which uses plastic grommets as retainers, the grommets should be replaced with new ones.*

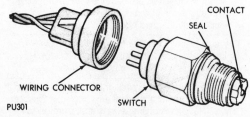

PU301

Neutral start and back-up light switch

1. Make sure that the adjustable swivel block is free to slide on the shift cable.
2. Place the shift lever in Park.
3. With the linkage assembled, and the swivel lock bolt loose, move the shift arm on the transaxle all the way to the front detent.
4. Hold the shift arm in this position with a force of about 10 lbs. and tighten the adjust swivel lock bolt to 8 ft. lb.
5. Check the linkage action.

NOTE: *The automatic transmission gear selector release buttom may pop up in the knob when shifting from PARK to DRIVE. This is caused by inadequate retension of the selector release knob retaining tab. The release button will always work but the loose button can be annoying. A sleeve (Chrysler Part No. 5211984) and washers (Chrysler Part No. 6500380) are available to cure this condition. If these are unavailable, do the following:*

1. Remove the release button.
2. Cut and fold a standard paper match stem as shown.
3. Using tweezers, insert the folded match as far as possible into the clearance slot as shown. The match should be below the knob surface.
4. Insert the button, taking care not to break the button stem.

1984-88

1. Put the gearshift in "PARK". Loosen the clamp bolt located on the gearshift cable bracket.
2. On column shifts, make sure that the preload adjustment spring engages the fork on the transaxle bracket.
3. Pull the shift lever (on the transmission) all the way to the front detent position (which puts the transmission in "PARK"). Then, tighten the lockbolt to 90 ft. lbs. on 1984-87 models and 100 ft. lbs. on 1988 cars.
4. Check the adjustment as follows:
    a. The detent positions of the transmission shift lever for "NEUTRAL" and "DRIVE" should be within the limits of the corresponding gate stops on the hand shift lever.
    b. The starter must operate with the key only if the shift lever is in "PARK" or "NEUTRAL" position.

THROTTLE CABLE ADJUSTMENT

1981-85

NOTE: *This adjustment should be performed while the engine is at normal operating temperature. Make sure that the carburetor is not on fast idle by disconnecting the choke.*

1. Loosen the adjustment bracket lock screw.

2. To insure proper adjustment, the bracket must be free to slide on its slot.

3. Hold the throttle lever firmly to the left (toward the engine) against its internal stop and tighten the adjusting bracket lock to 105 in. lbs. (8¾ ft. lbs.).

4. Reconnect the choke. Test the cable operation by moving the throttle lever forward and slowly releasing it to confirm it will return fully rearward.

1986-88

1. Make sure the engine is at operating temperature. On carbureted cars, disconnect the choke to make sure the throttle is completely off the fast idle cam.

2. Loosen the bracket lock screw that is mounted on the cable.

3. The bracket should be positioned with both its alignment tabs touching the surface of the transaxle. If not, position it that way. Then tighten the lock bolt to 105 in. lbs.

4. Release the cross lock on the cable assembly by pulling it upward. Make sure that the cable is then free to slide all the way toward the engine (until it is against its stop).

5. Now turn the transaxle throttle control lever fully clockwise—until it hits its internal stop. Press the cross lock downward and into its

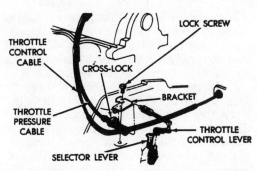

Adjusting the transmission throttle cable on 1986–88 cars

locked position. This will automatically remove all cable backlash.

6. Reconnect the choke, if it has been disconnected. Turn the transaxle throttle lever forward (or counterclockwise) and then slowly release it. It should return to the full clockwise position, indicating that the cable operates freely.

FRONT (KICKDOWN) BAND ADJUSTMENT

NOTE: *A spoecial tool #C-3380-A may facilitate adjustment of the front band. It is not absolutely necessary that it be used, however.*

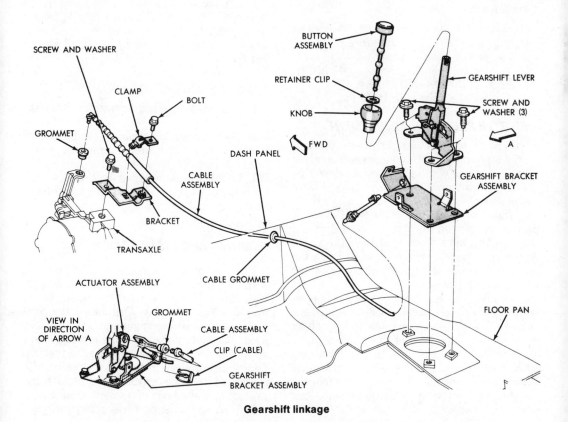

Gearshift linkage

The kickdown band adjusting screw is located on the left side (top front) on the transaxle case.

1. Loosen the locknut and back off the nut approximately 5 turns. Test the adjusting screw for free turning in the transaxle case.

2. Using special tool #C-3380-A or its equivalent, tighten the adjusting screw to 72 in. lbs. If adapter C-3705 is used with the tool, tighten the adjusting screw to 50 in. lbs.

3. Back off the adjusting screw 3 turns (A-404); 2½ turns (A-413 and A-470). Hold the adjusting screw in this position and tighten the locknut to 35 ft. lbs.

LOW/REVERSE (REAR) BAND ADJUSTMENT

A-404

1. Remove the oil pan and pressurize the low/reverse servo with 30 psi of air pressure.

2. Measure the gap between the band ends. If the gap is less than 2mm, the band has worn excessively and should be replaced. Band replacement is best left to a qualified repair facility.

3. Loosen and back off the locknut approximately 5 turns.

4. Tighten the adjusting screw to 41 in. lbs.

5. Back off the adjusting screw 3½ turns.

6. Tighten the locknut to 20 ft. lbs.

A-413 & A-470

NOTE: *Prior to adjustment, check the endgap as in the A-404 procedure.*

1. Loosen the locknut 5 turns.

2. Tighten the adjusting screw to 41 in. lbs.

3. Back off the screw 3½ turns.

4. Tighten the locknut to 10 ft. lbs.

THROTTLE PRESSURE ADJUSTMENT

NOTE: *To perform this procedure, you will need a special tool #C-3763 or equivalent for use of a gauge pin; and a special adapter C-4553 or equivalent to turn the throttle lever stop screw.*

1. Insert the gauge pin of the tool C-3763 or equivalent between the throttle lever cam and the kickdown valve. Then, push in on the tool to compress the kickdown valve against its spring until the throttle valve is positively bottomed inside the valve body.

2. Holding the kickdown valve in this position, install the adapter C-4553 or equivalent onto the throttle lever stop screw and turn it by its handle until the head of this screw touches the throttle lever tang. The throttle lever cam must touch the tool and the throttle valve must be bottomed at the same time the screw touches the throttle lever tang; if all these conditions are met, the adjustment is complete.

Neutral Safety and Backup Lamp Switch

TESTING

1. Make sure the transmission shift cable is properly adjusted.

2. Pull the wiring connector off the switch. Put the transaxle in "PARK".

3. With a battery powered continuity tester, test for continuity between the center pin of the switch and the transaxle case. Repeat the test with the transmission in "NEUTRAL".

4. Test to make sure there is *no* continuity in all other gear lever positions.

5. Now, shift the tester to the two outside terminals of the switch. Have someone shift the gear lever to all positions and make sure there is continuity *only* in the "REVERSE" position. Repeat this test with the tester hooked up between either pin and the case. There should be *no* continuity between either outside terminal and the case in any gear lever position.

6. Place a container underneath to catch draining fluid. Then, unscrew the switch and remove it from the transaxle case. Have someone move the gearshift to "PARK" and "NEUTRAL" positions while watching to see that the switch operating fingers inside the case are centered in the opening in which the switch is mounted.

7. Replace the switch if it fails any of the tests and if the shift cable and actuating fingers are okay. Make sure to reinstall the switch with a new seal, torque it to 24 ft. lbs. and replace lost fluid.

REMOVAL AND INSTALLATION

1. Remove the wiring connector from the switch.

2. Place a drain pan underneath the switch to catch drain fluid and unscrew the switch from the case.

3. Install the new switch with a new seal, torque it to 24 ft. lbs. and replace lost fluid.

Transaxle

REMOVAL AND INSTALLATION

The automatic transaxle can be removed with the engine installed in the car, but the transaxle and torque converter must be removed as an assembly. Otherwise, the drive plate, pump bushing or oil seal could be damaged. The drive plate will not support a load— no weight should be allowed to bear on the drive plate as the unit is removed; it must be fully disconnected from the converter before the transmission is shifted out of its normal position.

1. Disconnect the positive battery cable.

2. Disconnect the throttle and shift linkage from the transaxle.

3. Put a drain pan underneath and then disconnect both the upper and lower oil cooler hoses. If the car has a lockup converter, unplug the electrical connector, which is located near the dipstick.

4. Install a positive means of supporting the engine, such as a support fixture that runs across between the two front fenders.

5. Remove the upper bolts—those that are accessible from above from the bell housing.

6. For 1986 and later vehicles, refer to the appropriate procedure earlier in this chapter to remove or install the driveshafts. This will include removing both front wheels and raising the car and supporting it securely so it can be worked on from underneath. On 1985 and earlier vehicles, remove the driveshafts as follows:

  a. Remove the left splash shield. Drain the differential and remove the cover.

  b. Remove the speedometer adapter, cable and gear.

  c. Remove the sway bar.

  d. Remove both lower ball joint-to-steering knuckle bolts.

  e. Pry the lower ball joint from the steering knuckle.

  f. Remove the driveshaft from the hub.

  g. Rotate both driveshafts to expose the circlip ends. Note the flat surface on the inner ends of both axle tripod shafts. Pry the circlip out.

  h. Remove both driveshafts.

7. On 1986 and later vehicles, remove the left side splash shield.

8. Remove the dust cover from under the torque converter. Remove the access plug in the right splash shield to rotate the engine. Matchmark the torque converter and drive plate. Then, remove the torque converter mounting

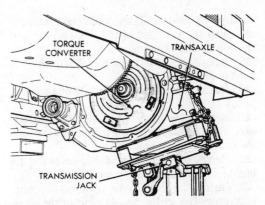

Lowering the transaxle out of the car. Note that the transmission support jig must support the unit by the corners of the oil pan, and not by the pan itself

bolts, rotating the engine after each bolt is removed for access to the next one.

9. Disconnect the plug for the neutral safety/backup light switch.

10. Remove the engine mount bracket from the front crossmember.

11. Support the transmission from underneath. It must be supported in a positive manner and without the weight resting on the pan; it should be supported by its corners.

12. Remove the front mount insulator through-bolts.

13. Remove the long through-bolt from the left hand engine mount.

14. Remove the starter. Then, remove any bell housing bolts that are still in position.

15. Pry the transaxle away from the engine to ensure that the torque converter will clear the drive plate. If removing a manual transaxle, slide the transaxle directly away from the engine so the transmission input shaft will slide smoothly out of the bearing in the flywheel and the clutch disc. Lower the transaxle and remove it from the engine compartment.

16. To install the transaxle, first support the unit securely and raise it into precise alignment with the engine block. Then, move it toward the block, inserting the transmission input shaft into the clutch disc, if it is a manual transaxle (turn the input shaft slightly, if necessary, to get the splines to engage). With automatic units, make sure to align the lower boltholes in the transaxle bell housing with those in the block.

17. Install the lower bell housing bolts and the starter. Bell housing bolts are torqued to 105 in. lbs.

18. Turn the engine via the crankshaft pulley bolt as necessary to align the torque converter boltholes with those in the flex drive plate. Make sure the matchmarks made prior to disassembly are aligned. Install each bolt and torque it to 40 ft. lbs. on 1981–85 models, and 55 ft. lbs.

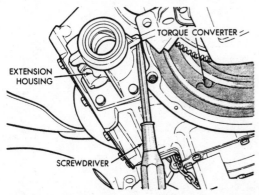

Prying the transaxle away from the engine for clearance. Use a blunt instrument rather than a screwdriver if you can on 1986–88 models. Then, turn the crank for access to the next set of boltholes and install the bolt in that position.

19. Install the long through-bolt into the left hand engine mount.

20. Install the front mount insulator through-bolts.

21. Remove the jack supporting the transmission. Then, install the engine mount bracket onto the front crossmember.

22. Reconnect the electrical connector for the backup light/neutral safety switch.

23. Install the dust cover under the torque converter. Install the access plug in the right splash shield.

24. Install the driveshafts by reversing the removal procedure. Install the left side splash shield.

25. With the wheels remounted and the car back on the floor, install the remaining bell housing bolts and torque them to 105 in. lbs.

26. Remove the engine support fixture.

27. Connect both the upper and lower oil cooler hoses. If the car has a lockup converter, replug the electrical connector.

28. Reconnect the throttle and shift cables and adjust them.

29. Install the differential cover on those transmission from which it was removed. Form a new gasket from RTV sealant when installing the cover. See Chapter 1. Fill the differential or combined transmission and differential with the approved automatic transmission fluid. Reconnect the battery.

Halfshafts

Removal and installation and overhaul procedures for all halfshafts, whether used with automatic or manual transmissions, are covered above, under the appropriate portions of the Manual Transaxle section.

Suspension and Steering

FRONT SUSPENSION

Chrysler front wheel drive cars use a Mac-Pherson Type front suspension, with vertical shock absorbers attached to the upper fender reinforcement and the steering knuckle. Lower control arms, attached inboard to a cross-member and outboard to the steering knuckle through a ball joint, provide lower steering knuckle position. During steering manuevers, the upper strut and steering knuckle turn as an assembly.

MacPherson Struts (Shock Absorbers)

REMOVAL AND INSTALLATION

NOTE: *A large C-clamp (4" or larger) is needed to perform this operation.*

1. Loosen the wheel nuts. Jack up the vehicle and support it with jackstands.

2. Remove the wheel.

3. If the same strut and knuckle will be re-used together, mark the cam adjusting bolt except on Sundance, Shadow, Lancer, and LeBaron GTS. On those models, mark the outline of the strut on the knuckle.

4. Remove the cam adjusting bolt, through bolt, washer plates, and brake hose bracket screw.

5. Have someone support the strut from underneath. Remove the strut mounting nuts and washers from the fender well. Lower and remove the strut.

6. Install the strut by raising it into position and then supporting it from underneath. Have someone support the strut at the bottom as you do this and hold it until it can be bolted to the knuckle. Install the washers and nuts and torque the nuts to 20 ft. lbs.

7. Position the neck of the knuckle in between the strut brackets, and install the cam

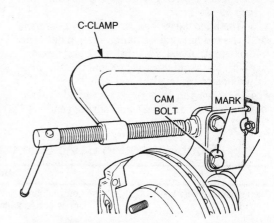

Using a C-clamp to position the lower end of the strut on the neck of the knuckle

and knuckle bolts and, if there are any washers, those also. Attach the brake hose retainer to the damper and torque the mounting bolt to 10 ft. lbs.

8. Index the strut to align the mark made on the knuckle neck at disassembly with the edge of the strut bracket.

9. Install a C-clamp onto the strut so as to pull the strut onto the knuckle neck. The rotating part of the clamp should rest against the neck. While tightenening the clamp, constantly check the fit of the knuckle neck into the strut, feeling for looseness. At the point where looseness is just eliminated, stop tightening the clamp. Make sure the index marks made earlier are aligned. If necessary, loosen the clamp and change the position of the strut to align them, and then retighten the clamp.

10. Torque the bolts to 75 ft. lbs. on 1984 and later models, 45 ft. lbs. on 1983 and earlier models. Then, turn them another ¼ turn. Remove the C-clamp.

11. Install the wheel and tire and torque the

bolts to 95 ft. lbs. on 1985 and later models and 80 ft. lbs. on 1981-84 models.

OVERHAUL

NOTE: *To perform this procedure, a special spring compressor such as Tool C-4838 (C-4514 on 1981-82 models) or equivalent is required. Also needed is a special large socket and adapter L-4558 and L-4558-1 which must be used to produce correct torque on the strut rod retaining nut.*

1. Remove the strut as previously outlined.
2. Compress the spring, using a reliable coil spring compressor.

CAUTION: *Make sure the spring is locked securely into the compressor and that all tension has been removed before beginning the next step.*

3. Install a large box or open-end wrench onto the rod nut and a smaller wrench onto the end of the strut rod. Hold the strut rod stationary with the small box wrench and use the larger wrench to remove the rod nut.
4. Remove the isolator, dust shield, jounce bumper, spacer (if used), and spring seat.

5. Remove the spring. Mark the spring as to "RIGHT" or "LEFT" side of the vehicle as they are *not* interchangeable from side to side.
6. Inspect the strut damper mount assembly for severe deterioration of the rubber isolator, cracked retainers, and distorted retainers and isolators or those with a failure of the bond holding rubber and metal parts together. Inspect the bearings for noise, roughness, or looseness. Pull the shock through its full stroke

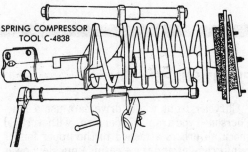

SPRING COMPRESSOR TOOL C-4838

Using a spring compressor to remove all tension from the strut spring

Troubleshooting Basic Steering and Suspension Problems

Problem	Cause	Solution
Hard steering (steering wheel is hard to turn)	• Low or uneven tire pressure	• Inflate tires to correct pressure
	• Loose power steering pump drive belt	• Adjust belt
	• Low or incorrect power steering fluid	• Add fluid as necessary
	• Incorrect front end alignment	• Have front end alignment checked/adjusted
	• Defective power steering pump	• Check pump
	• Bent or poorly lubricated front end parts	• Lubricate and/or replace defective parts
Loose steering (too much play in the steering wheel)	• Loose wheel bearings	• Adjust wheel bearings
	• Loose or worn steering linkage	• Replace worn parts
	• Faulty shocks	• Replace shocks
	• Worn ball joints	• Replace ball joints
Car veers or wanders (car pulls to one side with hands off the steering wheel)	• Incorrect tire pressure	• Inflate tires to correct pressure
	• Improper front end alignment	• Have front end alignment checked/adjusted
	• Loose wheel bearings	• Adjust wheel bearings
	• Loose or bent front end components	• Replace worn components
	• Faulty shocks	• Replace shocks
Wheel oscillation or vibration transmitted through steering wheel	• Improper tire pressures	• Inflate tires to correct pressure
	• Tires out of balance	• Have tires balanced
	• Loose wheel bearings	• Adjust wheel bearings
	• Improper front end alignment	• Have front end alignment checked/adjusted
	• Worn or bent front end components	• Replace worn parts
Uneven tire wear	• Incorrect tire pressure	• Inflate tires to correct pressure
	• Front end out of alignment	• Have front end alignment checked/adjusted
	• Tires out of balance	• Have tires balanced

to make sure its resistance is even. Replace all defective parts.

7. If the spring is being replaced, carefully unscrew and then remove the compressor. Then, compress the new spring in the same manner as the original was compressed—until it will fit onto the strut and permit assembly of all parts without interference. Install the spring with the single small coil at the top. The end of the lower coil must line up with the recess in the seat.

8. Install the spring seat, spacer (if used), jounce bumper, dust shield, and isolator.

9. Torque rod nut to 55 ft. lbs. before remov-

1. FRONT SUSPENSION CROSSMEMBER
2. FRONT PIVOT BOLT
3. LOWER CONTROL ARM
4. SWAY ELIMINATOR SHAFT ASSEMBLY
5. LOWER ARM BALL JOINT ASSEMBLY
6. STEERING GEAR
7. TIE ROD ASSEMBLY
8. DRIVE SHAFT
9. STEERING KNUCKLE
10. STRUT DAMPER ASSEMBLY
11. COIL SPRING
12. UPPER SPRING SEAT
13. REBOUND STOP
14. UPPER MOUNT ASSEMBLY
15. JOUNCE BUMPER
16. DUST SHIELD

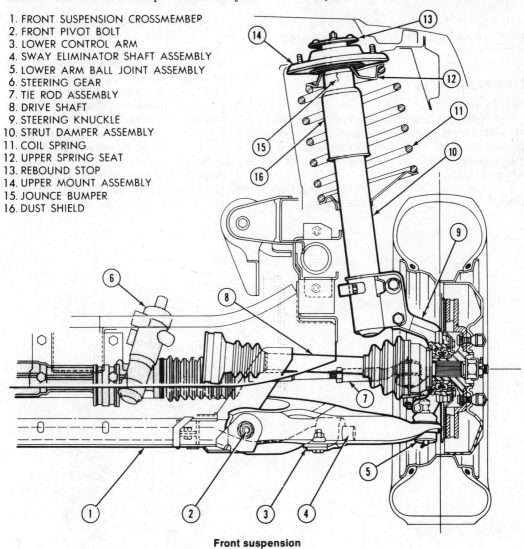

Front suspension

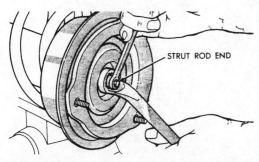

Hold the strut rod stationary as you remove the retaining nut

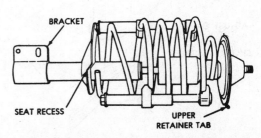

Installing/locating the spring. Note that the lower end of the spring must align with the seat recess.

ing the spring compressor. Be sure the lower coil end of the spring is seated in the recess. Use a crow's foot adaptor L-4558-1 to tighten the nut while holding the rod with an open end wrench.

NOTE: *The use of the adapter is necessary to ensure the proper torque is actually applied to the nut.*

10. Release the tension on the spring compressor. Install the strut back into the car as described above.

Lower Ball Joints

INSPECTION

The lower front suspension ball joints operate with no free play. The ball joint housing is pressed into the lower control arm with the joint stud retained in the steering knuckle with a (clamp) bolt.

With the weight of the vehicle resting on the ground, grasp the ball joint grease fitting with the fingers, and attempt to move it. If the ball joint is worn the grease fitting will move easily. If movement is noted, replacement of the ball joint is recommended.

REMOVAL AND INSTALLATION

1. Pry off the seal.
2. Position a receiving cup, special tool #C-4699-2 or its equivalent to support the lower control arm.
3. Install the $^{11}/_{16}$" deep-well socket over the stud and against the joint upper housing.
4. Press the joint assembly from the arm.
5. To install, position the ball joint housing into the control arm cavity.
6. Position the assembly in a press with special tool #C-4699-1 or its equivalent, supporting the control arm.
7. Align the ball joint assembly, then press it until the housing ledge stops against the control arm cavity down flange.

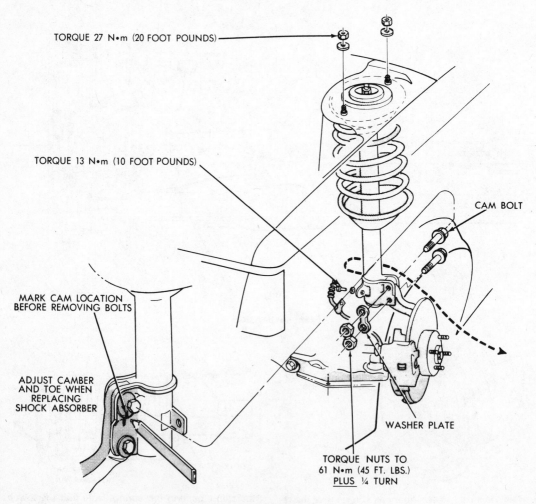

TORQUE 27 N•m (20 FOOT POUNDS)

TORQUE 13 N•m (10 FOOT POUNDS)

CAM BOLT

MARK CAM LOCATION BEFORE REMOVING BOLTS

ADJUST CAMBER AND TOE WHEN REPLACING SHOCK ABSORBER

WASHER PLATE

TORQUE NUTS TO 61 N•m (45 FT. LBS.) PLUS ¼ TURN

Strut removel

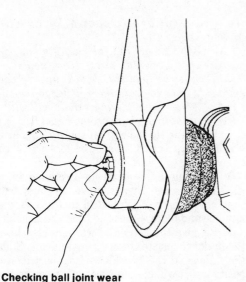

Checking ball joint wear

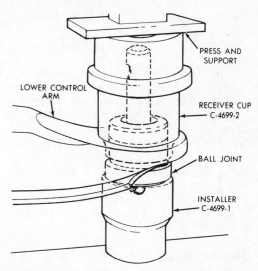

Installing ball joint

8. To install a new seal, support the ball joint housing with tool #C-4699-2 and place a new seal over the stud, against the housing.

9. With a 1½″ socket, press the seal onto the joint housing with the seat against the control arm.

Sway Bar

REMOVAL AND INSTALLATION

1. Raise the vehicle and support it in a secure manner.

2. Remove the nuts, bolts, and retainers at the ends of the sway bar—where it meets the control arms.

3. Remove the bolts from the mounting clamps attached to the crossmember and remove the swaybar.

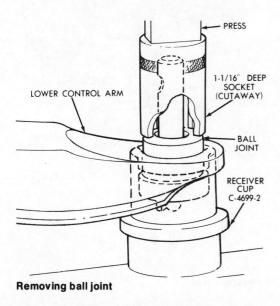

Removing ball joint

4. Put the busings that attach the swaybar to the crossmember into position on the swaybar with the curved surface facing upward and the slit facing forward.

5. Raise the swaybar into position and install the mounting clamps and their bolts.

6. Position the outboard retainers at the control arms, and install the bolts and nuts.

7. Lower the vehicle to the ground and make sure it is at design height by loading it normally. Then, torque the bolts to 25 ft. lbs. on 1981-87 models and 30 ft. lbs. on 1988 models.

Lower Control Arm

REMOVAL AND INSTALLATION

1. Jack up your vehicle and support it with jackstands.

2. Remove the front inner pivot through bolt, and rear stub strut nut, retainer and bushing, and the ball joint-to-steering knuckle clamp bolts.

3. Separate the ball joint stud from the steering knuckle by prying between the ball stud retainer on the knuckle and the lower control arm.

CAUTION: *Pulling the steering knuckle out from the vehicle after releasing it from the ball joint can separate the inner CV-joint.*

4. Remove the sway bar-to-control arm nut and reinforcement and rotate the control arm over the sway bar. Remove the rear stub strut bushing, sleeve and retainer.

NOTE: *The substitution of fasteners other than those of the grade originally used is not recommended.*

5. Install the retainer, bushing and sleeve on the stub strut.

6. Position the control arm over the sway bar

and install the rear stub strut and front pivot into the crossmember.

7. Install the front pivot bolt and loosely install the nut.

8. Install the stub strut bushing and retainer and loosely assemble the nut.

9. Install the ball joint stud into the steering knuckle and install the clamp bolt. Torque the clamp bolt to 70 ft. lb.

10. Position the sway bar bracket and stud through the control arm and install the retainer nut. Tighten the nut to 25 ft. lb.

11. Lower the car so that it is resting on the wheels. Tighten the front pivot bolt to 105 ft. lb. (95 ft. lbs. on 1986 and later cars) and the stub strut nut to 70 ft. lb.

Steering Knuckle and Spindle
REMOVAL AND INSTALLATION

1. Remove the cotter pin, nut lock and spring washer from the threaded outer end of the driveshaft.

2. The car should be resting on the floor with brakes applied. Loosen the hub nut. Then, raise the vehicle and remove the wheel.

3. Remove the hub nut. Then, raise the vehi-cle and support it securely by the crossmembers.

CAUTION: *In all the following steps, be aware that stretching stresses on the drive-shaft must be avoided. Avoid moving the knuckle so as to avoid them. Prior to removing it, make sure the driveshaft will slide freely out of the splines on the knuckle.*

4. Press the tie rod end off the steering arm with an appropriate tool (C-3894 or equivalent).

5. Disconnect the brake hose retainer from the strut damper. Then, remove the clamp bolt that holds the ball joint stud in the steering knuckle and remove the stud from the knuckle.

6. Remove the bolts and washers attaching the brake caliper to the steering knuckle. Slide the caliper off the knuckle and support it in a position that will not put excess pressure on the brake hose.

7. Slide the rotor off the wheel studs. Mark the cam adjusting bolt except on Sundance, Shadow, Lancer, and LeBaron GTS. On those models, mark the outline of the strut on the knuckle. Remove the cam adjusting bolt, through bolt, and washer plates attaching the knuckle to the bottom of the strut.

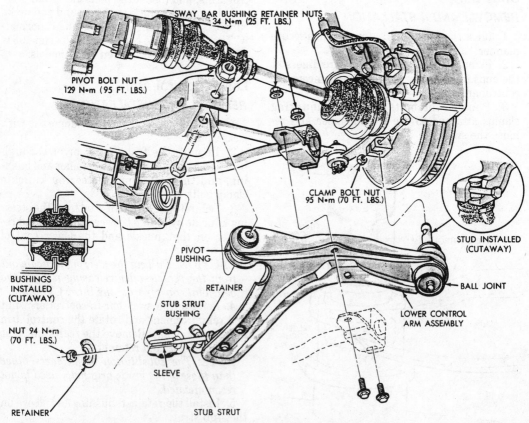

The lower control arm and mounts

8. Slide the driveshaft out of the center of the knuckle *without putting any stretching stresses on it.* If necessary, lightly tap the center of the driveshaft to ease it out of the knuckle. Remove the knuckle.

9. Clean the knuckle wear sleeve and the related seal. Lubricate the entire circumference of the seal and wear sleeve with Multi-Purpose grease. To install the steering knuckle, slide the splined outer end of the driveshaft through the splined center of the hub and then position the knuckle neck into the lower end of the strut. Install a C-clamp onto the strut so as to pull the strut onto the knuckle neck. The rotating part of the clamp should rest against the neck. While tightenening the clamp, constantly check the fit of the knuckle neck into the strut, feeling for looseness. At the point where looseness is just eliminated, stop tightening the clamp. Make sure the index marks made earlier are aligned. If necessary, loosen the clamp and change the position of the strut to align them, and then retighten the clamp. Install the bolts, washer and nuts. Torque the bolts to 75 ft. lbs. on 1984 and later models, 45 ft. lbs. on 1983 and earlier models. Then, turn them another ¼ turn.

10. Install the lower ball joint stud through the aperture in the steering knuckle and then install the knuckle clamp bolt and nut, torquing to 70 ft. lbs.

11. Install the stud of the tie rod end into the steering arm. Install the nut and torque it to 35 ft. lbs. Then, install a new cotter pin.

12. Install the brake disc over the wheel studs. Then, install the brake caliper over the disc. Position the caliper adapter over the steering knuckle. Install the bolts and torque them to 160 ft. lbs.

13. Attach the brake hose retainer to the strut damper and tighten its mounting screw to 10 ft. lbs. Install the washer and axle hub nut. Then, have someone appply the brakes and torque the hub nut to 180 ft. lbs. Install the spring washer, nut lock, and a new cotter pin (the nut lock has a slot in the outer edge which must line up with the hole through the end of the driveshaft). Finally, wrap the two ends of the cotter pin tightly around the end of the nut lock.

14. Install the wheel and tire and torque the wheel nuts to 95 ft. lbs.

Front Hub and Bearing

REMOVAL, REPACKING, AND INSTALLATION

NOTE: *It is not necessary to disassemble and repack wheel bearings. In fact, the bearings must be broken to disassemble them. This procedure is for replacement of damaged or worn bearings only. This procedure requires a set of special tools C-4811 or equivalent.*

1. Remove the knuckle assembly from the car as described above.

2. Back one of the bearing retainer screws out of the hub and install bracket C-4811-17 or equivalent between the head of the screw and the retainer. Then, insert the thrust button C-4811-6 or equivalent into the bore of the hub.

3. Position C-4811-14 so its two bolts will screw into the caliper mounting threads on the knuckle, passing through the tapped brake adapter extensions. Install the tool's nut and washer onto the bracket bolt of the tool. Then, tighten the bolt to pull the hub off the bearing.

4. If the outboard race stays on the hub, use a C-clamp and universal puller to remove it. Use the thrust button and the fabricated washer from C-4811-6 or equivalent used above; use the C-clamp to keep the puller jaws over the edges of the outboard inner race.

5. Remove the tool and attach the bolts from the steering knuckle.

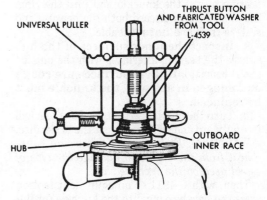

Removing the inner race with a universal puller and C-clamp

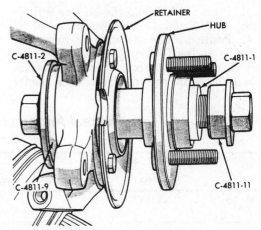

Pressing a new bearing into the knuckle with a toolset such as C-4811

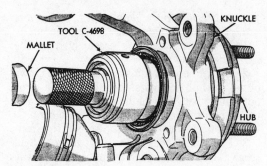

MALLET

TOOL C-4698

KNUCKLE

HUB

Installing a new seal in the bearing recess. Assemble the tool as shown.

6. Remove its three retaining screws and remove the bearing retainer from the steering knuckle.

7. Pry the bearing seal out of the machined recess in the knuckle, being careful not to scratch the surfaces of the recess.

8. Install a tool set such as C-4811 through the knuckle hub. Hold the nut with one wrench as you turn the bolt with another to pull the bearing out of the knuckle and into the ring. Then, be sure to discard both the bearing and seal, as they **are not** reuseable.

9. Inspect the inner surfaces of the hub (where the bearing interfaces with the outside of the bearing). **If these surfaces are rough or damaged in any way, the knuckle must be replaced.**

10. Turn the bearing so that the **Red** seal will face outward and be located near the brake disc. WARNING: *Failure to do this would cause heat from the brakes to damage the type of seal used on the opposite side.*

Then, with C-4811 or an equivalent toolset, press the new bearing into the knuckle until it seats. Install a new seal and the bearing retainer and then torque the retainer bolts to 20 ft. lbs.

11. Press the hub into the bearing with C-4811-1, -2, -9 and -11 or equivalent.

12. Position a new seal into the recess and then install Tool C-4698. Note that this tool has a handle and dual-purpose drive head provided for installing the seal into the knuckle and for

installing the wear sleeve into the CV-Joint housing. Assemble the tool as shown, make sure it and the seal are positioned squarely, and then lightly tap the seal into place with a light-weight mallet.

13. Lubricate the entire circumference of the seal and wear sleeve with Multi-Purpose grease.

14. Install the driveshaft into the knuckle and install the knuckle back into the car as described above.

Front End Alignment

Front wheel alignment is the proper adjustment of all the inter-related suspension angles affecting the running and steering of the front wheels. There are six basic factors which are the foundation of front wheel alignment. These are: height, caster, camber, toe-in, steering axis inclination, and toe-out/toe-in on turns. Of these basic factors, only camber and toe-out/toe-in are mechanically adjustable.

CAMBER ADJUSTMENT

1. Check the tire air pressure. Adjust if necessary.

2. Check the front wheels for radial run out.

3. Inspect the lower ball joints and steering linkage for looseness.

4. Check for broken or weak springs, front and rear.

5. Loosen the cam and through bolts.

6. Rotate the upper cam bolt to move the wheel in or out to the specified camber.

7. Tighten the bolts to 45 ft. lbs. plus ¼ turn.

TOE-IN ADJUSTMENT

1. Follow steps 1-4 from the previous procedure.

2. Center the steering wheel and hold it.

3. Loosen the tie rod lock nuts. Rotate the rods to align the toe to specifications. CAUTION: *Do not twist the tie rod to steering gear rubber boots during alignment.*

4. Tighten the tie rod lock nuts to 55 ft. lbs.

Wheel Alignment Specifications
(Caster is not adjustable)

Year	Front Camber		Rear Camber		Toe-Out (in.)	
	Range (deg.)	Preferred	Range (deg.)	Preferred	Front	Rear
'81–'85	¼N to ¾P	5/16P	1N-O	½N	7/32 out to ⅛ in	3/16 out to 3/16 in
'86–'88	¼N to ¾P	5/16P	1¼N–¼P	½N	7/32 in to ⅛ out	1/16 in

REAR SUSPENSION

All these cars use a flexible beam axle with trailing links and coil springs. One shock absorber on each side is mounted outside the coil spring and attached to the body and the beam axle. Wheel spindles are bolted to the outer ends of the axle.

Coil Springs
REMOVAL AND INSTALLATION

1. Jack up the vehicle and support it with jackstands.
2. Support the rear axle with a floor jack.
3. Remove the bottom bolt from both rear shock absorbers.
4. Lower the axle assembly until the spring and support isolator can be removed.
NOTE: *Do not stretch the brake hoses.*
5. Remove the spring and isolator.
6. Installation is the reverse of removal. Torque the lower shock bolts to 40 ft. lb.

Shock Absorbers
TESTING

Shock absorbers require replacement if the car fails to recover quickly after hitting a large bump or if it sways excessively following a directional change.

A good way to test the shock absorbers is to intermittently apply downward pressure to the side of the car until it is moving up and down for almost its full suspension travel. Release it and observe its recovery. If the car bounces once or twice after having been released and then comes to a rest, the shocks are alright. If the car continued to bounce, the shocks will probably require replacement.

REMOVAL AND INSTALLATION

1. Jack up the vehicle and support it with jackstands.
2. Support the rear axle with a floor jack.
3. Remove the top and bottom shock absorber bolts.

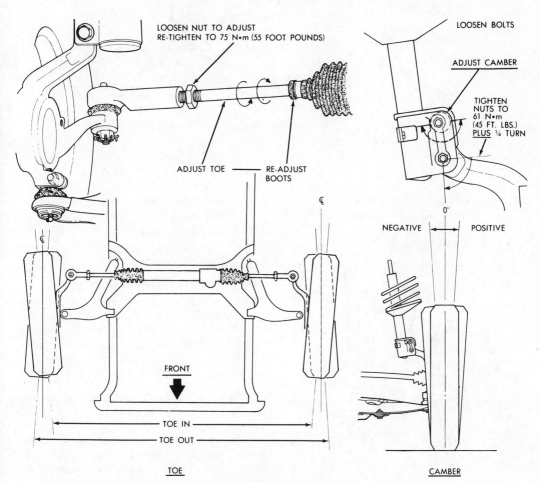

Alignment—camber/toe

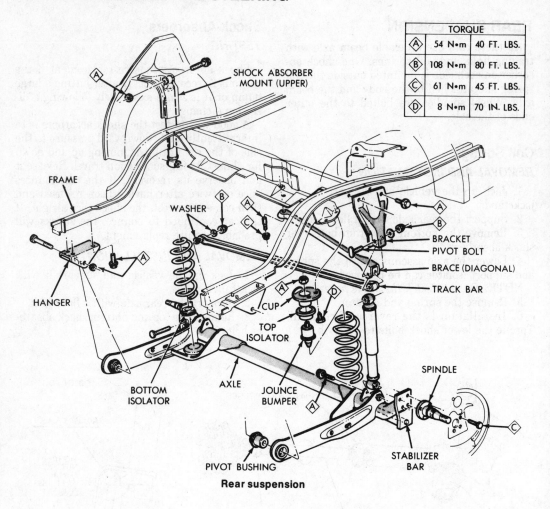

TORQUE		
Ⓐ	54 N•m	40 FT. LBS.
Ⓑ	108 N•m	80 FT. LBS.
Ⓒ	61 N•m	45 FT. LBS.
Ⓓ	8 N•m	70 IN. LBS.

SHOCK ABSORBER MOUNT (UPPER)

FRAME

WASHER

HANGER

BOTTOM ISOLATOR

AXLE

CUP

TOP ISOLATOR

JOUNCE BUMPER

BRACKET

PIVOT BOLT

BRACE (DIAGONAL)

TRACK BAR

SPINDLE

PIVOT BUSHING

STABILIZER BAR

Rear suspension

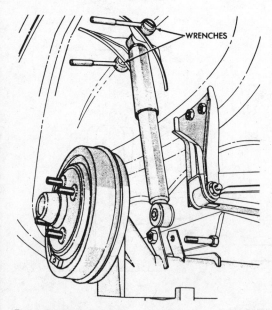

WRENCHES

Rear shock absorbers

4. Remove the shock absorbers.

5. Installation is the reverse of removal. Torque the upper and lower bolts to 40 ft. lb.

Track Bar

REMOVAL AND INSTALLATION

1. Raise the vehicle and support it securely by the body. Then, raise the rear axle to approximately its normal curb height and support it *securely* with an axle stand under either side.

2. If the car has a load-leveling system, disconnect the link from the sensor to the track bar.

3. Remove the track bar-to-axle pivot bolt and the track bar-to-frame pivot bolt. Then, remove the track bar.

4. To install, connect the track bar to the diagonal brace with the nut and bolt and torque them to 70 ft. lbs. Then, loosen the rearward assemble pivot bolt/nut on the rear side.

5. Attach the other end of the track bar to

the bracket on the axle and install the nut and bolt, torquing to 70 ft. lbs. Now, torque the nut on the track bar-to-frame bolt to 55 ft. lbs.

6. Attach the link from the sensor to the track bar. Carefully remove the axle stands and then lower the car.

Rear Wheel Bearings

REPLACEMENT

Drum Brakes

CAUTION: *Brake linings contain asbestos. Avoid using compressed air or any other means to remove dust from the drum or brake shoes or areas nearby. Failure to heed this warning could cause inhalation of asbestos fibers, a known carcinogen!*

1. Raise the car and support it securely. Remove the wheel and tire.

2. Remove the grease cap, cotter pin, nut lock and retaining nut.

3. Slide the washer off the spindle. Refer to Chapter 9 and adjust the rear brakes away from the drum. Then, pull the brake drum and outer bearing off the spindle. Remove the bearing from the drum.

4. Slide the inner bearing cone off the spindle. Slide the seal off the spindle.

5. Inspect the bearing rollers. If they turn roughly or the surfaces are cracked, rough or brinneled, replace them.

6. Inspect the inner diameter of the brake drum where the bearing rolls. If the surface is cracked, rough or brinneled, replace the drum.

7. Inspect the cone-shaped bearing surface of the spindle. If it is cracked, rough or brinneled, replace the spindle.

8. If the spindle must be replaced:

a. Disconnect the brake hydraulic tube from the back of the wheel cylinder. Disconnect the parking brake cable at the adjustment. Remove the four mounting bolts and remove the brake backing plate, spindle, and seal.

b. Route the parking brake cable through the trailing arm opening and route the brake tube over the trailing arm. Put the spindle, seal, and backing plate into position on the axle (with boltholes aligned). Install the four bolts and tighten them finger tight to position all parts. Then, torque them to 55 ft. lbs. Bleed the brake system as described in the next chapter.

9. Make sure all spindle surfaces and the inner diameter bearing surface in the brake drum are clean.

10. Very thoroughly pack the wheel bearings with *wheel bearing grease* (ordinary Multi-Purpose grease is *not* satisfactory). Work the grease

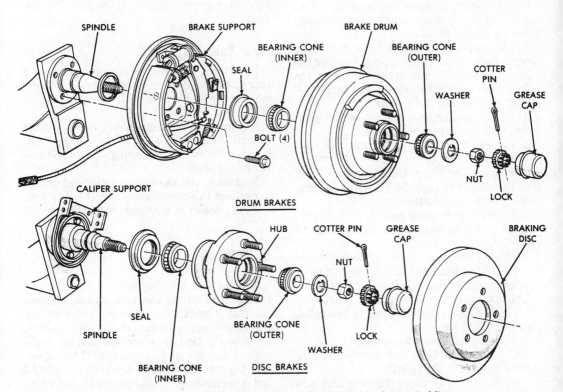

Exploded views of drum (above) and disc (below) brake assemblies

thoroughly into the spaces between the rollers by forcing grease through them repeatedly.

11. Install the seal, inner bearing cone, brake drum, and outer bearing cone onto the spindle. Note that the inner cone's larger diameter goes on first, while the outer cone's outer diameter goes on last.

12. Align the tab in the washer with the groove in the threaded portion of the spindle and slide it on. Screw the nut onto the spindle threads.

13. Rotating the drum, torque the nut to 240-300 in. lbs. Then back off the nut until preload is completely eliminated (the nut turns freely). Then, finger tighten the nut.

14. Install the nut lock until it touches the wheel bearing nut. Then, turn it backward *just* until the next slot aligns with the cotter pin hole.

15. Reconnect the parking brake cable and adjust it as described in Chapter 9.

16. Clean and install the grease cap. Install the wheel and tire and lower the vehicle to the floor.

Rear Disc Brakes

CAUTION: *Brake linings contain asbestos. Avoid using compressed air or any other means to remove dust from the rotor or brake calipers or linings or areas nearby. Failure to heed this warning could cause inhalation of asbestos fibers, a known carcinogen!*

1. Raise the car and support it securely. Remove the wheel and tire.

2. Disconnect the brake hose mounting bracket from the caliper support. Remove the parking brake cable and brake hose from the caliper assembly. Then, remove the caliper assembly as described in Chapter 9.

3. Unbolt and remove the caliper adapter. Slide the disc off the wheel studs.

4. Remove the grease cap, cotter pin, nut lock and retaining nut.

5. Remove the outer bearing cone. Then, slide the hub off the spindle. Remove the inner bearing cone. Remove the inner seal.

6. Inspect the bearing rollers. If they turn roughly or the surfaces are cracked, rough or brinneled, replace them.

7. Inspect the inner diameter of the brake hub where the bearing rolls. If the surface is cracked, rough or brinneled, replace the hub.

8. Inspect the cone-shaped bearing surface of the spindle. If it is cracked, rough or brinneled, replace the spindle.

9. If the spindle must be replaced:

a. Remove the bolts and remove the caliper support and the spindle.

b. Position the caliper support and new spindle onto the axle with the boltholes

aligned. Install the four retaining bolts finger tight. Then, torque to 55 ft. lbs.

10. Make sure all spindle surfaces and the inner diameter bearing surface in the brake hub are clean.

11. Very thoroughly pack the wheel bearings with *wheel bearing grease* (ordinary Multi-Purpose grease is *not* satisfactory). Work the grease thoroughly into the spaces between the rollers by forcing grease through them repeatedly.

12. Install the caliper adapter. Install the seal, inner bearing cone, brake hub and outer bearing cone onto the spindle. Note that the inner cone's larger diameter goes on first, while the outer cone's outer diameter goes on last.

13. Align the tab in the washer with the groove in the threaded portion of the spindle and slide it on. Screw the nut onto the spindle threads.

14. Install the rotor onto the wheel studs. Rotating the rotor, torque the nut to 240-300 in. lbs. Then back off the nut until preload is completely eliminated (the nut turns freely). Then, finger tighten the nut.

15. Install the nut lock until it touches the wheel bearing nut. Then, turn it backward *just* until the next slot aligns with the cotter pin hole.

16. Install the caliper as described in Chapter 9.

17. Clean and install the grease cap. Install the wheel and tire and lower the vehicle to the floor.

Rear Axle Alignment

Chrysler K- and E-Cars are equipped with a rear suspension, using wheel spindles, thereby making it possible to align the camber and toe of the rear wheels.

Alignment adjustment, if required, is made by adding shims (Part #5205114 or equivalent) between the spindle mounting surface and axle mounting plate.

Because of the specialized equipment needed to perform this procedure it is best left to your Chrysler dealer or a reliable repair facility.

STEERING

The manual steering system consists of a tube which contains the toothed rack, a pinion, the rack slipper, and the rack slipper spring. Steering effect is transmitted to the steering arms by the tie rods which are coupled to the ends of the rack, and tie rods ends. The connection between the ends of the rack and the tie rod is protected by a bellows type oil seal which retains the gear lubricant.

Troubleshooting the Steering Column

Problem	Cause	Solution
Will not lock	• Lockbolt spring broken or defective	• Replace lock bolt spring
High effort (required to turn ignition key and lock cylinder)	• Lock cylinder defective	• Replace lock cylinder
	• Ignition switch defective	• Replace ignition switch
	• Rack preload spring broken or deformed	• Replace preload spring
	• Burr on lock sector, lock rack, housing, support or remote rod coupling	• Remove burr
	• Bent sector shaft	• Replace shaft
	• Defective lock rack	• Replace lock rack
	• Remote rod bent, deformed	• Replace rod
	• Ignition switch mounting bracket bent	• Straighten or replace
	• Distorted coupling slot in lock rack (tilt column)	• Replace lock rack
Will stick in "start"	• Remote rod deformed	• Straighten or replace
	• Ignition switch mounting bracket bent	• Straighten or replace
Key cannot be removed in "off-lock"	• Ignition switch is not adjusted correctly	• Adjust switch
	• Defective lock cylinder	• Replace lock cylinder
Lock cylinder can be removed without depressing retainer	• Lock cylinder with defective retainer	• Replace lock cylinder
	• Burr over retainer slot in housing cover or on cylinder retainer	• Remove burr
High effort on lock cylinder between "off" and "off-lock"	• Distorted lock rack	• Replace lock rack
	• Burr on tang of shift gate (automatic column)	• Remove burr
	• Gearshift linkage not adjusted	• Adjust linkage
Noise in column	• One click when in "off-lock" position and the steering wheel is moved (all except automatic column)	• Normal—lock bolt is seating
	• Coupling bolts not tightened	• Tighten pinch bolts
	• Lack of grease on bearings or bearing surfaces	• Lubricate with chassis grease
	• Upper shaft bearing worn or broken	• Replace bearing assembly
	• Lower shaft bearing worn or broken	• Replace bearing. Check shaft and replace if scored.
	• Column not correctly aligned	• Align column
	• Coupling pulled apart	• Replace coupling
	• Broken coupling lower joint	• Repair or replace joint and align column
	• Steering shaft snap ring not seated	• Replace ring. Check for proper seating in groove.
	• Shroud loose on shift bowl. Housing loose on jacket—will be noticed with ignition in "off-lock" and when torque is applied to steering wheel.	• Position shroud over lugs on shift bowl. Tighten mounting screws.
High steering shaft effort	• Column misaligned	• Align column
	• Defective upper or lower bearing	• Replace as required
	• Tight steering shaft universal joint	• Repair or replace
	• Flash on I.D. of shift tube at plastic joint (tilt column only)	• Replace shift tube
	• Upper or lower bearing seized	• Replace bearings
Lash in mounted column assembly	• Column mounting bracket bolts loose	• Tighten bolts
	• Broken weld nuts on column jacket	• Replace column jacket
	• Column capsule bracket sheared	• Replace bracket assembly

Troubleshooting the Steering Column (cont.)

Problem	Cause	Solution
Lash in mounted column assembly (cont.)	• Column bracket to column jacket mounting bolts loose	• Tighten to specified torque
	• Loose lock shoes in housing (tilt column only)	• Replace shoes
	• Loose pivot pins (tilt column only)	• Replace pivot pins and support
	• Loose lock shoe pin (tilt column only)	• Replace pin and housing
	• Loose support screws (tilt column only)	• Tighten screws
Housing loose (tilt column only)	• Excessive clearance between holes in support or housing and pivot pin diameters	• Replace pivot pins and support
	• Housing support-screws loose	• Tighten screws
Steering wheel loose—every other tilt position (tilt column only)	• Loose fit between lock shoe and lock shoe pivot pin	• Replace lock shoes and pivot pin
Steering column not locking in any tilt position (tilt column only)	• Lock shoe seized on pivot pin	• Replace lock shoes and pin
	• Lock shoe grooves have burrs or are filled with foreign material	• Clean or replace lock shoes
	• Lock shoe springs weak or broken	• Replace springs
Noise when tilting column (tilt column only)	• Upper tilt bumpers worn	• Replace tilt bumper
	• Tilt spring rubbing in housing	• Lubricate with chassis grease
One click when in "off-lock" position and the steering wheel is moved	• Seating of lock bolt	• None. Click is normal characteristic sound produced by lock bolt as it seats.
High shift effort (automatic and tilt column only)	• Column not correctly aligned	• Align column
	• Lower bearing not aligned correctly	• Assemble correctly
	• Lack of grease on seal or lower bearing areas	• Lubricate with chassis grease
Improper transmission shifting—automatic and tilt column only	• Sheared shift tube joint	• Replace shift tube
	• Improper transmission gearshift linkage adjustment	• Adjust linkage
	• Loose lower shift lever	• Replace shift tube

Troubleshooting the Ignition Switch

Problem	Cause	Solution
Ignition switch electrically inoperative	• Loose or defective switch connector	• Tighten or replace connector
	• Feed wire open (fusible link)	• Repair or replace
	• Defective ignition switch	• Replace ignition switch
Engine will not crank	• Ignition switch not adjusted properly	• Adjust switch
Ignition switch wil not actuate mechanically	• Defective ignition switch	• Replace switch
	• Defective lock sector	• Replace lock sector
	• Defective remote rod	• Replace remote rod
Ignition switch cannot be adjusted correctly	• Remote rod deformed	• Repair, straighten or replace

The power steering system consists of four major parts: the power gear, power steering pump, pressure hose and the return hose. As with the manual system, the turning of the steering wheel is converted into linear travel through the meshing of the helical pinion teeth with the rack teeth. Power assist is provided by an open center, rotary type, three-way control valve which directs fluid to either side of the rack control piston.

Troubleshooting the Turn Signal Switch

Problem	Cause	Solution
Turn signal will not cancel	• Loose switch mounting screws • Switch or anchor bosses broken • Broken, missing or out of position detent, or cancelling spring	• Tighten screws • Replace switch • Reposition springs or replace switch as required
Turn signal difficult to operate	• Turn signal lever loose • Switch yoke broken or distorted • Loose or misplaced springs • Foreign parts and/or materials in switch • Switch mounted loosely	• Tighten mounting screws • Replace switch • Reposition springs or replace switch • Remove foreign parts and/or material • Tighten mounting screws
Turn signal will not indicate lane change	• Broken lane change pressure pad or spring hanger • Broken, missing or misplaced lane change spring • Jammed wires	• Replace switch • Replace or reposition as required • Loosen mounting screws, reposition wires and retighten screws
Turn signal will not stay in turn position	• Foreign material or loose parts impeding movement of switch yoke • Defective switch	• Remove material and/or parts • Replace switch
Hazard switch cannot be pulled out	• Foreign material between hazard support cancelling leg and yoke	• Remove foreign material. No foreign material impeding function of hazard switch—replace turn signal switch.
No turn signal lights	• Inoperative turn signal flasher • Defective or blown fuse • Loose chassis to column harness connector • Disconnect column to chassis connector. Connect new switch to chassis and operate switch by hand. If vehicle lights now operate normally, signal switch is inoperative • If vehicle lights do not operate, check chassis wiring for opens, grounds, etc.	• Replace turn signal flasher • Replace fuse • Connect securely • Replace signal switch • Repair chassis wiring as required
Instrument panel turn indicator lights on but not flashing	• Burned out or damaged front or rear turn signal bulb • If vehicle lights do not operate, check light sockets for high resistance connections, the chassis wiring for opens, grounds, etc. • Inoperative flasher • Loose chassis to column harness connection • Inoperative turn signal switch • To determine if turn signal switch is defective, substitute new switch into circuit and operate switch by hand. If the vehicle's lights operate normally, signal switch is inoperative.	• Replace bulb • Repair chassis wiring as required • Replace flasher • Connect securely • Replace turn signal switch • Replace turn signal switch
Stop light not on when turn indicated	• Loose column to chassis connection • Disconnect column to chassis connector. Connect new switch into system without removing old.	• Connect securely • Replace signal switch

Troubleshooting the Turn Signal Switch (cont.)

Problem	Cause	Solution
Stop light not on when turn indicated (cont.)	Operate switch by hand. If brake lights work with switch in the turn position, signal switch is defective.	
	• If brake lights do not work, check connector to stop light sockets for grounds, opens, etc.	• Repair connector to stop light circuits using service manual as guide
Turn indicator panel lights not flashing	• Burned out bulbs • High resistance to ground at bulb socket • Opens, ground in wiring harness from front turn signal bulb socket to indicator lights	• Replace bulbs • Replace socket • Locate and repair as required
Turn signal lights flash very slowly	• High resistance ground at light sockets • Incorrect capacity turn signal flasher or bulb • If flashing rate is still extremely slow, check chassis wiring harness from the connector to light sockets for high resistance • Loose chassis to column harness connection • Disconnect column to chassis connector. Connect new switch into system without removing old. Operate switch by hand. If flashing occurs at normal rate, the signal switch is defective.	• Repair high resistance grounds at light sockets • Replace turn signal flasher or bulb • Locate and repair as required • Connect securely • Replace turn signal switch
Hazard signal lights will not flash—turn signal functions normally	• Blow fuse • Inoperative hazard warning flasher • Loose chassis-to-column harness connection • Disconnect column to chassis connector. Connect new switch into system without removing old. Depress the hazard warning lights. If they now work normally, turn signal switch is defective. • If lights do not flash, check wiring harness "K" lead for open between hazard flasher and connector. If open, fuse block is defective	• Replace fuse • Replace hazard warning flasher in fuse panel • Conect securely • Replace turn signal switch • Repair or replace brown wire or connector as required

Troubleshooting the Manual Steering Gear

Problem	Cause	Solution
Hard or erratic steering	• Incorrect tire pressure • Insufficient or incorrect lubrication • Suspension, or steering linkage parts damaged or misaligned • Improper front wheel alignment • Incorrect steering gear adjustment • Sagging springs	• Inflate tires to recommended pressures • Lubricate as required (refer to Maintenance Section) • Repair or replace parts as necessary • Adjust incorrect wheel alignment angles • Adjust steering gear • Replace springs

Troubleshooting the Manual Steering Gear *(cont.)*

Problem	Cause	Solution
Play or looseness in steering	• Steering wheel loose	• Inspect shaft spines and repair as necessary. Tighten attaching nut and stake in place.
	• Steering linkage or attaching parts loose or worn	• Tighten, adjust, or replace faulty components
	• Pitman arm loose	• Inspect shaft splines and repair as necessary. Tighten attaching nut and stake in place
	• Steering gear attaching bolts loose	• Tighten bolts
	• Loose or worn wheel bearings	• Adjust or replace bearings
	• Steering gear adjustment incorrect or parts badly worn	• Adjust gear or replace defective parts
Wheel shimmy or tramp	• Improper tire pressure	• Inflate tires to recommended pressures
	• Wheels, tires, or brake rotors out-of-balance or out-of-round	• Inspect and replace or balance parts
	• Inoperative, worn, or loose shock absorbers or mounting parts	• Repair or replace shocks or mountings
	• Loose or worn steering or suspension parts	• Tighten or replace as necessary
	• Loose or worn wheel bearings	• Adjust or replace bearings
	• Incorrect steering gear adjustments	• Adjust steering gear
	• Incorrect front wheel alignment	• Correct front wheel alignment
Tire wear	• Improper tire pressure	• Inflate tires to recommended pressures
	• Failure to rotate tires	• Rotate tires
	• Brakes grabbing	• Adjust or repair brakes
	• Incorrect front wheel alignment	• Align incorrect angles
	• Broken or damaged steering and suspension parts	• Repair or replace defective parts
	• Wheel runout	• Replace faulty wheel
	• Excessive speed on turns	• Make driver aware of conditions
Vehicle leads to one side	• Improper tire pressures	• Inflate tires to recommended pressures
	• Front tires with uneven tread depth, wear pattern, or different cord design (i.e., one bias ply and one belted or radial tire on front wheels)	• Install tires of same cord construction and reasonably even tread depth, design, and wear pattern
	• Incorrect front wheel alignment	• Align incorrect angles
	• Brakes dragging	• Adjust or repair brakes
	• Pulling due to uneven tire construction	• Replace faulty tire

Troubleshooting the Power Steering Gear

Problem	Cause	Solution
Hissing noise in steering gear	• There is some noise in all power steering systems. One of the most common is a hissing sound most evident at standstill parking. There is no relationship between this noise and performance of the steering. Hiss may be expected when steering wheel is at end of travel or when slowly turning at standstill.	• Slight hiss is normal and in no way affects steering. Do not replace valve unless hiss is extremely objectionable. A replacement valve will also exhibit slight noise and is not always a cure. Investigate clearance around flexible coupling rivets. Be sure steering shaft and gear are aligned so flexible coupling rotates in a flat plane and is not distorted as shaft rotates. Any metal-to-metal contacts through flexible cou-

Troubleshooting the Power Steering Gear (cont.)

Problem	Cause	Solution
Hissing noise in steering gear (cont.)		pling will transmit valve hiss into passenger compartment through the steering column.
Rattle or chuckle noise in steering gear	• Gear loose on frame • Steering linkage looseness • Pressure hose touching other parts of car • Loose pitman shaft over center adjustment **NOTE:** A slight rattle may occur on turns because of increased clearance off the "high point." This is normal and clearance must not be reduced below specified limits to eliminate this slight rattle. • Loose pitman arm	• Check gear-to-frame mounting screws. Tighten screws to 88 N·m (65 foot pounds) torque. • Check linkage pivot points for wear. Replace if necessary. • Adjust hose position. Do not bend tubing by hand. • Adjust to specifications • Tighten pitman arm nut to specifications
Squawk noise in steering gear when turning or recovering from a turn	• Damper O-ring on valve spool cut	• Replace damper O-ring
Poor return of steering wheel to center	• Tires not properly inflated • Lack of lubrication in linkage and ball joints • Lower coupling flange rubbing against steering gear adjuster plug • Steering gear to column misalignment • Improper front wheel alignment • Steering linkage binding • Ball joints binding • Steering wheel rubbing against housing • Tight or frozen steering shaft bearings • Sticking or plugged valve spool • Steering gear adjustments over specifications • Kink in return hose	• Inflate to specified pressure • Lube linkage and ball joints • Loosen pinch bolt and assemble properly • Align steering column • Check and adjust as necessary • Replace pivots • Replace ball joints • Align housing • Replace bearings • Remove and clean or replace valve • Check adjustment with gear out of car. Adjust as required. • Replace hose
Car leads to one side or the other (keep in mind road condition and wind. Test car in both directions on flat road)	• Front end misaligned • Unbalanced steering gear valve **NOTE:** If this is cause, steering effort will be very light in direction of lead and normal or heavier in opposite direction	• Adjust to specifications • Replace valve
Momentary increase in effort when turning wheel fast to right or left	• Low oil level • Pump belt slipping • High internal leakage	• Add power steering fluid as required • Tighten or replace belt • Check pump pressure. (See pressure test)
Steering wheel surges or jerks when turning with engine running especially during parking	• Low oil level • Loose pump belt • Steering linkage hitting engine oil pan at full turn • Insufficient pump pressure • Pump flow control valve sticking	• Fill as required • Adjust tension to specification • Correct clearance • Check pump pressure. (See pressure test). Replace relief valve if defective. • Inspect for varnish or damage, replace if necessary

Troubleshooting the Power Steering Gear (cont.)

Problem	Cause	Solution
Excessive wheel kickback or loose steering	• Air in system	• Add oil to pump reservoir and bleed by operating steering. Check hose connectors for proper torque and adjust as required.
	• Steering gear loose on frame	• Tighten attaching screws to specified torque
	• Steering linkage joints worn enough to be loose	• Replace loose pivots
	• Worn poppet valve	• Replace poppet valve
	• Loose thrust bearing preload adjustment	• Adjust to specification with gear out of vehicle
	• Excessive overcenter lash	• Adjust to specification with gear out of car
Hard steering or lack of assist	• Loose pump belt	• Adjust belt tension to specification
	• Low oil level **NOTE:** Low oil level will also result in excessive pump noise	• Fill to proper level. If excessively low, check all lines and joints for evidence of external leakage. Tighten loose connectors.
	• Steering gear to column misalignment	• Align steering column
	• Lower coupling flange rubbing against steering gear adjuster plug	• Loosen pinch bolt and assemble properly
	• Tires not properly inflated	• Inflate to recommended pressure
Foamy milky power steering fluid, low fluid level and possible low pressure	• Air in the fluid, and loss of fluid due to internal pump leakage causing overflow	• Check for leak and correct. Bleed system. Extremely cold temperatures will cause system aeriation should the oil level be low. If oil level is correct and pump still foams, remove pump from vehicle and separate reservoir from housing. Check welsh plug and housing for cracks. If plug is loose or housing is cracked, replace housing.
Low pressure due to steering pump	• Flow control valve stuck or inoperative	• Remove burrs or dirt or replace. Flush system.
	• Pressure plate not flat against cam ring	• Correct
Low pressure due to steering gear	• Pressure loss in cylinder due to worn piston ring or badly worn housing bore	• Remove gear from car for disassembly and inspection of ring and housing bore
	• Leakage at valve rings, valve body-to-worm seal	• Remove gear from car for disassembly and replace seals

Troubleshooting the Power Steering Pump

Problem	Cause	Solution
Chirp noise in steering pump	• Loose belt	• Adjust belt tension to specification
Belt squeal (particularly noticeable at full wheel travel and stand still parking)	• Loose belt	• Adjust belt tension to specification
Growl noise in steering pump	• Excessive back pressure in hoses or steering gear caused by restriction	• Locate restriction and correct. Replace part if necessary.
Growl noise in steering pump (particularly noticeable at stand still parking)	• Scored pressure plates, thrust plate or rotor	• Replace parts and flush system
	• Extreme wear of cam ring	• Replace parts

Troubleshooting the Power Steering Pump (cont.)

Problem	Cause	Solution
Groan noise in steering pump	• Low oil level • Air in the oil. Poor pressure hose connection.	• Fill reservoir to proper level • Tighten connector to specified torque. Bleed system by operating steering from right to left—full turn.
Rattle noise in steering pump	• Vanes not installed properly • Vanes sticking in rotor slots	• Install properly • Free up by removing burrs, varnish, or dirt
Swish noise in steering pump	• Defective flow control valve	• Replace part
Whine noise in steering pump	• Pump shaft bearing scored	• Replace housing and shaft. Flush system.
Hard steering or lack of assist	• Loose pump belt • Low oil level in reservoir **NOTE:** Low oil level will also result in excessive pump noise • Steering gear to column misalignment • Lower coupling flange rubbing against steering gear adjuster plug • Tires not properly inflated	• Adjust belt tension to specification • Fill to proper level. If excessively low, check all lines and joints for evidence of external leakage. Tighten loose connectors. • Align steering column • Loosen pinch bolt and assemble properly • Inflate to recommended pressure
Foaming milky power steering fluid, low fluid level and possible low pressure	• Air in the fluid, and loss of fluid due to internal pump leakage causing overflow	• Check for leaks and correct. Bleed system. Extremely cold temperatures will cause system aeriation should the oil level be low. If oil level is correct and pump still foams, remove pump from vehicle and separate reservoir from body. Check welsh plug and body for cracks. If plug is loose or body is cracked, replace body.
Low pump pressure	• Flow control valve stuck or inoperative • Pressure plate not flat against cam ring	• Remove burrs or dirt or replace. Flush system. • Correct
Momentary increase in effort when turning wheel fast to right or left	• Low oil level in pump • Pump belt slipping • High internal leakage	• Add power steering fluid as required • Tighten or replace belt • Check pump pressure. (See pressure test)
Steering wheel surges or jerks when turning with engine running especially during parking	• Low oil level • Loose pump belt • Steering linkage hitting engine oil pan at full turn • Insufficient pump pressure • Sticking flow control valve	• Fill as required • Adjust tension to specification • Correct clearance • Check pump pressure. (See pressure test). Replace flow control valve if defective. • Inspect for varnish or damage, replace if necessary
Excessive wheel kickback or loose steering	• Air in system	• Add oil to pump reservoir and bleed by operating steering. Check hose connectors for proper torque and adjust as required.
Low pump pressure	• Extreme wear of cam ring • Scored pressure plate, thrust plate, or rotor	• Replace parts. Flush system. • Replace parts. Flush system.

Troubleshooting the Power Steering Pump (cont.)

Problem	Cause	Solution
Low pump pressure (cont.)	• Vanes not installed properly • Vanes sticking in rotor slots • Cracked or broken thrust or pressure plate	• Install properly • Freeup by removing burrs, varnish, or dirt • Replace part

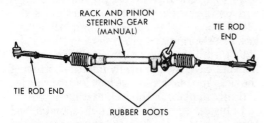

Manual steering gear

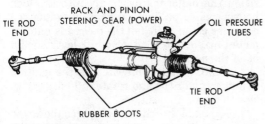

Power steering gear

Steering Wheel
REMOVAL AND INSTALLATION

1. Remove the horn button and horn switch.
2. Remove the steering wheel nut, and, on cars with automatic transmisison, the damper.
3. Using a steering wheel puller, remove the steering wheel. On cars with a sport steering wheel, two ⅜-18 SAE x 5″ bolts will be needed with the puller.
4. Align the master serration in the wheel hub with the missing tooth on the shaft. Torque the shaft nut to 60 ft. lbs. on 1981 models; 45 ft. lbs. on 1982 and later models.
CAUTION: *Do not torque the nut against the steering column lock or damage will occur.*
5. Replace the horn switch and button.

Turn Signal Switch
REMOVAL AND INSTALLATION
Without Tilt Wheel

1. Disconnect the negative battery terminal.
2. Remove the steering wheel as described earlier.
3. On vehicles equipped with intermittend wipe or intermittend wipe with speed control, remove the two screws that attach the turn signal lever cover to the lock housing and remove the turn signal lever cover.
4. Remove the wash/wipe switch assembly.
5. Pull the hider up the control stalk and remove the two screws that attach the control stalk sleeve to the wash/wipe shaft.
6. Rotate the control stalk shaft to the full clockwise position and remove the shaft from the switch by pulling straight out of the switch.
7. Remove the turn signal switch and upper bearing retainer screws. Remove the retainer and lift the switch up and out.

With Tilt Wheel

1. Disconnect the negative battery terminal.
2. Remove the steering wheel as previously described.
3. Remove the tilt lever and push the hazard warning knob in and unscrew it to remove it.
4. Remove the ignition key lamp assembly.
5. Pull the knob off the wash/wipe switch assembly.
6. Pull the hider up the stalk and remove the two screws that attach the sleeve to the wash/wipe switch and remove the sleeve.
7. Rotate the shaft in the wiper switch to the full clockwise position and remove the shaft by pulling straight out of the wash/wipe switch.

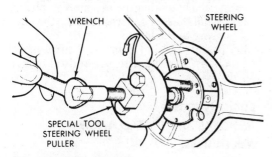

Steering wheel removal

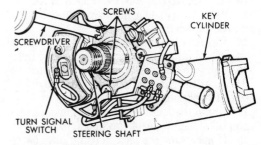

Turn signal switch removal

8. Remove the plastic cover from the lock plate. Depress the lock plate with tool C-4156 and pry the retaining ring out of the groove. Remove the lock plate, canceling cam and upper bearing spring.

9. Remove the switch actuator screw and arm.

10. Remove the three turn signal switch attaching screws and place the shift bowl in low position. Wrap a piece of tape around the connector and wires to prevent snagging then remove the switch and wires.

11. Installation is the reverse of removal.

Ignition Switch and Keylock
REMOVAL AND INSTALLATION

Without Tilt Wheel

1. Follow the turn signal switch removal procedure previously described.

2. Unclip the horn and key light ground wires.

3. Remove the retaining screw and move the ignition key lamp assembly out of the way.

4. Remove the four screws that hold the bearing housing to the lock housing.

5. Remove the snapring from the upper end of the steering shaft.

6. Remove the bearing housing from the shaft.

7. Remove the lock plate spring and lock plate from the steering shaft.

8. Remove the igniton key, then remove the screw and lift out the buzzer/chime switch.

9. Remove the two screws attaching the igniton switch to the column jacket.

10. Remove the ignition switch by rotating the switch 90 degrees on the rod then sliding off the rod.

11. Remove the two mounting screws from the dimmer switch and disengage the switch from the actuator rod.

12. Remove the two screws that mount the bellcrank and slide the bellcrank up in the lock housing until it can be disconnected from the ignition switch actuator rod.

13. To remove the lock cylinder and lock levers places the cylinder in the lock position and remove the key.

14. Insert a small diameter screwdriver or similar tool into the lock cylinder release holes and push into the release spring loaded lock retainers. At the same time pull the lock cylinder out of the housing bore.

15. Grasp the lock lever and spring assembly and pull straight out of the housing.

16. If necessary the lock housing may be removed from the column jacket by removing the hex head retaining screws.

17. Installation is the reverse of removal. If the lock housing was removed tighten the lock housing screws to 90 in. lbs.

18. To install the dimmer switch, firmly seat the push rod into the switch. Compress the switch until two $^3/_{32}$" drill shanks can be inserted into the alignment holes. Reposition the upper end of the push rod in the pocket of the wash/wipe switch. With a light rearward pressure on the switch, install the two screws.

19. Grease and assemble the two lock levers, lock lever spring and pin.

20. Install the lock lever assembly in the lock housing. Seat the pin firmly into the bottom of the slots and make sure the lock lever spring leg is firmly in place in the lock casting notch.

21. Install the ignition switch actuator rod from the bottom through the oblong hole in the lock housing and attach it to the bellcrank. Position the bellcrank assembly into the lock housing while pulling the ignition switch rod down the column, install the bellcrank onto its mounting surface. The gearshift lever should be in the park position.

22. Place the ignition switch on the ignition switch actuator rod and rotate it 90 degrees to lock the rod into position.

23. To install the ignition lock, turn the key to the lock position and remove the key. Insert the cylinder far enough into the housing to contact the switch actuator. Insert the key and press inward and rotate the cylinder. When the parts align the cylinder will move inward and lock into the housing.

24. With the key cylinder in the lock position and the ignition switch in the lock position (second detent from top) tighten the igniton switch mounting screws.

25. Feed the buzzer/chime switch wires behind the wiring post and down through the space between the housing and the jacket. Remove the igniton key and position the switch in the housing and tighten the mounting screws. The igniton key should be removed.

26. Install the lock plate on the steering shaft.

27. Install the upper bearing spring, then the upper bearing housing.

28. Install the upper bearing snapring on the steering shaft, locking the assembly in place.

29. Install the four screws attaching the bearing housing to the lock housing.

30. Install the key lamp and turn signal switch, following the procedure given previously.

Lock Cylinder
REMOVAL AND INSTALLATION

With Tilt Wheel

1. Remove the turn signal switch as previously described.

2. Place the lock cylinder in the lock position.

3. Insert a thin tool into the slot next to the switch mounting screwing boss (right hand slot) and depress the spring latch at the bottom of the slot and remove the lock.

4. Installation is the reverse of removal. Turn the ignition lock to the **Lock** position and remove the key. Insert the cylinder until the spring loaded retainer snaps into place.

Ignition Switch

REMOVAL AND INSTALLATION

With Tilt Wheel

1. Remove the turn signal switch as described above. Remove the ignition lock cylinder as described above.

CAUTION: *If the wedge spring described in the next step is dropped, it could drop into the column, requiring complete disassembly. Follow the directions and work carefully to avoid dropping it.*

2. Bend a paper clip or similar type of wire into a hook. Insert the curved end of the hook into the exposed loop of the buzzer/chime switch wedge spring. Pull the wire hook straight up to remove both the buzzer/chime switch and the spring.

3. Remove the three housing cover screws and remove the housing cover. Then, remove the wash/wipe switch.

4. Adjust the column into the full up position. Then, to remove the tilt spring retainer, insert a large Phillips screwdriver into the tilt spring opening, press the lockscrew in about $3/16$" and then turn it approximately ⅛ turn clounterclockwise to align the ears with the grooves in the housing. Remove the spring and guide.

5. Pull the actuating rod out of the dimmer switch. Remove the dimmer switch mounting screws and remove the switch.

6. Push the upper steering shaft inward far enough to remove the inner race and inner race seat, and remove both.

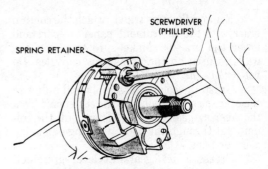

Removing the tilt spring retainer

7. Turn the ignition switch to the **ACCESSORY** position, remove its mounting screws, and remove it.

8. To install the new switch, first turn it to the **ACCESSORY** position and slide it into place. Install the mounting screws.

9. Hold the steering shaft inward and replace the inner race seat and inner race.

10. Put the dimmer switch into position and then install its retaining screws. Install the actuating rod.

11. Install the tilt spring and guide. Put the tilt spring retainer into position. Then, use a Phillips screwdriver to re-engage the spring retainer lockscrew.

12. Install the wash/wipe switch. Install the housing cover and install the three housing cover screws.

13. Insert the curved end of the hook used in removal into the loop of the buzzer/chime switch wedge spring. Use it to install both the buzzer/chime switch and the spring without allowing the spring to drop into the column.

14. Install the ignition lock cylinder as described above. Install the turn signal switch as described above.

Steering Column

REMOVAL AND INSTALLATION

1. Disconnect the negative battery cable.

2. If the car has a column shift, disconnect the cable rod by prying the rod out of the grommet in the shift lever. On these cars, also remove the cable clip and remove the cable from the lower bracket.

3. Disconnect the wiring connectors at the steering column jacket. Remove the steering wheel center pad assembly. Disconnect the horn wires.

4. Remove the steering wheel as described above.

5. Remove the instrument panel steering column cover and lower reinforcement. Disconnect the bezel.

6. Remove the indicator set screw and gearshift indicator pointer from the shift housing.

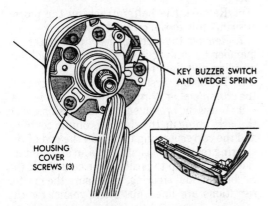

KEY BUZZER SWITCH AND WEDGE SPRING

HOUSING COVER SCREWS (3)

Location of the housing cover screws

7. Remove the nuts which attach the column bracket to the instrument panel support and lower the bracket. Make sure to retain the washers used on the breakaway capsules. *Do not remove the roll pin!*

8. Grasp the column assembly and pull it to the rear so as to disconnect the stub shaft from the steering gear coupling. Then, pull the column out through the door, avoiding damaging paint or trim.

9. Grease a *new* gearshift lever grommet. The grommet must be forced into place with a pair of pliers, working so as to install it from the side of the lever. Close the pair of pliers around the portion of the lever where the grommet goes and the grommet, with a washer located between the one jaw of the pair of pliers and the grommet to protect it from the teeth.

10. To install the column, position it in the car, align the stub shaft with the coupling in the steering gear, and gently thrust it forward to engage the two.

11. Raise the column and engage it with the 5 studs. Put the bracket in place below the column. Loosely install the 5 nuts, making sure to install washers on the breakaway capsules. Exert a force which will pull the column to the rear and then torque the nuts to 105 in. lbs.

12. Connect the gearshift cable rod to the shift lever on column shift-equipped cars. Grease the cable rod and then use a pair of pliers to force the rod to snap into the grommet. Check the linkage adjustment as described in Chapter 7.

13. Install the steering wheel as described above.

Steering Linkage
REMOVAL AND INSTALLATION
Tie Rod Ends

1. Jack up your car and support it with jackstands.

2. Loosen the jam nut which connects the tie rod end to the rack.

3. Mark the tie rod position on the threads.

4. Remove the tie rod cotter pin and nut.

5. Using a puller, remove the tie rod from the steering knuckle.

6. Unscrew the tie rod end from the rack.

7. Install a new tie rod end, and retighten the jam nut.

8. Recheck the wheel alignment.

Inner Tie Rod

NOTE: *To perform this procedure a 63 mm crow'sfoot adapter and a torque wrench are required*

1. Remove the tie rod end as described above. Install a backup open-end wrench onto the flat at the end of the steering rack to oppose torque that will be applied. Install another wrench onto the flats on the tie rod housing.

2. Being careful to keep the torques in balance so as to avoid twisting the rack, turn the inner tie rod housing until the rod separates from the rack.

3. Clean the threads on the rack and on the inside of the inner ball joint housing. Then, apply Loctite® No. 271, No. 277, or equivalent to the threads inside the inner ball joint housing.

4. Start the threads of the inner tie rod into the rack and turn the rod until it bottoms inside the rack. Turn the ball joint outward, if necessary, to keep it from contacting the rack and keeping the rod from bottoming.

5. Using a back-up wrench on the rack, and using the adapter and a torque wrench on the inner tie rod pivot housing, torque the housing to 60 ft. lbs.

Manual and Power Steering Gear
REMOVAL AND INSTALLATION

NOTE: *An assistant will be needed to perform this procedure.*

1. Loosen the wheel nuts. Raise the vehicle and support it securely by the body.

2. Detach the tie rod ends at the steering knuckles as described above.

3. Support the lower front suspension crossmember securely with a jack. Then, remove all four suspension crossmember attaching bolts. Lower the crossmember with the jack until it is possible to gain access to the steering gear and the lower steering column. Slide the gear off the steering column coupling.

4. Remove the splash shields and boot seal shields.

5. If the car has power steering, remove the fasteners from the hose locating bracket attachment points. Get a drain pan and disconnect both hoses at the opening nearest the steering gear and drain them into the pan. Discard the O-rings.

6. Remove the bolts attaching the power steering unit to the crossmember.

7. Remove the steering gear from the crossmember by pulling it off the steering column coupling and then removing it.

8. To install, first bolt the steering gear to the crossmember, torquing them to 250 in. lbs.

9. Raise the crossmember into position with the jack, lining up the steering column coupling and the corresponding fitting on the end of the steering rack pinion shaft. Have an assistant inside the car help to position the column. If the car has manual steering, make sure the master serrations are lined up. Then, maneuver the

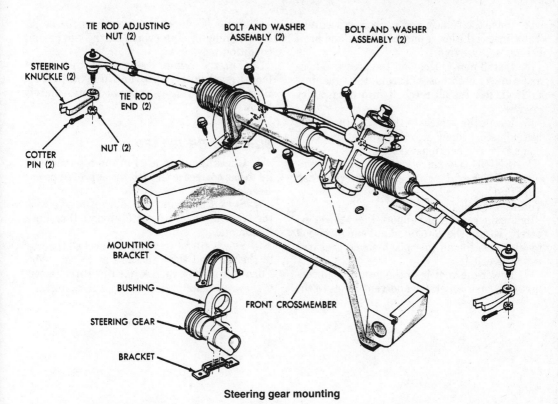

Steering gear mounting

crossmember/rack assembly so as to engage the column coupling and pinion shaft.

10. Position the crossmember so the boltholes will line up. Install the bolts, but do not tighten them—merely start the threads. Tighten the right rear bolt, which serves as a pilot bolt to properly located the crossmember. Then, torque all four bolts to 90 ft. lbs.

11. Reconnect the tie rod ends, as described above.

12. Wipe the ends of the power steering pump hoses and the ports in the steering gear. Install new O-rings on the hose tube ends and coat them with power steering fluid. Then, route the hose carefully in all clips and in such a way as to avoid kinks or close proximity to any exhaust system parts.

13. Make the hose connections and torque them to 25 ft. lbs. Refill the power steering pump with approved fluid.

14. Adjust toe in. Bleed the power steering system. Run the engine and check for leaks.

Power Steering Pump

REMOVAL AND INSTALLATION

1. Disconnect the vapor separator hose from the carburetor. If the car has air conditioning, disconnect the two wires from the air conditioning clutch cycling switch.

2. Remove the drive belt adjustment lockbolt

from the front of the power steering pump. Remove the pump end hose bracket nut, if the pump has one.

3. Raise the vehicle and support it securely.

4. Place a drain pan under the pump. Disconnect the return hose from the tube on the steering gear and and lower the end of the hose into the pan to drain the fluid from the pump (fluid will continue to drain during the next step).

5. Remove the right side splash shield (this protects the drive belts).

6. Disconnect both power steering hoses from the pump.

7. Cap the open hose ends as well as the ports in the pump to keep dirt out of the system.

8. Remove the lower stud nut and the pivot bolt from the pump.

9. Lower the vehicle. Remove the belt from the pump pulley.

10. Remove the pump rearward and to clear the mounting bracket and remove the adjusting bracket.

11. Rotate the pump clockwise so the pulley faces the rear of the vehicle and pull it upwards to remove it.

12. To replace the pump, position it as it was when it came out (pulley to the rear) and lower it into position. Then, turn it to its normal orientation. Install the adjustment bracket onto the pump with the tab in the lower left mounting hole in the front of the housing.

13. Raise the vehicle and support it securely. Then, install the lower pump stud nut and pivot bolt *only finger tight*.

14. Install new O-rings on the pressure hose and connect both hoses. Torque the tube nuts to 25 ft. lbs. Install the belt into both pulley grooves.

15. Lower the vehicle to the floor. Install the belt adjusting screw into the bracket and then and adjust the belt tension.

WARNING: *Do not pry on the pump reservoir. Be careful not to create excessive belt tension*

Torque the bolt to 30 ft. lbs.

16. Again raise and support the vehicle securely. Torque the lower stud nut and pivot bolt to 40 ft. lbs. Install the splash shield that protects the belt.

17. Lower the vehicle to the ground and connect the vapor separator and vent hoses to the carburetor. Connect the two wires to the air conditioning cycling switch, if the car has air conditioning.

18. Fill the pump reservoir to the correct (cold) level with approved fluid (not ATF). Bleed the system as described immediately below.

BLEEDING THE SYSTEM

1. Check the fluid level in the reservoir and fill to the correct level with the approved power steering fluid.

2. Start the engine and allow it to idle with the transmission in Neutral (manual) or Park (automatic).

3. Slowly turn the steering wheel all the way to the left and then all the way to the right. Turn it from lock to lock like this through several cycles. Then, refill the fluid reservoir.

BASIC OPERATING PRINCIPLES

Hydraulic systems are used to actuate the brakes of all automobiles. The system transports the power required to force the frictional surfaces of the braking system together from the pedal to the individual brake units at each wheel. A hydraulic system is used for two reasons.

First, fluid under pressure can be carried to all parts of an automobile by small pipes and flexible hoses without taking up a significant amount of room or posing routing problems.

Second, a great mechanical advantage can be given to the brake pedal end of the system, and the foot pressure required to actuate the brakes can be reduced by making the surface area of the master cylinder pistons smaller than that of any of the pistons in the wheel cylinders or calipers.

The master cylinder consists of a fluid reservoir and a double cylinder and piston assembly. Double type master cylinders are designed to separate the front and rear braking systems hydraulically in case of a leak.

Steel lines carry the brake fluid to a point on the vehicle's frame near each of the vehicle's wheels. The fluid is then carried to the calipers and wheel cylinders by flexible tubes in order to allow for suspension and steering movements.

In drum brake systems, each wheel cylinder contains two pistons, one at either end, which push outward in opposite directions.

In disc brake systems, the cylinders are part of the calipers. One cylinder in each caliper is used to force the brake pads against the disc.

All pistons employ some type of seal, usually made of rubber, to minimize fluid leakage. A rubber dust boot seals the outer end of the cylinder against dust and dirt. The boot fits around the outer end of the piston on disc brake calipers, and around the brake actuating rod on wheel cylinders.

The hydraulic system operates as follows: When at rest, the entire system, from the piston(s) in the master cylinder to those in the wheel cylinders or calipers, is full of brake fluid. Upon application of the brake pedal, fluid trapped in front of the master cylinder piston(s) is forced through the lines to the wheel cylinders. Here, it forces the pistons outward, in the case of drum brakes, and inward toward the disc, in the case of disc brakes. The motion of the pistons is opposed by return springs mounted outside the cylinders in drum brakes, and by spring seals, in disc brakes.

Upon release of the brake pedal, a spring located inside the master cylinder immediately returns the master cylinder pistons to the normal position. The pistons contain check valves and the master cylinder has compensating ports drilled in it. These are uncovered as the pistons reach their normal position. The piston check valves allow fluid to flow toward the wheel cylinders or calipers as the pistons withdraw. Then, as the return springs force the brake pads or shoes into the released position, the excess fluid reservoir through the compensating ports. It is during the time the pedal is in the released position that any fluid that has leaked out of the system will be replaced through the compensating ports.

Dual circuit master cylinders employ two pistons, located one behind the other, in the same cylinder. The primary piston is actuated directly by mechanical linkage from the brake pedal through the power booster. The secondary piston is actuated by fluid trapped between the two pistons. If a leak develops in front of the secondary piston, it moves forward until it bottoms against the front of the master cylinder, and the fluid trapped between the pistons will operate the rear brakes. If the rear brakes develop a leak, the primary piston will move forward until direct contact with the secondary piston takes place, and it will force the second-

Troubleshooting the Brake System

Problem	Cause	Solution
Low brake pedal (excessive pedal travel required for braking action.)	• Excessive clearance between rear linings and drums caused by in-operative automatic adjusters	• Make 10 to 15 alternate forward and reverse brake stops to adjust brakes. If brake pedal does not come up, repair or replace adjuster parts as necessary.
	• Worn rear brakelining	• Inspect and replace lining if worn beyond minimum thickness specification
	• Bent, distorted brakeshoes, front or rear	• Replace brakeshoes in axle sets
	• Air in hydraulic system	• Remove air from system. Refer to Brake Bleeding.
Low brake pedal (pedal may go to floor with steady pressure applied.)	• Fluid leak in hydraulic system	• Fill master cylinder to fill line; have helper apply brakes and check calipers, wheel cylinders, differential valve tubes, hoses and fittings for leaks. Repair or replace as necessary.
	• Air in hydraulic system	• Remove air from system. Refer to Brake Bleeding.
	• Incorrect or non-recommended brake fluid (fluid evaporates at below normal temp).	• Flush hydraulic system with clean brake fluid. Refill with correct-type fluid.
	• Master cylinder piston seals worn, or master cylinder bore is scored, worn or corroded	• Repair or replace master cylinder
Low brake pedal (pedal goes to floor on first application—o.k. on subsequent applications.)	• Disc brake pads sticking on abutment surfaces of anchor plate. Caused by a build-up of dirt, rust, or corrosion on abutment surfaces	• Clean abutment surfaces
Fading brake pedal (pedal height decreases with steady pressure applied.)	• Fluid leak in hydraulic system	• Fill master cylinder reservoirs to fill mark, have helper apply brakes, check calipers, wheel cylinders, differential valve, tubes, hoses, and fittings for fluid leaks. Repair or replace parts as necessary.
	• Master cylinder piston seals worn, or master cylinder bore is scored, worn or corroded	• Repair or replace master cylinder
Decreasing brake pedal travel (pedal travel required for braking action decreases and may be accompanied by a hard pedal.)	• Caliper or wheel cylinder pistons sticking or seized	• Repair or replace the calipers, or wheel cylinders
	• Master cylinder compensator ports blocked (preventing fluid return to reservoirs) or pistons sticking or seized in master cylinder bore	• Repair or replace the master cylinder
	• Power brake unit binding internally	• Test unit according to the following procedure: (a) Shift transmission into neutral and start engine (b) Increase engine speed to 1500 rpm, close throttle and fully depress brake pedal (c) Slow release brake pedal and stop engine (d) Have helper remove vacuum check valve and hose from power unit. Observe for backward movement of brake pedal. (e) If the pedal moves backward, the power unit has an internal bind—replace power unit

Troubleshooting the Brake System (cont.)

Problem	Cause	Solution
Spongy brake pedal (pedal has abnormally soft, springy, spongy feel when depressed.)	• Air in hydraulic system	• Remove air from system. Refer to Brake Bleeding.
	• Brakeshoes bent or distorted	• Replace brakeshoes
	• Brakelining not yet seated with drums and rotors	• Burnish brakes
	• Rear drum brakes not properly adjusted	• Adjust brakes
Hard brake pedal (excessive pedal pressure required to stop vehicle. May be accompanied by brake fade.)	• Loose or leaking power brake unit vacuum hose	• Tighten connections or replace leaking hose
	• Incorrect or poor quality brakelining	• Replace with lining in axle sets
	• Bent, broken, distorted brakeshoes	• Replace brakeshoes
	• Calipers binding or dragging on mounting pins. Rear brakeshoes dragging on support plate.	• Replace mounting pins and bushings. Clean rust or burrs from rear brake support plate ledges and lubricate ledges with molydisulfide grease. **NOTE:** If ledges are deeply grooved or scored, do not attempt to sand or grind them smooth—replace support plate.
	• Caliper, wheel cylinder, or master cylinder pistons sticking or seized	• Repair or replace parts as necessary
	• Power brake unit vacuum check valve malfunction	• Test valve according to the following procedure: (a) Start engine, increase engine speed to 1500 rpm, close throttle and immediately stop engine (b) Wait at least 90 seconds then depress brake pedal (c) If brakes are not vacuum assisted for 2 or more applications, check valve is faulty
	• Power brake unit has internal bind	• Test unit according to the following procedure: (a) With engine stopped, apply brakes several times to exhaust all vacuum in system (b) Shift transmission into neutral, depress brake pedal and start engine (c) If pedal height decreases with foot pressure and less pressure is required to hold pedal in applied position, power unit vacuum system is operating normally. Test power unit. If power unit exhibits a bind condition, replace the power unit.
	• Master cylinder compensator ports (at bottom of reservoirs) blocked by dirt, scale, rust, or have small burrs (blocked ports prevent fluid return to reservoirs).	• Repair or replace master cylinder **CAUTION:** Do not attempt to clean blocked ports with wire, pencils, or similar implements. Use compressed air only.
	• Brake hoses, tubes, fittings clogged or restricted	• Use compressed air to check or unclog parts. Replace any damaged parts.
	• Brake fluid contaminated with improper fluids (motor oil, transmission fluid, causing rubber components to swell and stick in bores	• Replace all rubber components, combination valve and hoses. Flush entire brake system with DOT 3 brake fluid or equivalent.
	• Low engine vacuum	• Adjust or repair engine

Troubleshooting the Brake System (cont.)

Problem	Cause	Solution
Grabbing brakes (severe reaction to brake pedal pressure.)	• Brakelining(s) contaminated by grease or brake fiuid	• Determine and correct cause of contamination and replace brakeshoes in axle sets
	• Parking brake cables incorrectly adjusted or seized	• Adjust cables. Replace seized cables.
	• Incorrect brakelining or lining loose on brakeshoes	• Replace brakeshoes in axle sets
	• Caliper anchor plate bolts loose	• Tighten bolts
	• Rear brakeshoes binding on support plate ledges	• Clean and lubricate ledges. Replace support plate(s) if ledges are deeply grooved. Do not attempt to smooth ledges by grinding.
	• Incorrect or missing power brake reaction disc	• Install correct disc
	• Rear brake support plates loose	• Tighten mounting bolts
Dragging brakes (slow or incomplete release of brakes)	• Brake pedal binding at pivot	• Loosen and lubricate
	• Power brake unit has internal bind	• Inspect for internal bind. Replace unit if internal bind exists.
	• Parking brake cables incorrrectly adjusted or seized	• Adjust cables. Replace seized cables.
	• Rear brakeshoe return springs weak or broken	• Replace return springs. Replace brakeshoe if necessary in axle sets.
	• Automatic adjusters malfunctioning	• Repair or replace adjuster parts as required
	• Caliper, wheel cylinder or master cylinder pistons sticking or seized	• Repair or replace parts as necessary
	• Master cylinder compensating ports blocked (fluid does not return to reservoirs).	• Use compressed air to clear ports. Do not use wire, pencils, or similar objects to open blocked ports.
Vehicle moves to one side when brakes are applied	• Incorrect front tire pressure	• Inflate to recommended cold (reduced load) inflation pressure
	• Worn or damaged wheel bearings	• Replace worn or damaged bearings
	• Brakelining on one side contaminated	• Determine and correct cause of contamination and replace brakelining in axle sets
	• Brakeshoes on one side bent, distorted, or lining loose on shoe	• Replace brakeshoes in axle sets
	• Support plate bent or loose on one side	• Tighten or replace support plate
	• Brakelining not yet seated with drums or rotors	• Burnish brakelining
	• Caliper anchor plate loose on one side	• Tighten anchor plate bolts
	• Caliper piston sticking or seized	• Repair or replace caliper
	• Brakelinings water soaked	• Drive vehicle with brakes lightly applied to dry linings
	• Loose suspension component attaching or mounting bolts	• Tighten suspension bolts. Replace worn suspension components.
	• Brake combination valve failure	• Replace combination valve
Chatter or shudder when brakes are applied (pedal pulsation and roughness may also occur.)	• Brakeshoes distorted, bent, contaminated, or worn	• Replace brakeshoes in axle sets
	• Caliper anchor plate or support plate loose	• Tighten mounting bolts
	• Excessive thickness variation of rotor(s)	• Refinish or replace rotors in axle sets
Noisy brakes (squealing, clicking, scraping sound when brakes are applied.)	• Bent, broken, distorted brakeshoes	• Replace brakeshoes in axle sets
	• Excessive rust on outer edge of rotor braking surface	• Remove rust

Troubleshooting the Brake System (cont.)

Problem	Cause	Solution
Noisy brakes (squealing, clicking, scraping sound when brakes are applied.) (cont.)	• Brakelining worn out—shoes contacting drum of rotor	• Replace brakeshoes and lining in axle sets. Refinish or replace drums or rotors.
	• Broken or loose holddown or return springs	• Replace parts as necessary
	• Rough or dry drum brake support plate ledges	• Lubricate support plate ledges
	• Cracked, grooved, or scored rotor(s) or drum(s)	• Replace rotor(s) or drum(s). Replace brakeshoes and lining in axle sets if necessary.
	• Incorrect brakelining and/or shoes (front or rear).	• Install specified shoe and lining assemblies
Pulsating brake pedal	• Out of round drums or excessive lateral runout in disc brake rotor(s)	• Refinish or replace drums, re-index rotors or replace

ary piston to actuate the front brakes. In either case, the brake pedal moves farther when the brakes are applied, and less braking power is available.

All dual circuit systems use a switch to warn the driver when only half of the brake system is operational. This switch is located in a valve body which is mounted on the firewall or the frame below the master cylinder. A hydraulic piston receives pressure from both circuits, each circuit's pressure being applied to one end of the piston. When the pressures are in balance, the piston remains stationary. When one circuit has a leak, however, the greater pressure in that circuit during application of the brakes will push the piston to one side, closing the switch and activating the brake warning light.

In disc brake systems, this valve body also contains a metering valve and, in some cases, a proportioning valve. The metering valve keeps pressure from traveling to the disc brakes on the front wheels until the brake shoes on the rear wheels have contacted the drums, ensuring that the front brakes will never be used alone. The proportioning valve controls the pressure to the rear brakes to lessen the chance of rear wheel lock-up during very hard braking.

Warning lights may be tested by depressing the brake pedal and holding it while opening one of the wheel cylinder bleeder screws. If this does not cause the light to go on, substitute a new lamp, make continuity checks, and, finally, replace the switch as necessary.

The hydraulic system may be checked for leaks by applying pressure to the pedal gradually and steadily. If the pedal sinks very slowly to the floor, the system has a leak. This is not to be confused with a springy or spongy feel due to the compression of air within the lines. If the system leaks, there will be a gradual change in the position of the pedal with a constant pressure.

Check for leaks along all lines and at wheel cylinders. If no external leaks are apparent, the problem is inside the master cylinder.

Disc Brakes

BASIC OPERATING PRINCIPLES

Instead of the traditional expanding brakes that press outward against a circular drum, disc brake systems utilize a disc (rotor) with brake pads positioned on either side of it. Braking effect is achieved in a manner similar to the way you would squeeze a spinning phonograph record between your fingers. The disc (rotor) is a casting with cooling fins between the two braking surfaces. This enables air to circulate between the braking surfaces making them less sensitive to heat buildup and more resistant to fade. Dirt and water do not affect braking action since contaminants are thrown off by the centrifugal action of the rotor or scraped off the by the pads. Also, the equal clamping action of the two brake pads tends to ensure uniform, straight line stops. Disc brakes are inherently self-adjusting.

There are three general types of disc brake:
1. A fixed caliper.
2. A floating caliper.
3. A sliding caliper.

The fixed caliper design uses two pistons mounted on either side of the rotor (in each side of the caliper). The caliper is mounted rigidly and does not move.

The sliding and floating designs are quite similar. In fact, these two types are often lumped together. In both designs, the pad on the inside of the rotor is moved into contact with the rotor by hydraulic force. The caliper, which is not held in a fixed position, moves slightly, bringing the outside pad into contact with the rotor. There are various methods of attaching floating calipers. Some pivot at the bottom or top, and some slide on mounting bolts. In any event, the end result is the same.

All the cars covered in this book employ the sliding caliper design.

Drum Brakes
BASIC OPERATING PRINCIPLES

Drum brakes employ two brake shoes mounted on a stationary backing plate. These shoes are positioned inside a circular drum which rotates with the wheel assembly. The shoes are held in place by springs. This allows them to slide toward the drums (when they are applied) while keeping the linings and drums in alignment. The shoes are actuated by a wheel cylinder which is mounted at the top of the backing plate. When the brakes are applied, hydraulic pressure forces the wheel cylinder's actuating links outward. Since these links bear directly against the top of the brake shoes, the tops of the shoes are then forced against the inner side of the drum. This action forces the bottoms of the two shoes to contact the brake drum by rotating the entire assembly slightly (known as servo action). When pressure within the wheel cylinder is relaxed, return springs pull the shoes back away from the drum.

Most modern drum brakes are designed to self-adjust themselves during application when the vehicle is moving in reverse. This motion causes both shoes to rotate very slightly with the drum, rocking an adjusting lever, thereby causing rotation of the adjusting screw.

Power Boosters

Power brakes operate just as non-power brake systems except in the actuation of the master cylinder pistons. A vacuum diaphragm is located on the front of the master cylinder and assists the driver in applying the brakes, reducing both the effort and travel he must put into moving the brake pedal.

The vacuum diaphragm housing is connected to the intake manifold by a vacuum hose. A check valve is placed at the point where the hose enters the diaphragm housing, so that during periods of low manifold vacuum brake assist vacuum will not be lost.

Depressing the brake pedal closes off the vacuum source and allows atmospheric pressure to enter on one side of the diaphragm. This causes the master cylinder pistons to move and apply the brakes. When the brake pedal is released, vacuum is applied to both sides of the diaphragm, and return springs return the diaphragm and master cylinder pistons to the released position. If the vacuum fails, the brake pedal rod will butt against the end of the master cylinder actuating rod, and direct mechanical application will occur as the pedal is depressed.

The hydraulic and mechanical problems that apply to conventional brake systems also apply to power brakes, and should be checked for if the tests below do not reveal the problem.

Test for a system vacuum leak as described below:

1. Operate the engine at idle without touching the brake pedal for at least one minute.
2. Turn off the engine, and wait one minute.
3. Test for the presence of assist vacuum by depressing the brake pedal and releasing it several times. Light application will produce less and less pedal travel, if vacuum was present. If there is no vacuum, air is leaking into the system somewhere.

Test for system operation as follows:

1. Pump the brake pedal (with engine off) until the supply vacuum is entirely gone.
2. Put a light, steady pressure on the pedal.
3. Start the engine, and operate it at idle. If the system is operating, the brake pedal should fall toward the floor if constant pressure is maintained on the pedal.

Power brake systems may be tested for hydraulic leaks just as ordinary systems are tested.

BRAKE SYSTEM

A conventional front disc/rear drum setup is used. The front discs are single piston caliper types; the rear drums are activated by a conventional top mounted wheel cylinder. Disc brakes require no adjustment, the drum brakes are self adjusting by means of the parking brake cable. The system is diagonally balanced, that is, the front left and right rear are on one system and the front right and left rear on the other. No proportioning valve is used. Power brakes are optional.

Adjustments
DRUM BRAKES

The brakes are self-adjusting and require no periodic adjustment. If the pedal is low and there are no apparent hydraulic problems, the rear drum brake linings are excessively worn or the automatic adjusters may be defective. The brakes are adjusted (the automatic adjusters are actuated) after drum removal or lining replacement.

In removing or installing the drums, the adjusters will have been adjusted down so the linings will be located well inside the drum. First, pump the pedal through its full stroke and with firm pressure repeatedly until the adjusters bring the linings out to fit the drum (the pedal comes up to a normal level). Then, adjust the parking brake cable as described later in this chapter. Finally, drive the car and stop normally several times to allow the adjusters to reach their final position.

Brake Light Switch

REMOVAL AND INSTALLATION

1. The stop lamp switch is incorporated with its mounting bracket. To replace the switch, first disconnect the negative battery cable. Then, unplug the two connector plugs.
2. Remove the wiring harness for the switch from the clip. Remove the nut and washer from the mounting bracket stud and remove the mounting bracket.
3. Install the switch/retaining bracket and install the nut and lockwasher. Tighten the retaining nut for the bracket. Connect the electrical connector plugs and route the wire through the retainer clip.
4. Push the switch forward as far as it will go (this will cause the brake pedal to move forward slightly).
5. Gently pull backward on the brake pedal until the pedal lever rests against the stop. This will ratchet the switch back to its properly adjusted position.

Master Cylinder

REMOVAL AND INSTALLATION

With Power Brakes

1. Disconnect the primary and secondary brake lines from the master cylinder. Plug the openings.

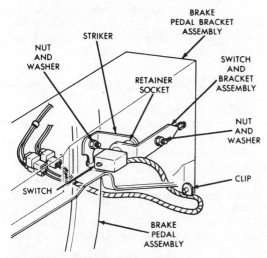

Mounting of the stop light switch.

Labels: NUT AND WASHER — STRIKER — BRAKE PEDAL BRACKET ASSEMBLY — SWITCH AND BRACKET ASSEMBLY — RETAINER SOCKET — NUT AND WASHER — CLIP — SWITCH — BRAKE PEDAL ASSEMBLY

2. Remove the nuts attaching the cylinder to the power brake booster.
3. Slide the master cylinder straight out, away from the booster.
4. Installation is the reverse of removal. Torque the mounting bolts to 15-25 ft. lbs.
5. Remember to bleed the brake system.

With Non-Power Brakes

1. Disconnect the primary and secondary brake lines and install plugs in the master cylinder openings.
2. Disconnect the stoplight switch mounting bracket from under the instrument panel. Pull the stop light switch out of the way to prevent switch damage.
3. Pull the brake pedal backward to disengage the pushrod from the master cylinder piston.

NOTE: *This will destroy the grommet.*

4. Remove the master cylinder-to-firewall nuts.
5. Slide the master cylinder out and away from the firewall. Be sure to remove all pieces of the broken grommet.
6. Install the boot on the pushrod.
7. Install a new grommet on the pushrod.
8. Apply a soap and water solution to the grommet and slide it firmly into position in the primary piston socket. Move the pushrod from side to side to make sure it's seated.
9. From the engine side, press the pushrod through the master cylinder mounting plate and align the mounting studs with the holes in the cylinder.
10. Install the nuts and torque them to 250 in. lbs.
11. From under the instrument panel, place the pushrod on the pin on the pedal and install a new retaining clip.

CAUTION: *Be sure to lubricate the pin.*

12. Install the brake lines on the master cylinder.
13. Bleed the system.

OVERHAUL

1. Remove the master cylinder as previously outlined.
2. Clean the housing and reservoir.
3. Remove the caps and empty the brake fluid.
4. Remove the reservoir by rocking it from side to side.
5. Remove the housing-to-reservoir grommets.
6. Use needle-nose pliers to remove the secondary piston stop pin from inside the master cylinder housing.
7. Remove the snapring from the outer end of the cylinder bore.

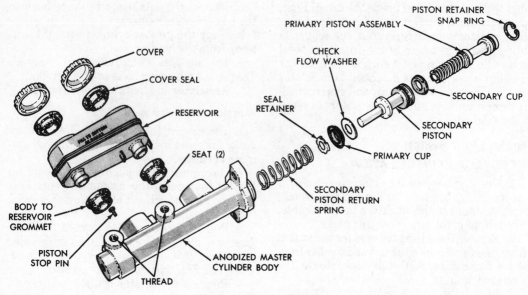

Master cylinder assembly

8. Slide the piston out of the cylinder bore.

9. Gently tap the end of the master cylinder on the bench to remove the secondary piston.

NOTE: *If the piston sticks in the bore use air pressure to force the piston out. New cups must be installed, if air pressure is used to force the piston out as the old cups will be damaged.*

10. Remove the rubber cups from the pistons (except the primary cup of the primary piston), after noting the position of the cup lips.

NOTE: *Do not remove the primary cup of the primary piston. If the cup is damaged, the entire piston assembly must be replaced.*

Install new piston cups in every case but the primary cup of the primary piston, unless it is certain that cups are in perfect condition. They must be flexible and free of cracks or wear, especially at the outer edges.

11. If the brass tube seats are not

reuseable, remove them with an Easy-out®, and insert new ones.

12. Wash the cylinder bore with clean brake fluid. Check for scoring, pitting or scratches. If any of these conditions exist replace the master cylinder. Replace the pistons if they are corroded. Replace the cups and seals. Discard all used rubber parts.

13. During installation, coat all components with clean brake fluid. This will protect them from corrosion and moisture and permit assembly without damaging rubber cups and seals.

14. With the rubber cups and master cylinder bore thoroughly lubricated, slide the secondary piston back into the bore. Follow it with the primary piston.

15. Install the snapring into the outer end of the cylinder bore. Then, use needle-nose pliers to install the secondary piston stop pin from inside the master cylinder housing.

MASTER CYLINDER BLEEDING

1. Place the master cylinder in a vise.

2. Connect two lines to the fluid outlet orifices, and into the reservoir.

3. Fill the reservoir with brake fluid.

4. Using a wooden dowel, depress the pushrod slowly, allowing the pistons to return. Do this several times until the air bubbles are all expelled.

5. Remove the bleeding tubes from the master cylinder, plug the outlets and install the caps.

NOTE: *It is not necessary to bleed the entire*

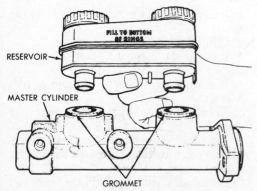

Removing the reservoir

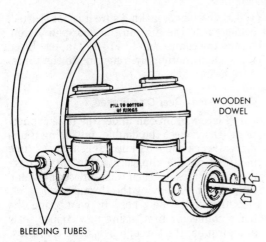

Bleeding the master cylinder

system after replacing the master cylinder, provided the master cylinder has been bled and filled upon installation.

Power Brake Booster

REMOVAL AND INSTALLATION

1. Remove the brake lines from the master cylinder.

2. Remove the nuts attaching the master cylinder to the brake booster, and remove the master cylinder.

3. Release its tension with a pair of pliers and slide the vacuum hose retaining clamp back from the check valve. Then, disconnect the vacuum line supplying the brake booster at the check valve. *Do not remove the check valve.* On 1985 and later models with a manual transmission: Remove the clutch cable mounting bracket and then pull the wiring harness away from and up the strut tower.

4. Working underneath the instrument panel, remove the retainer clip from the brake pedal pin. To do this, position a small, bladed instrument between the center tang of the retainer clip and the pin on the brake pedal and twist it. Use this method to cause the tang on the clip to pass over the end of the brake pedal pin. Discard the retainer clip because it will no longer lock safely.

5. Remove the brake light switch and striker plate.

6. Remove the four power booster attaching nuts.

7. Remove the booster from the car.

WARNING: *The power brake booster is not repairable. Do not attempt to disassemble it.*

8. To install, first postion the booster on its mounting bracket and install its four mounting nuts. Torque them to 250 in. lbs.

9. Coat the load bearing surface of the brake

pedal pin with Lubriplate® or equivalent to reduce wear. Then, connect the pushrod to the pedal pin and install a new retaining clip through the end. Lock the retaining clip securely.

10. Position the master cylinder onto the brake booster, install the mounting nuts and torque them to 250 in. lbs.

11. Route the vacuum hose carefully to the booster, ensuring that it is not kinked or pinched. Then, position its retaining clamp carefully.

12. Install each brake hydraulic tube into its correct master cylinder opening and torque the retaining flare nut to 145 in. lbs.

13. Slide the wiring harness down over the strut tower and reinstall the retaining clips. On 1985 and later models with a manual transmission, install the clutch cable mounting bracket.

14. Bleed the brake system, making sure to keep the master cylinder full of the approved brake fluid throughout the procedure. Make sure the unit is filled to the correct level when bleeding is completed.

Combination Control Valve

REMOVAL AND INSTALLATION

1. Unplug the electrical connector from the valve.

2. Place a drain pan underneath the valve. Disconnect all six hydraulic line flare nuts.

3. Remove the mounting bolt and remove the valve from the fender well.

4. To install: bolt the new valve onto the fender well.

5. Reconnect all six flare nut fittings. Torque to 145 in. lbs.

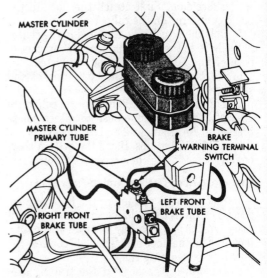

Mounting and hydraulic line identification for the brake combination valve

6. Reconnect the electrical connector.

7. Thoroughly bleed the brake system as described below. Then, repeatedly stop the vehicle with firm application on the pedal to center the warning switch spool valve and extinguish the brake light.

Brake Hoses

It is important to use quality brake hose intended specifically for the application. Hose of less than the best quality, or hose not made to the specified length will tend to fatigue and may therefore create premature leakage and, consequently, a potential for brake failure. Note also that brake hose differs from one side of the car to the other and should therefore be ordered specifying the side on which it will be installed.

Make sure hose end mating surfaces are clean and free of nicks and burrs, which would prevent effective sealing. Use new copper seals on banjo fittings. Torque brake tubing connections to 115-170 in. lbs.; hose-to-caliper connections to 19-29 ft. lbs.; and front brake hose-to-intermediate bracket fittings to 75-115 in. lbs.

REMOVAL AND INSTALLATION

Front Brake Hose

1. Place a drain pan under the hose connections. First, disconnect the hose where it connects to the body bracket and steel tube.

2. Unbolt the hose bracket from the strut assembly.

3. Remove the bolt to disconnect the banjo connection at the caliper.

4. Position the new hose, noting that the body bracket and the body end of the hose are keyed to prevent installation of the hose in the wrong direction. First attach the hose to the banjo connector on the caliper.

5. Bolt the hose bracket located in the center of the hose to the strut, allowing the bracket to position the hose so it will not be twisted.

6. Attach the hose to the body bracket and steel brake tube.

7. Torque the banjo fitting on the caliper to 19-29 ft. lbs.; the front hose to intermediate bracket to 75-115 in. lbs.; and the hose to brake tube to 115-170 in. lbs. Bleed the system thoroughly, referring to the procedure below.

Rear Brake Hose (Trailing Arm-to-Floor Pan)

1. Place a drain pan under the hose connections. Disconnect the double nut (using a primary wrench and a backup wrench) at the tube mounted on the floor pan. Then, disconnect the hose at the retaining clip.

2. Disconnect the hose at the trailing arm tube. Install the new tube to the trailing arm connection first. Torque the connection to 115-

170 in. lbs. Then, making sure it is not twisted, connect it to the tube on the floor pan. Again, torque the connection to 115-170 in. lbs. Bleed the system thoroughly, referring to the procedure below.

Caliper Hose—Rear Disc Brakes

1. Place a drain pan under the hose connections. Disconnect the double nut (using a primary wrench and a backup wrench) at the tube mounted on the clip, located on the caliper-mounted bracket. Then, disconnect the banjo connector by removing the through bolt.

2. Install the new hose by connecting the banjo connector first, using new copper seals and torquing the through-bolt to 19-29 ft. lbs.

3. Making sure the hose is not twisted, make the connection to the tube, torquing to 115-170 in lbs.

4. Secure the hose to the bracket with the retaining clip. Bleed the system thoroughly, referring to the procedure below.

Bleeding The System

The purpose of bleeding the brakes is to expel air trapped in the hydraulic system. The system must be bled whenever the pedal feels spongy, indicating that compressible air has entered the system. It must also be bled whenever the system has been opened or repaired. You will need a helper for this job.

WARNING: *Never reuse brake fluid which has been bled from the brake system. It contains moisture and corrosion products and should therefore always be replaced with fresh fluid.*

1. The sequence for bleeding is right rear, left front, left rear and right front. If the car has power brakes, remove the vacuum by applying the brakes several times. Do not run the engine while bleeding the brakes.

2. Clean all the bleeder screws. You may want to give each one a shot of penetrating solvent to loosen it up; seizure is a common problem with bleeder screws, which then break off, sometimes requiring replacement of the part to which they are attached.

3. Fill the master cylinder with DOT 3 brake fluid.

WARNING: *Brake fluid absorbs moisture from the air. Don't leave the master cylinder or the fluid container uncovered any longer than necessary. Be careful handling the fluid—it eats paint.*

Check the level of the fluid often when bleeding, and refill the reservoirs as necessary. Don't let them run dry, or you will have to repeat the process.

4. Attach a length of clear vinyl tubing to the

bleeder screw on the wheel cylinder. Insert the other end of the tube into a clear, clean jar half filled with brake fluid.

5. Have your assistant slowly depress the brake pedal. As this is done, open the bleeder screw ⅓-½ turn, and allow the fluid to run through the tube. Then close the bleeder screw before the pedal reaches the end of its travel. Have your assistant slowly release the pedal. Repeat this process until no air bubbles appear in the expelled fluid.

6. Repeat the procedure on the other three brakes, checking the lever of fluid in the master cylinder reservoir often.

After finishing, there should be no feeling of sponginess in the brake pedal. If there is, either there is still air in the line, in which case the process must be repeated, or there is a leak somewhere, which, of course, must be corrected before the car is moved.

FRONT DISC BRAKES

CAUTION: *Brake shoes contain asbestos, which has been determined to be a cancer-causing agent. Never clean the brake surfaces with compressed air! Avoid inhaling any dust from any brake surface! When cleaning brake surfaces, use a commercially available brake cleaning fluid.*

Brake Pads
INSPECTION

Measure lining wear by measuring the combined thickness of the shoe and lining at the thinnest point. It must be $\frac{5}{16}''$ on front disc brakes.

Disc Brake Pads and Calipers
REMOVAL AND INSTALLATION
ATE System

1. Raise and support the front end on jackstands.

2. Remove the front wheels.

3. Remove the caliper holddown spring by pushing in on the center of the spring and pushing outward.

4. Loosen but do not remove the guide pins, until the caliper is free. Remove the guide pins only if the bushings are being replaced.

5. Lift the caliper away from the rotor. The inboard pad will remain with the caliper. Remove the pad by pulling it away from the caliper piston to unsnap the retaining clip.

6. Remove the outboard pad by simply pulling it away from the caliper adapter.

7. If the caliper is being removed, disconnect and cap the brake line. If only the pads are being removed, support the caliper with wire in such a way that the brake line will not be stressed.

8. Lubricate both bushing channels with silicone lubricant.

9. Remove the protective backing from the noise suppression gasket on the inner pad assembly.

10. Install the new inboard pad in the caliper, centering the retainer in the piston bore.

11. Remove the protective backing from the noise suppression gasket on the outboard pad and position the pad on the adapter.

12. Carefully lower the caliper over the rotor and inboard pad.

13. Install the guide pins and torque to 18-22 ft. lbs.

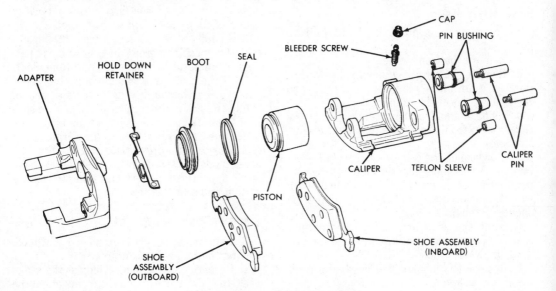

Exploded view—disc brake caliper

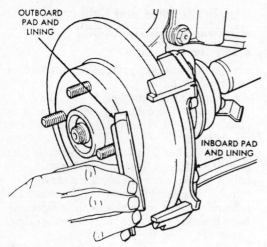

Outer disc pad

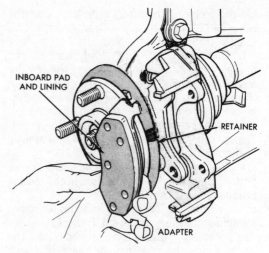

Inner disc pad

CAUTION: *It is easy to crossthread the guide pins. Start them carefully, turning them gently and allowing them to find their own angle.*

14. Install the holddown spring.

15. Install the wheels and torque the lugs to ½ torque in a crossing pattern, then torque them to the full torque of 95 ft. lbs. If the caliper was removed, bleed the system throroughly, as described above. Pump the brake pedal several times to ensure that the brake pads seat against the rotor. *The pedal must give resistance at the normal position before attempting to drive the car.* Drive the car at moderate speeds in an isolated area in order to apply the brakes several times to test the system and seat the new linings.

Kelsey-Hayes System

1. Raise and support the front end on jackstands.

2. Remove the front wheels.

3. Remove the caliper guide pin. To do this, unscrew it until it is free from the threads and then pull it out of the caliper adapter.

4. Using a small prybar, gently wedge the caliper away from the rotor, breaking the adhesive seals.

5. Slowly slide the caliper away from the rotor and off the caliper adapter. Support the caliper securely by hanging it from the body with wire (this is necessary to keep its weight from damaging the brake hose).

6. Slide the outboard pad off the caliper adapter. Then remove the disc by simply sliding it off the wheel studs.

7. Remove the inboard pad by sliding it off the caliper adapter.

8. If the caliper is to be removed, disconnect

and cap the brake line. Then, remove it from the hanger and remove it.

9. Lubricate both bushing channels with silicone grease.

10. Remove the protective paper backing from the anti-squeal surfaces on both pads. Install the inboard pad on the adapter. Be careful to keep grease from the bushing channels from getting onto the pad as you do this.

11. Install the rotor onto the wheel studs of the steering knuckle. Install the outboard pad in the caliper and carefully slide it into place over the rotor.

12. If necessary, reconnect the brake line or remove the caliper from the hanger. Lower the caliper into position over the rotor and pads. Install the guide pin and torque it to 35 ft. lbs.

CAUTION: *It is easy to crossthread the guide pin. Start it carefully, turning it gently and allowing it to find its own angle.*

13. Install the wheels and torque the lugs to half the specified torque in a criss-cross pattern. Then, torque the lugs to full torque (95 ft. lbs.). If the brake line was disconnected, bleed the system thoroughly as described above. Pump the brake pedal several times to ensure that the brake pads seat against the rotor. *The pedal must give resistance at the normal position before attempting to drive the car.* Drive the car at moderate speeds in an isolated area in order to apply the brakes several times to test the system and seat the new linings.

CALIPER OVERHAUL

1. Remove the caliper as previously outlined, leaving the brake line connected.

2. Carefully have a helper depress the brake pedal to hydraulically push the piston out of the bore. When the piston has passed out of the

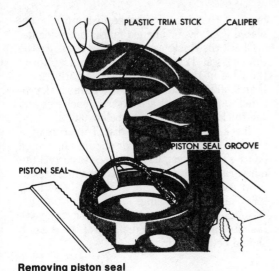

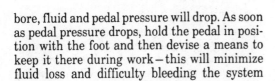

Removing piston seal

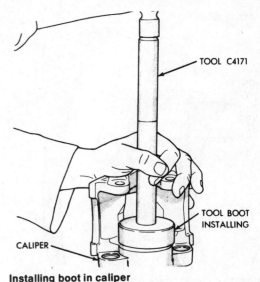

Installing boot in caliper

bore, fluid and pedal pressure will drop. As soon as pedal pressure drops, hold the pedal in position with the foot and then devise a means to keep it there during work – this will minimize fluid loss and difficulty bleeding the system later.

CAUTION: *Under no condition should air pressure be used to remove the piston. Personal injury could result from this practice.*

3. Disconnect the flexible brake line at the frame bracket and immediately plug the open end of the line. If the piston from the caliper on the opposite side of the car must now be removed, it can be removed in the same way. When the piston has been removed, disconnect and plug the other flexible line.

4. Place the caliper in a vise which has soft jaws, clamping it as lightly as possible.

WARNING: *Excessive vise pressure will cause bore distortion and piston binding.*

5. Remove the dust boot and discard it.

6. Use a plastic rod to work the piston seal out of its groove in the piston bore. Discard the old seal.

NOTE: *Do not use a metal tool for this procedure, because of the possiblity of scratching the piston bore or damaging the edges of the seal.*

7. Remove the bushings from the caliper by pressing them out, using a suitable tool. Discard the old bushings. If a Teflon® sleeve is used, discard this also.

8. Clean all parts using alcohol and blow dry with compressed air.

NOTE: *Whenever a caliper has been disassembled, a new boot and seal must be installed.*

9. Inspect the piston bore for scoring or pitting. Bores with light scratches can be cleaned

up. If the bore is scratched beyond repair, the caliper should be replaced.

10. Dip the new piston seal in clean brake fluid and install it in the bore groove.

CAUTION: *Never use an old piston seal.*

11. Coat the new piston with clean brake fluid, leaving a generous amount inside the boot.

12. Position the dust boot over the piston.

13. Install the piston into the bore, pushing it past the piston seal until it bottoms in the bore.

CAUTION: *Force must be applied uniformly to avoid cocking the piston.*

14. Position the dust boot in the counterbore.

15. Using tools #C-4689 and C-4171 or their equivalents install the dust boot.

16. Remove the Teflon® sleeves from the guide pin bushings before installing the bushings into the caliper. After the new bushings are installed in the caliper, reinstall the Teflon® sleeves into the bushings.

17. Be sure the flanges extend over the caliper casting evenly on both sides.

18. When reinstalling the calipers use new seal washers and torque the brake hose connections to the specified torque. Follow the installation procedure above.

19. Bleed the brake system. Pump the brake pedal several times to ensure that the brake pads seat against the rotor. *The pedal must give resistance at the normal position before attempting to drive the car.* Drive the car at moderate speeds in an isolated area in order to apply the brakes several times to test the system.

Brake Disc

REMOVAL AND INSTALLATION

1. Raise and support the front end on jackstands.

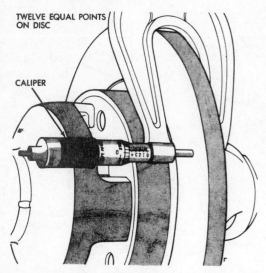

TWELVE EQUAL POINTS ON DISC

CALIPER

Checking disc for thickness

2. Remove the caliper from the rotor, but do not disconnect the brake line.

3. Suspend the caliper out of the way with wire. Do not put stress on the brake hose.

4. On ATE systems, remove the adapter from the knuckle.

5. Remove the rotor from the drive flange studs.

6. Coat both sides of the rotor with alcohol and slide it onto the studs.

7. Install the adapter (ATE systems).

8. Install the caliper as described above.

INSPECTION

Light scoring is acceptable. Heavy scoring or warping will necessitate refinishing or replace-

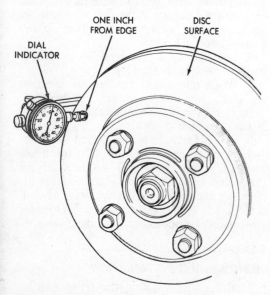

ONE INCH FROM EDGE

DISC SURFACE

DIAL INDICATOR

Checking disc for run-out

ment of the disc. The brake disc must be replaced if cracks or burned marks are evident.

Check the thickness of the disc. Measure the thickness at 12 equally spaced points 1″ from the edge of the disc. If thickness varies more than 0.0005″. the disc should be refinished, provided equal amounts are out from each side and the thickness does not fall below 0.882″.

Check the run-out of the disc. Total runout of the disc installed on the car should not exceed 0.005″. The disc can be resurfaced to correct minor variations as long as equal amounts are cut from each side and the thickness is at least 0.882″ after resurfacing.

Check the run-out of the hub (disc removed). It should not be more than 0.002″. If so, the hub should be replaced.

REAR DRUM BRAKES

CAUTION: *Brake shoes contain asbestos, which has been determined to be a cancer-causing agent. Never clean the brake surfaces with compressed air! Avoid inhaling any dust from any brake surface! When cleaning brake surfaces, use a commercially available brake cleaning fluid.*

Brake Drums

REMOVAL AND INSTALLATION

1. Jack up the car and support it with jack stands.

2. Remove the rear wheels.

3. On 1984 and later models, loosen the parking brake cable adjustment by backing off the adjusting nut. On all models, remove the plug from the support plate and insert a brake spoon or similar tooal and release the brake shoe drag. Do this by moving up on the left side and down on the right side on 1981-83 models, and by using an upward motion on both sides on later models.

4. Remove the grease cap.

5. Remove the cotter pin, locknut, and washer.

6. Remove the brake drum and bearings.

7. Installation is the reverse of removal. Adjust the wheel bearings as descriibed in Chapter 8.

INSPECTION

Measure drum run-out and diameter. If the drum is not to specifications, have the drum resurfaced. The run-out should not exceed 0.006″. The diameter variation (ovalness) of the drum must not exceed 0.0025″ in 30° or 0.0035″ in 360°. All brake drums will show markings of the maximum allowable diameter.

Once the drum is off, clean the shoes and springs with a damp rag to remove the accumulated brake dust.

CAUTION: *Do not use compressed air to blow brake dust off the linings or other brake system parts. Brake dust contains asbestos, a known cancer causing agent.*

Grease on the shoes can be removed with alcohol or fine sandpaper.

After cleaning, examine the brake shoes for glazed, oily, loose, cracked or improperly (unevenly) worn linings. Light glazing is common and can be removed with fine sandpaper. Linings that are worn improperly or below $\frac{1}{16}"$ above rivet heads or brake shoe should be replaced. The NHSTA advises states with inspection programs to fail vehicles with brake linings less than $\frac{1}{32}"$. A good "eyeball" test is to replace the linings when the thickness is the same as or less than the thickness of the metal backing plate (shoe).

Wheel cylinders are a vital part of the brake system and should be inspected carefully. Gently pull back the rubber boots; if any fluid is visible, it's time to replace or rebuild the wheel cylinders. Boots that are distorted, cracked or otherwise damaged, also point to the need for service. Check the flexible brake lines for cracks, chafing or wear.

Check the brake shoe retracting and holddown springs; they should not be worn or distorted. Be sure that the adjuster mechanism moves freely. The points on the backing plate where the shoes slide should be shiny and free of rust. Rust in these areas suggests that the brake shoes are not moving properly.

Brake Shoes

REMOVAL AND INSTALLATION

WARNING: *If you are not thoroughly familiar with the procedures involved in brake replacement, disassemble and assemble one side at a time, leaving the other wheel intact, as a reference. This will reduce the risk of assembling brakes incorrectly.*

1981-83 Models

1. Remove the brake drum. See the procedure earlier in this chapter.
2. Unhook the parking brake cable from the secondary (trailing) shoe.
3. Remove the shoe-to-anchor springs (retracting springs). They can be gripped and unhooked with a pair of pliers.
4. Remove the shoe hold down springs: compress them slightly and slide them off of the hold down pins.
5. Remove the adjuster screw assembly by

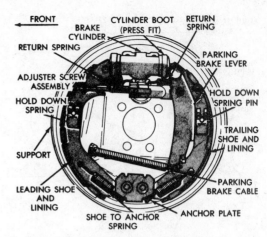

Left rear wheel brake system—1981–83 cars

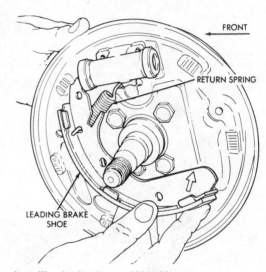

Installing brake drum—1981–83 cars

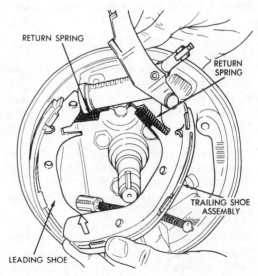

Installing trailing brake shoe and lever—1981–83 cars

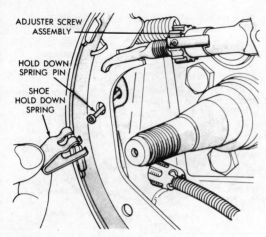

Installing shoe holddown spring—1981–83 cars

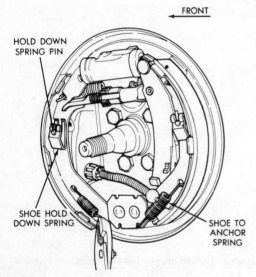

Installing shoe-to-anchor springs—1981–83 cars

spreading the shoes apart. The adjuster nut must be fully backed off.

6. Raise the parking brake lever. Pull the secondary (trailing) shoe away from the backing plate so pull-back spring tension is released.

7. Remove the secondary (trailing) shoe and disengage the spring end from the backing plate.

8. Raise the primary (leading) shoe to release spring tension. Remove the shoe and disengage the spring end from the backing plate.

9. Inspect the brakes (see procedures under Brake Drum Inspection).

10. Lubricate the six shoe contact areas on the brake backing plate and the web end of the brake shoe which contacts the anchor plate. Use a multi-purpose lubricant or a high temperature brake grease made for this purpose.

11. Chrysler recommends that the rear wheel

bearings be cleaned and repacked whenever the brakes are renewed. Be sure to install a new bearing seal.

12. With the leading shoe return spring in position on the shoe, install the shoe at the same time as you engage the return spring in the end support.

13. Position the end of the shoe under the anchor.

14. With the trailing shoe return spring in position, install the shoe at the same time as you engage the spring in the support (backing plate).

15. Position the end of the shoe under the anchor.

16. Spread the shoes and install the adjuster screw assembly making sure that the forked end that enters the shoe is curved down.

17. Insert the shoe hold down spring pins and install the hold down springs.

18. Install the shoe-to-anchor springs.

19. Install the parking brake cable onto the parking brake lever.

20. Replace the brake drum and tighten the nut to 240-300 in. lbs. while rotating the wheel.

21. Back off the nut enough to release the bearing preload and position the locknut with one pair of slots aligned with the cotter pin hole.

22. Install the cotter pin. The end play should be 0.001-0.003″.

23. Install the grease cap.

1984-88 Models

1. Remove the brake drum as described above. Remove the automatic adjuster spring by disconnecting the upper hook with a pair of pliers and then disconnecting it at the bottom. Then, remove the automatic adjuster lever.

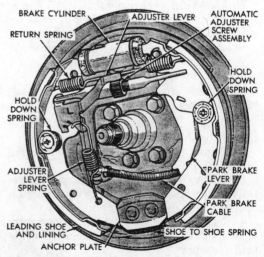

Drum brake system for 1984–88 models

2. Rotate the adjuster screw assembly to move each shoe out far enough to be free of the wheel cylinder boots.

3. Disconnect the parking brake cable from the parking brake actuating lever located at the brake mounting plate.

4. Remove the two shoe holddown springs by depressing and then turning each mounting washer so the narrow cut in the center of the clip is lined up with the locking bar. When the washer is properly lined up, slowly remove the tension and then remove the washer and spring.

5. Rock the shoes away from the wheel cylinder at the top and then loosen the adjustment on the automatic adjuster until tension is removed from the brake return spring (linking the tops of the shoes). Then, unhook and remove this spring. Unhook the shoe-to-shoe spring from the bottoms of the shoes, too.

6. Pull the shoes down and away from the support plate and remove them. In the case of the trailing shoe, use a suitable small lever to pull the C-clip off the retaining post. Remove the C-clip and the wave washer underneath, and then disconnect the parking brake lever at the shoe.

7. Clean the metal parts of the brake shoes and inspect them to ensure that they are not bent or severely worn. Inspect the lining to make sure it contacts the drum evenly. Also inspect it to make sure that the minimum lining thickness requirement shown in the Brake Specifications chart and any applicable state inspection standards for lining thickness are met.

8. Clean and inspect the brake support plate and the self-adjuster threads. Apply Multipur-

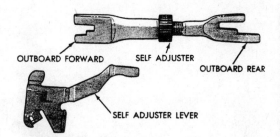

The self adjuster and lever used on 1984–88 models. Note that the adjuster must be installed only in the proper direction and with each end turned so the stepped side is outboard.

pose grease to the threads. Replace the self-adjuster if the threads are corroded. Inspect the springs for overheating (signs are burned paint or distorted end coils) and replace as necessary.

9. Lubricate all 8 contact areas of the support plate with Multipurpose grease. Insert the post of the parking brake lever through the trailing shoe. Install the wave washer and a new C-clip.

10. Attach the return (upper) spring between the two shoe assemblies; then install the brake automatic adjuster with the two stepped sides of the forks facing to the front or outboard sides of the shoes. The longer fork must face toward the rear.

11. Connect the shoe-to-shoe spring to the bottoms of the shoes. Then, expand the automatic adjuster assembly by turning the screw until the shoes are far enough apart that they will not disturb the wheel cylinder boots when installing them. Move the shoes upward and into position on the support plate, sliding the bottoms under the retaining clip at the bottom of the plate.

12. Install the holddown springs by forcing the locks over the retainers and then turning them 90° to ensure they lock positively.

13. Install the automatic adjuster lever and its retaining spring. Connect the parking brake cable to the parking brake actuating lever on the mounting plate.

14. Adjust the automatic adjuster well inward so the brake drum can be installed without resistance.

CAUTION: *Make sure the adjuster nut stays in contact with the tubular strut of the adjuster when you do this.*

15. Install the brake drum. Readjust the wheel bearings as described in Chapter 8 and install a new cotter pin. Install the wheel and torque the bolts.

16. After lowering the car, pump the brake pedal several times to adjust the brakes. When there is adequate pedal, road test the car in an isolated area at lower speeds applying the

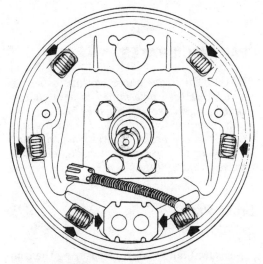

Apply Multipurpose grease to the eight areas shown on 1984–88 models to ensure smooth brake operation

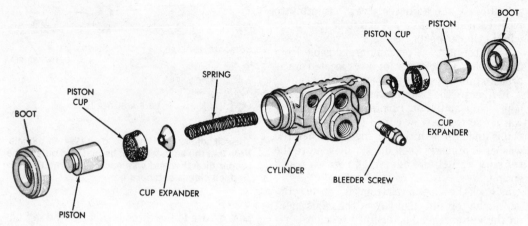

Rear wheel cylinder

brakes repeatedly to ensure that they are performing well and to complete the adjustment.

Wheel Cylinders

REMOVAL AND INSTALLATION

1. Jack up your vehicle and support it with jack stands.
2. Remove the brake drums as previously outlined.
3. Visually inspect the wheel cylinder boots for signs of excessive leakage. Replace any boots that are torn or broken.
  NOTE: A slight amount of fluid on the boots may not be a leak but may be preservative fluid used at the factory.
4. If a leak has been discovered, remove the brake shoes and check for contamination. Replace the linings if they are soaked with grease or brake fluid.
5. Disconnect the brake line from the wheel cylinder.
6. Remove the wheel cylinder attaching bolts, then pull the wheel cylinder out of its support.
7. Installation is the reverse of removal. Torque the wheel cylinder mounting bolts to 75 in. lbs. and the brake line connection to 115-170 in. lbs.
8. Bleed the brake system.

OVERHAUL

1. Pry the boots away from the cylinder and remove the boots and piston as an assembly.
2. Disengage the boot from the piston.
3. Slide the piston into the cylinder bore and press inward to remove the other boot and piston. Also remove the spring with it the cup expanders.
4. Wash all parts (except rubber parts) in clean brake fluid thoroughly. Do not use a rag; lint will adhere to the bore.

5. Inspect the cylinder bores. Light scoring can usually be cleaned up with crocus cloth. Black stains are caused by the piston cups and are no cause of concern. Bad scoring or pitting means that the wheel cylinder should be replaced.
6. Dip the pistons and new cups in clean brake fluid prior to assembly.
7. Coat the wheel cylinder bore with clean brake fluid.
8. Install the expansion spring with the cup expanders.
9. Install the cups in each end of the cylinder with the open ends facing each other.
10. Assemble new boots on the piston and slide them into the cylinder bore.
11. Press the boot over the wheel cylinder until seated.
12. Install the wheel cylinder.

REAR DISC BRAKES

CAUTION: *Brake shoes contain asbestos, which has been determined to be a cancer-causing agent. Never clean the brake surfaces with compressed air! Avoid inhaling any dust from any brake surface! When cleaning brake surfaces, use a commercially available brake cleaning fluid.*

Brake Pads

INSPECTION

Measure lining wear by measuring the combined thickness of the shoe and lining at the thinnest point. It must be $9/32$ on rear disc brakes.

Brake Caliper and Pads
REMOVAL AND INSTALLATION

NOTE: *You'll need a metric size Allen wrench (4mm) to perform this operation.*

1. Raise the vehicle and support it securely by the body structure or rear axle. Remove the rear wheels.

2. There is an access plug on the inboard side of the caliper that looks like an ordinary bolt. It is located just under the parking brake cable lever. Clean the plug and the area around it to keep dirt out of the caliper and then remove it.

3. Install the 4 mm Allen wrench into the access hole and turn it counterclockwise to retract the pads from the disc. Turn the retractor a few turns—until there is daylight between the disc and the pads.

4. Remove the anti-rattle spring by prying it off the outside of the caliper with a small, blunt instrument. Be careful to pry outward on the spring just far enough to release it, in order to avoid damaging it.

5. Clean the guide pins and the areas around them of dirt and then unscrew them. Pull them out just far enough to free the caliper from the adapter if it is not necessary to replace the caliper bushings. If the bushings are to be replaced, remove the guide pins.

6. Lift the caliper (and the inboard pad, which will remain with it) upward and away from the braking disc and then suspend it securely on a piece of wire, so as to prevent putting stress on the brake hose.

7. Pull the inboard pad away from the caliper piston and remove it. Pull the outboard pads off the caliper adapter.

WARNING: *In the following step, be careful to retract the piston very slowly and carefully and by using only a minimum of effort. The use of excessive force will damage the retraction and actuation shafts.*

8. Insert the Allen wrench into the access hole and retract the piston all the way by rotating the wrench *very gently just until the rotating effort increases very slightly.*

9. Install a new inboard brake pad to the bore of the caliper piston. Then, install a new outboard pad marked "L" or "R", according to the side of the vehicle you are working on. This pad is installed by sliding it onto the caliper adaptor

10. Lower the caliper over the disc and outboard pad. Gently and cautiously turn the guide pins *in order to start them in their threads without cross-threading them.* Use a minimum amount of force and allow the pins to find their own angle so the threads will not be damaged. Torque the guide pins to 18-26 ft. lbs.

11. Install the anti-rattle spring. Then, insert the Allen wrench back through the access hole and turn the retraction shaft clockwise just until there is a slight amount of tension on it and the clearance between the pads and disc has been removed. Then, retract the shaft $\frac{1}{3}$ of a turn.

12. If the brake line has been disconnected, bleed the brake system. Pump the brake pedal several times to ensure that the brake pads seat against the rotor. *The pedal must give resistance at the normal position before attempting to drive the car.* Drive the car at moderate speeds in an isolated area in order to apply the brakes several times to test the system.

Brake Caliper
OVERHAUL

Rear disc brake calipers are not overhauled, but are replaced. Only the dust boots and guide pin bushings are serviced, as described here. If a new caliper assembly complete with dust boots and guide pin bushings is to be installed, make sure to transfer useable pads and related parts and replace those which are worn, as described above, and to follow Steps 1 and 9.

1. Disconnect and plug the brake line. Disconnect the parking brake cable retaining clips from the hanger bracket and caliper. Disconnect the cable at the parking brake lever. Then, remove the caliper as described above.

2. Check the caliper dust boot and inboard pad area for piston seal leaks. If there is a visible leak, the caliper must be replaced (they are not serviceable).

3. Inspect the dust boot and the caliper pin bushings. Replace them if they are damaged, dry, or embrittled.

4. Clean the area around the dust boot with alcohol or a suitable solvent and wipe it dry. Re-

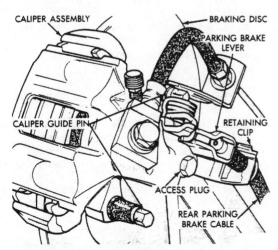

The caliper used on rear disc brakes

move the dust boot retainer with a finger or a blunt instrument and remove the dust boot from the caliper and piston grooves and discard it.

5. Clean the grooves in the piston and caliper and then coat a new boot with clean brake fluid, leaving a heavy coating inside. Position the boot over the piston and into the grooves of both piston and caliper. Install a boot retainer over the groove in the caliper.

6. Pry the bushings from the caliper with a small, dull tool. Discard the bushings and Teflon® sleeves.

7. Remove the Teflon® sleeves from new bushings. Install the bushings by putting pressure on their flanges with the fingers to press them in until seated. Reinstall the Teflon® sleeves.

8. Install the caliper as described above. Connect the brake hose, torquing the banjo bolt to 19-29 ft. lbs.

9. Bleed the brake system as described above. Pump the brake pedal several times to ensure that the brake pads seat against the rotor. *The pedal must give resistance at the normal position before attempting to drive the car.* Drive the car at moderate speeds in an isolated area in order to apply the brakes several times to test the system.

Brake Disc Rotor
REMOVAL AND INSTALLATION

Remove the brake caliper and pads as described above. Unbolt and remove the caliper adapter. The disc is held in place by the wheel and wheel nuts. Before removing the disc, mark it and one adjacent wheel stud so it may be installed in the same position. It may be simply pulled off the studs once the caliper and pads have been removed. Install in reverse order, torquing the caliper adapter mounting bolts to 130-190 ft. lbs.

INSPECTION

Inspect the disc for scoring, rust, impregnated lining material and ridges, and replace or machine it if serious problems in these areas are visible. Take the following specific measurements:

1. With the wheel removed, install the lugnuts to hold the disc snugly in place against the hub. Then, mount a dial indicator so it will read runout about 1″ from the outer edge of the rotor. Zero the indicator, rotate the disc, and read the maximum reading. It must be 0.005″ or less.

2. If the specification is excessive, remove the rotor and repeat the process, this time mounting the indicator so as to measure the runout of the hub. This must not exceed 0.003″.

If it does, the hub requires replacement (see Chapter 8). If hub runout meets the specification and disc runout does not, replace the disc or have it machined, if it can be trued up while maintaining minimum thickness specifications (stamped on an unmachined surface). Note that this specification includes 0.030″ wear beyond the maximum machining limit of 0.030″ from original thickness.

3. Use a micrometer to measure disc thickness at 4 locations. Thickness variation must not exceed 0.0005″. If thickness variation can be corrected by machining the disc while maintaining maximum thickness limits, this may be done.

PARKING BRAKE

Cable
ADJUSTMENT

NOTE: *The service brakes must be properly adjusted before adjusting the parking brake.*

1. Release the parking brake lever, then back off the parking brake cable adjuster so there is slack in the cable.

2. Clean and lubricate the adjuster threads.

3. Use a brake spoon to turn the star-wheel adjuster until there is light shoe-to-drum contact. Back off the adjuster until the wheel rotates freely with not brake drag.

4. Tighten the parking brake adjsuter until a slight drag is felt while rotating the wheels.

5. Loosen the cable adjusting nut until the rear wheels can be rotated freely, then back the cable adjuster nut off 2 full turns.

6. Test the parking brake. The rear wheels should rotate freely without dragging.

REMOVAL AND INSTALLATION
Front Cable

1. Jack up your car and support it with jack stands.

2. Loosen the cable adjusting nut and disengage the cable from the connectors.

3. Lift the floor mat for access to the floor pan.

4. Remove the floor pan seal panel.

5. Pull the cable end forward and disconnect it from the clevis.

6. Pull the cable assembly through the hole.

7. Installation is the reverse of removal.

8. Adjust the service and parking brakes.

Rear Cable

1. Jack up your vehicle and support it with jack stands.

2. Remove the rear wheels.

3. Remove the brake drums.

4. Back off the cable adjuster to provide slack in the cable.

5. Compress the retainers on the end of the

cable and remove the cable from the chassis mount. A worm gear type hose clamp can be used for this procedure.

6. Disconnect the cable from the brake shoe lever.

7. Use another hose clamp to assist in re- moving the cable housing from the support clamp. Remove the hose clamp when the cable has been removed.

8. Pull the brake cable from the rear axle.

9. Installation is the reverse of removal.

10. Adjust the service and parking brakes.

Brake Specifications

All measurements given are (in.) unless noted

| Model | Lug Nut Torque (ft. lb.) | Master Cylinder Bore | Brake Disc | | Brake Drum | | | Minimum Lining Thickness | |
			Minimum Thickness	Maximum Run-Out	Diameter	Max. Machine O/S	Max. Wear Limit	Front	Rear
1981–85	95	.827	.882	.004	7.87 ②	①	①	.300	⁵⁄₁₆ ④
1986–88	95	.827	.930–.940	.005	7.87 ③	①	①	⁵⁄₁₆	⁵⁄₁₆ ④

NOTE: Minimum lining thickness is as recommended by the manufacturer. Because of variations in state inspection regulations, the minimum allowable thickness may be different than recommended by the manufacturer.

① See figure stamped on the drum.

② Caravelle, 600 and New Yorker: 8.66

③ Caravelle, 600 and New Yorker, and Daytona, Aries, Reliant, Le Baron and Town and Country with Heavy Duty Brakes and towing option: 8.66

④ Applies to drum brakes. Rear disc: ⁹⁄₃₂

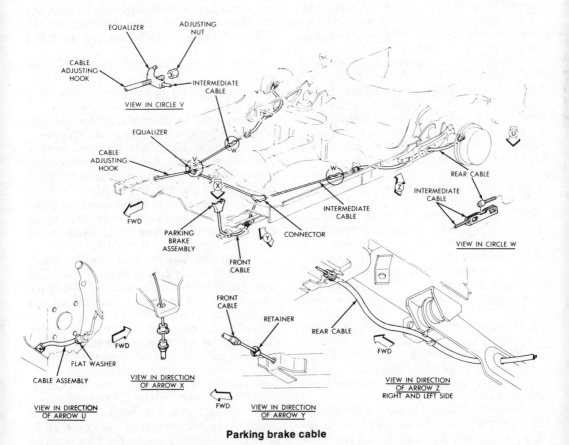

Parking brake cable

Body

10

EXTERIOR

Doors

REMOVAL AND INSTALLATION

All Chrysler Front Wheel Drive cars are equipped with doors whose hinges are welded to both the door panel and the door pillar. Doors are removed and installed basically by disconnecting them at the hinges.

NOTE: *To perform this procedure, you'll need a hinge alignment tool C-4741 and a removal tool C-4614 or C-4716 (depending on the size of the hinge). It will also be helpful to have a grinding wheel.*

1. Disconnect the negative battery cable. If there is any kind of wiring harness to the door, remove the door panel as described later in this chapter. Then, label all electrical connectors. Unplug each connector. Route the harness through the grommet in the edge of the door, coil it and tape it in a spot where it will be kept away from the area of the door hinges.

2. Open the door and, using a padded device of some kind, support it securely from underneath near the outer end.

3. Use the hinge removal tool to remove the *lower* hinge pin. Then, immediately install the hinge alignment tool in place of the hinge pin.

4. Make sure the door is steadied against falling over. Use the appropriate sized hinge removal tool to remove the upper hinge pin. Then, remove the alignment tool and remove the door.

5. Grind a chamfer on the lower end of both hinge pins to ease installation.

6. Position the door so as to fit its hinge-halves into the hinge-halves welded to the body. Align the door precisely and install two hinge alignment tools.

7. Position the upper hinge pin under the upper hinge and use a small hammer to tap it upward and through the hinge. Install the lower

hinge pin from the upper side of the lower hinge in a similar manner. Remove the two alignment tools.

8. Route the wiring harness through the door, connecting all connectors to their original locations. Install the door panel as described later in this section.

ADJUSTMENT

The door hinges are welded to both the door panels and door pillars. Because of this fact, adjustments can be performed only through the use of a special door hinge adjusting tool (C-4736), which bends the hinges in a controlled way.

Before adjusting either hinge, check these items:

• The alignment of the striker plate. Is it correct?

• The fit and condition of the hinge roll pins. If there is looseness, they must be replaced.

• The installation of the door seal. Sealing problems which may seem to be door misalignment may actually be due to irregular/incorrect positioning of the seal on the body.

1. If it is necessary to adjust the striker plate:

a. Scribe around the striker plate to mark its location against the door jamb. Then, loosen the mounting screws just slightly.

b. Open and close the door slowly to watch engagement of the door with the striker. The door should not rise or fall as it is closed. Reposition the striker vertically to ensure that this requirement is met.

c. Close the door and inspect its outer surface to see if it is flush with adjacent sheet metal. If not, adjust the striker inward or outward until the door rests in a flush position.

d. Tighten the striker adjustments securely.

2. If these other checks fail to resolve door alignment problems, it is necessary to bend the hinges. Keep in mind that this process must be done gradually to fine tune the door position.

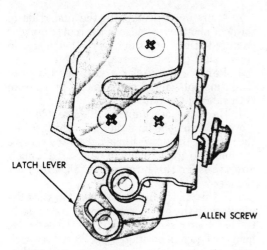

LATCH LEVER

ALLEN SCREW

Adjusting the door latch

First, determine the exact angle/area of misalignment.

3. Slip the hinge bending tool *completely* over the hinge to be bent. Then, slowly and gradually apply pressure so the change in door position can be monitored accurately. Stop the process and check the point of misalignment frequently.

LATCH ADJUSTMENT

The latch adjustment affects both the smoothness of doorlatch operation and the door handle-to-skin position.

1. Insert a $\frac{5}{32}''$ Allen wrench through the access hole in the end of the door and engage it with the Allen screw in the latch mechanism. Slide the screw up or down in the slot to adjust the latch position and then tighten the Allen screw to about 30 in. lbs. Remove the wrench.

2. Close the door and check the operation of the latch as well as the door handle position.

3. Readjust as described in Steps 1 and 2 until the door closes smoothly and the door handle is flush.

Hood

REMOVAL AND INSTALLATION

NOTE: *To perform this operation a cover that will protect both the windshield and the two fenders is required, as well as an assistant.*

1. Scribe a mark around each hinge where it connects to the underside of the hood for reinstallation with a minimum of adjustment.

2. Protect the windshield and fenders with a cover. Then, place blocks of wood behind the hood—between it and the windshield to protect the windshield in case the hood should slide to the rear.

3. As an assistant supports the hood, remove the hood bolts. With one person on either side, remove the hood from the car. If the hood is being replaced with a new one, transfer the latch striker and safety catch by removing the attaching bolts and reinstalling these components onto the new hood with them.

4. To install the hood, first position it as precisely as possible—with the boltholes of the upper hinge and the hood lined up. Then, with the assistant both supporting the front of the hood and keeping the assembly from sliding back toward the windshield, install the bolts until their heads are just a turn or two below the lower hood surface.

5. Shift the hood on both sides to align the matchmarks and hinges precisely. Tighten one bolt on either side gradually, checking that the hood remains in position and shifting it to maintain alignment as necessary. Tighten one bolt on either side to hold the hood in position.

6. Have the assistant hold the hood up as you tighten all the remaining bolts slightly. Then, torque all bolts to 105 in. lbs.

7. Remove the cover and blocks.

ALIGNMENT

1. Inspect the clearances between the hood edges in relation to the cowl, fenders and grille panel.

2. If the hood requires adjustment, loosen the mounting bolts located on the underside of the hood.

3. Shift the hood forward or rearward to change the dimension between its rear and the cowl first, if this adjustment is necessary. Once this is correct, shift the hood right or left as necessary.

4. Torque the bolts to 105 in. lbs.

Trunk Lid

REMOVAL AND INSTALLATION

NOTE: *This operation requires the help of an assistant to prevent possible physical injury or damage to the rear window and fenders.*

1. Scribe a mark around each hinge where it connects to the underside of the trunk lid for reinstallation with a minimum of adjustment.

2. As an assistant supports the trunk lid remove the bolts (2 on on either side) which fasten it to the outer arm of the hinge. Then, with one person on either side, remove the lid from the car. If a new trunk lid is to be installed, unbolt and transfer the lock cylinder, Chrysler medallion and gasket, lock cylinder and gasket, and latch.

3. To install the trunk lid, first position it as precisely as possible—with the boltholes of the upper hinge and the lid lined up. Then, with the

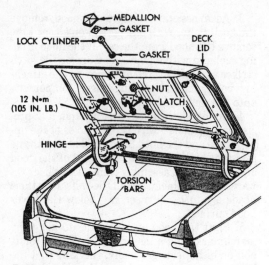

MEDALLION
GASKET
LOCK CYLINDER
GASKET
DECK LID
12 N•m
(105 IN. LB.)
NUT
LATCH
HINGE
TORSION BARS

Replacing the trunk lid

assistant both supporting the rear of the lid and keeping the assembly from sliding forward toward the rear window, install the bolts until their heads are just a turn or two below the lower hood surface.

4. Shift the lid on both sides to align the matchmarks and hinges precisely. Tighten one bolt on either side gradually, checking that it remains in position and shifting it to maintain alignment as necessary. Tighten one bolt on either side to hold the trunk lid in position.

5. Have the assistant hold it up as you tighten all the remaining bolts slightly. Then, torque all bolts to 105 in. lbs.

ADJUSTMENT

1. Inspect the clearances between the edges of the trunk lid in relation to the rear of the body under the rear window, the fenders, and the rear panel.

2. If the lid requires adjustment, loosen the mounting bolts located on its underside.

3. Shift the lid forward or rearward to change the dimension between its front end and the fore and after seals first, if this adjustment is necessary. Once this is correct, shift the hood right or left as necessary.

4. Torque the bolts to 105 in. lbs.

Hatch or Liftgate

REMOVAL AND INSTALLATION

NOTE: *It is necessary to use an assistant to perform this procedure without risking damage to areas of the body adjacent to the hatch. Masking tape and rope type sealer are also required.*

1. Securely support the hatch in the wide-open position. Mark the outline of each hinge where it contacts the underside of the hatch.

2. Apply masking tape to the underside of the door and the rear edge of the roof to prevent damage to these areas in case the hatch should slip or shift during removal.

3. Remove the upper and lower lift prop mounting bolts and remove the lift props from both sides of the hatch.

4. Have the assistant hold the hatch. Remove the two bolts on either side which fasten the hatch to the upper hinge halves and remove the hatch. If the hatch is to be re-used, unbolt and transfer the bumper, latch, and lock cylinder.

5. To install the hatch, position it against the hinges with the holes in the hinges and those in the hatch precisely aligned. Have the assistant hold the hatch in position. Apply rope type sealer to the outer edges of the hinges where they will fit against the hatch.

6. Install the hinge mounting bolts and tighten them alternately and evenly.

7. Locate one of the lift props, having the assistant adjust the height of the hatch so hinge holes will align. Install the attaching bolts. Have the assistant hold the opposite side as you install the prop and bolts on the other side.

8. Remove the masking tape installed to protect various areas of the car body.

Bumpers

ADJUSTMENT

It is possible to adjust the bumper's side-to-side or vertical location. Loosen the bumper-to-energy absorber (outer) attaching nuts or bolts. Shift the bumper as necessary, use a helper or an infinitely adjustable jack to hold it in position and torque to 105 inch lbs. on 1981-85 models and 250 inch lbs. on later models.

REMOVAL AND INSTALLATION

WARNING: *Energy absorbing units may become stuck in the retracted position because of an impact. DO NOT DRILL THE ABSORBER TO REMOVE PRESSURE. This could result in the release of this pressure — 10,000 psi worth! If loosening the bolts or nuts at either end to relieve torque on the energy absorber does not cause it to expand, it MUST BE DISCARDED.*

1. Place supports under the bumper. If the bumper has a fascia, remove the retaining nuts and remove it.

2. Remove the bumper-to-energy absorber (outer end) retaining nuts or bolts. Then, lower the bumper to the floor.

3. To install the bumper, raise it into its normal position and install the retaining nuts/bolts loosely. Now, shift the bumper as necessary, use a helper or an infinitely adjustable jack to hold it in position and then torque that attach-

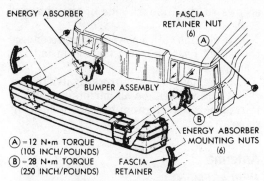

ENERGY ABSORBER

FASCIA
RETAINER NUT
(6) A

BUMPER ASSEMBLY

B

ENERGY ABSORBER
MOUNTING NUTS
(6)

A = 12 N•m TORQUE
(105 INCH/POUNDS)
B = 28 N•m TORQUE
(250 INCH/POUNDS)

FASCIA
RETAINER

Replacing the bumper on a 1981 K-car

ing nuts or bolts to 105 in. lbs. on 1981-85 models and 250 in. lbs. on later models.

4. Install the bumper fascia and retaining nuts, if the car has one.

Grille

REMOVAL AND INSTALLATION

K- and E-Cars

The grille on these cars is retained by 2 mounting screws at the top and two return springs at the bottom. The use of springs at the bottom permits the grille to flex during a parking lot type of low-speed collision.

To replace the grille, all that is necessary is to open the hood, remove the two top mounting screws, disconnect the two return springs at the bottom, and pull the grille out. Reverse this procedure to install it.

H-Body Cars: Lancer, LeBaron GTS

The grille on these models is retained very simply. There is once screw on either side, ac-

cessible from in front of the car. Simply remove both these screws to remove the grille. Install it in reverse order.

G-Body: Daytona & Laser

The grille on the Daytona & Laser is retained by two screws at the top (reached from in front of the car) and two at the bottom, accessible from above and by going behind the grille. These screws are accessible once the hood is open. Remove the four screws and remove the grille. Replace the grille in reverse order.

P-Body: Sundance and Shadow

1. Open the hood. Then remove the headlamp bezel by removing the screws and rotating it upward at the bottom and then out of the grille.

2. Remove the headlamps as described in Chapter 6.

3. Loosen the bolts attaching the grille to the outboard mounting brackets. Remove the bolts attaching the grille to the radiator panel.

4. Remove the grille. To install the grille, position the slotted ends over the bolts in the outboard mounting brackets and then carefully shift the grille from left to right to create even spacing on either side.

5. Install the bolts attaching the grille to the brackets in the radiator panel.

6. Tighten the bolts attaching the grille to the outboard grille brackets.

7. Insert the headlamps through the grille openings and install them to the radiator panel.

8. Install the headlamp bezels by starting them at the top and then rotating them downward.

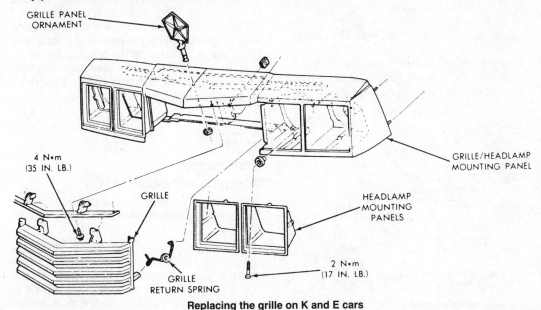

GRILLE PANEL
ORNAMENT

4 N•m
(35 IN. LB.)

GRILLE

GRILLE
RETURN SPRING

GRILLE/HEADLAMP
MOUNTING PANEL

HEADLAMP
MOUNTING
PANELS

2 N•m
(17 IN. LB.)

Replacing the grille on K and E cars

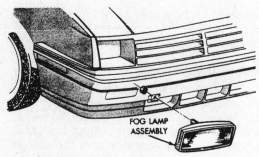

Removal/installation of the factory-installed fog lamps used on 1988 models

Fog Lights
REMOVAL AND INSTALLATION

1. Disconnect the 2 pin wiring connector for the fog light. It is located in the engine compartment, rearward of the radiator panel.
2. Remove the fog lamp mounting nut from behind the fog lamp. Pull the lamp and wiring out of the bumper.
3. Installation is the reverse of removal.

Mirrors
REMOVAL AND INSTALLATION

1. Remove the mirror bezel mounting screw to release the bezel from the channel bracket. If the mirror is the remote control type, loosen the bezel set screw (this will release the cable control).
2. If the mirror is the power type, remove the door trim panel, and then disconnect the mirror wiring harness at the connector.
3. Remove the 3 screws from the inboard side of the channel bracket.
4. Remove the 2 screws from the door frame. Release the mirror and seal from the channel bracket.
5. To install the mirror, assemble the mirror and seal to the channel bracket. Install the 2 screws to the door frame and then install the 3

screws to the inboard side of the channel bracket.
6. If working with a power mirror, reconnect the wiring harness connector and install the trim panel.
7. On remote control mirrors, tighten the bezel set screw. Then, on all mirrors, install the mirror bezel-to channel bracket mounting screw.

Antenna
REPLACEMENT

NOTE: *To perform this operation, a special antenna cap nut (much like a socket wrench), Tool C-4816, is required.*

1. The radio must be removed from the car to gain access to the antenna connection. Remove the radio as described in Chapter 6. Then, unplug the antenna lead at the radio.
2. Use an open-end wrench of appropriate size across the flats at the bottom of the antenna mast to unscrew the mast from the antenna adapter. Then, remove the mast.
3. Use the special tool to unscrew the antenna cap nut from the fender. Then, remove the cap nut and the adapter and gasket underneath it.
4. If access to the antenna body from underneath the fender is blocked by an inner fender shield, remove the 3 screws from the reat of the shield and bend it away to gain access.
5. Then, remove the antenna lead and body assembly.
6. To install the antenna, first insert the antenna body and cable through the hole in the fender from underneath. Then, install the gasket, adapter and cap nut. torquing the cap nut to 100-150 inch lbs. with the special tool.
7. Screw the antenna mast into the antenna body. Tighten it with the open-end wrench until its sleeve bottoms on the antenna body.
8. Route the antenna cable to the radio, connect it to the radio and then reinstall the radio as described in Chaper 6.

INTERIOR

Door Panels
REMOVAL AND INSTALLATION

Aries, Reliant, LeBaron, Town & Country, Caravelle, 600, New Yorker Turbo, Sundance and Shadow

NOTE: *If the watershield must be removed to work on the window mechanism or other items mounted inside the door, you will need a soft, water-resistant material designed to retain the watershield to the door metal.*

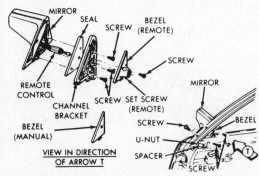

Rear view mirror mounting

CHILTON'S
AUTO BODY
REPAIR TIPS

Tools and Materials • Step-by-Step Illustrated Procedures
How To Repair Dents, Scratches and Rust Holes
Spray Painting and Refinishing Tips

With a little practice, basic body repair procedures can be mastered by any do-it-yourself mechanic. The step-by-step repairs shown here can be applied to almost any type of auto body repair.

TOOLS & MATERIALS

You may already have basic tools, such as hammers and electric drills. Other tools unique to body repair — body hammers, grinding attachments, sanding blocks, dent puller, half-round plastic file and plastic spreaders — are relatively inexpensive and can be obtained wherever auto parts or auto body repair parts are sold. Portable air compressors and paint spray guns can be purchased or rented.

Auto Body Repair Kits

The best and most often used products are available to the do-it-yourselfer in kit form, from major manufacturers of auto body repair products. The same manufacturers also merchandise the individual products for use by pros.

Kits are available to make a wide variety of repairs, including holes, dents and scratches and fiberglass, and offer the advantage of buying the materials you'll need for the job. There is little waste or chance of materials going bad from not being used. Many kits may also contain basic body-working tools such as body files, sanding blocks and spreaders. Check the contents of the kit before buying your tools.

BODY REPAIR TIPS

Safety

Many of the products associated with auto body repair and refinishing contain toxic chemicals. Read all labels before opening containers and store them in a safe place and manner.

• Wear eye protection (safety goggles) when using power tools or when performing any operation that involves the removal of any type of material.

• Wear lung protection (disposable mask or respirator) when grinding, sanding or painting.

Sanding

1 Sand off paint before using a dent puller. When using a non-adhesive sanding disc, cover the back of the disc with an overlapping layer or two of masking tape and trim the edges. The disc will last considerably longer.

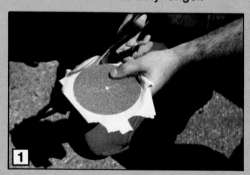

2 Use the circular motion of the sanding disc to grind *into* the edge of the repair. Grinding or sanding away from the jagged edge will only tear the sandpaper.

3 Use the palm of your hand flat on the panel to detect high and low spots. Do not use your fingertips. Slide your hand slowly back and forth.

WORKING WITH BODY FILLER

Mixing The Filler

Cleanliness and proper mixing and application are extremely important. Use a clean piece of plastic or glass or a disposable artist's palette to mix body filler.

1 Allow plenty of time and follow directions. No useful purpose will be served by adding more hardener to make it cure (set-up) faster. Less hardener means more curing time, but the mixture dries harder; more hardener means less curing time but a softer mixture.

2 Both the hardener and the filler should be thoroughly kneaded or stirred before mixing. Hardener should be a solid paste and dispense like thin toothpaste. Body filler should be smooth, and free of lumps or thick spots.

Getting the proper amount of hardener in the filler is the trickiest part of preparing the filler. Use the same amount of hardener in cold or warm weather. For contour filler (thick coats), a bead of hardener twice the diameter of the filler is about right. There's about a 15% margin on either side, but, if in doubt use less hardener.

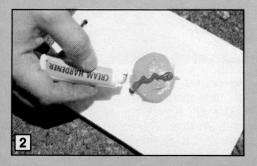

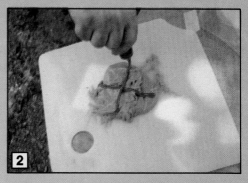

3 Mix the body filler and hardener by wiping across the mixing surface, picking the mixture up and wiping it again. Colder weather requires longer mixing times. Do not mix in a circular motion; this will trap air bubbles which will become holes in the cured filler.

Applying The Filler

1 For best results, filler should not be applied over 1/4″ thick.

Apply the filler in several coats. Build it up to above the level of the repair surface so that it can be sanded or grated down.

The first coat of filler must be pressed on with a firm wiping motion.

Apply the filler in one direction only. Working the filler back and forth will either pull it off the metal or trap air bubbles.

REPAIRING DENTS

Before you start, take a few minutes to study the damaged area. Try to visualize the shape of the panel before it was damaged. If the damage is on the left fender, look at the right fender and use it as a guide. If there is access to the panel from behind, you can reshape it with a body hammer. If not, you'll have to use a dent puller. Go slowly and work the metal a little at a time. Get the panel as straight as possible before applying filler.

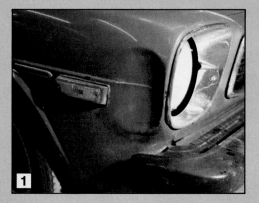

1 This dent is typical of one that can be pulled out or hammered out from behind. Remove the headlight cover, headlight assembly and turn signal housing.

2 Drill a series of holes ½ the size of the end of the dent puller along the stress line. Make some trial pulls and assess the results. If necessary, drill more holes and try again. Do not hurry.

3 If possible, use a body hammer and block to shape the metal back to its original contours. Get the metal back as close to its original shape as possible. Don't depend on body filler to fill dents.

4 Using an 80-grit grinding disc on an electric drill, grind the paint from the surrounding area down to bare metal. Use a new grinding pad to prevent heat buildup that will warp metal.

5 The area should look like this when you're finished grinding. Knock the drill holes in and tape over small openings to keep plastic filler out.

6 Mix the body filler (see Body Repair Tips). Spread the body filler evenly over the entire area (see Body Repair Tips). Be sure to cover the area completely.

7 Let the body filler dry until the surface can just be scratched with your fingernail. Knock the high spots from the body filler with a body file ("Cheesegrater"). Check frequently with the palm of your hand for high and low spots.

8 Check to be sure that trim pieces that will be installed later will fit exactly. Sand the area with 40-grit paper.

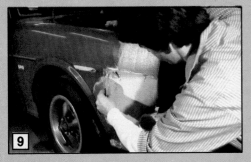

9 If you wind up with low spots, you may have to apply another layer of filler.

10 Knock the high spots off with 40-grit paper. When you are satisfied with the contours of the repair, apply a thin coat of filler to cover pin holes and scratches.

11 Block sand the area with 40-grit paper to a smooth finish. Pay particular attention to body lines and ridges that must be well-defined.

12 Sand the area with 400 paper and then finish with a scuff pad. The finished repair is ready for priming and painting (see Painting Tips).

Materials and photos courtesy of Ritt Jones Auto Body, Prospect Park, PA.

REPAIRING RUST HOLES

There are many ways to repair rust holes. The fiberglass cloth kit shown here is one of the most cost efficient for the owner because it provides a strong repair that resists cracking and moisture and is relatively easy to use. It can be used on large and small holes (with or without backing) and can be applied over contoured areas. Remember, however, that short of replacing an entire panel, no repair is a guarantee that the rust will not return.

1 Remove any trim that will be in the way. Clean away all loose debris. Cut away all the rusted metal. But be sure to leave enough metal to retain the contour or body shape.

2 Grind away all traces of rust with a 24-grit grinding disc. Be sure to grind back 3-4 inches from the edge of the hole down to bare metal and be sure all traces of paint, primer and rust are removed.

3 Block sand the area with 80 or 100 grit sandpaper to get a clear, shiny surface and feathered paint edge. Tap the edges of the hole inward with a ball peen hammer.

4 If you are going to use release film, cut a piece about 2-3" larger than the area you have sanded. Place the film over the repair and mark the sanded area on the film. Avoid any unnecessary wrinkling of the film.

5 Cut 2 pieces of fiberglass matte to match the shape of the repair. One piece should be about 1" smaller than the sanded area and the second piece should be 1" smaller than the first. Mix enough filler and hardener to saturate the fiberglass material (see Body Repair Tips).

6 Lay the release sheet on a flat surface and spread an even layer of filler, large enough to cover the repair. Lay the smaller piece of fiberglass cloth in the center of the sheet and spread another layer of filler over the fiberglass cloth. Repeat the operation for the larger piece of cloth.

7 Place the repair material over the repair area, with the release film facing outward. Use a spreader and work from the center outward to smooth the material, following the body contours. Be sure to remove all air bubbles.

8 Wait until the repair has dried tack-free and peel off the release sheet. The ideal working temperature is 60°-90° F. Cooler or warmer temperatures or high humidity may require additional curing time. Wait longer, if in doubt.

9

Sand and feather-edge the entire area. The initial sanding can be done with a sanding disc on an electric drill if care is used. Finish the sanding with a block sander. Low spots can be filled with body filler; this may require several applications.

10

When the filler can just be scratched with a fingernail, knock the high spots down with a body file and smooth the entire area with 80-grit. Feather the filled areas into the surrounding areas.

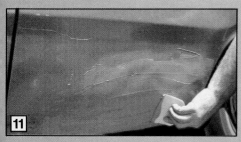

11

When the area is sanded smooth, mix some topcoat and hardener and apply it directly with a spreader. This will give a smooth finish and prevent the glass matte from showing through the paint.

12

Block sand the topcoat smooth with finishing sandpaper (200 grit), and 400 grit. The repair is ready for masking, priming and painting (see Painting Tips).

Materials and photos courtesy Marson Corporation, Chelsea, Massachusetts

PAINTING TIPS

Preparation

1

SANDING — Use a 400 or 600 grit wet or dry sandpaper. Wet-sand the area with a ¼ sheet of sandpaper soaked in clean water. Keep the paper wet while sanding. Sand the area until the repaired area tapers into the original finish.

2

CLEANING — Wash the area to be painted thoroughly with water and a clean rag. Rinse it thoroughly and wipe the surface dry until you're sure it's completely free of dirt, dust, fingerprints, wax, detergent or other foreign matter.

3

MASKING — Protect any areas you don't want to overspray by covering them with masking tape and newspaper. Be careful not get fingerprints on the area to be painted.

4

PRIMING — All exposed metal should be primed before painting. Primer protects the metal and provides an excellent surface for paint adhesion. When the primer is dry, wet-sand the area again with 600 grit wet-sandpaper. Clean the area again after sanding.

Painting Techniques

Paint applied from either a spray gun or a spray can (for small areas) will provide good results. Experiment on an old piece of metal to get the right combination before you begin painting.

SPRAYING VISCOSITY (SPRAY GUN ONLY) — Paint should be thinned to spraying viscosity according to the directions on the can. Use only the recommended thinner or reducer and the same amount of reduction regardless of temperature.

AIR PRESSURE (SPRAY GUN ONLY) — This is extremely important. Be sure you are using the proper recommended pressure.

TEMPERATURE — The surface to be painted should be approximately the same temperature as the surrounding air. Applying warm paint to a cold surface, or vice versa, will completely upset the paint characteristics.

THICKNESS — Spray with smooth strokes. In general, the thicker the coat of paint, the longer the drying time. Apply several thin coats about 30 seconds apart. The paint should remain wet long enough to flow out and no longer; heavier coats will only produce sags or wrinkles. Spray a light (fog) coat, followed by heavier color coats.

DISTANCE — The ideal spraying distance is 8″-12″ from the gun or can to the surface. Shorter distances will produce ripples, while greater distances will result in orange peel, dry film and poor color match and loss of material due to overspray.

OVERLAPPING — The gun or can should be kept at right angles to the surface at all times. Work to a wet edge at an even speed, using a 50% overlap and direct the center of the spray at the lower or nearest edge of the previous stroke.

RUBBING OUT (BLENDING) FRESH PAINT — Let the paint dry thoroughly. Runs or imperfections can be sanded out, primed and repainted.

Don't be in too big a hurry to remove the masking. This only produces paint ridges. When the finish has dried for at least a week, apply a small amount of fine grade rubbing compound with a clean, wet cloth. Use lots of water and blend the new paint with the surrounding area.

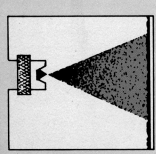

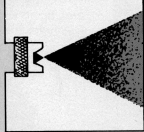

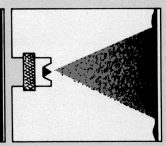

WRONG	CORRECT	WRONG
Thin coat. Stroke too fast, not enough overlap, gun too far away.	*Medium coat. Proper distance, good stroke, proper overlap.*	*Heavy coat. Stroke too slow, too much overlap, gun too close.*

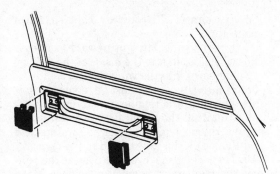

Removing the pull strap appliques ("K"-Body cars)

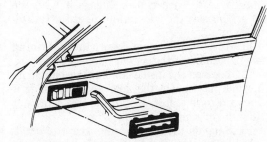

Removing the remote bezel from the right side door ("K"-Body cars)

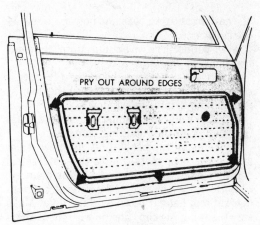

Door panel retaining clip locations

Since rain water that gets into the window slit drains down inside the door, it is necessary to seal the watershield carefully so there will not be leakage inside the car.

1. Unsnap the plastic appliques from the door pull strap and the remote bezel. Then, pull the front edge of the bezel outward and push the bezel backward to release it.

2. Remove the mounting screws at either end of the pull strap and remove it from the door panel.

3. Note the installation angle of the window crank handle and then remove it. To do this, use an Allen wrench to remove the Allen screw from the center of the window mechanism shaft.

4. Remove the retaining screws from the lower side of the door handle and remove it.

5. There are spring clips mounted to the door panel which slip into holes drilled into the door metal. Using a flat stick, gently pry the panel off the door at front, back and bottom to release the clips.

6. Lift the panel straight upward to release clips which retain it to the inside of the door by running down into the window slot.

7. If the watershield must be removed, carefully pull it off the retaining material.

8. To install the panel, first run new sealer around the door metal under the watershied and then stick the watershield to the door.

9. Hook the panel over the door at the win-

dow slit and hang it down over the door. Make sure the retaining clips line up with their corresponding holes and then press the panel inward directly over each clip to engage it with the door.

10. Install the door handle with the retaining screws if the car has one.

11. Install the window crank handle at the same angle by engaging its internal splines with those on the window mechanism shaft. Then, install the retaining screw and tighten it with the Allen wrench.

12. Install the pull strap, its retaining screws and the bezels.

13. install the remote bezel. '

G-Body Cars: Daytona & Laser

1. Lower the window all the way. Disconnect the battery negative cable.

2. If the car has manual windows, remove the Allen screw from the end of the window mechanism shaft and remove the crank handle.

3. With a piece of thin, relatively soft material (such as a strip of wood), gently pry the electric mirror/door lock bezel out of the armrest. Then, disconnect the wiring connectors for the electric mirror and the door lock switch.

4. Remove the bezel surrounding the remote lock/latch release switches.

5. Disconnect the four armrest electrical plugs at the armrest. Remove the screw located behind each plug and the single screw in the opening of the switch bezel.

6. Rotate the armrest to release it and remove it.

7. Remove the one remaining trim panel retaining screw from the area of the door near the body pillar.

8. There are spring clips mounted to the door panel which slip into holes drilled into the door metal. Using a flat stick, gently pry the panel

off the door at front, back and bottom to release the clips.

9. Disconnect the wire connector at the courtesy lamp.

10. Lift the panel straight upward to release clips which retain it to the inside of the door by running down into the window slot.

11. If the watershield must be removed, carefully pull it off the retaining material.

12. To install the panel, first run new sealer around the door metal under the watershield and then stick the watershield to the door.

13. Hook the panel over the door at the window slit and hang it down over the door. Make sure the retaining clips line up with their corresponding holes and then press the panel inward directly over each clip to engage it with the door. Connect the wire connector at the courtesy lamp.

14. Install the trim panel retaining screw located in the area of the door near the body pillar.

15. Rotate the armrest into position.

16. Install the screw located behind the location of each plug in the armrest and the single screw in the opening of the switch bezel. Connect the four armrest electrical plugs.

17. Install the bezel surrounding the remote lock/latch release switches.

18. Connect the wiring connectors for the electric mirror and the door lock switch. Then, install the electric mirror/door lock bezel into the armrest.

19. If the car has manual windows, install the crank handle and then install the Allen screw into the end of the window mechanism shaft.

20. Reconnect the negative battery cable.

H-Body Cars: Lancer, LeBaron GTS
WITH MANUAL WINDOW REGULATORS

1. Lower the window glass all the way. Note the crank handle installation angle. Then, remove the regulator crank handle retaining screw from the regulator shaft with an Allen wrench.

2. Unsnap the mirror remote control bezel and remove it.

3. Remove the two screws at the mirror remote control. Then slide the inside handle bezel rearward to release it and remove it.

4. Remove the single trim panel retaining screw located at the forward/upper corner.

5. There are spring clips mounted to the door panel which slip into holes drilled into the door metal. Using a flat stick, gently pry the panel off the door at the bottom, at the rear and half way up the front. Then, flex the panel at the forward, upper corner to to disengage the two additional clips located there.

6. Disconnect the courtesy light electrical connector.

7. Lift the panel straight upward to release clips which retain it to the inside of the door by running down into the window slot.

8. If the watershield must be removed, carefully pull it off the retaining material.

9. To install the panel, first run new sealer around the door metal under the watershield and then stick the watershield to the door.

10. Hook the panel over the door at the window slit and hang it down over the door. Make sure the retaining clips line up with their corresponding holes and then press the panel inward directly over each clip to engage it with the door. Connect the wire connector at the courtesy lamp.

11. Install the single trim panel retaining screw located at the forward/upper corner.

12. Position the inside handle bezel behind its normal position in the door and then slide it forward to install it. Install the two screws at the mirror remote control.

13. Snap on the mirror remote control bezel.

14. Install the regulator crank handle onto regulator shaft at its original installation angle. Install the retaining screw with an Allen wrench.

H-Body: Lancer, LeBaron GTS
FRONT DOOR WITH MANUAL WINDOW REGULATOR

1. Roll the window all the way down. With an Allen wrench, remove the window crank handle retaining screw. Note the installation angle of the handle and remove it.

2. Snap off the mirror remote control bezel. Then, remove the two screws at the mirror remote control. Slide the inside handle bezel rearward and remove it.

3. Remove the door panel retaining screw from the forward/upper corner of the panel. There are spring clips mounted to the door panel which slip into holes drilled into the door metal. Using a flat stick, gently pry the panel off the door at the bottom, at the rear and half way up the front. Then, flex the panel at the forward, upper corner to to disengage the two additional clips located there.

4. Disconnect the courtesy light electrical connector.

5. Lift the panel straight upward to release clips which retain it to the inside of the door by running down into the window slot.

6. If the watershield must be removed, carefully pull it off the retaining material.

7. To install the panel, first run new sealer around the door metal under the watershield and then stick the watershield to the door.

8. Hook the panel over the door at the window slit and hang it down over the door. Make

sure the retaining clips line up with their corresponding holes and then press the panel inward directly over each clip to engage it with the door. Connect the wire connector at the courtesy lamp.

9. Install the door panel retaining screw to the forward/upper corner of the panel.

10. Slide the inside handle bezel rearward and install it. Install the two screws at the mirror remote control. Snap the mirror remote control bezel back on.

11. Reinstall the crank handle at its original angle.

H-Body: Lancer, LeBaron GTS
FRONT DOOR WITH ELECTRIC WINDOW REGULATOR

1. Lower the glass all the way. Then, disconnect the negative battery cable.

2. Remove the single retaining screw located at the electric window switch plate's forward edge. Lift the switch plate off the door panel, note how the connectors are hooked up, and then disconnect the connectors.

3. Follow Steps 2 through 6 of the procedure above to complete removal. Then, follow 7 through 10.

4. Remake the electrical connections to the window switch. Then, slip the switchplate into the door panel. Install the switchplate retaining screw. Reconnect the battery.

H-Body: Lancer, LeBaron GTS
REAR DOOR WITH MANUAL REGULATOR

1. Roll the glass all the way down. Disconnect the negative battery cable.

2. Using an Allen wrench, remove the retaining screw for the window crank handle from the regulator shaft. Note the angle of the crank handle and remove it.

3. Remove the retaining screw from the pull cup behind the armrest. Then, slide the remote control bezel rearward to remove it.

4. There are spring clips mounted to the door panel which slip into holes drilled into the door metal. Using a flat stick, gently pry the panel off the door at the bottom, at the rear and half way up the front (there are 6 clips).

5. Disconnect the courtesy lamp electrical connector.

6. Lift the panel straight upward to release clips which retain it to the inside of the door by running down into the window slot.

7. If the watershield must be removed, carefully pull it off the retaining material.

8. To install the panel, first run new sealer around the door metal under the watershield and then stick the watershield to the door.

9. Hook the panel over the door at the window slit and hang it down over the door. Make

sure the retaining clips line up with their corresponding holes and then press the panel inward directly over each clip to engage it with the door. Connect the wire connector at the courtesy lamp.

10. Position the remote control bezel into the panel and slide it forward to install it. Install the retaining screw into the pull cup behind the armrest.

11. Install the crank handle at its original installation angle. Reconnect the battery.

H-Body: Lancer, LeBaron GTS
REAR DOOR WITH ELECTRIC REGULATOR

1. Roll the glass all the way down. Disconnect the negative battery cable.

2. Unsnap the window lift bezel and pull the switch out of the door panel just far enough to reach wiring. Note the wiring connector locations and disconnect them.

3. Follow Steps 2 through 10 of the procedure above.

4. Reconnect the electric window motor wiring connectors to the correct terminals. Locate the switch into the door panel and snap the bezel back in.

5. Reconnect the battery.

LeBaron

1. Lower the window all the way.

2. Remove the switch bezel and the radio speaker from the door.

3. Remove the screw from the opening in which the switch bezel was located.

4. Remove the 2 screws attaching the door panel from the through-slits in the carpeted area of the map pocket.

5. If the car has manually operated windows, remove the retaining Allen screw for the regulator handle from the center of the window regulator shaft. Note the installation angle of the regulator handle and then remove it. Remove the spacer behind the handle.

6. Pull the bottom of the trim panel outward carefully to disengage the the lower clips. Pull it out just far enough to gain access to the courtesy lamp connection. Then, reach behind the panel and disconnect the courtesy lamp wire.

7. Pull the panel in order to remove the remaining clips from the door. Lift the panel straight upward to release clips which retain it to the inside of the door by running down into the window slot.

8. If the watershield must be removed, carefully pull it off the retaining material.

9. To install the panel, first run new sealer around the door metal under the watershield and then stick the watershield to the door.

10. Hook the panel over the door at the win-

dow slit and hang it down over the door. Connect the wire connector at the courtesy lamp. Make sure the retaining clips line up with their corresponding holes and then press the panel inward directly over each clip to engage it with the door.

11. Reinstall the regulator handle at its original installation angle.

12. Install the 2 screws attaching the door panel working throught the slits in the carpeted area of the map pocket.

13. Install the panel retaining screw into the opening in which the switch bezel was located.

14. Install the switch bezel and the radio speaker into the door.

Door Locks

REMOVAL AND INSTALLATION

All Models Except Daytona & Laser

NOTE: *On Sundance, Shadow, Lancer and LeBaron GTS a Torx® screwdriver is required to remove the lock mechanism mounting screws.*

1. Raise the glass until it is up all the way. Remove the trim panel and plastic air shield as described above.

2. Disconnect the outside handle link and key cylinder link from the lock mechanism.

3. Disconnect the remote control link, remote latch lock link and, if the car has electric locks, the electric motor link.

4. Remove the three lock attaching screws and remove the lock through the access hole.

5. Reposition the lock inside the door through the access hole. Install the three attaching screws.

6. Reconnect the remote control link, remote latch lock link and, if the car has electric locks, the electric motor link.

7. Reconnect the outside handle link and key cylinder link from the lock mechanism.

8. Install the water shield and trim panel as described above. Adjust the latch as described above.

Daytona & Laser

NOTE: *If the car has electric door locks, you will need two short ¼-20 bolts and corresponding nuts.*

1. Roll the window down all the way. Disconnect the battery.

2. Remove the door panel as described above. Peel the water shield away at the top/rear to gain access to the hole located on the inside of the door and near the lock mechanism.

3. Raise the window all the way (if the car has electric windows, reconnect the battery to do this and then disconnect it again).

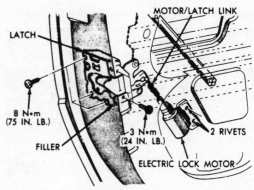

Door lock components on Daytona with electric locks

4. Disconnect the lock cylinder-to-lock link. Disconnect the outside handle-to-lock mechanism link.

5. Disconnect the inside handle-to-lock link and the inside remote lock actuator-to-lock link.

6. If the car is equipped with electric door locks, drill out the two rivets that retain the locking motor.

7. Remove the three bolts attaching the lock mechanism to the door. Remove the lock and, if the car has electric locks, the locking motor.

8. To install the mechanism, first transfer the locking motor to the new mechanism (on cars with electric locks).

9. Position the latach assembly on the door and install the three attaching bolts. Torque these bolts to 75 inch lbs.

10. If the car has electric locks, attach the locking motor to the door with two short ¼-20 bolts and corresponding nuts. Torque these to 90 inch lbs.

11. Connect the lock cylinder to the latch link.

12. Connect the outside handle to the latch link. Do the same with the inside handle.

13. Connect the inside lock remote switch to the latch link.

14. Lower the window all the way (temporarily connecting the battery on cars equipped with electric windows to do so). Then, install the air shield, water shield and trim panel as described above. Reconnect the battery.

Door Glass and Regulator

REMOVAL AND INSTALLATION

NOTE: *Window regulators are riveted to the door frame. The rivets must be drilled out and replaced by bolts or bolt/nut combinations of certain specification. Read through the procedure and make sure all parts are in hand before beginning work.*

Aries, Reliant, LeBaron, Town & Country

FRONT DOOR

1. Lower the glass all the way. Remove the trim panel as described above.

2. Gently pull the air and water shields off the door.

3. Remove the three nuts that attach the glass to the regulator channel. Then, lower the glass all the way.

4. Remove the outer glass-sealing weatherstrip by disengaging the spring clip tabs from the slots in the outer door panel. To do this, grasp the weatherstrip between the thumb and forefinger on either side of each spring clip. Pull out slightly and then up at each clip until the weatherstrip is free.

5. Work the glass off the mounting studs and remove it through the slot in the top of the lower door.

6. To remove the regulator, drive the center pin of each regulator mounting rivet out with a hammer and drift punch. Then, drill the rivets out with a ¼″ drill.

7. Disengage the regulator arm from the lift plate and then remove the regulator through the access hole in the inside of the door.

8. To install the new regulator, load it through the access hole and engage the access arm with the lift plate. Then, bolt the regulator to the door with ¼-20 nuts and short screws, *making sure these screws will not interfere with regulator operation.* Torque the screws and nuts to 90-115 inch lbs.

9. Install the new glass by lowering it into the door. Position the glass on the mounting studs.

10. Install the outer weatherstrip by sliding the clips into the door panel slots and sliding them downward until they lock.

11. Raise the glass to the top of its travel and then install the three retaining nuts, but without tightening them. Seat the glass fully in the upper glass run to adjust it, and then tighten the mounting nuts gently.

12. Install the air and water shields and the trim panel as described above.

Aries, Reliant, LeBaron, Town & Country, Caravelle, 600, New Yorker Turbo

REAR DOOR

1. Remove the trim panel as described above.

2. Remove the watershield and air shield. Remove the end seals from the front and rear of the door at the beltline.

3. Remove its two mounting bolts and remove the support bracket from underneath the fixed glass at the rear of the door.

4. Remove, from inside the door, the two

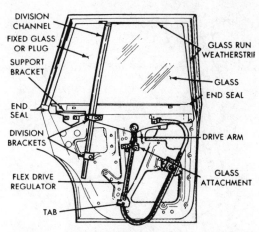

Rear door glass component locations on K and E models

brackets that attach the "division" channel (dividing the moveable and stationary glass sections).

5. Remove the glass run weatherstrip from the forward and top edges of the door where the moveable glass contacts it.

6. Remove the mounting screw from the top of the divison channel.

7. Remove the fixed glass.

8. Remove the outer glass-sealing weatherstrip by disengaging the spring clip tabs from the slots in the outer door panel. To do this, grasp the weatherstrip between the thumb and forefinger on either side of each spring clip. Pull out slightly and then up at each clip until the weatherstrip is free.

9. Remove the bolt (it has a shoulder on it) which attaches the glass to the drive arm of the flex drive mechanism.

10. Then, remove the division channel, moveable glass and drive arm together by raising the assembly. Rotate it 90 degrees, so the lower division channel bracket is parallel to the opening. Then, lift the assembly out through belt opening.

11. Drive the center pins from the 6 mounting rivets (7 with electric windows) for the regulator using a hammer and drift pin. Then drill the rivets out with a ¼″ drill. Then, rotate the regulator as necessary for clearance and remove it through the access hole in the door.

12. If re-using the same regulator, clean and lubricate the flex drive teeth. Then, orient the regulator so it can be installed through the access hole and locate it inside the door with its locating tab engaging the appropriate hole.

NOTE: *The torque sequence specified for the following step must be followed to prevent binding of the flex drive unit for the window.*

13. Use ¼-20 bolts and nuts to remount the

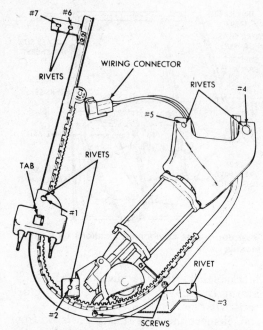

Follow the numerical sequence when remounting the rear door window regulator on K and E body cars

regulator, *tightening the nuts as specified in the illustration.* Torque to 90 inch lbs.

14. To install the new glass, start the bottom of the division channel, the glass, and the drive arm assembly into the belt opening. With the lower bracket parallel to the opening, lower the assembly into the door until the upper division channel bracket is near the belt opening.

15. Rotate the assembly 90 degrees to bring it into its normal orientation. Then, rest the channel on the bottom of the door.

16. Raise the glass by hand. Then, position the drive arm onto the flex drive and secure it with the bolt with the shoulder on it.

17. Install the outer glass-sealing weatherstrip.

18. Install the fixed-glass bracket, but do not tighten the bolts. Then, position the fixed-glass into the opening and rock it into position. Allow it to rest lightly on the support bracket.

19. Fit the rear edge of the division channel over the front edge of the fixed-glass. Then, install the mounting screw into the top of the division channel.

20. Install the glass run weatherstrip into the forward and top door channels.

21. Install the upper bracket retaining the division channel. Then, install the lower bracket retaining the division channel.

22. Push the fixed glass bracket upward and secure it in place.

23. Install the end seals at the belt opening. Install the air and water shields.

24. Install the door trim panel as described above.

G-Body: Daytona & Laser

CAUTION: *If the glass has shattered, wear gloves and work cautiously. Use a protective, heavy cloth to cover all painted surfaces, plastic parts, and interior trim near the glass. Remove the glass from the window frame before removing the gloves.*

1. Roll the window all the way down. Disconnect the battery.

2. Remove the trim panel and air and water shields as described above. Then, raise the glass until it is possible to work on the glass mounting nuts through the lower access hole (reconnecting the battery temporarily to operate the window motor, if the car has electric windows).

CAUTION: *If the glass is still in position, make sure to support it during the next step.*

3. Remove the three lift plate-to-glass attaching nuts.

4. Remove the two glass stabilizers. If the glass is intact, remove it through the window frame.

CAUTION: *If the glass has been shattered, wear gloves and goggles and then use a heavy duty vacuum to carefully remove all glass particles from the door and glass run at this point.*

5. Remove the lift plate-to-regulator screw and remove the lift plate from the door.

6. Using a hammer and drift punch, drive out the center pin in each of the 8 rivets (7 on cars with electric windows) that mount the regulator to the door. Then, drill out each rivet with a ¼″ drill.

7. Turn the regulator as necessary and then remove it through the access hole in the door.

8. Remove the flex window drive and install it onto the new regulator. Clean and lubricate the teeth.

9. Work the assembly back into the door through the access hole, and position it so its mounting holes line up with the holes where rivets where installed. Install ¼-20 bolts and

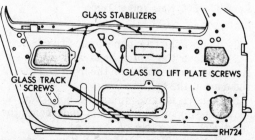

Location of components involved in removal/installation of door glass on Daytona and Laser

corresponding nuts to mount the regulator. Torque to 90 inch lbs.

10. Attach the lift plate to the regulator with an M6 x 25 bolt.

11. Attach the three glass-to-lift plate mounting studs to the new glass. Then, install the glass through the window opening. It must initially be cocked to the rear to work it into position and then leveled. Install the retaining nuts without tightening them.

12. Attach the two inner stabilizers without tightening them. Then, loosen the three glass track mounting screws.

13. Connect the battery if the car has electric windows and install the crank handle if it has manually operated windows. Then, guiding the glass, move the window up carefully until it has reached its uppermost position.

14. Tighten the three lift plate-to-glass attaching nuts, starting with the one in the middle, to 85 inch lbs.

15. Tighten the three glass track mounting screws to 115 inch lbs.

16. Adjust the inner glass stabilizers so they just touch the glass and then tighten them to 115 inch lbs.

17. Lower the glass and disconnect the battery or remove the window regulator handle. Install the door trim panel as described above.

Sundance & Shadow, Lancer, LeBaron, and LeBaron GTS

FRONT DOOR — MANUAL REGULATOR

WARNING *A special tool must be used to remove the glass, or the glass-run channel may be damaged. Use Miller Tool No. C-4867 or equivalent.*

1. Remove the door trim panel as described above. Carefully remove the watershield as described there also.

2. Lower the glass to gain the best possible access to the rear glass sliders. Then, use the special tool to disengage the sliders from the rear glass guide, holding the glass to keep it from rotating and falling.

3. Rotating the glass on the regulator roller, slide it rearward and lower the rear until it reaches a 45 degree angle. Then, remove it.

4. Temporarily install the regulator handle and set the position of the unit for easy access to the regulator mounting rivets (just below the position where the window would normally be all the way up).

5. Drill out the three rivets on the regulator with a ¼" drill. Then, slide the regulator off the glass lift channel. Cock the regulator to an appropriate angle and remove it through the access hole.

6. To install, angle the regulator appropri-

ately and work it through the access hole in the door.

7. Line up the regulator mounting and rivet holes and then install short ¼-20 bolts and nuts (it may be easier to install the bolts if you reset the position of the regulator by temporarily installing the handle). Torque the bolts to 90-115 in. lbs. and make sure they are short enough that they will not interfere with the moving parts as the window is raised and lowered.

8. Transfer the lift channel and sliders to the new glass. Then, slide the glass back into the door at the angle at which it was removed.

9. Rotate the glass to its normal position and slide it forward on the regulator roller in reverse of the removal procedure.

10. Position the glass for best possible access to the rear sliders, holding it to keep it from rotating and falling. Then, use the special tool to engage the sliders with the rear glass guide.

11. Install the watershield and trim panel as described above.

FRONT DOOR ELECTRIC REGULATOR

WARNING: *A special tool must be used to remove the glass, or the glass-run channel may be damaged. Use Miller Tool No. C-4867 or equivalent.*

1. Remove the door trim panel as described above. Carefully remove the watershield as described there also.

2. Follow Steps 2-3 of the procedure above to remove the glass from the door.

3. Adjust the position of the regulator until there is access to all the regulator mounting rivets (this is just below the position where the glass is all the way up).

4. Disconnect the negative battery cable. Then, disconnect the window motor electrical connector.

5. Drill out the 6 regulator mounting rivets with a ¼" drill. Then, slide the regulator off the glass channel.

6. Remove the motor from the regulator. Then, remove the regulator from the door, turning it as necessary so it will fit easily through the access hole.

7. If the regulator is being re-used, clean and lubricate the teeth on the flex drive rack. Then, load the regulator assembly through the door access panel.

8. Install the motor onto the regulator. Then, engage the regulator roller with the lift channel.

9. Line up the regulator mounting and rivet holes and then install short ¼-20 bolts and nuts (it may be easier to install the bolts if you reset the position of the regulator by temporarily installing the handle). Torque the bolts to

90-115 in. lbs. and make sure they are short enough that they will not interfere with the moving parts as the window is raised and lowered.

10. Connect the regulator wiring connector and the negative battery cable. Install the window as described in Steps 8-10 of the procedure above.

11. Install the watershield and trim panel as described above.

REAR DOOR MANUAL REGULATOR

Follow the procedure above for the front door, noting that there are only 34 mounting rivets for the regulator.

REAR DOOR ELECTRICAL REGULATOR

Follow the procedure above for the front door through Step 4. Remove the regulator-to-regulator arm bolt; then proceed with the remaining steps of the procedure. Note that the rear door electric window regulator is retained by only 5 mounting rivets.

Electric Window Motor
REMOVAL AND INSTALLATION
Conventional (Gear Type) Regulators

CAUTION: *The electric window regulator incorporates a very powerful spring which forces the window toward the top of the window frame at all times. Failure to ensure that the window is in this position before beginning this operation could result in a dangerous situation. The same is true of failing to support the window upward, in case a malfunction of this spring should occur.*

1. Remove the trim panel as described in the appropriate procedure above. Lower the window until it is in the full up position. Then, *securely* prop the window in this position.

2. Disconnect the negative battery cable. Then, disconnect the electric window motor electrical connector (located about 11 inches away from the motor in the wiring harness).

3. Remove the 3 mounting screws which attach the motor gearbox to the window regulator. On most models, there are three holes in the inner panel to provide access to these screws. On J body cars, go in through the opening in the inner panel and reach around to the rear of the regulator to gain access to these screws.

4. Remove the motor from the regulator by grabbing the motor housing and pulling it toward either the inner or outer panel.

CAUTION: *Keep fingers well away from the gears while disengaging the motor. Gears may turn a small amount, and could pinch!*

Rock or twist the motor as necessary to get it to disengage from the regulator.

5. To install the motor, position it onto the regulator, gaining access as during removal. Work the motor into a position that will ensure the motor gear engages the regulator sector teeth *and* the center post on the motor gearbox enters the pilot hole in the mounting plate. As the motor approaches its final position, rock it to ensure easy engagement of the gearteeth.

6. Align the motor screw holes with those in the mounting plate. Install the 3 motor gearbox screws and the single tiedown bracket screw. Torque them to 50-60 in. lbs.

7. Remove the blocking device. Connect the multiprong connector and then the battery.

Flex-Drive Type Regulators

NOTE: *To perform this procedure, a center punch, a ¼" drill, and 7 #8-32 x ½" screws are required.*

1. Remove the trim panel as described in the appropriate procedure above. Then, the screw that attaches the flexible rack to the drive arm must be removed. Adjust the position of the window up and down until the position is right for access to this screw and then remove it. Now, *securely* prop the window in this position. If the motor will not operate on its own, try assisting it cautiously. If this fails, see the note below.

2. Disconnect the battery. Disconnect the motor electrical connector.

3. Remove the regulator/ motor attaching rivets by knocking out the rivet center mandrels with a hammer and the center punch. Then, drill the rivets out with the ¼" drill.

4. Start the motor end of the flex drive regu-

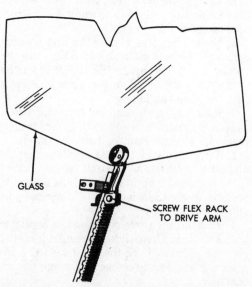

GLASS

SCREW FLEX RACK TO DRIVE ARM

The location of the flexible rack-to-drive arm screw

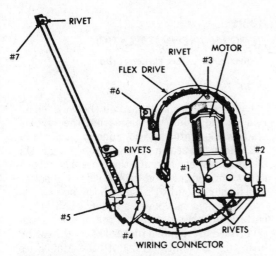

Follow the numerical sequence when remounting the flex-drive regulator with screws

lator out through the largest access hole in the door panel, maneuvering and rotating the unit out. Remove the screws attaching the motor to the flexible track.

NOTE: *If the motor will not move, it will be necessary follow steps 2 and 3 to drill out the attaching rivets. Then, move the motor/flexible drive assembly as necessary to gain access to the screws mounting the motor to the flex drive. Manually lift the window upward until it is possible to access the screw that attaches the flexible rack to the drive arm and then remove it.*

6. Remove the 2 screws attaching the motor to the flex drive.

7. To install the motor, feed the top of the flexible drive track into the access hole and then rotate it toward the door pillar until the motor is horizontal. Then, rotate the assembly in the opposite direction to align the bracket tab with the slot in the inner door panel.

8. Install the mounting screws and torque them to 40 inch lbs. in the sequence shown.

9. Connect the motor electrical connector. Reconnect the battery. Position the window drive so the flex rack fitting lines uop with the window drive arm. Install the screw and torque to 40 in. lbs. Remove the window prop.

Inside Rear View Mirror
REPLACEMENT

The mirror is mechanically attached to the mirror button, and if it should become cracked or develop a a mechanical problem which prevents easy adjustment, it can be replaced very simply by disconnecting it from the button. The button, in turn, serves to mount the mirror to the windshield. If it should be damaged or the adhesive bond should become partly broken, it can be removed and replaced after the mirror is detached. Note that removal of the button and/ or remaining adhesive requires the use of a controllable electric heat gun. Also needed, if the button must be replaced, are a rag soaked in alcohol, ordinary kitchen cleanser, and fine-grit sandpaper. The new button is installed using a special adhesive kit 4054099 or an equivalent available in the aftermarket.

1. Loosen the setscrew with a standard screwdriver until all tension is removed. Slide the base of the mirror upward and off the mounting button.

2. If the mirror mounting button must be removed, first mark the location of the button on the outside of the windshield with a wax pencil. Then, apply low heat with the electric heat gun to soften the vinyl. When it is soft, peel the button off the glass.

3. Clean the surface of the windshield where the button was mounted with a rag soaked in alcohol and the cleanser. Then, wipe the surface with an alcohol soaked rag. Do not touch this area of the windshield glass!

4. Crush the vial in the plastic housing of the accelerator in the new button kit to saturate the applicator.

5. Remove the paper sleeve and then apply a generous amount of the accelerator to the onto the mounting surface of the mirror button.

6. Allow the accelerator to dry for 5 minutes; during this time, be careful not to touch the mounting surface of the button.

7. Apply a thin film of the accelerator to the iner surface of the windshield where the button will be mounted. Allow this to dry for 1 minute.

8. Apply one drop of the adhesive to the center of the mounting surface of the button.

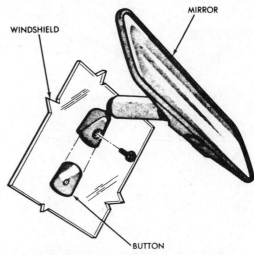

The mounting of the rearview mirror to the button and windshield

Then, use the bottom of the adhesive tube, distribute the adhesive evenly over the entire button bonding surface.

NOTE: *Precise alignment of the button is essential in the following step from the beginning, as the adhesive sets up very fast!*

9. Position the bottom edge of the button against the lower edge of the mark made earlier with the button lined up side-to-side. Then, rock the button upward until it touches the windshield over its entire surface. Press it firmly to the glass and hold it there firmly for 1 full minute.

10. Remove the pressure, but allow 5 minutes more time for the button mounting adhesive to dry.

11. With an alcohol-dampened cloth, remove any adhesive which may have spread beyond the mounting surface of the button.

WARNING: *Be careful not to overtighten the mirror mounting screw in the following procedure, as the mirror mounting button could be distorted, destroying its bond with the windshield.*

12. Slide the mirror downward and over the mount. Tighten the screw gently!

Seats

REMOVAL AND INSTALLATION

Caravelle, 600, New Yorker Turbo

FRONT

1. Move the seat forward all the way. Then, remove the mounting nuts from the vertical studs welded into the floor (one on each side).

2. Move the seat all the way to the rear. On all but power bench seats, there are 2 bolts, oriented horizontally, on either side (on power bench there is only 1). Remove the bolts.

3. If the car has power seats, disconnect the battery and then disconnect the motor electrical connector. Remove the seat from the car by lifting upward on the rear until the stud clears the mounting hole in the frame and then lifting and angling the seat as necessary to maneuver it out. If the seat must be detached from the mounting frame, remove the four nuts from the studs and separate the two.

4. To install the seat, first, attach it to the frame and install the attaching nuts, torquing them to 250 inch lbs. Then, install the assembled seat into the car, positioning the forward

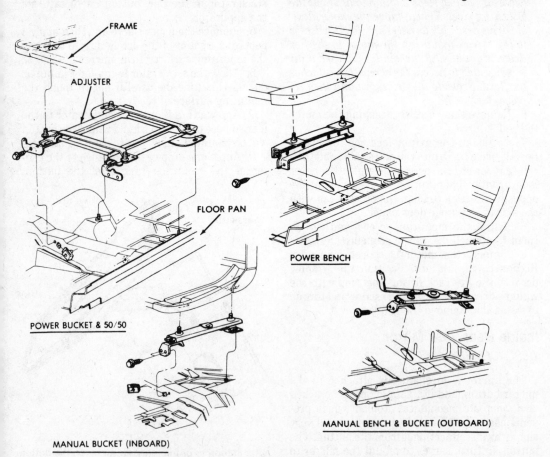

E-Body seat mountings for 1986–88 models

mount over the beam on the floor, shifting the seat side-to-side to line up the boltholes in the frame and beam. Then, tilt the seat rearward to cause the rear of the frame to sit down over the stud. Install the bolts and nuts and torque to 250 inch lbs.

Aries, Reliant, LeBaron, Town & Country

FRONT

1. Move the seat forward all the way. Then, remove the mounting bolts from the crossmember. Note that bucket seats use a nut and washer, accessible from underneath, to retain the bolt at the rear.
2. Move the seat all the way to the rear. Remove the bolts (one on either side) that retain the seat adjuster frame at the front. These sit in a horizontal postion.
3. If the car has power seats, disconnect the battery and then disconnect the motor electrical connector. Remove the seat from the car by lifting it upward and out. If the seat must be detached from the mounting frame, remove the four nuts from the studs and separate the two.
4. To install the seat, first, attach it to the frame and install the attaching nuts, torquing them to 250 inch lbs. Then, install the assembled seat into the car, positioning the forward mount over the beam on the floor, shifting the seat side-to-side to line up the boltholes in the frame and beam. Install the bolts and nuts and torque to 250 inch lbs.

1986-88
Caravelle, 600, New Yorker Turbo Aries, Reliant, LeBaron, Town & Country

REAR BENCH SEAT

1. To remove the rear cushion, remove the 2 screws from the underside of the front of the rear seat cushion. Remove the cushion from the vehicle.
2. To remove the seat back, remove the 2 screws from the bottom/rear of the seat back. Then, unsnap the 2 seatbelt retainers. Lift the seat back upward to disengage the seatback wires from the support pockets.
3. Install the seatback and rear cushion by reversing the removal procedure.

Daytona, Laser, Lancer, LeBaron GTS, LeBaron, Sundance & Shadow

FRONT SEAT

1. Move the seat forward all the way. Remove the mounting nuts attaching the seat to the floor at the rear.
2. Move the seat all the way to the rear and remove the two seat frame-to-crossmember bolts, located horizontally, from the front on either side. Remove the seat.

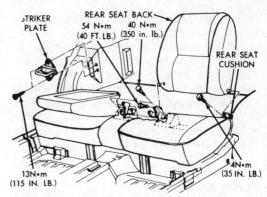

Rear seat mountings on Daytona and Laser

3. Install in reverse order, torquing the nuts/bolts to 250 inch lbs.

Daytona and Laser

REAR SEAT

The seat backs are hinged. The hinge mounting bolts are accessible directly under the seat back. Remove the bolt on either side to remove the seat back. To install, reverse the procedure, torquing the bolt to 350 inch lbs.

The seat cushions are bolted to the floor pan. Remove the mounting bolt at the rear on either side and remove the seat cushion. Reverse the procedure to install, torquing the bolts to 40 ft. lbs.

1986-88
Lancer, LeBaron GTS, Sundance, Shadow, LeBaron

REAR SEAT CUSHION

The rear seat cushion is bolted to the floorpan. Simply remove the bolts and remove the cushion. Install in reverse order.

REAR BENCH SEAT BACK

1. Peel back the corner of the carpet from the back of the rear seat by pulling it free from the Velcro® retainers.
2. Remove the seat back-to-hinge arm screws from both sides. Remove the seat back.
3. Reverse this procedure to install the seat back.

REAR 60/40 SEAT BACK

To remove the seat back, simply remove the seat back-to-hinge arm screws from the seat back. Then, remove the seat back. Reverse the procedure to install the seat back.

1981-85 Cars

REAR SEAT CUSHION AND BACK

1. To remove the rear seat cushion, remove the 2 screws from the underside of the rear seat

cushion and remove it from the vehicle. Install it in reverse order.

2. To remove the seat back, first remove the 2 screws from the bottom of the seat back. Then, unsnap the 2 seat belt retainers.

3. Remove the seat back by lifting it upward so as to disengage the seatback retaining wires from the support pockets.

4. To install the seat back, lower it into position so as to engage the retaining wires.

Power Seat Motor

REMOVAL AND INSTALLATION

1. Move the seat adjuster as required for easy access to the mounting bolts, if possible. Remove the adjuster mounting bolts/nuts from the floor pan.

2. Disconnect the battery negative cable.

Disconnect the wiring harness motor connector at the carpet. Then, remove the seat from the car.

3. Lay the seat on its back on a clean surface. Then, remove the motor mounting screws from the motor bracket and the single mounting bolt from the adjuster.

4. Note the routing of cable to the motor. Then, carefully disconnect the housing and cables from the motor assembly. Remove the motor.

5. To install the motor, first position it in its mounted position. Then, connect the cables and the housing to the motor.

6. Install the transmission-to-motor mounting screws. Install the bolt fastening the motor to the adjuster. Then, install the seat in reverse of the removal procedure. Reconnect the wiring harness connector and the battery negative cable.

General Conversion Table

Multiply By	To Convert	To	
		LENGTH	
2.54	Inches	Centimeters	.3937
25.4	Inches	Millimeters	.03937
30.48	Feet	Centimeters	.0328
.304	Feet	Meters	3.28
.914	Yards	Meters	1.094
1.609	Miles	Kilometers	.621
		VOLUME	
.473	Pints	Liters	2.11
.946	Quarts	Liters	1.06
3.785	Gallons	Liters	.264
.016	Cubic inches	Liters	61.02
16.39	Cubic inches	Cubic cms.	.061
28.3	Cubic feet	Liters	.0353
		MASS (Weight)	
28.35	Ounces	Grams	.035
.4536	Pounds	Kilograms	2.20
—	To obtain	From	Multiply by

Multiply By	To Convert	To	
		AREA	
.645	Square inches	Square cms.	.155
.836	Square yds.	Square meters	1.196
		FORCE	
4.448	Pounds	Newtons	.225
.138	Ft./lbs.	Kilogram/meters	7.23
1.36	Ft./lbs.	Newton-meters	.737
.112	In./lbs.	Newton-meters	8.844
		PRESSURE	
.068	Psi	Atmospheres	14.7
6.89	Psi	Kilopascals	.145
		OTHER	
1.104	Horsepower (DIN)	Horsepower (SAE)	.9861
.746	Horsepower (SAE)	Kilowatts (KW)	1.34
1.60	Mph	Km/h	.625
.425	Mpg	Km/1	2.35
—	To obtain	From	Multiply by

Tap Drill Sizes

National Coarse or U.S.S.

Screw & Tap Size	Threads Per Inch	Use Drill Number
No. 5	40	.39
No. 6	32	.36
No. 8	32	.29
No. 10	24	.25
No. 12	24	.17
1/4	20	8
5/16	18	F
3/8	16	5/16
7/16	14	U
1/2	13	27/64
9/16	12	31/64
5/8	11	17/32
3/4	10	21/32
7/8	9	49/64

National Coarse or U.S.S.

Screw & Tap Size	Threads Per Inch	Use Drill Number
1	8	7/8
1 1/8	7	63/64
1 1/4	7	1 7/64
1 1/2	6	1 11/32

National Fine or S.A.E.

Screw & Tap Size	Threads Per Inch	Use Drill Number
No. 5	44	.37
No. 6	40	.33
No. 8	36	.29
No. 10	32	.21

National Fine or S.A.E.

Screw & Tap Size	Threads Per Inch	Use Drill Number
No. 12	28	.15
1/4	28	3
6/16	24	1
3/8	24	Q
7/16	20	W
1/2	20	29/64
9/16	18	33/64
5/8	18	37/64
3/4	16	11/16
7/8	14	13/16
1 1/8	12	1 3/64
1 1/4	12	1 11/64
1 1/2	12	1 27/64

Drill Sizes In Decimal Equivalents

Inch	Decimal	Wire	mm
1/64	.0156		.39
	.0157		.4
	.0160	78	
	.0165		.42
	.0173		.44
	.0177		.45
	.0180	77	
	.0181		.46
	.0189		.48
	.0197		.5
	.0200	76	
	.0210	75	
	.0217		.55
	.0225	74	
	.0236		.6
	.0240	73	
	.0250	72	
	.0256		.65
	.0260	71	
	.0276		.7
	.0280	70	
	.0292	69	
	.0295		.75
	.0310	68	
1/32	.0312		.79
	.0315		.8
	.0320	67	
	.0330	66	
	.0335		.85
	.0350	65	
	.0354		.9
	.0360	64	
	.0370	63	
	.0374		.95
	.0380	62	
	.0390	61	
	.0394		1.0
	.0400	60	
	.0410	59	
	.0413		1.05
	.0420	58	
	.0430	57	
	.0433		1.1
	.0453		1.15
3/64	.0465	56	
	.0469		1.19
	.0472		1.2
	.0492		1.25
	.0512		1.3
	.0520	55	
	.0531		1.35
	.0550	54	
	.0551		1.4
	.0571		1.45
	.0591		1.5
	.0595	53	
	.0610		1.55
1/16	.0625		1.59
	.0630		1.6
	.0635	52	
	.0650		1.65
	.0669		1.7
	.0670	51	
	.0689		1.75
	.0700	50	
	.0709		1.8
	.0728		1.85

Inch	Decimal	Wire	mm
	.0730	49	
	.0748		1.9
	.0760	48	
	.0768		1.95
5/64	.0781		1.98
	.0785	47	
	.0787		2.0
	.0807		2.05
	.0810	46	
	.0820	45	
	.0827		2.1
	.0846		2.15
	.0860	44	
	.0866		2.2
	.0886		2.25
	.0890	43	
	.0906		2.3
	.0925		2.35
	.0935	42	
3/32	.0938		2.38
	.0945		2.4
	.0960	41	
	.0965		2.45
	.0980	40	
	.0981		2.5
	.0995	39	
	.1015	38	
	.1024		2.6
	.1040	37	
	.1063		2.7
	.1065	36	
	.1083		2.75
7/64	.1094		2.77
	.1100	35	
	.1102		2.8
	.1110	34	
	.1130	33	
	.1142		2.9
	.1160	32	
	.1181		3.0
	.1200	31	
	.1220		3.1
1/8	.1250		3.17
	.1260		3.2
	.1280		3.25
	.1285	30	
	.1299		3.3
	.1339		3.4
	.1360	29	
	.1378		3.5
	.1405	28	
9/64	.1406		3.57
	.1417		3.6
	.1440	27	
	.1457		3.7
	.1470	26	
	.1476		3.75
	.1495	25	
	.1496		3.8
	.1520	24	
	.1535		3.9
	.1540	23	
5/32	.1562		3.96
	.1570	22	
	.1575		4.0
	.1590	21	
	.1610	20	

Inch	Decimal	Wire & Letter	mm
	.1614		4.1
	.1654		4.2
	.1660	19	
	.1673		4.25
	.1693		4.3
	.1695	18	
11/64	.1719		4.36
	.1730	17	
	.1732		4.4
	.1770	16	
	.1772		4.5
	.1800	15	
	.1811		4.6
	.1820	14	
	.1850	13	
	.1850		4.7
	.1870		4.75
3/16	.1875		4.76
	.1890		4.8
	.1890	12	
	.1910	11	
	.1929		4.9
	.1935	10	
	.1960	9	
	.1969		5.0
	.1990	8	
	.2008		5.1
	.2010	7	
13/64	.2031		5.16
	.2040	6	
	.2047		5.2
	.2055	5	
	.2067		5.25
	.2087		5.3
	.2090	4	
	.2126		5.4
	.2130	3	
	.2165		5.5
7/32	.2188		5.55
	.2205		5.6
	.2210	2	
	.2244		5.7
	.2264		5.75
	.2280	1	
	.2283		5.8
	.2323		5.9
	.2340	A	
15/64	.2344		5.95
	.2362		6.0
	.2380	B	
	.2402		6.1
	.2420	C	
	.2441		6.2
	.2460	D	
	.2461		6.25
	.2480		6.3
1/4	.2500	E	6.35
	.2520		6.
	.2559		6.5
	.2570	F	
	.2598		6.6
	.2610	G	
	.2638		6.7
17/64	.2656		6.74
	.2657		6.75
	.2660	H	
	.2677		6.8

Inch	Decimal	Letter	mm
	.2717		6.9
	.2720	I	
7/16	.2756		7.0
	.2770	J	
	.2795		7.1
	.2810	K	
9/32	.2812		7.14
	.2835		7.2
	.2854		7.25
	.2874		7.3
	.2900	L	
	.2913		7.4
	.2950	M	
	.2953		7.5
19/64	.2969		7.54
	.2992		7.6
	.3020	N	
	.3031		7.7
	.3051		7.75
	.3071		7.8
	.3110		7.9
5/16	.3125		7.93
	.3150		8.0
	.3160	O	
	.3189		8.1
	.3228		8.2
	.3230	P	
	.3248		8.25
	.3268		8.3
21/64	.3281		8.33
	.3307		8.4
	.3320	Q	
	.3346		8.5
	.3386		8.6
	.3390	R	
	.3425		8.7
11/32	.3438		8.73
	.3445		8.75
	.3465		8.8
	.3480	S	
	.3504		8.9
	.3543		9.0
	.3580	T	
	.3583		9.1
23/64	.3594		9.12
	.3622		9.2
	.3642		9.25
	.3661		9.3
	.3680	U	
	.3701		9.4
	.3740		9.5
3/8	.3750		9.52
	.3770	V	
	.3780		9.6
	.3819		9.7
	.3839		9.75
	.3858		9.8
	.3860	W	
	.3898		9.9
25/64	.3906		9.92
	.3937		10.0
	.3970	X	
	.4040	Y	
13/32	.4062		10.31
	.4130	Z	
	.4134		10.5
27/64	.4219		10.71

Inch	Decimal	mm
	.4331	11.0
7/16	.4375	11.11
	.4528	11.5
29/64	.4531	11.51
15/32	.4688	11.90
	.4724	12.0
31/64	.4844	12.30
	.4921	12.5
1/2	.5000	12.70
	.5118	13.0
33/64	.5156	13.09
17/32	.5312	13.49
	.5315	13.5
35/64	.5469	13.89
	.5512	14.0
9/16	.5625	14.28
	.5709	14.5
37/64	.5781	14.68
	.5906	15.0
19/32	.5938	15.08
39/64	.6094	15.47
	.6102	15.5
5/8	.6250	15.87
	.6299	16.0
41/64	.6406	16.27
	.6496	16.5
21/32	.6562	16.66
	.6693	17.0
43/64	.6719	17.06
11/16	.6875	17.46
	.6890	17.5
45/64	.7031	17.85
	.7087	18.0
23/32	.7188	18.25
	.7283	18.5
47/64	.7344	18.65
	.7480	19.0
3/4	.7500	19.05
49/64	.7656	19.44
	.7677	19.5
25/32	.7812	19.84
	.7874	20.0
51/64	.7969	20.24
	.8071	20.5
13/16	.8125	20.63
	.8268	21.0
53/64	.8281	21.03
27/32	.8438	21.43
	.8465	21.5
55/64	.8594	21.82
	.8661	22.0
7/8	.8750	22.22
	.8858	22.5
57/64	.8906	22.62
	.9055	23.0
29/32	.9062	23.01
59/64	.9219	23.41
	.9252	23.5
15/16	.9375	23.81
	.9449	24.0
61/64	.9531	24.2
	.9646	24.5
31/32	.9688	24.6
	.9843	25.0
63/64	.9844	25.0
1	1.0000	25.4

AIR/FUEL RATIO: The ratio of air to gasoline by weight in the fuel mixture drawn into the engine.

AIR INJECTION: One method of reducing harmful exhaust emissions by injecting air into each of the exhaust ports of an engine. The fresh air entering the hot exhaust manifold causes any remaining fuel to be burned before it can exit the tailpipe.

ALTERNATOR: A device used for converting mechanical energy into electrical energy.

AMMETER: An instrument, calibrated in amperes, used to measure the flow of an electrical current in a circuit. Ammeters are always connected in series with the circuit being tested.

AMPERE: The rate of flow of electrical current present when one volt of electrical pressure is applied against one ohm of electrical resistance.

ANALOG COMPUTER: Any microprocessor that uses similar (analogous) electrical signals to make its calculations.

ARMATURE: A laminated, soft iron core wrapped by a wire that converts electrical energy to mechanical energy as in a motor or relay. When rotated in a magnetic field, it changes mechanical energy into electrical energy as in a generator.

ATMOSPHERIC PRESSURE: The pressure on the Earth's surface caused by the weight of the air in the atmosphere. At sea level, this pressure is 14.7 psi at 32°F (101 kPa at 0°C).

ATOMIZATION: The breaking down of a liquid into a fine mist that can be suspended in air.

AXIAL PLAY: Movement parallel to a shaft or bearing bore.

BACKFIRE: The sudden combustion of gases in the intake or exhaust system that results in a loud explosion.

BACKLASH: The clearance or play between two parts, such as meshed gears.

BACKPRESSURE: Restrictions in the exhaust system that slow the exit of exhaust gases from the combustion chamber.

BAKELITE: A heat resistant, plastic insulator material commonly used in printed circuit boards and transistorized components.

BALL BEARING: A bearing made up of hardened inner and outer races between which hardened steel ball roll.

BALLAST RESISTOR: A resistor in the primary ignition circuit that lowers voltage after the engine is started to reduce wear on ignition components.

BEARING: A friction reducing, supportive device usually located between a stationary part and a moving part.

BIMETAL TEMPERATURE SENSOR: Any sensor or switch made of two dissimilar types of metal that bend when heated or cooled due to the different expansion rates of the alloys. These types of sensors usually function as an on/off switch.

BLOWBY: Combustion gases, composed of water vapor and unburned fuel, that leak past the piston rings into the crankcase during normal engine operation. These gases are removed by the PCV system to prevent the build-up of harmful acids in the crankcase.

BRAKE PAD: A brake shoe and lining assembly used with disc brakes.

BRAKE SHOE: The backing for the brake lining. The term is, however, usually applied to the assembly of the brake backing and lining.

BUSHING: A liner, usually removable, for a bearing; an anti-friction liner used in place of a bearing.

BYPASS: System used to bypass ballast resistor during engine cranking to increase voltage supplied to the coil.

CALIPER: A hydraulically activated device in a disc brake system, which is mounted straddling the brake rotor (disc). The caliper contains at least one piston and two brake pads. Hydraulic pressure on the piston(s) forces the pads against the rotor.

CAMSHAFT: A shaft in the engine on which are the lobes (cams) which operate the valves. The camshaft is driven by the crankshaft, via a belt, chain or gears, at one half the crankshaft speed.

CAPACITOR: A device which stores an electrical charge.

CARBON MONOXIDE (CO): a colorless, odorless gas given off as a normal byproduct of combustion. It is poisonous and extremely dangerous in confined areas, building up slowly to toxic levels without warning if adequate ventilation is not available.

CARBURETOR: A device, usually mounted on the intake manifold of an engine, which mixes the air and fuel in the proper proportion to allow even combustion.

CATALYTIC CONVERTER: A device installed in the exhaust system, like a muffler, that converts harmful byproducts of combustion into carbon dioxide and water vapor by means of a heat-producing chemical reaction.

CENTRIFUGAL ADVANCE: A mechanical method of advancing the spark timing by using flyweights in the distributor that react to centrifugal force generated by the distributor shaft rotation.

CHECK VALVE: Any one-way valve installed to permit the flow of air, fuel or vacuum in one direction only.

CHOKE: A device, usually a moveable valve, placed in the intake path of a carburetor to restrict the flow of air.

CIRCUIT: Any unbroken path through which an electrical current can flow. Also used to describe fuel flow in some instances.

CIRCUIT BREAKER: A switch which protects an electrical circuit from overload by opening the circuit when the current flow exceeds a predetermined level. Some circuit breakers must be reset manually, while other reset automatically

COIL (IGNITION): A transformer in the ignition circuit which steps of the voltage provided to the spark plugs.

COMBINATION MANIFOLD: An assembly which includes both the intake and exhaust manifolds in one casting.

COMBINATION VALVE: A device used in some fuel systems that routes fuel vapors to a charcoal storage canister instead of venting

them into the atmosphere. The valve relieves fuel tank pressure and allows fresh air into the tank as fuel level drops to prevent a vapor lock situation.

COMPRESSION RATIO: The comparison of the total volume of the cylinder and combustion chamber with the piston at BDC and the piston at TDC.

CONDENSER: 1. An electrical device which acts to store an electrical charge, preventing voltage surges.
2. A radiator-like device in the air conditioning system in which refrigerant gas condenses into a liquid, giving off heat.

CONDUCTOR: Any material through which an electrical current can be transmitted easily.

CONTINUITY: Continuous or complete circuit. Can be checked with an ohmmeter.

COUNTERSHAFT: An intermediate shaft which is rotated by a mainshaft and transmits, in turn, that rotation to a working part.

CRANKCASE: The lower part of an engine in which the crankshaft and related parts operate.

CRANKSHAFT: The main driving shaft of an engine which receives reciprocating motion from the pistons and converts it to rotary motion.

CYLINDER: In an engine, the round hole in the engine block in which the piston(s) ride.

CYLINDER BLOCK: The main structural member of an engine in which is found the cylinders, crankshaft and other principal parts.

CYLINDER HEAD: The detachable portion of the engine, fastened, usually, to the top of the cylinder block, containing all or most of the combustion chambers. On overhead valve engines, it contains the valves and their operating parts. On overhead cam engines, it contains the camshaft as well.

DEAD CENTER: The extreme top or bottom of the piston stroke.

DETONATION: An unwanted explosion of the air fuel mixture in the combustion chamber caused by excess heat and compression, advanced timing, or an overly lean mixture. Also referred to as "ping".

DIAPHRAGM: A thin, flexible wall separating two cavities, such as in a vacuum advance unit.

DIESELING: A condition in which hot spots in the combustion chamber cause the engine to run on after the key is turned off.

DIFFERENTIAL: A geared assembly which allows the transmission of motion between drive axles, giving one axle the ability to turn faster than the other.

DIODE: An electrical device that will allow current to flow in one direction only.

DISC BRAKE: A hydraulic braking assembly consisting of a brake disc, or rotor, mounted on an axle, and a caliper assembly containing, usually two brake pads which are activated by hydraulic pressure. The pads are forced against the sides of the disc, creating friction which slows the vehicle.

DISTRIBUTOR: A mechanically driven device on an engine which is responsible for electrically firing the spark plug at a predetermined point of the piston stroke.

DOWEL PIN: A pin, inserted in mating holes in two different parts allowing those parts to maintain a fixed relationship.

DRUM BRAKE: A braking system which consists of two brake shoes and one or two wheel cylinders, mounted on a fixed backing plate, and a brake drum, mounted on an axle, which revolves around the assembly. Hydraulic action applied to the wheel cylinders forces the shoes outward against the drum, creating friction and slowing the vehicle.

DWELL: The rate, measured in degrees of shaft rotation, at which an electrical circuit cycles on and off.

ELECTRONIC CONTROL UNIT (ECU): Ignition module, module, amplifier or igniter. See Module for definition.

ELECTRONIC IGNITION: A system in which the timing and firing of the spark plugs is controlled by an electronic control unit, usually called a module. These systems have not points or condenser.

ENDPLAY: The measured amount of axial movement in a shaft.

ENGINE: A device that converts heat into mechanical energy.

EXHAUST MANIFOLD: A set of cast passages or pipes which conduct exhaust gases from the engine.

FEELER GAUGE: A blade, usually metal, of precisely predetermined thickness, used to measure the clearance between two parts. These blades usually are available in sets of assorted thicknesses.

F-Head: An engine configuration in which the intake valves are in the cylinder head, while the camshaft and exhaust valves are located in the cylinder block. The camshaft operates the intake valves via lifters and pushrods, while it operates the exhaust valves directly.

FIRING ORDER: The order in which combustion occurs in the cylinders of an engine. Also the order in which spark is distributed to the plugs by the distributor.

FLATHEAD: An engine configuration in which the camshaft and all the valves are located in the cylinder block.

FLOODING: The presence of too much fuel in the intake manifold and combustion chamber which prevents the air/fuel mixture from firing, thereby causing a no-start situation.

FLYWHEEL: A disc shaped part bolted to the rear end of the crankshaft. Around the outer perimeter is affixed the ring gear. The starter drive engages the ring gear, turning the flywheel, which rotates the crankshaft, imparting the initial starting motion to the engine.

FOOT POUND (ft.lb. or sometimes, ft. lbs.): The amount of energy or work needed to raise an item weighing one pound, a distance of one foot.

FUSE: A protective device in a circuit which prevents circuit overload by breaking the circuit when a specific amperage is present. The device is constructed around a strip or wire of a lower amperage rating than the circuit it is designed to protect. When an amperage higher than that stamped on the fuse is present in the circuit, the strip or wire melts, opening the circuit.

GEAR RATIO: The ratio between the number of teeth on meshing gears.

GENERATOR: A device which converts mechanical energy into electrical energy.

HEAT RANGE: The measure of a spark plug's ability to dissipate heat from its firing end. The higher the heat range, the hotter the plug fires.

HUB: The center part of a wheel or gear.

HYDROCARBON (HC): Any chemical compound made up of hydrogen and carbon. A major pollutant formed by the engine as a byproduct of combustion.

HYDROMETER: An instrument used to measure the specific gravity of a solution.

INCH POUND (in.lb. or sometimes, in. lbs.): One twelfth of a foot pound.

INDUCTION: A means of transferring electrical energy in the form of a magnetic field. Principle used in the ignition coil to increase voltage.

INJECTION PUMP: A device, usually mechanically operated, which meters and delivers fuel under pressure to the fuel injector.

INJECTOR: A device which receives metered fuel under relatively low pressure and is activated to inject the fuel into the engine under relatively high pressure at a predetermined time.

INPUT SHAFT: The shaft to which torque is applied, usually carrying the driving gear or gears.

INTAKE MANIFOLD: A casting of passages or pipes used to conduct air or a fuel/air mixture to the cylinders.

JOURNAL: The bearing surface within which a shaft operates.

KEY: A small block usually fitted in a notch between a shaft and a hub to prevent slippage of the two parts.

MANIFOLD: A casting of passages or set of pipes which connect the cylinders to an inlet or outlet source.

MANIFOLD VACUUM: Low pressure in an engine intake manifold formed just below the throttle plates. Manifold vacuum is highest at idle and drops under acceleration.

MASTER CYLINDER: The primary fluid pressurizing device in a hydraulic system. In automotive use, it is found in brake and hydraulic clutch systems and is pedal activated, either directly or, in a power brake system, through the power booster.

MODULE: Electronic control unit, amplifier or igniter of solid state or integrated design which controls the current flow in the ignition primary circuit based on input from the pickup coil. When the module opens the primary circuit, the high secondary voltage is induced in the coil.

NEEDLE BEARING: A bearing which consists of a number (usually a large number) of long, thin rollers.

OHM: (Ω) The unit used to measure the resistance of conductor to electrical flow. One ohm is the amount of resistance that limits current flow to one ampere in a circuit with one volt of pressure.

OHMMETER: An instrument used for measuring the resistance, in ohms, in an electrical circuit.

OUTPUT SHAFT: The shaft which transmits torque from a device, such as a transmission.

OVERDRIVE: A gear assembly which produces more shaft revolutions than that transmitted to it.

OVERHEAD CAMSHAFT (OHC): An engine configuration in which the camshaft is mounted on top of the cylinder head and operates the valve either directly or by means of rocker arms.

OVERHEAD VALVE (OHV): An engine configuration in which all of the valves are located in the cylinder head and the camshaft is located in the cylinder block. The camshaft operates the valves via lifters and pushrods.

OXIDES OF NITROGEN (NOx): Chemical compounds of nitrogen produced as a byproduct of combustion. They combine with hydrocarbons to produce smog.

OXYGEN SENSOR: Used with the feedback system to sense the presence of oxygen in the exhaust gas and signal the computer which can reference the voltage signal to an air/fuel ratio.

PINION: The smaller of two meshing gears.

PISTON RING: An open ended ring which fits into a groove on the outer diameter of the piston. Its chief function is to form a seal between the piston and cylinder wall. Most automotive pistons have three rings: two for compression sealing; one for oil sealing.

PRELOAD: A predetermined load placed on a bearing during assembly or by adjustment.

PRIMARY CIRCUIT: Is the low voltage side of the ignition system which consists of the ignition switch, ballast resistor or resistance wire, bypass, coil, electronic control unit and pick-up coil as well as the connecting wires and harnesses.

PRESS FIT: The mating of two parts under pressure, due to the inner diameter of one being smaller than the outer diameter of the other, or vice versa; an interference fit.

RACE: The surface on the inner or outer ring of a bearing on which the balls, needles or rollers move.

REGULATOR: A device which maintains the amperage and/or voltage levels of a circuit at predetermined values.

RELAY: A switch which automatically opens and/or closes a circuit.

RESISTANCE: The opposition to the flow of current through a circuit or electrical device, and is measured in ohms. Resistance is equal to the voltage divided by the amperage.

RESISTOR: A device, usually made of wire, which offers a preset amount of resistance in an electrical circuit.

RING GEAR: The name given to a ring-shaped gear attached to a differential case, or affixed to a flywheel or as part a planetary gear set.

ROLLER BEARING: A bearing made up of hardened inner and outer races between which hardened steel rollers move.

ROTOR: 1. The disc-shaped part of a disc brake assembly, upon which the brake pads bear; also called, brake disc.
2. The device mounted atop the distributor shaft, which passes current to the distributor cap tower contacts.

SECONDARY CIRCUIT: The high voltage side of the ignition system, usually above 20,000 volts. The secondary includes the ignition coil, coil wire, distributor cap and rotor, spark plug wires and spark plugs.

SENDING UNIT: A mechanical, electrical, hydraulic or electromagnetic device which transmits information to a gauge.

SENSOR: Any device designed to measure engine operating conditions or ambient pressures and temperatures. Usually electronic in nature and designed to send a voltage signal to an on-board computer, some sensors may operate as a simple on/off switch or they may provide a variable voltage signal (like a potentiometer) as conditions or measured parameters change.

SHIM: Spacers of precise, predetermined thickness used between parts to establish a proper working relationship.

SLAVE CYLINDER: In automotive use, a device in the hydraulic clutch system which is activated by hydraulic force, disengaging the clutch.

SOLENOID: A coil used to produce a magnetic field, the effect of which is produce work.

SPARK PLUG: A device screwed into the combustion chamber of a spark ignition engine. The basic construction is a conductive core inside of a ceramic insulator, mounted in an outer conductive base. An electrical charge from the spark plug wire travels along the conductive core and jumps a preset air gap to a grounding point or points at the end of the conductive base. The resultant spark ignites the fuel/air mixture in the combustion chamber.

SPLINES: Ridges machined or cast onto the outer diameter of a shaft or inner diameter of a bore to enable parts to mate without rotation.

TACHOMETER: A device used to measure the rotary speed of an engine, shaft, gear, etc., usually in rotations per minute.

THERMOSTAT: A valve, located in the cooling system of an engine, which is closed when cold and opens gradually in response to engine heating, controlling the temperature of the coolant and rate of coolant flow.

TOP DEAD CENTER (TDC): The point at which the piston reaches the top of its travel on the compression stroke.

TORQUE: The twisting force applied to an object.

TORQUE CONVERTER: A turbine used to transmit power from a driving member to a driven member via hydraulic action, providing changes in drive ratio and torque. In automotive use, it links the driveplate at the rear of the engine to the automatic transmission.

TRANSDUCER: A device used to change a force into an electrical signal.

TRANSISTOR: A semi-conductor component which can be actuated by a small voltage to perform an electrical switching function.

TUNE-UP: A regular maintenance function, usually associated with the replacement and adjustment of parts and components in the electrical and fuel systems of a vehicle for the purpose of attaining optimum performance.

TURBOCHARGER: An exhaust driven pump which compresses intake air and forces it into the combustion chambers at higher than atmospheric pressures. The increased air pressure allows more fuel to be burned and results in increased horsepower being produced.

VACUUM ADVANCE: A device which advances the ignition timing in response to increased engine vacuum.

VACUUM GAUGE: An instrument used to measure the presence of vacuum in a chamber.

VALVE: A device which control the pressure, direction of flow or rate of flow of a liquid or gas.

VALVE CLEARANCE: The measured gap between the end of the valve stem and the rocker arm, cam lobe or follower that activates the valve.

VISCOSITY: The rating of a liquid's internal resistance to flow.

VOLTMETER: An instrument used for measuring electrical force in units called volts. Voltmeters are always connected parallel with the circuit being tested.

WHEEL CYLINDER: Found in the automotive drum brake assembly, it is a device, actuated by hydraulic pressure, which, through internal pistons, pushes the brake shoes outward against the drums.

ABBREVIATIONS AND SYMBOLS

A: Ampere

AC: Alternating current

A/C: Air conditioning

A-h: Ampere hour

AT: Automatic transmission

ATDC: After top dead center

μA: Microampere

bbl: Barrel

BDC: Bottom dead center

bhp: Brake horsepower

BTDC: Before top dead center

BTU: British thermal unit

C: Celsius (Centigrade)

CCA: Cold cranking amps

cd: Candela

cm^2: Square centimeter

cm^3, cc: Cubic centimeter

CO: Carbon monoxide

CO_2: Carbon dioxide

cu.in., in^3: Cubic inch

CV: Constant velocity

Cyl.: Cylinder

DC: Direct current

ECM: Electronic control module

EFE: Early fuel evaporation

EFI: Electronic fuel injection

EGR: Exhaust gas recirculation

Exh.: Exhaust

F: Fahrenheit

F: Farad

pF: Picofarad

μF: Microfarad

FI: Fuel injection

ft.lb., ft. lb., ft. lbs.: foot pound(s)

gal: Gallon

g: Gram

HC: Hydrocarbon

HEI: High energy ignition

HO: High output

hp: Horsepower

Hyd.: Hydraulic

Hz: Hertz

ID: Inside diameter

in.lb.; in. lb.; in. lbs: inch pound(s)

Int.: Intake

K: Kelvin

kg: Kilogram

kHz: Kilohertz

km: Kilometer

km/h: Kilometers per hour

$k\Omega$: Kilohm

kPa: Kilopascal

kV: Kilovolt

kW: Kilowatt

l: Liter

l/s: Liters per second

m: Meter

mA: Milliampere

mg: Milligram

mHz: Megahertz

mm: Millimeter

mm^2: Square millimeter

m^3: Cubic meter

MΩ: Megohm

m/s: Meters per second

MT: Manual transmission

mV: Millivolt

μm: Micrometer

N: Newton

N-m: Newton meter

NOx: Nitrous oxide

OD: Outside diameter

OHC: Over head camshaft

OHV: Over head valve

Ω: Ohm

PCV: Positive crankcase ventilation

psi: Pounds per square inch

pts: Pints

qts: Quarts

rpm: Rotations per minute

rps: Rotations per second

R-12: A refrigerant gas (Freon)

SAE: Society of Automotive Engineers

SO$_2$: Sulfur dioxide

T: Ton

t: Megagram

TBI: Throttle Body Injection

TPS: Throttle Position Sensor

V: 1. Volt; 2. Venturi

μV: Microvolt

W: Watt

∞: Infinity

<: Less than

>: Greater than

Index

Title: U is for undertow

Item ID: 3949910107S306

Due: 12/8/2012

Title: Chilton Book Company
          repair manual, Chrysler
          front wheel drive, 1981-
          88 : all U.S. and
          Canadian front wheel
          drive models of Dodge
          Aries, 400, 600,
          Daytona, Lancer,
          Shadow : Plymouth
          Caravelle, Reliant,
          Sundance : Chrysler E-
          Class, Executive sedan,
          4-

Item ID: 3949910076S901

Due: 12/8/2012

Title: Chilton's auto repair
          manual

Item ID: 3949910030S709

Due: 12/8/2012

Chilton's Repair & Tune-Up Guides

The Complete line covers domestic cars, imports, trucks, vans, RV's and 4-wheel drive vehicles.

RTUG Title	Part No.
AMC 1975-82	7199
Covers all U.S. and Canadian models	
Aspen/Volare 1976-80	6637
Covers all U.S. and Canadian models	
Audi 1970-73	5902
Covers all U.S. and Canadian models.	
Audi 4000/5000 1978-81	7028
Covers all U.S. and Canadian models including turbocharged and diesel engines	
Barracuda/Challenger 1965-72	5807
Covers all U.S. and Canadian models	
Blazer/Jimmy 1969-82	6931
Covers all U.S. and Canadian 2- and 4-wheel drive models, including diesel engines	
BMW 1970-82	6844
Covers U.S. and Canadian models	
Buick/Olds/Pontiac 1975-85	7308
Covers all U.S. and Canadian full size rear wheel drive models	
Cadillac 1967-84	7462
Covers all U.S. and Canadian rear wheel drive models	
Camaro 1967-81	6735
Covers all U.S. and Canadian models	
Camaro 1982-85	7317
Covers all U.S. and Canadian models	
Capri 1970-77	6695
Covers all U.S. and Canadian models	
Caravan/Voyager 1984-85	7482
Covers all U.S. and Canadian models	
Century/Regal 1975-85	7307
Covers all U.S. and Canadian rear wheel drive models, including turbocharged engines	
Champ/Arrow/Sapporo 1978-83	7041
Covers all U.S. and Canadian models	
Chevette/1000 1976-86	6836
Covers all U.S. and Canadian models	
Chevrolet 1968-85	7135
Covers all U.S. and Canadian models	
Chevrolet 1968-79 Spanish	7082
Chevrolet/GMC Pick-Ups 1970-82 Spanish	7468
Chevrolet/GMC Pick-Ups and Suburban 1970-86	6936
Covers all U.S. and Canadian 1/2, 3/4 and 1 ton models, including 4-wheel drive and diesel engines	
Chevrolet LUV 1972-81	6815
Covers all U.S. and Canadian models	
Chevrolet Mid-Size 1964-86	6840
Covers all U.S. and Canadian models of 1964-77 Chevelle, Malibu and Malibu SS; 1974-77 Laguna; 1978-85 Malibu; 1970-86 Monte Carlo; 1964-84 El Camino, including diesel engines	
Chevrolet Nova 1986	7658
Covers all U.S. and Canadian models	
Chevy/GMC Vans 1967-84	6930
Covers all U.S. and Canadian models of 1/2, 3/4, and 1 ton vans, cutaways, and motor home chassis, including diesel engines	
Chevy S-10 Blazer/GMC S-15 Jimmy 1982-85	7383
Covers all U.S. and Canadian models	
Chevy S-10/GMC S-15 Pick-Ups 1982-85	7310
Covers all U.S. and Canadian models	
Chevy II/Nova 1962-79	6841
Covers all U.S. and Canadian models	
Chrysler K- and E-Car 1981-85	7163
Covers all U.S. and Canadian front wheel drive models	
Colt/Challenger/Vista/Conquest 1971-85	7037
Covers all U.S. and Canadian models	
Corolla/Carina/Tercel/Starlet 1970-85	7036
Covers all U.S. and Canadian models	
Corona/Cressida/Crown/Mk.II/Camry/Van 1970-84	7044
Covers all U.S. and Canadian models	
Corvair 1960-69	6691
Covers all U.S. and Canadian models	
Corvette 1953-62	6576
Covers all U.S. and Canadian models	
Corvette 1963-84	6843
Covers all U.S. and Canadian models	
Cutlass 1970-85	6933
Covers all U.S. and Canadian models	
Dart/Demon 1968-76	6324
Covers all U.S. and Canadian models	
Datsun 1961-72	5790
Covers all U.S. and Canadian models of Nissan Patrol; 1500, 1600 and 2000 sports cars; Pick-Ups; 410, 411, 510, 1200 and 240Z	
Datsun 1973-80 Spanish	7083
Datsun/Nissan F-10, 310, Stanza, Pulsar 1977-86	7196
Covers all U.S. and Canadian models	
Datsun/Nissan Pick-Ups 1970-84	6816
Covers all U.S and Canadian models	
Datsun/Nissan Z & ZX 1970-86	6932
Covers all U.S. and Canadian models	
Datsun/Nissan 1200, 210, Sentra 1973-86	7197
Covers all U.S. and Canadian models	
Datsun/Nissan 200SX, 510, 610, 710, 810, Maxima 1973-84	7170
Covers all U.S. and Canadian models	
Dodge 1968-77	6554
Covers all U.S. and Canadian models	
Dodge Charger 1967-70	6486
Covers all U.S. and Canadian models	
Dodge/Plymouth Trucks 1967-84	7459
Covers all 1/2, 3/4, and 1 ton 2- and 4-wheel drive U.S. and Canadian models, including diesel engines	
Dodge/Plymouth Vans 1967-84	6934
Covers all 1/2, 3/4, and 1 ton U.S. and Canadian models of vans, cutaways and motor home chassis	
D-50/Arrow Pick-Up 1979-81	7032
Covers all U.S. and Canadian models	
Fairlane/Torino 1962-75	6320
Covers all U.S. and Canadian models	
Fairmont/Zephyr 1978-83	6965
Covers all U.S. and Canadian models	
Fiat 1969-81	7042
Covers all U.S. and Canadian models	
Fiesta 1978-80	6846
Covers all U.S. and Canadian models	
Firebird 1967-81	5996
Covers all U.S. and Canadian models	
Firebird 1982-85	7345
Covers all U.S. and Canadian models	
Ford 1968-79 Spanish	7084
Ford Bronco 1966-83	7140
Covers all U.S. and Canadian models	
Ford Bronco II 1984	7408
Covers all U.S. and Canadian models	
Ford Courier 1972-82	6983
Covers all U.S. and Canadian models	
Ford/Mercury Front Wheel Drive 1981-85	7055
Covers all U.S. and Canadian models Escort, EXP, Tempo, Lynx, LN-7 and Topaz	
Ford/Mercury/Lincoln 1968-85	6842
Covers all U.S. and Canadian models of FORD Country Sedan, Country Squire, Crown Victoria, Custom, Custom 500, Galaxie 500, LTD through 1982, Ranch Wagon, and XL; MERCURY Colony Park, Commuter, Marquis through 1982, Gran Marquis, Monterey and Park Lane; LINCOLN Continental and Towne Car	
Ford/Mercury/Lincoln Mid-Size 1971-85	6696
Covers all U.S. and Canadian models of FORD Elite, 1983-85 LTD, 1977-79 LTD II, Ranchero, Torino, Gran Torino, 1977-85 Thunderbird; MERCURY 1972-85 Cougar,	

continued on next page

RTUG Title	Part No.
1983-85 Marquis, Montego, 1980-85 XR-7; LINCOLN 1982-85 Continental, 1984-85 Mark VII, 1978-80 Versailles	
Ford Pick-Ups 1965-86	6913
Covers all $1/2$, $3/4$ and 1 ton, 2- and 4-wheel drive U.S. and Canadian pick-up, chassis cab and camper models, including diesel engines	
Ford Pick-Ups 1965-82 Spanish	7469
Ford Ranger 1983-84	7338
Covers all U.S. and Canadian models	
Ford Vans 1961-86	6849
Covers all U.S. and Canadian $1/2$, $3/4$ and 1 ton van and cutaway chassis models, including diesel engines	
GM A-Body 1982-85	7309
Covers all front wheel drive U.S. and Canadian models of BUICK Century, CHEVROLET Celebrity, OLDSMOBILE Cutlass Ciera and PONTIAC 6000	
GM C-Body 1985	7587
Covers all front wheel drive U.S. and Canadian models of BUICK Electra Park Avenue and Electra T-Type, CADILLAC Fleetwood and deVille, OLDSMOBILE 98 Regency and Regency Brougham	
GM J-Car 1982-85	7059
Covers all U.S. and Canadian models of BUICK Skyhawk, CHEVROLET Cavalier, CADILLAC Cimarron, OLDSMOBILE Firenza and PONTIAC 2000 and Sunbird	
GM N-Body 1985-86	7657
Covers all U.S. and Canadian models of front wheel drive BUICK Somerset and Skylark, OLDSMOBILE Calais, and PONTIAC Grand Am	
GM X-Body 1980-85	7049
Covers all U.S. and Canadian models of BUICK Skylark, CHEVROLET Citation, OLDSMOBILE Omega and PONTIAC Phoenix	
GM Subcompact 1971-80	6935
Covers all U.S. and Canadian models of BUICK Skyhawk (1975-80), CHEVROLET Vega and Monza, OLDSMOBILE Starfire, and PONTIAC Astre and 1975-80 Sunbird	
Granada/Monarch 1975-82	6937
Covers all U.S. and Canadian models	
Honda 1973-84	6980
Covers all U.S. and Canadian models	
International Scout 1967-73	5912
Covers all U.S. and Canadian models	
Jeep 1945-87	6817
Covers all U.S. and Canadian CJ-2A, CJ-3A, CJ-3B, CJ-5, CJ-6, CJ-7, Scrambler and Wrangler models	
Jeep Wagoneer, Commando, Cherokee, Truck 1957-86	6739
Covers all U.S. and Canadian models of Wagoneer, Cherokee, Grand Wagoneer, Jeepster, Jeepster Commando, J-100, J-200, J-300, J-10, J20, FC-150 and FC-170	
Laser/Daytona 1984-85	7563
Covers all U.S. and Canadian models	
Maverick/Comet 1970-77	6634
Covers all U.S. and Canadian models	
Mazda 1971-84	6981
Covers all U.S. and Canadian models of RX-2, RX-3, RX-4, 808, 1300, 1600, Cosmo, GLC and 626	
Mazda Pick-Ups 1972-86	7659
Covers all U.S. and Canadian models	
Mercedes-Benz 1959-70	6065
Covers all U.S. and Canadian models	
Mereceds-Benz 1968-73	5907
Covers all U.S. and Canadian models	

RTUG Title	Part No.
Mercedes-Benz 1974-84	6809
Covers all U.S. and Canadian models	
Mitsubishi, Cordia, Tredia, Starion, Galant 1983-85	7583
Covers all U.S. and Canadian models	
MG 1961-81	6780
Covers all U.S. and Canadian models	
Mustang/Capri/Merkur 1979-85	6963
Covers all U.S. and Canadian models	
Mustang/Cougar 1965-73	6542
Covers all U.S. and Canadian models	
Mustang II 1974-78	6812
Covers all U.S. and Canadian models	
Omni/Horizon/Rampage 1978-84	6845
Covers all U.S. and Canadian models of DODGE omni, Miser, 024, Charger 2.2; PLYMOUTH Horizon, Miser, TC3, TC3 Tourismo; Rampage	
Opel 1971-75	6575
Covers all U.S. and Canadian models	
Peugeot 1970-74	5982
Covers all U.S. and Canadian models	
Pinto/Bobcat 1971-80	7027
Covers all U.S. and Canadian models	
Plymouth 1968-76	6552
Covers all U.S. and Canadian models	
Pontiac Fiero 1984-85	7571
Covers all U.S. and Canadian models	
Pontiac Mid-Size 1974-83	7346
Covers all U.S. and Canadian models of Ventura, Grand Am, LeMans, Grand LeMans, GTO, Phoenix, and Grand Prix	
Porsche 924/928 1976-81	7048
Covers all U.S. and Canadian models	
Renault 1975-85	7165
Covers all U.S. and Canadian models	
Roadrunner/Satellite/Belvedere/GTX 1968-73	5821
Covers all U.S. and Canadian models	
RX-7 1979-81	7031
Covers all U.S. and Canadian models	
SAAB 99 1969-75	5988
Covers all U.S. and Canadian models	
SAAB 900 1979-85	7572
Covers all U.S. and Canadian models	
Snowmobiles 1976-80	6978
Covers Arctic Cat, John Deere, Kawasaki, Polaris, Ski-Doo and Yamaha	
Subaru 1970-84	6982
Covers all U.S. and Canadian models	
Tempest/GTO/LeMans 1968-73	5905
Covers all U.S. and Canadian models	
Toyota 1966-70	5795
Covers all U.S. and Canadian models of Corona, MkII, Corolla, Crown, Land Cruiser, Stout and Hi-Lux	
Toyota 1970-79 Spanish	7467
Toyota Celica/Supra 1971-85	7043
Covers all U.S. and Canadian models	
Toyota Trucks 1970-85	7035
Covers all U.S. and Canadian models of pickups, Land Cruiser and 4Runner	
Valiant/Duster 1968-76	6326
Covers all U.S. and Canadian models	
Volvo 1956-69	6529
Covers all U.S. and Canadian models	
Volvo 1970-83	7040
Covers all U.S. and Canadian models	
VW Front Wheel Drive 1974-85	6962
Covers all U.S. and Canadian models	
VW 1949-71	5796
Covers all U.S. and Canadian models	
VW 1970-79 Spanish	7081
VW 1970-81	6837
Covers all U.S. and Canadian Beetles, Karmann Ghia, Fastback, Squareback, Vans, 411 and 412	

Chilton's Repair & Tune-Up Guides are available at your local retailer or by mailing a check or money order for **$13.95** plus **$3.25** to cover postage and handling to:

Chilton Book Company
Dept. DM
Radnor, PA 19089

NOTE: When ordering be sure to include your name & address, book part No. & title.